Multinational Corporations and the Impact of Public Advocacy on Corporate Strategy

Nestle and the Infant Formula Controversy

Issues in Business Ethics

VOLUME 6

Multinational Corporations and the Impact of Public Advocacy on Corporate Strategy

Nestle and the Infant Formula Controversy

by

S. Prakash Sethi
Baruch College
The City University of New York

Kluwer Academic Publishers
Boston / Dordrecht / London

Distributors for North America:
Kluwer Academic Publishers
101 Philip Drive
Assinippi Park
Norwell, Massachusetts 02061 USA

Distributors for all other countries:
Kluwer Academic Publishers Group
Distribution Centre
Post Office Box 322
3300 AH Dordrecht, THE NETHERLANDS

Library of Congress Cataloging-in-Publication Data
Sethi, S. Prakash.
    Multinational corporations and the impact of public advocacy on
corporate strategy : Nestle and the infant formula controversy/by
S. Prakash Sethi.
        p. cm. — (Issues in business ethics ; v. 6)
    Includes bibliographical references and index.
    ISBN 0-7923-9378-3 (acid-free paper)
    1. Nestlé. 2. Baby foods industry — Developing countries.
3. Infants — Developing countries — Nutrition. 4. Infant
formulas — Nutrition. I. Title. II. Series.
HD9015.S93N387 1994
338.7′66462′091724 — dc20   93-32157
                                                                  CIP

Printed on acid-free paper.

Printed in the United States of America

Contents

This Book is Dedicated to the memory of

Father Theodore V. Purcell, S.J.

He was a dedicated scholar and a
compassionate human being who always
strove to search for truth with purity of
motives and integrity of means.

Preface

This book has been a labor of love, and has been lovingly labored at, for a period that has stretched for almost 10 years. And yet, this has been by far the most difficult, and physically and emotionally exhausting research project I have ever undertaken. The infant formula controversy has touched so many people, institutions, and nations at so many different levels, that coming to grips with the scope of the problem, defining its dimensions, and establishing causative and associational linkages becomes at once a highly complex and a dauntingly difficult proposition.

From its very inception, in the late 1960s, when the potential association between bottle-feeding and infant diseases and deaths first penetrated public consciousness in a significant manner, the issue has been highly emotionally charged. At the same time, the infant formula controversy has been mired in charges and countercharges of abuse of scientific and medical research, unethical and immoral behavior, exploitation of the poor and uninformed, and a suspicion of hidden agenda on the part of opposing parties. Each side is able to parade an impressive group of scientists, public health experts, and physicians, all with vast experience of working with the people of the Third World. And yet, there has been a problem in sorting out the elusive truths about the controversy. To wit, most of those who have had the best exposure to some facet of the problem are disqualified for that very reason. Using their particular prism, they view all alternative explanations as biased and tainted. One group argues for an objective, nonpartisan basis for evaluating field research data. Other groups, however, dismiss such statements by asserting that no science can be truly objective and value neutral, and that those advocating it, subscribe at best to a particular value orientation.

As is wont in the case of most questions of public policy, a discussion of the infant formula issue is further complicated by economic, social and religious, and national and international political perspectives. At the institutional level we have the infant formula industry and its constituent companies, largely multinational corporations, contending that they sell a safe product to mothers who are in need of it, and have, in any case, freely opted to purchase it for their own health and/or socioeconomic reasons, and generally under the advice and support of local health care personnel. The opponents encompass a wide variety of groups. They include scientific and health care personnel, social and community health workers and organizations, as well as national public health agencies and medical bodies. They also include public interest groups, both religious and nonsectarian, who gave the controversy its moral fervor and organizing skills, thereby setting this controversy into a category unto itself.

This controversy also marked the coming of age of international social activism where groups from the United States were able to build strong networks with their West European counterparts and also establish operational bases in Third World countries. An added element has been the involvement of most of the world's national governments and a number of international organizations, such as the World Health Organization (WHO), and United Nations International Children's Emergency Fund (UNICEF).

I first started work on the infant formula project in early 1976 as part of an ongoing effort to study the impact of corporate activities on the environment and other sociopolitical institutions. My interest in these issues arose out of my emotional attachment with people in the Third World since I was born in India and spent a part of my adult life there. I was equally attracted to the issue for intellectual reasons. The infant formula controversy provides a microcosm of the types of issues and players that are likely to dominate debate and action in the public policy arena in the coming decade as it pertains to the role of large multinational corporations in society.

The initial effort was reflected in a joint article with Dr. James Post of Boston University. However, after a year's work it became apparent to me that it was impossible to undertake research *as such* on this issue with any degree of objectivity and impartiality. Whether one liked it or not, one was either tagged as having been co-opted by the corporate critics and thereby labeled as an "activist scholar." Or, alternately, he/she was tagged as having been duped by the industry and had thereby become its unwitting mouthpiece. The problem was further compounded by the fact that a substantial portion of the data had to come from parties who had a continuing vital stake in the outcome of any research in terms of whether it would support or undermine their respective positions or preferred solutions. For these reasons, I decided to refrain from writing or publishing anything on the subject until such time that the issues had either been resolved or at least matured to a point where reasonable people could share information, exchange ideas, reflect on the events, and draw some conclusions as to their implications.

Late in 1983, two years after the passage of the World Health Organization (WHO) Code, I felt that the situation had calmed down to an extent that an attempt could be made to take a comprehensive look at the issue. I perceived the research design to have three important elements. The first step had to be the development of an analytical framework that would allow for a dynamic study of the events as they would unfold in order to understand cause–effect relationships. The situational dynamics created the two other necessary elements of my research design. I had to have access to primary data showing the internal processes by which decisions were made by various groups as events unfolded and various parties responded to each other's actions-reactions. Such data would also shed light on how the group interactions impacted the sociopolitical environment and public perceptions and changes in the nature of future options available to various participants. This was especially necessary for three reasons: (1) throughout the controversy it had been obvious to me that there was a large gap between public pronouncements of different parties as to what they would consider an acceptable proposition as a bargaining ploy versus what were their realistic expectations; (2) those expectations had changed over time as a consequence of changes in the external environment; and (3) the strategies and tactics were pursued by various groups during different phases of the controversy.

I was indeed fortunate in enlisting the cooperation of almost all the major groups and principal participants. I received access to most of the internal information, including confidential documents, strategy papers, and records and minutes of meetings previously not made public. By the time I was ready to start work on the project, the archival data alone had become a stack of reports and publications that occupied eight four-foot-wide drawers in two filing cabinets. The primary data alone, however, were not sufficient to fully understand the dynamics of social conflict. The written record, even in its raw form, presents a rationalized and often sanitized version of events. However, it does not explain the thought processes and reasoning employed by different actors as they were making real-time decisions. Thus, to supplement the archival data, I conducted over 250 hours of taped interviews with more than 40 individuals representing various constituencies and institutions.

My first and by far most difficult task was to enlist Nestle executives' cooperation on this project. Moreover, given Nestle's earlier experience with outsiders, it was not certain whether executives at Nestle, S.A. in Switzerland, could ever be dissuaded from their siege complex and persuaded to release inside corporate information or give interviews on record. My eventual success in securing Nestle's cooperation for this project was due primarily to the efforts of the late Mr. Rafael D. Pagan, Jr., then president of Nestle Coordination Center for Nutrition, Inc. (NCCN), in Washington, D.C. Early in 1984, there was visible movement toward the settlement of the infant formula controversy, and Nestle had become more flexible and forthcoming. It was through Mr. Pagan's efforts that the parent company's executives were persuaded to cooperate in this project. He also gave me his support, starting with on-the-record taped interviews lasting more than 20 hours and spread over 12 months. I received similar cooperation from the three other senior executives and top strategists at NCCN, namely, Dr. Thad Jackson, Mr. John O. Mongoven, and Dr. Niels Christiansen. In addition, with rare exceptions, I was provided with almost total access to NCCN's internal documents, including minutes of strategy meetings, position papers, and intracompany communications. This was also the time when highly sensitive discussions were going on between the company, activist groups, UNICEF and WHO toward the interpretation of various WHO Code provisions and their compliance by Nestle, discussions that ultimately led to the termination of the boycott. This was a real-life laboratory experience in terms of crisis management and stakeholder relations with tremendous stakes for the company's future.

I also interviewed various senior executives at Nestle, S.A. in Switzerland, some of whom had not given any other public interviews either on or off the record about their roles and activities at Nestle during the infant formula controversy. Foremost among them were Dr. Carl L. Angst, managing director of Nestle, S.A. Dr. Angst was ultimately to play a major role in committing Nestle to its new course following the enactment of the WHO Code. The second most important player in terms of changes in Nestle's home office strategy was Mr. Ernest Saunders, a Briton, who at that time was the executive in-charge of Nestle's Infant Foods and Dietetic Products Division and was, therefore, responsible for the company's worldwide sale of infant formula products. Other Nestle executives with deep involvement in the infant formula controversy were Mr. Geoffrey A. Fookes, Mr. Jacques Paternot, and Mr. Gerald Raffe. In the United States, another Nestle-related person whose support was critical to the success of this project was Mr. Tom Ward, an attorney and senior partner with the law firm of Ward, Lazarus, Grow & Cihlar. Mr. Ward had represented Nestle's interests in the United States for a number of years and had first-hand knowledge of Nestle's activities in the United States during some of the most difficult periods: for example, the Kennedy Hearing. Other former executives of Nestle, U.S.A., interviewed for this book were Mr. David E. Guerrant and Mr. Henry Ciocca. Mr. Guerrant, a marketing expert, headed Nestle's U.S. operations, and Mr. Ciocca, an attorney, was responsible for its public affairs activities during the early stages of the infant formula controversy in the United States and especially around the time of the Kennedy Hearing.

There were a number of people in the U.S.-based infant formula manufacturers who were helpful in providing information and discussing various aspects of the controversy as it involved their companies. They included Mr. Tom McCollough, director of Third World Research, and Mr. David O. Cox, former president of Ross Laboratories, a subsidiary of Abbott Laboratories. Acknowledgments are also due Mr. E. Steven Bauer, then vice president — corporate and governmental affairs; Ms. Beverly Halchak, director — maternal child health, Wyeth-Ayerst Laboratories, a subsidiary of American Home Products; and Ms. Margaret Maruschak, vice president, and Mr. Jerry Parrott, director of public relations, both of Bristol-Myers.

Clearly, this book would not have been possible had I not received similar support and cooperation from the many activist groups and individuals who played key roles in the infant formula controversy. Notable among them are: Mr. Timothy H. Smith, executive director of Interfaith Center on Corporate Responsibility (ICCR), and Ms. Leah Margulies, the founder of Infant Formula Action Coalition (INFACT). A strong note of thanks is due to Mr. Douglas A. Johnson, national chairperson of Infant Formula Action Coalition (INFACT), for his cooperation in this project. Mr. Johnson was perhaps one of the most important individuals in giving focus to the infant formula movement in the United States. There were other members of INFACT, International Nestle Boycott Committee (INBC), and International Baby Food Action Network (IBFAN) who cooperated in this project. Notable among them are (in alphabetical order): Mr. Edward Baer, Mr. Doug Clement, Dr. Robert McClean, Sister Regina Murphy, Sister Regina Rowan, Dr. Luther Tyson, Sister Marilyn Uline, Mr. Richard Ulrich, and Ms. Pat Young.

There were two other church leaders to whom I owe a deep debt of gratitude for their support and counsel through the entire period of research and writing of this book: Dr. Philip Wogaman and Dr. James Armstrong. Dr. Wogaman, a former dean and a faculty member of Weslyan Theological Seminary, was the head of the Methodist Task Force (MTF) appointed by that denomination to study all aspects of infant formula controversy and recommend to that body as to whether to join the boycott against Nestle. Other members of the Methodist Task Force cooperating in this project were Ms. Anita Anand, Dr. Robert Kegerreis, and Dr. Paul Minus. I am grateful to all of them for their support and encouragement.

Dr. James Armstrong, a former bishop of the Methodist Church and former president of the National Council of Churches (NCC), is presently the senior pastor of First Congregational Church in Winter Park, Florida. His vast experience as one of the top religious leaders in the United States, and his global perspective, were invaluable in understanding the evolving role of religious institutions as social activists. Other leaders of the Methodist Church cooperating in this project were: Dr. Norman E. DeWire, then general secretary, and Dr. Paul McCleary, then associate general secretary for research, General Council of Ministries, and currently president, Christian Children's Fund. They provided me with access to the in-house church documents and also assisted me in the interpretation of various church documents and the rules and procedures of the Methodist assemblies and conferences through which all decisions pertaining to that denomination are made.

There was another Nestle-related, and yet quite public, organization that played an important role in the latter stages of the infant formula controversy. This was the Nestle Infant Formula Audit Commission (NIFAC), chaired by former U.S. Senator and Secretary of State, Mr. Edmund Muskie. Senator Muskie provided me with details of his experiences with NIFAC but also on his views about the usefulness of NIFAC-like organizations in resolving similar business–society confrontations in the future. In addition, I was given access to in-house documents pertaining to NIFAC's activities.

Outside the United States, I was fortunate in receiving the support of many individuals with deep involvement in the infant formula controversy. Foremost among them was Mr. Andrew Chetley, formerly with War-on-Want and until recently the European director of IBFAN. Mr. Chetley, along with Mr. Mike Mueller, can genuinely take the credit for raising the issue of infant formula marketing practices and putting it on the international agenda. Mr. Chetley and Ms. Annalies Allain of International Organization of Consumer Unions (IOCU) were the foremost lobbyists and strategists for the activist groups during the phases when the infant formula issue had moved to the World Health Assembly in Geneva. Other individuals in various European organizations who were helpful in providing information included: Ms. Janice Mantell, Switzerland; Ms. Patricia Rundell and Ms. Lisa Woodburn, United Kingdom; Ms. Ann Margaret Yngue, Sweden; and Mr. Thomas Koch, West Germany. Their support and cooperation are gratefully acknowledged.

A number of administrators in the Department of Health and the Agency for International Development in the U.S. government were helpful with ideas and information. I am grateful for their cooperation. They included: Dr. Edward N. Brandt, former under secretary of health, and Ms. Rose Belmont, associate director of multilateral programs, Office of International Health and Human Services, both of the U.S. Department of Health and Human Services, and Dr. Carol A. Adelman, a research scientist in infant nutrition with the Agency of International Development (AID). Dr. Adelman was one of the very few people within the AID, who were in strong disagreement with AID's position both as to the scientific basis of the infant formula controversy, and also as to the charges laid by the activists against the infant formula manufacturers. Another AID scientist with views diametrically opposed to those of Dr. Adelman was Dr. Stephen C. Joseph. Dr. Joseph resigned from AID following this country's sole negative vote at the World Health Assembly (WHA). He provided me with information about the reasons for his resignation and commented on the workings of AID and the State Department, and the involvement of the White House officials in the deliberations that culminated in the U.S. negative vote. A number of other senior U.S. government officials provided on-the-record interviews and cooperated in the project. Their names and positions held at that time were as follows: Mr. Elliot Abrams, then under secretary, U.S. Department of State; Mr. Gordon Streeb, former deputy assistant secretary for international organizational affairs, and Mr. Neil Boyer, former deputy director for health and narcotics program, both of the U.S. Department of State. A number of other scientists and administrators associated with various U.S. government departments were also helpful with information but, for their own reasons, have preferred to remain anonymous. I am grateful to all of them for their encouragement and support.

Finally, I must record with a note of sadness and disappointment the al-most total lack of cooperation with which my efforts were met at the World Health Organization in Geneva. In fact, I was actively discouraged by Dr. J. Cohen, a policy advisor to the director general, and, from most accounts, one of the most influential persons in the WHO Secretariat, from undertak-ing the project. Dr. Cohen would talk to me only on the condition that the interview was not recorded. He indicated that a study, like my book, would not be in the best interest of WHO as it would expose the organization to external scrutiny and thereby jeopardize its effectiveness. However, when I persisted in my efforts, all the senior administrators and scientists with whom I had confirmed appointments either declined to meet with me or refused to offer any information under instructions from their superiors. Nevertheless, I was able to speak to a number of scientists and WHO offi-cials — both then current and former — with the promise that their identi-ties would not be revealed because they feared reprisals from their superiors and political repercussions from some of the member nations. Two former WHO officials provided on-the-record interviews. They were: Dr. M. Behar, a retired WHO scientist, who was deeply involved in the WHO work per-taining to the infant formula during its most intense phase; and Dr. Stanislas Flasche, former deputy director-general of WHO. On the other hand, I re-ceived tremendous cooperation from various scientists and administrators at the UNICEF headquarters in New York. UNICEF, along with WHO, was one of the agencies involved with the infant formula controversy. In partic-ular, I would like to acknowledge the assistance and cooperation of Dr. E.J.R. Hayward, Mr. Bertil Mathsson, Dr. Yoon Gu Lee, Dr. Les Tepley, and Dr. Max Milner. As a result of all these interviews, and with the help of many other people, agencies, and organizations from different parts of the world, I believe I was able to put together an accurate picture of the WHO activities pertaining to the infant formula controversy.

In coping with the enormous demands for data collection, library re-search, cross-checking of facts, and other support, I was ably and uncom-plainingly assisted by Mr. Leo Giglio and Ms. Linda Sama, two doctoral students at Baruch College, who worked as my research assistants during different phases of the project. To a minor extent, additional support was provided by Mr. Steven Papamarocs, Ms. Jill Abel, and Mr. B. Elango, also doctoral students at Baruch College. The primary burden of typing various versions of the "final" manuscript was carried out by Mr. Ruben Cardona, Ms. Julie Levine, Mr. Daniel Rarback, Ms. Beulah Babulal, Ms. Michelle Hunter, and other staff members of the Center for Management, Baruch College, and by Mrs. Ock Hee Hale at the Rochester Institute of Technol-ogy. I would like to thank them all for their assistance and support.

I am also grateful to many of my colleagues for their critical comments in reviewing various parts of the manuscript. They are: Professor Bharat Bhalla (Fairfield University), Professor Hamid Etemad (McGill University), Professor Cecilia Falbe (State University of New York — Albany), late

Professor K.A.N. Luther (Wake Forest University), Professor Karen Paul (Florida International University), late Father Theodore Purcell, S.J. (Georgetown University), Dr. Paul Steidlmeier (State University of New York — Binghamton), and Father Oliver Williams (University of Notre Dame).

It is inevitable that in a project lasting over a number of years I would have missed acknowledging contributions of many other supporters, friends, and colleagues. To them, I offer my deepest apologies. In almost every phase of this book, I have immensely benefited from association with scores of people who were willing to share information and give of their time, advice, and counsel. Nevertheless, I alone bear the sole responsibility for the views contained in this book.

S. Prakash Sethi
New York

THE SETTING

1 THE INFANT FORMULA CONTROVERSY AT CENTER STAGE

It was 8:00 A.M. on Thursday morning, October 4, 1984, in Washington, D.C. Nestle and the International Nestle Boycott Committee (INBC) had scheduled a joint press conference for 9 A.M. at the Mayflower Hotel. Both Nestle and INBC were to announce the termination of the latter's worldwide boycott of Nestle products. It had all started almost ten years ago, in 1974, when the infant formula controversy first entered the public consciousness in a major way with the publication of Mike Muller's *The Baby Killer.*[1] In the interim decade, a coalition of activist groups, Third World governments, and religious organizations had succeeded in having the World Health Organization (WHO), an agency of the United Nations, to enact for the first time an International Code of Breast-Milk Substitutes (the WHO Code) in 1981.[2] The coalition had also launched a worldwide boycott against Nestle's products and engaged in a host of other pressure tactics, to influence public opinion against Nestle and other infant formula manufacturers, to implement the provisions of the WHO Code in their marketing of infant formula products, and to accept INBC as a legitimate and important spokesperson for the affected people of the Third World.

It was only fitting that the press conference was taking place at the Mayflower Hotel, a venerable Washington landmark now owned by Nestle. The press conference was being moderated by Mark Siegel, a former aide to the U.S. Senator Edward M. Kennedy. Facing the audience on the right side were the members of INBC: Mrs. Patricia Young, national chairperson of INBC; Douglas A. Johnson, national chairperson of INFACT (Infant Formula Action Coalition); and Ms. Lisa Woodburn, European coordinator of

3

INBC. In the audience were such well-known activists as Tim Smith, executive director of the Interfaith Center on Corporate Responsibility (ICCR); Andrew Chetley, general administrator of International Baby Food Action Network and one of the leaders of European activists based in London; and Doug Clement, director of the Minneapolis office of INBC. However, conspicuous by their absence were Leah Margulies, one of the original founders of INFACT and, by some accounts, the creator of the Nestle boycott strategy; and Edward Baer, another member of the core group at ICCR that was responsible for masterminding the organized religious groups' opposition to the infant formula industry.

Seated on the left side nearest to the podium was Dr. Carl Angst, executive vice president of Nestle, U.S.A., whose ascendancy to power in the company was largely credited for a change in Nestle's strategy that led to the negotiated settlement of the boycott. On the far left side of the podium sat Mr. Rafael D. Pagan, Jr., president of Nestle Coordination Center for Nutrition, Inc. (NCCN) based in Washington, D.C., and the architect of Nestle's strategy over the last three years that culminated in the termination of the boycott. Occupying the middle seat was Mr. Edmund S. Muskie, a former U.S. Senator and Secretary of State, and chairman of the Nestle Infant Formula Audit Commission (NIFAC). A novel independent organization, NIFAC was created and funded by Nestle, and was responsible for the monitoring of Nestle's infant formula marketing practices in the Third World countries to ensure their compliance with the WHO Code.

To the participants and observers alike, it was an important event with its future implications most propitious or ominous depending on one's perspective. The critics of the infant formula industry were savoring their victory. If the activists were not behaving like victors, it was only because such behavior might appear unbecoming and inappropriate. But their sense of moral victory and political achievement could not be denied, and it was apparent to all but the most uninitiated.

Nestle also had ample reasons to be happy with the situation. For more than seven years, the company had been the target of severe criticism in the United States and abroad for its sale and promotion of infant formula products in Third World countries. Until three years ago, the company's public image and credibility with important segments of influential leadership in the United States — and to a lesser extent in certain other West European countries — was at a low ebb. And yet, starting in 1981, Nestle was able to effect such a complete turnaround in its situation that it must be considered one of the most successful crisis management stories — and one that is likely to become a classic — in the annals of business–society conflicts.

Mr. Siegel opened the press conference by welcoming everyone on "this historic day" on behalf of the Nestle Company and the International Nestle Boycott Committee (INBC). He then proceeded to describe the ground rules under which the press conference would be conducted:

I will first introduce the participants on the podium and then read to you the Joint Statement of Nestle and the International Nestle Boycott Committee. Following the reading of the statement, the representatives of the International Nestle Boycott Committee, Ms. Woodburn, Mr. Johnson, and Mrs. Young, will have a total of 10 minutes to make statements, to be followed by Mr. Muskie and Dr. Angst, who will also have 10 minutes in the aggregate. Following the statements, the participants will be open to questions from the press.[3]

If this all sounded very formal, indeed it was. The mechanics of organizing the press conference could not have been more complex and elaborate than high-level U.S.–Soviet disarmament talks. The moderator of the press conference, the selection of the people to sit on the podium, the order of their speaking, and their formal statements were all agreed upon beforehand, word by painstaking word, in negotiations that had lasted until the wee hours of the morning and that, on more than one occasion, were on the verge of breakdown. The fabric of cooperation was very fragile. It was based on a foundation of trust that was still tenuous and unstable.

As the drama unfolded, it became apparent that both sides were anxious to bury the hatchet, forget the acrimonious past, give credit to each other for progress, and herald a new era of cooperation. It was not, however, a marriage made in heaven. The threshold level of trust had improved, but the situation had remained unstable. As future events would show, it was not too long thereafter that the activists became disenchanted with the compliance efforts by Nestle and other companies; then renewed their criticism of the infant formula manufacturers and instituted new pressure tactics against major infant formula companies.

The joint statement referred to the progress made between January 1984 (when the initial agreement was signed to suspend the boycott) and October 1984, in resolving four major areas of disagreement concerning the code implementation. The joint statement, among other things, stated:

Recognizing the substantial progress Nestle has made in implementing the WHO International Code, INBC has voted to recommend full termination of the international boycott of the Company.

INBC shall continue to observe carefully Nestle's marketing practices and cooperate with NIFAC in the investigation of allegations of violations of the WHO International Code. Nestle shall continue to rely upon the Nestle Infant Formula Audit Commission to investigate allegations of deviations from established infant formula marketing policy.

Nestle and INBC are convinced that the steps they are committed to contribute to the safe and adequate nutrition for infants, protect and promote breast-feeding and ensure the proper use of breast milk substitutes, when these are necessary. . . . Lastly, Nestle and INBC call upon all concerned to join this process so that the application of the WHO Code can be more quickly achieved in all countries, and our joint commitment to improved infant health more tangibly realized.[4]

The joint statement reflected the tremendous emphasis INBC placed on the recognition of its being a "party of interest" in the negotiating process. It claimed to retain for itself an important role in the monitoring and evaluation of Nestle's compliance with the code. Furthermore, it asserted itself as an equal partner with WHO, member governments, and the infant formula manufacturers in ensuring a strict interpretation and implementation of the code. This concern for legitimacy and validation of rights was further reinforced through the written and oral statements of INBC members at the press conference. They went to great lengths in describing the unresolved issues and the process of consultation that had been established to deal with them in the future. The statements of INBC spokespersons complimented Nestle's efforts, recognizing that it was "not perfect" although it was "not the same company it was seven years ago." There was no comment, however, about any of the imperfections that might be attributed to the critics' actions or behavior during this period.[5]

The statements then turned their attention to the three U.S. companies, alleging that while Nestle had been making progress in complying with the code, Nestle's competitors were not doing so. "For ten years our field monitors investigated the marketing practices of the *entire* industry. What we found this summer was not encouraging." INBC charged that despite their pledges to the contrary, the three American companies were still violating the WHO Code in many Third World countries.

> It's bad enough for these and other companies to continue the marketing practices that the world's health authorities have identified as unsafe for babies. To steal that market from a company which has chosen to act ethically is most unconscionable, and deserving of public sanctions. The termination of the International Nestle Boycott now permits the international movement to redirect its energies to these companies.[6]

In his statement, Dr. Carl Angst, Nestle's executive vice president, expressed his satisfaction and happiness, not only because the boycott had ended but also because "it reflects the recognition by even our most severe critics that we have accomplished what we promised to do."[7] Dr. Angst's statement then briefly referred to the industry's perspective of the infant formula problem. He spoke of the needs of mothers who must feed their infants with non-breast-milk products, admitted to some of the mistakes the industry earlier made in underestimating the health problems associated with inappropriate and incorrect use of infant formulas, and also to the emotional and often abusive criticism to which Nestle was subjected to by its critics. He observed:

> There have always been mothers who cannot or will not breast-feed their babies. It is also a reality in infant feeding in many parts of the world today that formula is not just used as a total replacement for breast milk but rather as a supplement in a program of mixed feeding. For these reasons there has never been any ques-

tion in Nestle's mind throughout its history that breast milk substitutes fill a real need. . . . You therefore can imagine that it came as quite a shock to us when we became subject to the most severe — and frequently abusive — criticism. . . . Notwithstanding, I gladly admit that we learned quite a bit and above all that infant formula may be prepared in an inappropriate way more frequently than we suspected.

He went on to state that the infant formula issue must be placed in its proper context. Infant health in the developing world may be affected not just by marketing practices, but much more significantly by lack of hygiene, poverty, and inadequate health care. Until all these problems have been addressed, infant mortality will remain high in the Third World. He asserted that the WHO Code did not come even close to solving the problem, and that joint efforts of corporations, governments, churches, and other interested groups were required to solve these problems.[8]

Dr. Angst also recognized that some promotional practices by the industry posed the risk of discouraging mothers to breastfeed and were, therefore, wrong. It detailed the steps taken by Nestle in implementing the WHO Code and stated that the company would continue these efforts in the future "with the assistance of WHO, UNICEF, the Nestle Infant Formula Audit Commission (NIFAC), and many individual governments and interest groups."

An important turning point had been reached in the infant formula controversy. However, it was not the end of the controversy but the start of another phase, and a short-lived one at that. The inherent fragility of such multiparty agreements and the difficulty arriving at and maintaining a common interpretation of lengthy and complex understandings soon became apparent. The activists constantly complained of Nestle's breach of agreements and violation of code provisions in many Third World countries. These complaints were not confined to Nestle alone, however, but were also levied, to varying degrees, against other major international infant formula manufacturers as well. Finally, after years of recriminations and accusations of code violations, the activists again brought the issue to a new confrontational level. After a short truce and a boycott termination lasting less than four years, on October 4, 1988, the Action for Corporate Accountability (ACA) announced the resumption of its boycott of Nestle and a new boycott of AHP. Although ACA was a new organization, it was guided by the leadership of INFACT.[9] Based on their monitoring of industry's marketing practices in 42 developing countries, NGOs charged Nestle and American Home Products (AHP) with supplying free and low-cost infant formula to hospitals in violation of the code.[10]

An added reason for ACA's boycott activity was the recent entry of Nestle in the U.S. infant formula market. In June 1988, Carnation Company, a wholly owned subsidiary of Nestle, entered the U.S. infant formula foods market by introducing two infant nutrition products. Called Good Start H.A. and Good Nature, the two products were promoted as being more suitable for babies who were allergic to milk-based formulas. This targeted niche segment represented an extremely small percentage of all infants and should have been serviced only under close supervision by pediatricians. And yet, contrary to every established market practice in the United States, Carnation chose to advertise its products directly to consumers in print and television advertising and made them available for purchase in supermarkets instead of through pharmacies. In a sense of deja vu, Carnation's action raised a storm of protest, initiated enquiries from various regulatory agencies, vociferous complaints from medical professionals, and more adverse publicity than the company could handle. Importantly, while the Nestle Infant Formula Commission (NIFAC) found that "substantial controversy surrounds Carnation's marketing practices for these products,"[11] NIFAC also "determined that Nestle is largely in compliance with Nestle's publicly stated commitments to the WHO Code."[12] Finding that "ACA's expressed reasons for the boycott against Nestle were founded upon a different interpretation of the Guidelines and Resolution than is held by the Commission," NIFAC declined to support the renewed boycott.[13]

Similarly, in October 1989, Gerber Corporation, a producer of baby foods, also initiated direct consumer advertising for a new line of artificial infant formula product, called Gerber Baby Formula, under arrangement with Bristol-Myers Corporation.[14] During January–February 1991, both Nestle and AHP announced their decisions to stop providing free and low-cost samples to hospitals in Third World countries "except for the limited number of infants who need it." However, both companies planned to enforce this decision gradually. ACA was not satisfied with this gradual approach and decided to continue its boycott of both the companies until it felt satisfied with their full compliance.[15] Thus the entire controversy entered a new phase, with no end in sight.

It would be a worthwhile objective to create a comprehensive and factually accurate description of events surrounding the infant formula controversy. It would demonstrate the immense complexity that encumbers all significant issues of public policy and social import. More importantly, it would capture for the reader the very hazardous, unpredictable, and intense nature of the process through which these issues are handled and ultimately must be resolved. For they involve social institutions and human beings with all that is noble in them, and also the ignoble cruelty that afflicts all of us. Such a study should provide ample lessons for the corporate community, social activists, international organizations, and national governments, about the most effective strategies and tactics in dealing with similar issues.

In the broader context of business–society conflicts, the infant formula controversy might be viewed as one episode. It is, however, an important one, with many more preceding it and certainly many more to follow. Having studied scores of business–society conflicts in the last 20 years, and the infant formula controversy for almost 10 years,[16] this author is convinced that we have reached a watershed in the arena of conflict between business institutions and social groups. In the final analysis, they all represent some underlying concerns for a just and humane society, people's desire to determine their own destiny; and notions of distributive justice, rights, and entitlements.

No vision of the future is ever totally perfect, and only the passage of time and events will determine the impact of what has been wrought. We are captives of our imagination, which is constrained to a large extent by our living environment. Societies survive and civilizations flourish because people of wisdom can judiciously combine the lessons of the distant past with the human and material resource constraints of yesteryear. It would be presumptuous for someone who has lived through this period, and is so close to it, to declare that a lesson has been learned or to add up the gains and the losses from the experience. For this, we must await the objective judgment of history.

Instant history, however, has its uses. For neither now nor in the future can we ignore the recent past. It provides us with a point of departure from which we can measure progress or deflection therefrom. We are encumbered by it in our perceptual biases about the behavior and motives of the people and institutions we must deal with. And most importantly, it influences the goals we wish to achieve and the means we would like to employ. History repeats itself precisely because we have short memories.

An analysis of the infant formula controversy provides us with a mirror to see that our institutional stereotypes are no longer valid — both as institutions themselves perceive them and as their opponents portray them. Therefore, it is of paramount importance that we understand the changing nature of our sociopolitical environment, its impact on the relative power and authority of various institutions in commanding a society's physical and human resources, and the constraints it imposes on institutions in the exercise of that power. At the micro level, a failure to perceive accurately the changing nature of these power relationships can cause us to react and respond incorrectly to external challenges, with often disastrous results for all concerned. Even more fundamentally, at the macro level, changing institutional power relationships will not only affect business–society conflicts, they will influence and shape the very character of international and national geopolitical arrangements, and the nature of political order in democratic societies.

Finally, the findings of this study suggest some valuable lessons that could be put to good use by corporate executives and management students dealing with corporate strategy, organization structure, and decision-making processes, social issues management, stakeholder relations, business–government relations, and domestic and international public affairs. They should also provide us with an insight as to the impact of corporate culture on a company's response to external pressures and the extreme difficulties in bringing about changes in a corporation's culture, value orientation, and self-image.

Notes

1. Mike Muller, *The Baby Killer,* 2nd edition (London: War on Want, 1974), p. 2.

2. World Health Organization, *International Code of Marketing of Breast-Milk Substitutes* (Geneva, 1981).

3. Nestle Coordination Center for Nutrition, Inc., *Minutes of Press Conference,* October 4, 1984, p. 2.

4. "Joint Statement of Nestle and the International Nestle Boycott Committee," *Press Conference,* Washington, D.C., October 4, 1984, p. 2.

5. "Statement of Douglas A. Johnson, National Chairperson, Infant Formula Action Coalition (INFACT), and Lisa Woodburn, European Coordinator, International Nestle Boycott Committee," *Press Conference,* p. 3.

6. "Statement of Douglas A. Johnson," ibid., pp. 2–3.

7. "Remarks of Dr. Carl L. Angst, Executive Vice President, Nestle, S.A.," *Press Conference.*

8. *Ibid.,* pp. 2–4.

9. Alix M. Freedman, "Nestle Faces New Boycott Threat in Distribution of Infant Formula," *The Wall Street Journal,* June 29, 1988, p. 28; "Renewed Boycott of Nestle is Urged by Advocacy Groups," *The Wall Street Journal,* October 5, 1988, p. B10; "Boycott of Nestle to Resume," *The New York Times,* October 5, 1988, p. D2.

10. *Ibid.*

11. Nestle Infant Formula Audit Commission, *Report No. 13,* Washington, D.C., June 30, 1989, p. 7.

12. *Ibid.,* p. 8.

13. *Ibid.,* p.1.

14. For details, see Amal Kumar Naj, "Nestle To Sell Infant Formula In U.S.; Step Likely To Hurt Competitors' Profits," *The Wall Street Journal,* June 6, 1988, p. 5; Alix M. Freedman, "Nestle's New Infant Formula Line Introduced In A Bid For U.S. Market," *The Wall Street Journal,* June 28, 1988, p. 38; Milt Freudenheim, "A Safer Infant Formula Promised," *The New York Times,* June 28, 1988, p. D1, D22; Andrea Adelson, "Pediatricians On Carnation," *The New York Times,* June 29, 1988, p. D5; "Carnation's Move In Infant Formula," *The New York Times,* June 30, 1988, p. D8; "Carnation Won't Use Name In Infant Formula Campaign," *The Wall Street Journal,* July 15, 1988, p. 20; Steven Greenhouse, "Nestle's Time To Swagger," *The New York Times,* January 1, 1989; "FDA Rejects Nestle Unit's 'Good Start' Label Claim," *The Wall Street Journal,* February 3, 1989, p. B7; Alix M. Freedman, "Nestle's Bid To Crash Baby Formula Market in The U.S. Stirs A Row," *The Wall Street Journal,* February 16, 1989, pp. A1, A9; "Nestle Ad Claims For Baby Formula Probed In 3 States," *The Wall Street Journal,* March 2, 1989, p. B6; "Nestle To Drop Claim On Label Of Its Formula," *The Wall Street Journal,* March 13, 1989, p. B5; "Nestle Rejects Militant P.R. Plan To Combat Renewal Of Boycott," *The Wall Street Journal,* April 25, 1989, pp. B6–7; "Gerber Plan For Infant Formula," *The New York Times,* June 16, 1989, p. D5; Alix M. Freedman, "Gerber Unveils Its Baby Formula, Aims To Woo Parents Rather Than Doctors," *The Wall Street Journal,* June 16, 1989, p. B3; "Nestle's Carnation Co. Unit Settles Dispute Over Infant Formula Ads," *The Wall Street Journal,* July 7, 1989, p. B4; "Carnation Halts Formula Claims," *The New York Times,* July 7, 1989, p. D5; Michael Freitag, "The Infant Formula Debate Strikes Home," *The New York Times,* September 3, 1989, p. E5; Barry Meier, "Are Ads For Infant Formula Fit For The Eyes Of Parents?," *The New York Times,* December 29, 1990, p. 46; Julia Flynn Silver & David Woodruff, "The

Furor Over Formula Is Coming To A Boil," *Business Week,* April 9, 1990, pp. 52–53; "A Flap Over Formula Is Coming To A Boil," *Business Week,* January 1, 1991, p. 47.

15. For details of the latest controversy, see "Nestle to Restrict low-Cost Supplies Of Baby Food To Developing Nations," *The Wall Street Journal,* January 30, 1991, p. B6; and "American Home Infant Formula Giveaway To End," *The Wall Street Journal,* February 4, 1991, pp. B1, B5.

16. S. Prakash Sethi, "Inhuman Errors and Industrial Crises," *Columbia Journal of World Business* (Spring 1987), pp. 101–110; *The South African Quagmire: In Search for a Peaceful Path to Democratic Pluralism* (Cambridge, Mass.: Ballinger Publishing Co., 1987); *Up Against the Corporate Wall: Modern Corporations and Social Issues of the Eighties,* 4th Edition (Englewood Cliffs, N.J.: Prentice-Hall, 1982); "The Marketing of Infant Formula in Less Developed Countries: Public Consequences of Private Action," *California Management Review* (Summer, 1979), pp. 35–48; *Japanese Business and Social Conflict: A Comparative Analysis of Response Patterns With American Business* (Cambridge, Mass.: Ballinger, 1975); and *Business Corporations and the Black Man* (New York: Harper & Row, 1970).

2 THE SOCIETAL CONTEXT OF THE INFANT FORMULA CONTROVERSY

Globalization of Business–Society Conflict — Institutional and Structural Changes

The infant formula controversy, more so than any other event, has crystallized the growing internationalization of conflicts between corporations and host country governments, with the intervention of both international organizations and public interest groups representing different constituencies and viewpoints. Another case in point is the issue of the U.S. companies' operations in South Africa. These have been the subject of intense pressure from a variety of religious and other activist groups because of that country's apartheid policies. The U.S. government enacted legislation proscribing some types of activities on the part of the U.S. companies' operations in South Africa. Another impact of these pressures has been the establishment of the Sullivan Principles under which the subscribing companies agreed to abide by various rules of nondiscrimination and corporate social performance. Equally important, these companies have subjected themselves to outside monitoring and public reporting of their performance under these principles. Furthermore, as a consequence of these pressures, a large number of companies withdrew from doing business in South Africa.

Social activism, which until recently was a major force primarily in the United States, has now emerged as a significant element in Western Europe and is fast spreading in other parts of the world. Social activists are building effective networks across national borders to confront multinational corporations in the international arena. In the process, they have escalated the

Figure 2–1.   International sociopolitical environment of multinational corporations — pre-1970s

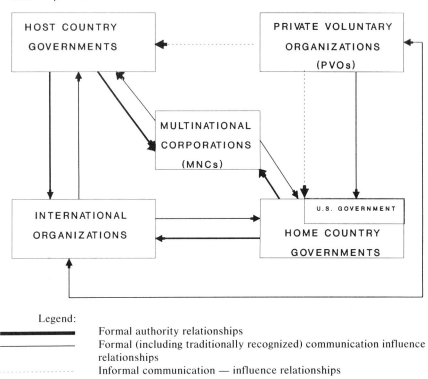

Legend:

▬▬▬▬▬	Formal authority relationships
───────	Formal (including traditionally recognized) communication influence relationships
·············	Informal communication — influence relationships

level of conflict both as to its diversity and magnitude; have built alliances with different governments; and above all, politicized many international organizations such as WHO, UNCTAD, UNICEF, UNESCO, and FAO that had previously been primarily technical or program-oriented agencies. A somewhat simplified version of the new external environment of multinational corporations (MNCs) is presented in Figures 2–1 and 2–2. The framework identifies four types of nonmarket intervenors.[1] They are: home country and host country governments, international political organizations, and private voluntary organizations.

Nonmarket Intervenors — Home Country and Host Country Governments

Figure 2–1 shows that up until the 1960s, the primary elements of the MNCs' external environment, with a measure of direct control over MNCs' behavior, were the host country and home country governments. Of the four com-

Figure 2–2. International sociopolitical environment of multinational corporations — post-1970s

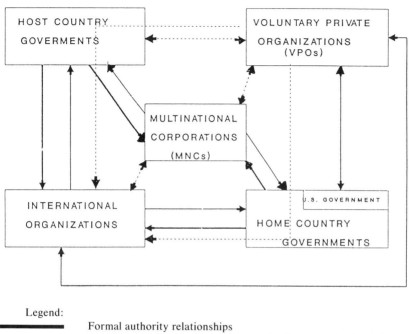

Legend:

▬▬▬▬▬	Formal authority relationships
————	Formal (including traditionally recognized) communication influence relationships
··············	Informal communication — influence relationships

ponents of the external environment, that is, nonmarket intervenors, the MNC has had a large measure of familiarity and experience in dealing with home country and host country governments. Hence, within the constraints of national sovereignty, MNCs have developed sophisticated coping mechanisms. They rely on the control of technological, financial, and marketing resources available to the MNCs; the host country's needs for these resources; and the options available to MNCs for investing their resources among countries seeking such investments.

Although there is a perception among the less developed countries (LDCs) that the balance of negotiating power, aided and abetted by MNCs' home country governments, has historically rested with the multinationals, this is not always the case. Multinational corporations are not a homogeneous group. They have different corporate goals, investment and marketing strategies, which are based on their asset dispersion, market penetration, and propensity to take risk. Thus, in many cases, a lack of bargaining power on the part of a host country may be the outcome of insufficient interest for MNCs to invest in a particular nation because of poor investment opportunities commensurate with perceived risk.[2]

LDCs also have available to them the resources of many international agencies — for example, the World Bank — and even private consulting firms of international repute, to provide legal and technical assistance in dealing with multinational corporations. Certainly, the Organization of Petroleum Exporting Countries (OPEC) nations have not lacked technical or marketing skills in dealing with the multinational corporations and Western governments on their own terms. A growing number of multinational corporations, based in developing countries such as South Korea, Taiwan, Philippines, India, and Pakistan, have been successfully competing in international markets with their Western counterparts.[3] Moreover, until recently, an anti-market growth ideology followed by many developing countries contributed to their lackluster economic performance and even economic decline. This situation was often aggravated through excessive regulation, poorly conceived macro economic policies, and corrupt administration. Under these circumstances, LDCs cannot escape at least partial blame for their poor economic showing and for the alleged misdeeds of MNC operations within their borders.[4]

Nonmarket Intervenors — International Organizations

The third type of nonmarket intervenors are various international organizations, notably United Nations' organizations and affiliated agencies. Until the beginning of the 1970s, there were only a few formal direct contacts between international organizations and MNCs. These were largely confined to such activities as standard setting and information sharing. The situation has significantly changed since then (see Figure 2–2). The addition of a large number of newly independent nations has altered the character of many of these organizations. Politically conscious, yet economically backward and sorely in need of technological and financial resources of the industrially advanced countries, the developing countries have been using their numerical power in the U.N.'s organizations and agencies to redress the economic imbalance that they perceive to be existing in the market place where capitalistic countries and private enterprises are said to hold inherently advantageous positions. These countries blamed most of their problems on the exploitative policies — both past and present — of the imperialist West. They have demanded a share of all the world's resources as a matter of historical and moral right. Even the repressive character of many of their authoritarian governments and poor management of their own economies are blamed on the Western governments and MNCs.

The politicization of many international organizations has been one manifestation of this approach. The WHO Code of infant formula marketing practices is one example of a more active and interventionist approach on the part of international organizations. Other examples can be found in the current efforts to develop a code of ethics for multinational corporations, and international codes for marketing pesticides and pharmaceuticals. The changing role of international organizations raises two important issues, those of process and outcomes. The new modus operandi of these international organizations has not yet fully developed. Therefore, an analysis of the evolution of the infant formula controversy and the role of various U.N. agencies, notably the UNICEF and WHO, should provide us with valuable insights as to their potential future role and impact in resolving technical and sociopolitical conflicts among the developing and developed countries, on the one hand, and among countries and multinational corporations, on the other hand.

Nonmarket Intervenors — PVOs

The fourth component, private voluntary organizations (PVOs), represents one of the most significant changes in the MNCs' external environment. One group of PVOs includes scientific and professional organizations with expertise and interest in issues involving their respective areas. Somewhere in the middle are institutions representing organized religion, and consumer and other groups representing the concerns of the poor and other unwary consumers and advocating causes on humanitarian and ethical grounds. Last are special interest groups and social activists whose sociopolitical and ideological orientations cover the entire spectrum of values and beliefs. These groups do not represent constituencies of people in the conventional sense of the word. Instead they represent constituencies of ideas or a vision of a different, and what they perceive to be a better, world. MNCs have become the focus of attention on the part of a large number of these activist groups because: (1) a great many issues of concern to these groups are rooted in the behavior and activities of the multinational corporations; and (2) MNCs also offer the most fertile cachet of resources that are claimed and desired by their constituencies.

Figure 2–2 shows the changing role of these groups in impacting international political and public agenda. The influence of these groups on domestic political decisions and national agenda in the United States has become amply manifest over the last two decades. The role of PVOs at the international level is more recent and not yet fully developed or well understood. And yet their impact on MNC operations can be even more far reaching and traumatic. This has been amply demonstrated in the case of the infant formula controversy and the Nestle boycott which is the subject of this enquiry.

An Analytical Framework for Understanding the Controversy — the Life-Cycle of an Issue

The adequacy and appropriateness of a strategic response to a changing social environment must be viewed within the context of the evolution of a social conflict. It requires an understanding of the impact of cultural and sociopolitical conditions on the introduction of a new phenomenon into a social system and the strategies pursued by the change agent and those who oppose it. It is, therefore, important to have a conceptual framework[5] that brings into focus the dynamics of the interaction between the elements of the external social environment and society's expectations of institutional behavior in dealing with specific issues.

The framework briefly developed here suggests a rationale by which the activities of infant formula manufacturers, private voluntary organizations, international agencies, and governments of various countries — especially those of LDCs — can be analyzed in terms of their effectiveness in introducing social change, that is, marketing of infant formula products, and their acceptance by other groups, both as to means employed and ends sought. This framework consists of three components: external environment, the institutions, and strategic response patterns.

1. *External environment* deals with the external context within which different institutions' strategies are introduced and evaluated. The focus is on the generalized external conditions created by a multitude of actions by various social actors that are essentially similar within a given contextual and temporal frame. The emphasis is on how an issue or a problem reaches successive stages of severity because of its cumulative effect, real or perceived, on the public's consciousness.

2. *Institutional characteristics* define the nature of the institution itself in terms of its value set, mission, and goals; leadership style; organizational structure and dynamics; physical and human resources; its vision of the future; and ways in which these characteristics influence an institutions or a group's strategic choices. The characteristics of an institution set the limits within which it will act, define its perception of the external environment and the relevant stage of an issue's life-cycle, and determine its response modes toward other groups' actions.

3. *Nature of strategic responses* component examines the diversity, adequacy, and effectiveness of strategic responses employed by different groups and institutions toward the achievement of their respective objectives.

The External Environment

The impact of the external environment on a problem and the effectiveness of an institution's response can best be evaluated in terms of the life-cycle of the problem. Each issue goes through various stages in terms of the public's awareness of its importance, saliency, magnitude for potential harm, scope and time available for corrective action, and private/governmental agencies that could undertake remedial action. To facilitate our understanding of the evolution of a social conflict, we can divide the elapsed time between the emergence of a problem and its solution and ultimate elimination into four categories or stages: (1) preproblem, (2) problem identification, (3) remedy and relief, and (4) prevention. There is some overlap among these categories because social problems do not fall neatly into discrete groups, nor can they always be solved in distinct successive steps.

The Preproblem Stage.   In the process of manufacturing and marketing, business firms are constantly engaged in a series of transactions that respond to two kinds of forces: market and nonmarket. In the case of market forces, a firm adapts by varying its product and service offerings to meet changing societal needs and expectations. Adequacy of response is measured in terms of a firm's ability to sell its products and services profitably in a competitive environment. All market actions, however, have some nonmarket or indirect consequences. These second-order effects are of two kinds. The first type pertains to the normal leakages found in any production and service activity and is unavoidable. The second type pertains to the unintended and unanticipated consequences of a firm's activities on other individuals and groups in society who were not a party to the market transactions and were unaware of the potential adverse effect to which they were exposed. These second-order effects, generally called externalities, traditionally have been borne by society as a whole. Taken individually, each action or incident is not significant in terms of its impact on the corporation or the affected parties. However, when undertaken by a large number of companies and continued over a long period of time, their cumulative effect is substantial. When that happens, a problem is born.

The preproblem stage has both cultural and sociopolitical dimensions. The capacity or willingness of a nation to accept and tolerate a level of societal degradation may keep a situation from accelerating to the problem identification stage. In many cases, the time lag between the creation of a problem and the emergence of its negative side effects may be quite long because the problem was too complex to be easily isolated or identified. In other instances, some influential groups are able to prevent information from being disseminated or prevent its recognition by governmental agencies and political organs. Conversely, an open communication system, the availability of mass media, and the existence of politically active and sophisticated groups can elevate a situation to the level of a crisis before all the necessary evidence is in.

The elapsed time at the preproblem stage is probably the longest of all four stages, although there is a tendency for the time span to become shorter with increasing industrialization. Most individuals and institutions respond to the problem passively. Their efforts are aimed at adaptation, and the problem is treated as a given. Elevation to the problem identification stage varies with different cultures and is based on the relative sociopolitical strength of the affecting and affected groups and the receptivity of the external environment.

Table 2–1 briefly summarizes significant events in the issue life cycle of the infant formula controversy. The preproblem phase of the infant formula controversy spanned nearly a decade from the early 1970s to May 1978. In the early 1970s, several U.N.-sponsored professional groups — for example, Protein Advisory Groups (PAG) — began to discuss the problem of infant health and nutrition. In July 1982, PAG issued a statement (No. 23) warning against the promotion of infant formula to "vulnerable groups" in the Third World. Around the same time, *The New Internationalist*[6] magazine published an article titled "The Baby Food Controversy." This was followed by the publication of a pamphlet *The Baby Killer*[7] by War on Want, a London-based public interest group involved in Third World development issues. Using Switzerland-based Nestle and England-based Cow and Gates as examples, this pamphlet accused infant formula companies with overpromoting their products to poor people in the Third World and thereby contributing to infant sickness and death. The publication of the book and its reprinting in Switzerland led Nestle to sue its critics for libel.

In the United States, a church-related group, Interfaith Center on Corporate Responsibility (ICCR), initiated a campaign to persuade U.S. corporations to curb their promotion and sale of infant formula to Third World countries. A coalition of activist groups, Infant Formula Action Coalition (INFACT), was organized that launched a boycott against Nestle in the United States. These efforts culminated in congressional hearings, chaired by U.S. Senator Edward Kennedy. The hearings became the catalyst that initiated the infant formula controversy into its next life-cycle stage — problem identification.

The Problem Identification Stage.   Once a problem has become large enough, and its impact significant enough, there is a drive among the affected groups to define it, identify its causes, and relate it to the source. This period is marked by extreme tension between opposing groups. Corporations try to delay the issue from reaching the problem identification stage while corporate critics seek to classify an issue as having reached the problem identification stage as soon as possible. This is one of the most difficult stages in the whole process. The causes of the problem may be varied, with each factor contributing only minutely to its overall impact. The definition of the problem necessarily involves conflict between vested interests and value orientations of individual groups. Thus, social activists may view all promotion of infant formula products as inherently undesirable because of its alleged adverse effect on breast-feeding. Infant formula manufacturers, on the other hand, may defend their right to sell their products to those mothers who for health, economic, or personal reasons may want to use the product, have the necessary means to buy it, and have sufficient information to use it properly.

Table 2–1.   Issue lifecycle of the infant formula controversy: significant levels

Pre-problem stage	Early 1970	Protein Advisory Group (PAG) meetings Bogota, Colombia, and Caribbean Food & Nutrition Institute meeting, Mona Jamaica
	July 4, 1977	Nestle Boycott begins
	June 1978	
Problem identification stage	July 1978	June 1978, U.S. Senate hearings chaired by Senator E. Kennedy
	May 1981	
Remedy & relief stage	May 1981	May 1981, WHO enacted a code U.S. casted the only negative vote
		Nestle announces compliance with WHO code in Third World countries
	Jan. 1984	
Prevention stage	Jan. 1984	Jan. 1984. Nestle, INBC signed agreement suspending boycott U.S. infant formula manufacturers announce WHO Code compliance in Third World countries Industry forms a new association: International Association of Infant Food Manufacturers (IFM) INBC-INFACT continues monitoring compliance by Nestle and other companies Progress in Third World countries to enact enabling legislation to conform with WHO code extremely slow Citing continued code violations, INBC's successor organization, Action for Corporate Accountability announces resumption of boycott against Nestle Direct consumer marketing of infant foods initiated in the U.S. by some companies
	Present	Nestle and American Home Products announce a gradual cessation of free distribution of samples to hospitals in Third World countries.

The problem identification stage of the infant formula controversy lasted approximately three years, from May 1978 to May 1981. Following the Kennedy hearings, both Senator Kennedy and the infant formula manufacturers agreed that the complexity and international character of the issue was such that it would be best resolved through an international agency with appropriate expertise in dealing with public health issues in the Third World.

Hence, with the concurrence of all concerned, the issue was made the responsibility of the Geneva-based World Health Organization (WHO). After extensive deliberations and heated political discussions lasting over three years, an International Code of Marketing of Breast-Milk Substitutes was enacted by the World Health Assembly (WHA), by a margin of 118–1, with United States casting the sole negative vote.

The Remedy and Relief Stage.   Once the causal linkages have been established, there arises the question of remedying the harm already inflicted on the injured parties, and imposing sanctions, penalties, or restraints on the culprits. This stage is marked by pragmatic negotiations and damage containment. It is not unusual for the previous adversaries to join in new alliances in order to find third parties — for example, government — to share the financial burden.

The remedy and relief stage of the infant formula controversy spanned the period between May 1981 and January 1984. The enactment of the Code put intensive pressure on the infant formula companies to comply with the Code. Nestle immediately announced its compliance with the Code which was soon followed by the three U.S. infant formula manufacturers. In Europe and Japan, major infant formula companies moved more cautiously and slowly. All companies, however, emphasized that they would confine their WHO Code compliance to Third World countries. In industrially advanced countries, they would address the problem in accordance with laws and regulations promulgated by the legislatures of those countries.

In the United States, INFACT intensified its boycott campaign against Nestle while continuing to put pressure on the U.S. companies through shareholder resolutions and other means of public advocacy. Nestle undertook a series of bold and quite innovative actions to meet the concerns of the company's critics. It established an audit commission, called Nestle Infant Formula Audit Commission (NIFAC), chaired by former U.S. Senator Edmund Muskie, to examine Nestle's policies for their compliance with the WHO Code and to investigate complaints of Nestle's noncompliance. This was a major step designed to gain credibility for the company's actions in compliance with the code. NIFAC thus advanced Nestle's strategy, first initiated with its decision to cooperate with the Methodist Task Force when this religious group initiated an investigation of Nestle's infant-formula-related activities in Third World countries and its compliance efforts with the WHO Code. The objective of this strategy was to reduce the level of hostility between the company and its critics by narrowing down and precisely defining the unresolved issues and creating a mechanism, or level playing field, where competing claims could be verified. The combined effect of all these efforts was the initiation of a dialogue between Nestle and INFACT, initiated under the auspices of UNICEF (United Nation's Children Fund). Consequently, an agreement was reached in January 1984 whereby Nestle's critics agreed to suspend their boycott.

The Prevention Stage.   At this stage of the issue life-cycle, the focus shifts on the development of long-range programs to prevent recurrence of the problem. These include the restructuring of organization and decision-making processes, the development of new processes, and the emergence of new special interest groups to bring about necessary changes in the sociopolitical and legal environment. The prevention stage is not sequential but generally overlaps with the problem identification and remedy and relief stages.

This stage is marked by a high degree of uncertainty and difficulty in making an accurate appraisal of potential costs and benefits of different solutions. The strategies to be pursued by society will, of necessity, involve unfamiliar sociopolitical arrangements. Each party tries to overestimate the benefits of its advocated solution while underestimating its costs. Each side enlarges its legitimacy by purporting to speak for groups that it does not directly represent, or can represent, for example, future generations, poor people of the Third World — or to foster alliances and allegiances with other groups. Preferred solutions by each party invariably provide for it a greater role in controlling the activities of other groups. It is not uncommon to find a high degree of self-righteousness in the pronouncements of various groups that are long on rhetoric but short on substance. Preventive measures may also lead to the creation of a "new issue cycle" through unforeseen negative side effects of adopted solutions.

The prevention stage of the infant formula controversy began in January 1984 and continues today. The industry efforts during the code enactment phase were coordinated by International Council of Infant Food Industry (ICIFI), a group dominated by Nestle. Thus following the enactment, although both Nestle and the ICIFI endorsed the code, this endorsement was met with almost universal skepticism. Member companies felt that ICIFI's role as the industry's voice had become ineffective because of (1) its past opposition to the code; (2) its close identification with Nestle; (3) its inability to achieve NGO status within WHO; and, (4) lack of credibility with the industry's critics, many Third World governments, and news media. Consequently, in 1983 the member companies decided to disband ICIFI. Instead, in February 1984, a new, more broad-based group was founded to represent industry's interests. Called International Association of Infant Food Manufacturers (IFM), the new organization is a member of International Society of Dietic Industries (ISDI), which has nongovernmental organization (NGO) status with WHO which enables it to make official representations to WHO on issues of interest to its members.

In the United States, Nestle had been expanding its areas of operations through acquisitions, the most notable of these being Stouffer Hotels and Carnation Co. Although, Nestle held almost 50 percent share of the worldwide infant formula sales, it did not manufacture or market infant formula products in the United States where companies like Abbott Laboratories, American Home Products, and Bristol Myers Squibb hold strong market positions and consumer franchises. However, in 1988, Nestle entered the

U.S. infant formula market through its Carnation subsidiary. In order to break the stranglehold of the U.S. manufacturers and gain customer acceptance, Nestle–Carnation introduced two products that were especially suited for infants and children who were allergic to milk or soy-based products. Moreover, the company decided to sell its products through supermarkets and also engaged in mass media direct consumer advertising. These practices immediately brought it under strong attack from the medical and health care professionals and also from the U.S. Food and Drug Administration for the products' therapeutic claims.

In October 1989 Bristol-Myers initiated a multimillion dollar consumer advertising campaign to promote a new artificial milk product for infants. This campaign was also criticized by doctors and hospitals. Many doctors have refused to recommend the product to their patients, and some have even refused to use other Bristol-Myers and Nestle products.

Ultimately, the agreement with Nestle to terminate the boycott was short-lived. Reflecting the inherent fragility of such multiparty agreements, the difficulty of arriving at and maintaining a common interpretation of lengthy and complex understandings, and the often disparate agendas of the interested parties, on October 4, 1988, the Action for Corporate Accountability (ACA) announced the resumption of the Nestle boycott and a new boycott of American Home Products. The two companies have denied the charges but the boycott has continued although with a great deal less public interest and involvement than the previous boycott.

In January 1991, under pressure from NIFAC, Nestle announced its decision to stop supplying infant formula, either free or at low cost, to hospitals and clinics in the Third World "except for the limited number of infants who need it." Within a week of Nestle's announcement, AHP also announced its plan to end all free supplies of infant formula to maternities and hospitals in developing countries within two years. In June 1991, NIFAC published its last report and decided to disband itself. It was felt that IFM, with its expanded activities and the appointment of an ombudsman, was better situated to handle activist complaints and coordinate the activities of not only Nestle but other infant formula manufacturers as well.

Notes

1. For a further discussion of the changing international sociopolitical environment as it impacts multinational corporation–Third World relations, and the role of market and non-market players, see: S. Prakash Sethi, "Opportunities and Pitfalls for Multinational Corporations in a Changed Political Environment," *Long Range Planning,* Vol. 20, No. 6 (December 1987), pp. 45–53; and, S. Prakash Sethi, Hamid Etemad, and K.A.N. Luther,"New Sociopolitical Focus: The Globalization of Conflict," *The Journal of Business Strategy* (Spring 1986), 24–31.

2. There is exhaustive literature on the role of multinational corporations in international trade and development as well as in Third World development. The latter body of literature

covers the entire spectrum, ranging from ideological, sociopolitical, and economic rationales. It would be well nigh impossible to cite even a small portion of this literature. However, following references are provided here for illustrative purposes only. See Thomas Donaldson, *The Ethics of International Business* (New York: Oxford University Press, 1989); Robert Gilpin, *U.S. Power and the Multinational Corporation* (New York: Basic Books, 1973); Norman G. Gluckman and Douglas P. Woodward, *The New Competitors* (New York: Basic Books, 1989); Stephen H. Hymar, *The International Operations of National Firms: A Study of Direct Foreign Investment* (Cambridge, Mass.: MIT Press, 1977); Robert Kutner, *The End of Laissez-Faire: National Purpose and the Global Economy After the Cold War* (New York: Knopf, 1991); Theodore H. Moran, ed., *Multinational Corporations and the Third World* (Lexington, Mass.: D.C. Heath, 1985); Kenichi Ohmae, *Borderless State* (New York: Harper, 1991); Michael E. Porter, ed., *Competition in Global Industries* (Boston, Mass.: HBS Press, 1986); Daniel K. Tarullo, "Logic, Myth and the International Economic Order," *Harvard International Law Journal,* Vol. 26, No. 2 (Spring 1985), 533–552; Raymond A. Vernon, *Storm Over the Multinationals* (Cambridge, Mass.: Harvard University Press, 1976); and, Raymond A. Vernon, "Sovereignty at Bay: Ten Years After," *International Organization* (Summer 1981).

3. See, for example: Michael E. Porter, *The Competitive Advantage of Nations* (New York: Free Press, 1990); "A Survey of the Third World: Poor Man's Burden," *The Economist,* (September 23, 1989); Louis T. Wells, Jr., *Third World Multinationals: The Rise of Foreign Investment from Developing Countries* (Cambridge, Mass.: MIT Press, 1983); and, Richard N. Farmer, ed., *Advances in International Comparative Management,* Vol. 1 (Greenwich, Conn.: Jai Press, 1984).

4. For examples of relevant literature on these and related issues, see: Carol C. Adelman, ed., *International Regulation* (San Francisco: Institute for Contemporary Studies, 1988); P.T. Bauer, *Equality, The Third World and Economic Delusion* (Cambridge, Mass.: Harvard University Press, 1981); Phillip Berryman, *Liberation Theology* (New York: Orbis, 1987); S.R. Clegg and S.G. Redding, eds., *Capitalism in Contrasting Cultures* (New York: Walter de Gruyter, 1990); Robert A. Dahl, *Democracy and its Critics* (New Haven, Conn.: Yale University Press, 1989); Robert Klitgaard, *Tropical Gangsters: One Man's Experience with Development and Decadence in Deepest Africa* (New York: Basic Books, 1990); Theodore H. Moran and contributors, *Investing in Development: New Role for Private Capital* (Washington, D.C.: Overseas Development Council, 1986); S. Prakash Sethi and Bharat B. Bhalla, "Free Market Orientation and Economic Growth: Some Lessons for the Developing Countries and Multinational Corporations," *Business in the Contemporary World,* Vol. III, No. 2 (Winter 1991), 86–101; S. Prakash Sethi and Paul Steidlmeier, "A New Paradigm of the Business/Society Relationship in the Third World: The Challenge of Liberation Theology," in Lee E. Preston, ed., *Research in Corporate Social Performance and Policy, Vol. 10* (Greenwich, Conn.: Jai Press, 1988), pp. 29–43; Hernando de Soto, *The Other Path: The Invisible Revolution in the Third World* (New York: Harper, 1989); and United Nations Development Program (UNDP), *Human Development Report 1990* (New York: Oxford University Press, 1990).

5. The discussion of the conceptual framework is based on and expanded from the author's earlier work in S. Prakash Sethi, "A Conceptual Framework for Environmental Analysis of Social Issues and Evaluation of Business Response Patterns," *The Academy of Management Review* (January 1979), 63–74, and S. Prakash Sethi, "An Analytical Framework for Making Cross-Cultural Comparisons of Business Responses to Social Pressures," in Lee E. Preston, ed., *Research in Corporation Social Performance and Policy,* Vol. 1 (Greenwich, Conn.: Jai Press, 1978), pp. 233–267.

6. H. Geach, "The Baby Food Controversy," *The New Internationalist* (August 1973); and A. Chetley, *The Baby Killer Scandal* (London: War on Want, 1979).

7. M. Muller, *The Baby Killer* (London: War on Want, 1974).

3 THE INSTITUTIONAL CONTEXT OF THE INFANT FORMULA CONTROVERSY

Core Values, Organizational Characteristics, and Strategic Options

All business activities carry with them certain second-order effects, called externalities, on society. In a market economy, a firm makes every effort, within the prevailing legal system, to externalize as much of its costs to society as possible and thereby improve its internal efficiencies and profits. The operation of the market economy assures that these second-order effects of a firm's activities are in the public domain and so must be handled by government agencies, or absorbed by various communities and groups, leaving individual firms to pursue their self-interest unfettered by external considerations.

Industrialization and economic growth have been accompanied by a tremendous increase in such costs as deterioration of human relationships within and without the organization, loss of individual freedom, and business influence on government and the political process. This has created a public feeling that business institutions, through a variety of influences, have been able to avoid paying a fair share of social costs emanating from their activities. Moreover, an increasingly large portion of these costs are being inflicted on groups who are least able to bear them and who stand to gain minimal benefits from business activities that gave rise to these costs in the first place. It is business's strategy for introducing economic, and its concomitant, social change, and its response to nonmarket forces seeking modification in corporate behavior, that has increasingly come to define the nature and scope of business–society conflicts.

It was earlier suggested that business–society conflicts are influenced by three sets of factors, namely, external environment, institutional characteristics of the groups involved, and the types of strategies and tactics they pursue in achieving their goals and objectives. The external conditions refer to the economic, social, and political environments in which a firm operates. Among the economic factors, an important element is the industry structure within which a firm operates and competitive conditions with which it must contend. A reduction in market uncertainty arising out of reduced competition yields "above normal" profits, or in economic terms, "monopoly rent," to the dominant firm or firms with secure market niches. The resultant resources provide the management with strategic slack or greater degrees of freedom with which to respond to potential changes in a firm's external environment. Under these circumstances an organization's internal factors become more important in determining corporate responses to demands for changes in its behavior from the external environment. We now turn our attention to these internal factors in the context of our analytical framework.

Nature of the Institutions Involved

The nature of an institution incorporates three distinct components. They are: the intellectual core or value set of the institution; its mission and goals, leadership style; and organizational structure and dynamics. The infant formula controversy involved four sets of players. They were the business institutions, private voluntary organizations, international agencies, and national governments. However, the primary conflict centered around the business institutions and private voluntary organizations. The remaining two groups played either supporting roles, provided legitimacy to different parties for their actions, or created arenas where strategies and tactics of opposing groups for resolving conflicts were played out. Therefore, the focus of our analysis is directed to the two primary players, that is, the corporation and private voluntary groups.

Nature of the Institutions Involved — The Corporation[1]

The *intellectual core* and *value set* of the corporate entity lie in the basic right of individuals to combine their resources — in a manner that is legal — to produce goods and services that the society needs and at prices that are competitively determined in the marketplace. The success of a corporation is determined in direct proportion to its ability to serve public needs. Profits are a measure of corporation's reward for doing a job well. In the strict sense of the word, the most profitable corporation is also the most socially responsible corporation because it has satisfied the needs of a large segment of society.

This is, however, a very narrow construction of the social role of capitalism in general and corporations in particular. Market system is not a perfect mechanism. It requires a certain degree of state supervision to enforce the rules of the game. Moreover, as Irving Kristol observes, historically the virtue of capitalism was measured: (1) in terms of its ability to maximize production of goods and services and provide people with maximum freedom to pursue their self-interest; and (2) to create a distributive system of social rewards and benefits that people considered just, fair, and equitable. Kristol suggests that modern defenders of capitalism have been emphasizing the former, while the survival of the system depends on the public's perception of capitalism's ability to deliver the latter. Devoid of its moral and aesthetic core, capitalism would be likely to lose its ethical mooring and social legitimacy.[2]

A *corporation's goals* are reasonably well defined both from the perspective of the corporation's traditional external constituencies — for example, current and potential investors — and its internal constituencies, e.g., management and employees. One of the most important characteristics of these goals is that they are *embodied* in the institution of the corporation itself. In this respect, the corporation is quite similar to certain other social institutions such as the Catholic church or the army. Although there may be marginal differences between various constituencies as to the magnitude and rate of goal achievement, the overall identity with the institution's goals remains unchallenged. This monolithic intensity provides the corporation with the power over those who serve it, to shape their outlook and character for its own ends.

Conventional wisdom would suggest that the primary goal of the corporation is to maximize the returns to its owners, that is, shareholders, commensurate with some measure of risk. However, in practice this is far from true. There is ample evidence to suggest that managers do not always act in the best interests of stockholders. The rapid turnover in stockholders and the increasingly institutional character of stockholding make stockholder governance less than effective. Top managers hold most of the cards in controlling the destiny of the corporation and, except in dire circumstances, are hard to replace by discontented stockholders.

Given the undemocratic character of the corporation and strong control exercised by top management over its affairs, we must view corporate goals in behavioral terms. Viewed in this light, managerial objectives can be defined as: (1) maximize and protect management's discretionary authority; (2) minimize risk to corporate survival; and (3) avoid conflict with other socio-political groups. These goals are hierarchical, that is, top management would not sacrifice its autonomy to minimize economic risk to the corporation or avoid social conflict with other constituent groups. Thus where tradeoffs are to be made, they must be made in favor of managerial autonomy and at the expense of the other two goals in descending order.[3]

Corporate goals are also defined in specific terms measurable both in terms of quantity and over time. Rewards for individual performance are closely tied to the achievement of corporate goals. One consequence of this approach is that managers emphasize the development of qualities that are narrowly specialized and have a high degree of relevance to corporate functions. Another consequence of this narrow specialization is a relative lack of interest in ideas that are not of immediate relevance to the business in hand.

The *organizational structure* of the corporation is essentially hierarchical in character. Increased authority for action runs parallel to an ever-enlarging responsibility for performance and rests in successively fewer hands. Although entry by individual employees into the system is voluntary, there are high exit barriers created through a system of rewards and penalties which increase with length of tenure. Therefore, within broad limits, the top management, especially the chief executive, sets not only the rhythm and work style for the corporation but also the moral tone and how it relates to its external constituencies and responds to changing societal expectations.

Corporate management is also trained to think in terms of specific problems and specific solutions, neatly partitioned to measure success over time. This is an important attribute and helps management to make efficient use of its scarce resources by providing a sharper focus on problems at hand and the means to solve them. However, this characteristic also makes managers reluctant to undertake problems that are not clearly definable or opt for solutions where performance or success is not easily measurable, if at all, within a reasonable time horizon. Unfortunately, most of the business–society issues fall into this category.

Nature of Institutions Involved — Private Voluntary Organizations[4]

Private voluntary organizations (PVOs) represent a broad spectrum of entities ranging from fairly large organized groups to informal ad hoc groups consisting of a few individuals. They also encompass a variety of ideological orientations and cover a multitude of activities. Nevertheless, PVOs can be grouped into four broad categories.

1. A large number of PVOs are either organs of sectarian organizations or are affiliated with them. Their activity agenda is invariably an extension of the goals and purposes of their parent organizations. Such a PVO is an

organizational convenience designed to provide a more focused approach to the achievement of the parent's goals. Where differences exist they are more in the nature of specific activities and the means to achieve them. Examples of these groups are: Catholic Health Association, Moral Majority, Christian Children's Fund, and Interfaith Center on Corporate Responsibility (ICCR).

2.   Another significant category includes groups of nonsectarian, professional organizations that advocate causes which directly relate to the values and goals of that profession or expertise of its members. Examples of this genre are Union of Concerned Scientists, American Medical Association, Trial Lawyers for Public Justice, and 9 to 5 National Association of Working Women.

3.   A third category consists of groups that are bound by the issues they espouse and the causes they advocate. Although they are primarily secular in nature, they may receive support from both sectarian and nonsectarian sources. Among the most notable groups in this category are The Sierra Club, Planned Parenthood, National Rifle Association, and Natural Resources Defense Fund.

4.   A fourth category is comprised of ad hoc groups that are formed by individuals in response to certain situational crises which the group members view as a threat to certain values they consider vital for their community or society as a whole. PVOs in this category include groups like Infant Formula Action Coalition (INFACT), Action on Smoking and Health (ASH), Mothers Against Drunk Driving (MADD), and National Coalition for the Homeless.

The *intellectual core* and *value set* of PVOs are loaded with symbols of high moral content, altruism, and social good. These are projected against forces of selfishness, greed, and narcissism in society. This value set has four important components that at once make PVOs a formidable force in society and a fearsome adversary to its opponents. They are also the source of a PVO's vulnerability and offer extremely tenuous hold on its existence and survival.

1.   PVOs espouse causes and represent concerns that have inherent "worthiness," thereby providing them with a built-in aura of social legitimacy and moral authority. This is important because in most cases PVOs do not or cannot receive exclusive or even explicit mandate or right of representation from those they purport to serve. Cases in point are those of safeguarding the environment, wildlife protection, pollution control, serving the poor and homeless, fighting apartheid in South Africa, or protecting the health of infants and children in the Third World. In issues like environment and wildlife, there is no natural constituency of people to protect, while in other cases, like the homeless or infants and children in the Third World, the right to representation is rarely sought or directly received. In these cases,

representational rights are self-assumed through the righteousness of the advocate in defending a just cause and in providing a needed service.

2.   The social rationale of these causes has a large ideological and moral component. Issues are seen in sharp relief as either right or wrong. Their high moral content and self-righteousness leaves little room for self-doubt or compromise, thereby making conflicts highly contentious and difficult to resolve.

3.   PVOs represent causes and serve groups with infinite and insatiable demand but with little or no economic resources to meet that demand. The environment cannot protect itself; the homeless do not have the means to acquire shelter; and the poor of the Third World are too poor to help themselves. At the same time, in order to redress these social problems and correct social wrongs, PVOs must ask for resources from others who may have had little to do with the creation of these ills except in a an indirect manner as members of society, or from those who are being accused of being the culprits and are, therefore, immediate and direct adversaries.

This approach is in sharp contrast to the operational context of a business organization where both the providers and the users of a firm's products and services command a firm's resources in direct proportion to their willingness and ability to pay for them. Thus a firm constantly strives to make efficient use of resources and provide services to only those whose needs are considered to be of highest priority because they are willing to pay more for them than anyone else. PVOs, on the other hand, give priority to providing services to those users who are least able to pay for them. Thus there is an ever-expanding demand for these services with little built-in constraints. And yet, these needs cannot be served without imposing costs on other segments of society or sacrificing other social needs. Unfortunately, the PVO system of advocacy consists of "special interest pleading," notwithstanding its moral overtones, and as such largely ignores alternative priorities.

4.   Given that the providers of resources to PVOs do not gain any direct or concrete benefits, PVOs must constantly devote an inordinate amount of energy and expense to rally people to their causes and urge them to give voluntarily of their time and money. This calls for creating a high profile for the cause, imbuing it with intense emotional content, and providing it with an adversary who is formidable and must be conquered, whether it be self-guilt or another institution, such as bad corporation or big government.

Sources of Legitimacy.   PVOs draw their *legitimacy* from four sources: intrinsic, contractual, functional, and constituency-based. These categories are not mutually exclusive. A given group may assert legitimacy for its actions based on one or more of these rationale either simultaneously or sequentially. Intrinsic legitimacy accrues when a group undertakes an activity with a high moral and ethical content and inherent worthiness: for example, animal welfare rights, Sierra Club, Infant Formula Action Coalition, Pro Life and Pro Choice advocacy groups. Contractual legitimacy arises when a group is asked to perform certain actions under contract from another group, whether a PVO or for-profit organization: for instance, legal aid to indigent people, Investor Responsibility Research Center (IRRC). Functional legitimacy accrues to a group when it undertakes activities with a high component of social need but which are insufficiently performed: for example, foster care, fine arts, culture enhancement activities. Constituency-based legitimacy is accrued through a direct mandate from the people being represented by the PVO, and organizations that are supported by people and institutions who agree with their programs and action agenda but have no contractual relations. Examples of PVOs in this category include American Association of Retired Persons, National Rifle Association, Common Cause, Council on Economic Priorities, Natural Resources Defense Council, and World Wildlife Fund.

PVOs follow divergent paths in designing their *organizational structures* based on size, task complexity, financial resources, and length of time a PVO has been in existence. In general, large well-established organizations are likely to have more formal, hierarchical structures. Organizations that undertake a variety of tasks requiring a multiplicity of skills and resource combinations, and/or cover diverse geopolitical regions, are likely to have organization structures that mimic divisional structures followed by business corporations with diversified products and regions.

The *decision-making style* of most PVO groups is consensual in which a great deal of effort is expended in following democratic procedures for decision making. This is done from sheer necessity because PVO workers draw a large measure of their compensation in terms of psychic satisfaction from doing something worthwhile, "making a difference," or being part of a movement. Therefore, they must be seen as being meaningful participants in the groups' decision-making processes. Clearly, this process is more apparent and less real when a PVO grows in size, involves a large number of people, and deploys many types of professionals. Similarly, all PVOs must, of necessity, devote inordinate time and resources in raising funds to support their activities. Therefore, PVOs develop elaborate systems — both formal and informal — to keep their constituents informed of their activities and keep them involved, to ensure their continuous support and participation.

A consensual or participative approach to internal decision making and external constituency building is more vital to the survival of PVOs that depend on grassroots level activity and volunteer support. These groups face a conflicting dilemma. They must allow for maximum discussion and democratic decision making to ensure a continuously high level of involvement on the part of participants. At the same time, they must also have a strong and disciplined leadership that would mobilize an essentially volunteer mass with differing and changing levels of motivation. These groups also have a high rate of turnover and must depend on a relatively small but dedicated core of professional organizers and charismatic leaders to keep the organization's agenda in focus and get things moving. The end result is that these groups display a large measure of apparent and ritualistic group discussion and consensual decision making. And yet in reality more decisions are made by a small coterie of core individuals and is approved by the body politic after lengthy discussions where everyone is allowed to have his/her say and made to feel that his/her views have been heard. In this sense, internal communications and decisionmaking procedures display a strong similarity to the ritualistic communications — prior to formal decisions — in the Japanese management system.[5]

Nature of Strategic Options

The dynamics of social change create environmental uncertainty where an institution must constantly defend its turf and justify its modus operandi. In a changing sociopolitical environment, the performance of a corporation, or for that matter any other social institution, must be, to a large extent, culturally and temporally determined. In the final analysis, all organizations must depend on society for their existence, continuity, and growth. Thus given the organic and dynamic nature of social systems, institutions must constantly strive to pattern their activities so that they are in congruence with the goals of the overall system.[6] The strategic response patterns of competing organizations in a given societal conflict situation can be classified into four broad categories. These are: domain defense, domain offence-encroachment, domain expansion, and domain integration.[7]

Domain Defense

The objective of this strategy is to maintain: (1) the sanctity of an organization's activity domain, that is, its raison d'etre and goal legitimacy; and (2) to preserve managerial autonomy in choosing means to accomplish organization goals. Domain defense includes *both* the organization's persona, that is, its right to exist, and its functional mode of operations. The critical element in domain defense is maintaining the integrity of an organization's core values and the means which the organization has *traditionally* used (historical prerogatives) to maintain and expand those core values. It is not crucial whether these core values have their original sanctification from legal, sociopolitical, or historical bases. They may even have been acquired through a derivative process, that is, through an affiliation, legal or implied: for example, "halo effect" with another organization possessing societal acceptance of its core values.

In issues of public policy, involving business–society conflicts, the concept of legitimacy is very important and incorporates both legal and nonlegal legitimacy. While legal legitimacy connotes a sense of current societal consensus as to the nature and scope of an organization's activity domain, nonlegal legitimacy, that is, changing public attitudes, suggests the future direction of societal expectations as to that organization's behavior. The latter concept is more dynamic and represents a greater challenge to the organization in defending its activity domain and anticipating potential threats from other groups. An erosion in societal acceptance of the legitimacy of an organization's core values could be fatal to its survival and future growth. It may also legitimize the right of other groups to challenge its activity domain.

Domain Offense — Encroachment

An organization seeking to create a new activity domain or expand an existing one has two approaches at its disposal which it may pursue in any combination: (1) it may stake out as its activity domain an area of activity or a group of people that is not being currently served; and (2) it may displace another group and take over its activity domain. The former may come about because a particular activity/issue or group has not been deemed economically or politically important by existing organizations. However, to make this group or activity viable, the group leadership will have to enhance its influence in the environment, thereby making it more of a threat to the activity domain of another organization. The second approach is designed to remove a particular activity away from the domain of an existing organization and thereby threaten its survival and growth or, at a minimum, reduce its potential competitive strength and operational autonomy.

Domain Expansion

In business–society conflicts, strategies of domain defense and offense assume a clearly delineated activity domain where any gain for one group must come at the expense of some other group. The conflict is thus viewed as a zero-sum game by all parties concerned. Domain expansion occurs when opposing groups seek to expand the scope of a particular domain where incrementally added activities offer opportunities for cooperation and coalition building, and thereby devise new and more creative solutions to conflict resolution. There are two important points to remember with regard to the strategy of domain expansion: (1) the organization following the strategy of domain defense, for instance, the corporation, does not yield any variation in its domain specifications or restrict its operational autonomy.[8] Instead, it agrees to cooperate with opposing groups in entirely new areas of activity that had previously not been part of its domain; and (2) this domain expansion may consist of marginal or peripheral activities that would not appreciably alter the characteristics of an organization's primary activity domain. Thus domain expansion may have more symbolic than substantive value, and the opposing groups may often use it as a face-saving device when the conflict appears unresolvable and the dominant group prefers to minimize the potential for future conflict by creating an aura of amiability or cooperation. Where domain expansion is significant in scope and potential impact, it almost invariably comes at the expense of third parties who were either unaware of this potential assault on their activity domain or were too weak to defend themselves against this encroachment.

Domain Integration

The strategy of domain integration calls for a proactive approach to conflict resolution where opposing parties do not seek to enhance their position and activity domain at the expense of others, either those who are directly involved in the conflict or other third parties. Instead, this approach seeks to incorporate, or reconcile, conflicting objectives of the opposing groups in a manner that produces a unified set of goals and operational strategies that yield a larger positive gain for all concerned. It is in a sense a "win-win" solution. For domain integration strategy to work, four things are necessary: (1) opposing groups must develop a high threshold level of trust for each other's motives and integrity; (2) they must not seek to challenge each other's core values or absolute minimum goals necessary for the organization's survival and well being; (3) they must be willing to yield on less important goals in order to achieve their major aims and also help their opponents to maintain the integrity of their core values; (4) in conflict resolution, they seek innovative solutions that redefine the nature of the problem itself and thereby generate high positive goal achievement values not only for the groups involved but also for the broader community. Pruitt (1981)[9] makes a distinction between compromises and integrative agreements. The former is based on specific tradeoffs where opposing parties attempt to match their relative gains and losses to ensure that each one maximizes its relative gain when adjusted for one's bargaining and risk of loss from delayed or postponed agreements. Integrative solutions, on the other hand, attempt to fashion agreements that have the potential of yielding higher combined positive values while minimizing the losses on issues that are most important to various parties to the conflict. According to Pruitt,[10] integrative solutions are preferable where:

- both sides have a large number of nonnegotiable demands, and conflict resolution is not possible unless a way can be found to reconcile all parties' interests;

- compromises have been forced under pressure of time or other factors but without resolving the underlying sources of contention. They become unsatisfactory to both parties and cause issues to resurface at a future date. Domain integration offers greater long-term stability;
- domain integration creates mutually rewarding arrangements and thereby strengthens relations between parties; and
- domain integration fashions solutions that are least disruptive, and are accommodative of the interests of parties, both inside and outside the conflict. They have the potential for contributing to the welfare of the broader community.

Linkages Between Strategic Options and Managerial Choices

Corporations must constantly cope with environmental risk and uncertainty arising out of economic and competitive factors. In business–society conflicts, additional elements of uncertainty result from sociopolitical considerations. Management's perception of environmental risk and uncertainty comes about from (1) its knowledge, and capacity to learn, about *objective* environmental factors, and (2) its *perception* of risks associated with changes in those factors.[11] The former relates to an assessment of the magnitude of the environmental risk. The latter relates to the management's perception of its ability to manage and propensity to take that risk.

An organization's ability to respond to changes in its external environment and its choice of particular response patterns would depend on the degree of *strategic slack* available to the firm, as well as *managerial uniqueness,* that is, internal factors of organization structure, corporate culture, and leadership style that distinguish a firm's response patterns to external forces from those of other firms.[12]

Strategic slack includes two components: economic slack and organizational slack.[13] Strategic slack is a measure of firm's resources and market power, however achieved, that allows it "a window of opportunity to initiate changes in its operations in socially desirable directions. Alternately, it can provide the corporation with the resources with which to defy the external environment, or delay changes sought by the external environment in a corporation's goals and operational strategies."[14] To the extent that a firm can insulate itself from market forces, it achieves above-normal returns on its investment and thereby provides its management with extra resources compared with those of the firm's competitors. In economic and market terms, "slack" implies excess resources that a firm commands in the marketplace resulting from superior performance in comparison with other firms competing in the marketplace for consumer patronage and supply of capital and other resources. A firm must make every effort to generate economic slack, "defined as above-market rent, that a firm is able to extract from the use of its resources. This above-market rent may come as a result of a firm or industry's dominant position in certain markets, protected niches either through regulation or other such factors as brand loyalty, copyrights, patents, etc."[15] Clearly, a large measure of economic slack available to a firm's management increases its discretion as to choice of strategies that it may use both in dealing with economic and noneconomic issues.

A decline in market uncertainty also causes organizational slack and inertia where internal factors become more important in determining corporate responses to demands for changes in its behavior from the external environment.[16] These internal factors include corporate assets, resources (physical and human), market knowledge and experience, corporate culture and institutional memory, management expertise, management's self-image and management's belief in the rightness of its position, management's perception of hostility in the environment, and its evaluation of the relative strength of its opponents — both governmental agencies and nongovernmental groups.[17]

Existence of strategic slack is a prerequisite to managerial discretion in decision making. Therefore, managers would seek every possible way to maximize this slack even in the absence of economic slack. This is often possible where managers have control of internal organization and have insulated themselves from the pressures of stockholders or other claimants on a company's resources. It is easily seen in situations when an entrenched management rewards itself with additional compensation and other perquisites of office even in the face of poor corporate earnings and lower market valuation of a firm's stock.

It is important to note that while a large measure of strategic slack increases a management's discretion, the manner in which that discretion is used impacts a firm's conceptualization of its strategic options and its preference for a particular option. The latter factor is determined by what we call "managerial uniqueness," the sum total factors that define the corporate personality. Strategic slack affords management the arrogance of power to respond negatively to external forces of change. Thus, a self-assured and self-righteous management may be willing to tolerate a high degree of mismatch between corporate behavior and external environmental expectations, thereby causing a higher level and an extended period of dissonance between the corporation and its adversaries.[18] Alternately, strategic slack may provide management with an opportunity to experiment, fashion innovative solutions, and respond proactively to external forces of change. Thus, a self-assured and yet tolerant management, when cushioned with a high level of current profits, may be willing to take a longer term perspective of the situation and move more rapidly to reduce the level of mismatch than called for by immediate and predictable changes in external environment. Both of these response patterns may involve short-term economic considerations, that is, impact on market structure and competitive prices; and long-term considerations of a corporation's ability to continue to operate in a nonhostile economic and sociopolitical environment.[19] In the discussion that follows in subsequent chapters, we analyze strategies and tactics of Nestle and the infant formula industry, and those of their opponents, within the framework of domains of strategic option, strategic slack, and management uniqueness.

Notes

1. The discussion in this section is partly drawn and adapted from, S. Prakash Sethi, "A Strategic Framework for Dealing with Schism Between Business and Academe," *Public Affairs Review,* IV (1983), 4–59.

2. Irving Kristol, "When Virtue Loses All Her Loveliness: Some Reflections on Capitalism and The Free Society," *The Public Interest* (Fall 1970), 3–16.

3. S. Prakash Sethi and Cecilia Falbe, "Determinants of Corporate Social Performance," paper presented at the Stanford Business Ethics Workshop, Graduate School of Business, Stanford University, Stanford, Calif., August 14–17, 1985.

4. Although social activism has had a long history in the United States, it has been only during the last 20 years or so that it has begun to receive serious systematic attention from researchers and scholars. For a representative sample of readings covering different and often opposing views on social activism, see: Sanford D. Horwitt, *Let Them Call Me Rebel: Saul Alinsky — His Life and Legacy* (New York: Random House, 1991); S. Prakash Sethi, "The Corporation and the Church: Institutional Conflict and Social Responsibility," *California Management Review,* XV, 1 (1972), 63–74; Michael Novak, *This Hemisphere of Liberty: A Philosophy of the Americas* (Washington, D.C.: The AEI Press, 1990); Ernest W. Lefever, *Amsterdam to Nairobi: The World Council of Churches and the Third World* (Washington, D.C.: Ethics and Public Policy Center, 1979).

5. S. Prakash Sethi, Nobuaki Namiki, and Carl S. Swanson, *The False Promise of the Japanese Miracle* (New York: Harper & Row, 1985), 37–39.

6. S. Prakash Sethi, "A Conceptual Framework for Environmental Analysis of Social Issues and Evaluation of Corporate Response Patterns," *The Academy of Management Review,* 4, 1 (January 1979), 63–74. See also Barry D. Baysinger, "Domain Maintenance as an Objective of Business Political Activity: An Extended Typology," *Academy of Management Review,* 9, 2 (1984), 248–254; Robert H. Miles, *Coffin Nails and Corporate Strategies* (Englewood Cliffs, N.J.: Prentice-Hall, 1982); C. Perrow, *Complex Organizations: A Critical Essay,* 2nd ed. (Glenview, Ill.: Scott, Foresman, 1979); and J. Dowling and J. Pfeffer, "Organizational Legitimacy: Social Values and Organizational Behavior," *Pacific Sociological Review,* 18, 1, (1975), 22–136.

7. In developing a typology here, I owe a debt of gratitude to Barry Baysinger (1984, *op. cit.,* supra note 6), and Robert Miles (1982, *op. cit.,* supra note 6) for their work. However, although the nomenclature in the current study is rather similar in important parts to that of Baysinger and Miles, the typologies developed here are substantially different as to their content and applications. For example in Baysinger (1984), there are three types of activity domains: domain management, domain defense, and domain maintenance. He makes a distinction between domain defense and domain maintenance in that the former is concerned with defending the organization's goals and purposes; the latter is concerned with the methods by which the organization pursues its goal and purposes. In my analysis, I make no such distinction. Based on an extensive study of a large number of business and society conflicts,

I have found that both corporations and their adversaries may use similar tactics while pursuing different strategies. See S. Prakash Sethi and Paul Steidlmeier, *Up Against the Corporate Wall: Modern Corporations and Social Issues of the Nineties*, 5th ed. (Englewood Cliffs, N.J.: Prentice-Hall, 1991). Thus in my classificatory schema, domain defense and domain maintenance are merged, thereby making a major departure from the logic of Baysinger's typology. Baysinger's concept of domain management is somewhat similar to my category of domain offense with the difference that I do not make any distinction between means. Miles (1982, pp. 52–53) suggests a three-part classification; domain defense, domain offense, and domain creation. While his notion of domain defense is quite similar to the one suggested here, his other two categories are quite different. Domain offense, according to Miles, is a competitive notion and incorporates both market displacement and internal efficiencies that would provide the organization with further resources with which to defend its activity domain. In my classification, domain offense is defined primarily in terms of its objective, that is, to attack and encroach on one's adversary's activity domain *regardless* of the means used to achieve such a purpose. Miles's concept of domain creation essentially focuses on diversification strategies wherein organizations seek out new areas that offer greater growth potential or a more hospitable operational environment. As has been shown in the text, this concept varies significantly with the concepts of domain expansion and domain integration that have more specific meaning and carry distinct implications for organizational strategies and tactics.

8. Domain expansion, as developed here, shares some apparent attributes with Baysinger's typology of domain management (1984, p. 249), with some significant differences. Baysinger visualized cooperative activities primarily among one type of groups — for example, business organizations lobbying together, while our classification visualizes domain expansion coming through cooperation with opposing types of organizations even while conflict continues among similar organizations. An example of this situation is where one or more companies breaks ranks from the industry held joint positions, and instead forms alliances with activist groups opposing them.

9. Dean G. Pruitt, "Achieving Integrative Agreements," in Max H. Bazerman and Roy J. Lewicki, eds., *Negotiating in Organizations* (Beverly Hills, Calif.: Sage Publications, 1983), p. 36.

10. Dean G. Pruitt, *Negotiating Behavior* (New York: Academic Press, 1981), pp. 137–162; See also Dean G. Pruitt, "Achieving Integrative Agreements," in Max H. Bazerman and Roy J. Lewicki, eds., *Negotiating in Organizations, ibid.*, pp. 35–50.

11. Masoud Yasai-Ardekani, "Structural Adaptations to Environments," *Academy of Management Review,* 11, 1 (1986), 9–21.

12. Sethi and Falbe, "Determinants of Corporate Social Performance," supra note 3.

13. Cecilia M. Falbe and S. Prakash Sethi, "The Concept of Strategic Slack: Implications for Strategic Response Patterns by Corporations to Public Policy Options," paper presented at the 9th Annual International Conference of Strategic Management Society, San Francisco, Calif., October 11–14, 1989. See also Mark P. Sharfman, Gerrit Wolf, Richard B. Chase, and David A. Tansik, "Antecedents of Organizational Slack," *Academy of Management Review,* 13, 4 (1988), 601–614; J.L. Bourgeois and J. Singh, "Organizational Slack and Political Behavior Within Top Management Teams," *Academy of Management Proceedings* (1983), 43–47; R.M. Cyert and J.G. March, *A Behavioral Theory of the Firm* (Englewood Cliffs, N.J.: Prentice-Hall, Inc., 1963); Yasai-Ardekani, *op. cit.,* supra note 11; Miles, *op. cit.,* supra note 6; Robert H. Miles, *Managing the Corporate Social Performance: A Grounded Theory* (Englewood Cliffs, N.J.: Prentice-Hall, 1987).

14. Sethi and Falbe, *op. cit.,* supra note 3.

15. Falbe and Sethi, *op.cit.,* supra note 13.

16. R.E. Caves and M.E. Porter, "Market Structure, Oligopoly, and Stability of Market Shares," *The Journal of Industrial Economics,* 26 (1978), 289–313; R.B. Duncan, "Characteristics of Organizational Environments and Perceived Environmental Uncertainty," *Ad-*

ministrative Science Quarterly, 17 (1972), 313–327; Peter H. Grinyar, "Strategy, Structure, Size and Bureaucracy," *Academy of Management Journal* 24, 3 (1981), 471–486; L.G. Hrebniak and C.C. Snow, "Industry Differences in Environmental Uncertainty and Organizational Characteristics Related to Uncertainty," *Academy of Management Journal,* 23 (1980), 750–759; R.E. Miles and C.C. Snow, *Organizational Strategy, Structure and Process* (New York: McGraw Hill, 1978); J. Pfeffer and H. Leblebici, "The Effort of Competition on Some Dimensions of Organizational Structure," *Social Forces,* 52 (1973), 268–279; J. Pfeffer and G.R. Salancik, *The External Control of Organizations* (New York: Harper & Row, 1978); and W.H. Starbuck, "Organizations and their Environments," in M.D. Dunnette (ed.), *Handbook of Industrial Organizational Psychology* (Chicago, Ill.: Rand McNally, 1976), pp. 1069–1123.

17. J. Child, "Managerial and Organizational Factors Associated with Company Performance — Part II: A Contingency Analysis," *Journal of Management Studies,* 12 (1975), 12–28; B.L.T. Hedberg, P.C. Nystrom, and W.H. Starbuck, "Camping on Seesaws: Prescriptions for a Self-Designing Organization," *Administrative Science Quarterly,* 21 (1976), 41–56; M.W. McCall, Jr., "Making Sense with Nonsense: Helping Frames of Reference Clash," in P.C. Nystrom and W.H. Starbuck (eds.), *Prescriptive Models of Organizations* (Amsterdam: North-Holland, 1977), pp. 111–123; P.C. Nystrom and W.H. Starbuck, "Managing Beliefs in Organizations," *Journal of Behavioral Science,* 20 (1984), 277–287; and W.H. Starbuck, "Congealing Oil: Investing Ideologies to Justify Acting Ideologies Out," *Journal of Management Studies,* 18 (1981), 3–27.

18. R.M. Cyert and J.G. March, *op. cit.,* supra note 13; R. Leifer and G.P. Huber, "Relations Among Perceived Environmental Uncertainty, Organizational Structure and Boundary Spanning Behavior," *Administrative Science Quarterly,* 22 (1977), 235–247; J.R. Montanari, "Operationalizing Strategic Choice," in J.H. Jackson and C.P. Morgan, eds., *Organization Theory: A Macro Perspective for Management* (Englewood Cliffs, N.J.: Prentice-Hall, Inc., 1978); P.C. Nystrom and W.H. Starbuck, "To Avoid Organizational Crisis, Unlearn," *Organizational Dynamics,* 12, 4 (1984), 53–65; A.M. Pettigrew, *The Politics of Organizational Decision-Making* (London: Tavistock, 1973); W.H. Starbuck and J.M. Dutton, "Designing Adaptive Organizations," *Journal of Business Policy,* 3, 4 (1978), 21–28; and W.H. Starbuck, A. Greve, and B.L.T. Hedberg, "Responding to Crises," *Journal of Business Strategy,* 9, 2 (1978), 111–137.

19. Sethi and Falbe, "Determinants of Corporate Social Performance," *op. cit.,* supra note 3; R.B. Duncan, "Characteristics of Organizational Environments and Perceived Environmental Uncertainty," *op.cit.,* supra note 16; L.G. Hrebniak and C.C. Snow, "Industry Differences in Environmental Uncertainty and Organizational Characteristics Related to Uncertainty," *op. cit.,* supra note 16; J. Pfeffer and G. R. Salancik, *op. cit.,* supra note 16; W. H. Starbuck, *op. cit.,* supra note 16; and Masoud Yasai-Ardekani, "Structural Adaptations to Environments," *op. cit.,* supra note 11.

II THE GATHERING STORM

4 SOWING THE SEEDS OF THE CONTROVERSY: THE EUROPEAN SCENE

Why are mothers abandoning breast feeding in countries where it is part of the culture? Are we helping to promote the trend? What is the responsibility of the baby food industry? What are we doing to prevent avoidable malnutrition?[1]

This was the provocative beginning of a report entitled *The Baby Killer*,* published in March 1974, by Mike Muller and War on Want, a London-based, nonprofit, activist group that deals with hunger, poverty, and other problems of the Third World. The report was headlined "A War on Want Investigation into the Promotion and Sale of Powdered Milk in the Third World." Investigation it certainly was. The report castigated the entire infant food industry for its marketing and promotion practices in Third World countries. Nestle, as the largest marketer of such products in the Third World, came in for special scorn and criticism. In addition to Nestle, the report also made a particular mention of the marketing and promotional activities of Cow and Gate, a multinational company headquartered in the United Kingdom with operations in a large number of Third World countries.

---

*All references to *The Baby Killer* in this chapter will often be made as "The Report" followed by appropriate page numbers.

In strong language that dripped with an extreme sense of moral outrage, the opening paragraph of the report summarized its conclusion by stating:

> Third World babies are dying because their mothers bottle-feed them with Western style infant milk. Many that do not die are drawn into a vicious cycle of malnutrition and disease that will leave them physically and intellectually stunted for life.
>
> The frightening fact is that this suffering is avoidable. The remedy is available to all but the small minority of mothers who cannot breast feed, because mother's milk is accepted by all to be the best food for any baby under six months old.
>
> Although even the baby food industry agrees that this is correct, more and more Third World mothers are turning to artificial foods during the first few months of their babies' lives. In the squalor and poverty of the new cities of Africa, Asia and Latin America, the decision is often fatal.
>
> The baby food industry stands accused of promoting their products in communities which cannot use them properly; of using advertising, sales girls dressed up in nurses' uniforms, give away samples and free gift gimmicks that persuade mothers to give up breast feeding. [The Report, p. 2]

With this salvo, War on Want believed that by opening the subject to public debate, a solution might be found faster than through silence. But what it opened was much more than a debate. It started a movement that saw, among other things, an internationalization of social conflict involving transnational corporations, national governments, and international organizations. It forced industry and business groups to recognize, in addition to their owners or stockholders, a larger set of stakeholders: employees, customers, local governments, and public interest groups, to name a few. The chain of events started by *The Baby Killer* and the ensuing events thrust voluntary private organizations into playing the roles of catalysts, instigators, power brokers, and oversight monitors. Finally, it demonstrated the power of organized religion to forge alliances and build coalitions among activist groups of different persuasions and bring about changes in their behavior and in the direction of their activities.

The introductory sentence of the report disclaimed any intention "to prove that baby milk kills babies." It observed that "in optimum conditions, with proper preparation and hygiene, they can be a perfectly adequate infant food." The report goes on to state that the conditions in the Third World, however, are far from ideal. Under conditions of utmost poverty, illiteracy, squalor, unsanitary conditions, and almost nonexistent basic health care facilities, "the choice of an artificial substitute for breast milk is in reality a choice between health and disease" and "baby milks can be killers." [The Report, p. 5]

The report stated that for almost two decades the infant food companies have been expanding into less developed countries, aided with consumer

advertising campaigns in mass media and other unsavory marketing and promotional tactics. These include:

- Use of medically unqualified salesgirls who are hired and dressed in
  nurses' uniforms.
- Mothers being encouraged to bottle-feed their babies while they are breastfeeding them satisfactorily.
- Payment to qualified nurses on a sales-related basis, thereby belying their
  educational role.
- Use of mass media consumer advertising suggesting that feeding babies
  with the sponsoring company's brand of infant formula would cause babies
  to grow up healthy.
- Provision of free samples to mothers in hospitals encouraging them to use
  a company's product.
- Labels that associate healthy baby pictures with the use of infant food.
- Promotional gimmicks and sales incentives to induce people to buy and
  use infant formula products.
- Free gifts to doctors and also free samples of infant foods to induce them
  to use them in their hospitals and recommend them to new mothers.
- Educational literature widely displayed in hospitals that associates bottle
  feeding and infant formula with healthy babies. [The Report, p. 13]

Representatives of Nestle and other companies mentioned in *The Baby
Killer* strongly denied these allegations. They all expressed their agreement
that most infants should be breast-fed and claimed that this was their intent
in the educational materials distributed by the companies in maternity wards
of hospitals and to the medical profession. They further asserted that all
promotional activities were directed at consumers who had already made a
choice, for whatever reason, to use infant formula foods. The following comments by a Nestle spokesman typifies the industry response *at that time* to
the questions raised by the critics of the infant formula industry.

> We have milk on the market; naturally that milk is going to be available to the
> people. We do not deny that there is a trend to use that milk for feeding babies
> but we can say that there are good reasons for doing so in some cases. If the
> mother comes to a decision not to breastfeed because she has to use an alternative
> for some reason, then this is not our promotion against breastfeeding.
>   This problem of misuse of baby foods which causes gastroenteritis: we know
> the whole cycle, over-dilution, bad bottle hygiene and all that. Nobody is trying
> to deny that it happens and we deplore the fact that it does. It is a very bad
> advertisement for our product if it happens with our product. So we would like to
> be able to control the consumption to those people who can afford our product.
> It's good business to do so. Our problem is how do you stop that product from
> getting to people who shouldn't be using it. [The Report, p. 13]

The Baby Killer did not believe that industry would voluntarily put more emphasis on infant nutrition and health at the expense of its sales and profits. As evidence, the report cited Nestle's annual report (1973) indicating that although sales growth in developed countries was lagging in line with declining birth rates, they were doing well in developing countries "thanks to the growth of population and improved living standards" (p. 21). *The Baby Killer* made a series of recommendations for industry to follow. They were to set the stage for confrontation in the ensuing months and years between War on Want and Nestle, and eventually between infant formula food manufacturers and country governments, various international organizations, and a variety of public interest and religious groups. The recommendations, among others, included:

• A ban on all consumer advertising in poor countries.
• A ban on promotion to the medical profession.
• Companies should refrain from all consumer advertising, promotion to the medical profession, and all other activities that might discourage mothers from breastfeeding their infants.
• They should also work with international organizations on the problems of infant and child nutrition.
• Governments of developing countries were urged to curtail importation, distribution, and promotion of infant foods where these foods made little useful contribution to infant nutrition and health. (The Report, p. 18)

Antecedents to the Controversy: The Protein Advisory Group

The publication of *The Baby Killer* galvanized media attention and focused world opinion not only on infant malnutrition, but also the activities of the infant formula industry in general and those of Nestle–Switzerland in particular. Thousands of requests were received for the report, and over 20,000 copies of the English version were distributed worldwide. It was also translated into many different languages around the world.

The Baby Killer was the catalyst in making the infant formula controversy highly politicized and heightened in public consciousness. The antecedents of the controversy, however, can be traced back more than 30 years in the work of various United Nations agencies through their ad hoc coalition, the Protein Advisory Group. In the 1940s, pediatricians, nutrition specialists, and U.N. agencies became cognizant of the problems of infant nutrition in tropical and subtropical regions. The condition, identified as protein malnutrition, sparked an effort on the part of these agencies to develop potential uses of supplemental protein from fish, peanuts, sesame, soy, and skim milk. As an area of concern, infant malnutrition, however, did not fit into existing niches in any particular agency such as FAO, WHO, or UNICEF. Therefore, UNICEF took the initiative and proposed the creation of an ad hoc committee of tripartite sponsorship composed of UNICEF, WHO, and FAO. This led to two informative conferences sponsored by the Macy Foundation in Jamaica in 1953, and in Princeton in 1955. Among the recommendations of the Princeton conference was that:

> an independent advisory body be formed and provide guidance to the relevant international agencies for the development, testing, and utilization of protein sources available indigenously. The conference specifically mentioned the need to develop quality criteria for protein foods suitable for feeding infant and young children.[2]

The Protein Advisory Group (PAG) was organized in 1955. The membership of PAG was drawn from various U.N. agencies, Third World governments, academic institutions, and private sector companies involved in the manufacturing and sale of infant foods; it consisted primarily of well-known pediatricians and clinicians. The PAG meetings brought together officials from WHO, FAO, UNICEF, Infant Formula producers, pediatricians, and nutritionists.[3] The PAG effort spanned over 22 years from 1955 to 1977, with over 50 members, including six different chairmen and three different vice chairmen. The early period of PAG work was distinguished for its cooperative nature where people represented different constituencies. The problem was essentially viewed in scientific and resource availability terms. However, as the years passed, and with the turnover in PAG membership and staff personnel, the focus shifted somewhat toward the role of various institutions, notably the producers of infant formula foods. New members stressed the importance of breastfeeding and proper weaning practices for infant nutrition. They formed a subgroup within PAG called the "Working Group on Feeding the Preschool Child." The group's name became Protein Calorie Advisory Group in the early 1970s. Thus, rather than looking at the totality of the problem, increasing attention was paid to the marketing practices of infant formula compounds in the Third World. The process became somewhat adversarial, with companies being accused of contributing to the problem of infant morbidity and mortality through overpromotion of breast milk substitutes.

At this time, Dr. Derrick B. Jelliffe, an expert in infant nutrition and a participant in the group's forums, wrote a paper entitled "The Urban Avalanche and Child Nutrition."[4] This paper documented the trend of declining breastfeeding and its effect on infant mortality. Also suggested was the catalytic role that industry advertising played in this trend. This was followed by another paper, "Commerciogenic Malnutrition?" in *Nutrition Review.*[5] Dr. Jelliffe, a PAG consultant, was the director of the Caribbean Food & Nutrition Institute at that time. In "Commerciogenic Malnutrition?" Jelliffe states that "malnutrition in young children in developing countries has a highly complex etiology, varying from area to area, and indeed changing in pattern with time. At the moment, the infant food industry is not helping and, on balance, probably is a deleterious force in regard to the nutrition of young children in technically developing countries."[6]

These papers were to have a profound effect on the nature of debate both within PAG and also in broader sociopolitical circles on the infant formula controversy. Increasingly, the infant formula companies were seen as the villains and the Third World countries as the victims. Coming into the meetings, the infant formula companies were aware that their marketing practices were considered an important factor on the agenda for the meetings. They were, however, unaware of the extent to which they would be criticized and the heights to which the issue would escalate.[7]

On July 18, 1972, approximately one month after the second PAG conference in Paris, the PAG drafted "Recommendations for Groups." These guidelines, entitled *PAG Statement 23,* were aimed at governments, physicians, and industry alike. Specific issues addressed in the *PAG Statement 23* were:[8]

Governments were called to:

- Encourage industrial investment, for the development of highly nutritious foods;
- Reduce fiscal burdens on processed infant formulas and weaning foods;
- Consider subsidy programs (including free distribution) to provide nutritious infant formulas and weaning foods to the poorest groups; and
- Stimulate the use of mass media channels for both education and responsible product promotion.

Pediatricians and other physicians, for their part, were urged to:

- Keep informed of developments in infant and child feeding, including the promotion of breastfeeding; and,
- Meet with representatives of the food industry to discuss progress in child nutrition, with particular emphasis on the needs of low-income populations.

Industry was asked to:

- Assure that breastfeeding be stressed in its own employee training programs and that sales and promotional methods discouraging appropriate breastfeeding be avoided;
- Avoid direct promotion to new mothers;
- Develop "unambiguous" standard directions for the preparation of commercial formulas, taking into account the needs of illiterate persons; and,
- Use product labels and literature as a means of encouraging better hygiene practices in infant food preparation.

PAG Statement 23 provided the industry with some breathing room and an opportunity to put its house in order. The recommendations were indeed conciliatory in nature and did not go beyond suggestions and exhortations. PAG's statement, although recognized as being a step in the right direction, was criticized as being too lenient and vague, by industry critics and many pediatricians and nutritional specialists. In response to the statement, Nestle ordered an audit of marketing practices used by its companies in the developing nations and consulted health officials in the less developed countries (LDCs) concerning Nestle's role in the education of mothers. The only change suggested by the audit was that Nestle should put greater stress on the primacy of breastfeeding in their advertisements. The American companies producing infant formula, like Bristol-Myers and Abbott Laboratories, thought the PAG code was too lenient and drafted their own more stringent codes of marketing ethics for developing countries. The mood and dynamics of the subsequent two conferences did not change much in adding significantly to the context or scope of the debate.

Polarization of the Debate

In August of 1973, a British Journal, the *New Internationalist,* published an article entitled, "The Baby Food Tragedy."[9] This article was based on an interview with Dr. R.G. Hendrickse and Dr. David Morely, two child health care specialists with many years of experience in LDCs. The two experts claimed that the marketers of infant formula had contributed to diarrheal disease and subsequent malnutrition among infants in Third World countries. They argued that low family incomes led to the misuse of formulas by mothers as they tried to stretch small quantities of the powdered formula by adding more water than recommended. Because of poor sanitary conditions, the water was often contaminated, culminating in infant illness. The doctors supported breastfeeding as the preferred method of nutrition. The article's emotional impact was severe and widespread as copies were sent to over 3,000 hospitals in developing nations. The Nestle company was singled out in the article for that company's aggressive, and potentially harmful, marketing practices.

Nestle's Response to the New Internationalist

Nestle was extremely unhappy with the article and with the tactics of the magazine's editors in publicizing it. *The New Internationalist* had sent advance photocopies of the article to physicians and health care professionals around the world. Nestle, on the other hand, received the article only after it was published, with a note from the editors offering to publish a "fair

representation of your views on this distressing matter." The company, however, interpreted it to mean that "fair representation would inevitably be
equated with an admission of guilt on the part of the company.*"[10] Nestle's
top management also believed that the "errors and misrepresentations in the
report were obvious not only to those familiar with the actual situations described, but that even the uninitiated exposed to the issues for the first time
would be able to tell from the way in which the article was presented that it
was intended to be more than straight forward reportage."[11] The company
believed that rather than illuminating or discussing an otherwise complex
issue, the *New Internationalist* was intent on keeping the "pot boiling."[12]

The company's position was printed in the October 1973 issue of *The New
Internationalist*.[13] This printed response was edited and abbreviated by the
editors prior to its publication. The company strongly believed that its activities had been misrepresented and that it was going to take more than a letter
to the editor to correct this misunderstanding. To try to resolve the issue,
Nestle management invited the editors to the company's headquarters in
Switzerland with a view to engaging in a broad-ranging discussion that was
"obviously" needed to provide a "fair representation." *The New Internationalist* responded with an editorial that disparaged Nestle's efforts. The
editors refused the invitation, claiming that PAG 23 was being violated, and
ran an editorial also in the October 1973 issue entitled "Milk and Murder."[14]
Instead, they called for a stepped-up campaign that was picked up by others.

---

*The details of Nestle's version of the dispute with the *New Internationalist,* the publishers
of "The Baby Food Tragedy," and also the Berne Trial are drawn, in part, from a confidential monograph prepared for Nestle and authored by Maggie McComas, Geoffrey Fookes,
and George Taucher, entitled *The Infant Formula Controversy — Nestle and the Dilemma
of Third World Nutrition* (Nestle, S.A., Switzerland,1982). To the best of our knowledge,
this monograph was never officially released although a limited number of copies seemed to
be circulating in various circles.

In 1988, this monograph was reincarnated and published under the title of *Infant Feeding: Anatomy of a Controversy 1973–1984* (New York: Springer-Verlag, 1988). This new
version, considerably expanded, appeared under the editorship of Dr. John Dobbing, a well-
known British pediatric research scientist. This new book dropped the two authors from the
previous version. These were: Mr. Geoffrey Fookes, one of the Nestle executives with perhaps the longest association and involvement in the infant formula controversy, and Mr.
George Taucher, professor of business administration, International Management Development Institute (IMEDE), Lausanne, Switzerland. The third author, Ms. Maggie McComas,
remained as a contributor to the new volume. Her materials appear to have been transferred
more or less intact from the previous version. The new version also includes four chapters
written by Mr. Gabriel Veraldi, a free-lance writer-journalist based in France. Of the 11
chapters, Dr. John Dobbing was responsible for only one, "Medical and Scientific Commentary on Charges Made Against the Infant Formula Industry." In his preface to the book,
Dr. Dobbing states: "Although I feel reasonably qualified to discuss the medical and scientific aspects, I was less confident when it came to things which concern the media, politics,
international affairs and public attitudes" (p. xi).

Nestle's Response to the Baby Killer

Earlier in this chapter, the contents of *The Baby Killer* were discussed. In response to this attack, Nestle felt that Mr. Mike Muller had intentionally reported the negative aspects of the situation without recognizing information obtained from his interviews with Nestle employees. During the course of preparing his report, Mike Muller had visited Nestle's headquarters in Switzerland and spoke to a number of corporate executives, including G.A. Fookes from Nestle's infant and dietetic products division. Nestle's top managers felt that the company had fully cooperated with Mr. Muller and expected to see an objective and serious discussion of the issues. Instead, they considered their trust abused by Mr. Muller's one-sided depiction of the issue. However, they were restrained in their public comments. Mr. Arthur Furer, Nestle's managing director, stated: ". . . that marketing needed to be handled with great care in order to avoid misuse of these important food products. I am personally glad to have read Mike Muller's report which gave me an opportunity to rethink the whole problem."[15] Responding to the report, Nestle initiated an extensive investigation of its marketing practices which led to some modifications. These included more stringent controls on the distribution of samples to health professionals, strict avoidance of direct contact between company representatives (mothercraft nurses) and mothers where such a policy was suggested by local authorities, and suspension of advertising not meeting with the approval of local health officials.[16]

The pamphlet, *The Baby Killer,* was translated into German by the Third World Action Group (TWAG) in Switzerland and published in May 1974. The translated version, a 32-page booklet, was retitled *Nestle Kills Babies* (*Nestle Totet Babys*). In the translation, it was maintained that Nestle was responsible for the death or the permanent damage of thousands of children and was using unethical methods in Third World countries, especially with respect to advertising.

Nestle's response was almost immediate and massive when compared with the relative obscurity of the sponsoring group, TWAG, and the modest distribution of the pamphlet. On June 2, 1974, Nestle sued all those involved with the translation and its publication. Nestle was incensed by the accusation: "No one has the right to assert that we are pursuing unethical and immoral sales practices . . . this is why we brought libel actions against TWAG."[17] The company cited four specific reasons for the suit:

- the title;
- the charge that the practices of Nestle and other companies were unethical and immoral;
- the accusation of being responsible for the death or the permanent physical and mental damage of thousands of babies by its sales promotion policy;
- and the accusation that in developing countries, the sale representatives

for baby food are dressed like nurses to give the sales promotion a scientific appearance.[18]

Nestle decided to pursue a libel suit because it considered it to be the only viable option available to the company. In response to a question, Mr. Paternot of Nestle observed that using a media campaign to counter adverse publicity by the booklet at that time would have been the wrong thing to do because the article was published in a very obscure journal and was not available to the general public. Thus a media campaign would have focused the public's attention to something which people would otherwise not ordinarily be aware of.*

As it turned out, the libel trial created exactly the same situation. It gave the Swiss group the opportunity to publicize their efforts. They had no money and their campaign was created with funds that they raised. The more Nestle pursued the case, the more the Swiss group gained in public recognition. Soon after the media events unfolded, Nestle realized the blunder it had committed. The ferocity of Nestle's response, in terms of the law suit, filed with great fanfare, ended up providing the previously small and obscure group with a large measure of legitimacy, and made the issue and the group into an international cause celebre.

Soon thereafter, Nestle offered to settle the case out of court, provided that the Third World Action Group:

• apologize publicly and withdraw the statements against Nestle;
• pay an amount to be determined by the judge to a charity;
• pay all legal costs; destroy all copies of the report;
• and guarantee that they would not spread further accusations against the company.[19]

The TWAG refused to accept the offer: "We prefer the trial and we will evoke evidence of the truth. . . . The trial about the consequences of processed baby food in developing countries will be of public interest." Later in 1974, and again in November 1975, Nestle extended its suit to include other authors and a publication on the same subject (*The Gentle Killer*). The authors of *The Gentle Killer* were acquitted as the judicial authorities accepted the defendants' position that the title referred to the infant formula itself and not to the Nestle Company.

---

*Mr. Jacques Paternot, Nestle, S.A. Switzerland. Interview with the author. Unless otherwise specifically stated, all direct quotes or paraphrased statements of various people cited herein are based on personal on-the-record interviews or written communication with the author.

The Berne Trial

The trial, which grew specifically out of *The Baby Killer* controversy, was held in Berne, Switzerland (1974–1976). The proceeding went through three hearings: November 1975, and February and June 1976. TWAG immediately began holding press conferences paneled by Mr. Mike Muller, the World Council of Churches, and TWAG leaders. The activists' arguments and accusations evoked strong public response and added an emotional component to the debate. Nestle waited to hold its first press conference until after the initial hearings (1975). Managing director Furer, head of research Prof. Q. Mauron, and Dr. Hans Miller (an infant food expert) defended the need for quality infant formula products in Third World countries; using facts and figures, they refuted criticism of Nestle's marketing policies. Nestle's case at the trial centered around disclaiming the truth of the title "Nestle Kills Babies." The TWAG defense was built around the argument that the use of infant formula was causing malnutrition and disease in infants. Dr. Jelliffe testified at the trial on behalf of TWAG and reiterated his thesis that although there were other reasons as to why mothers were gravitating toward bottle feeding, the commercial promotion of infant formula was the primary reason for the decline of breastfeeding in developing countries. The trial turned out to be a TWAG show in all respects, thereby putting Nestle on the defensive. Just before the start of the last hearing, Nestle withdrew three of the charges, leaving the one concerning the title.

In July 1976, Nestle won a technical victory when the judge found the 30 members of TWAG guilty of libel. The judge explained the verdict by saying: the adequate causal connection between the sale or any other type of distribution of powdered milk and the death of infants fed with such products is interrupted by the action of third parties, for which the complainant, in terms of criminal law, cannot be held responsible. In this sense, there is no negligent or even intentional killing.[21]

The members of the group were each fined 300 Swiss francs ($150 U.S.). However, the presiding judge did not entirely clear Nestle. He chastised the company for its advertising and marketing practices.

> The need ensues for the Nestle Company to fundamentally rethink its advertising practices in developing countries as concerns bottle feeding, for its advertising practice up to now can transform a life-saving product into one that is dangerous and life-destroying. If Nestle S.A. in the future, wants to be spared the accusations of immoral and unethical conduct, it will have to change its advertising practices.[22]

Results of the Berne Trial — Consequences for Nestle

Notwithstanding the outcome of the trial, the company quite predictably refused to acknowledge that its marketing and promotion practices were in any way immoral or unethical. A few days after the trial, Nestle's managing director, Mr. Arthur Furer, issued a circular in which he said that he had personally investigated the marketing practices of the company and "was able to see that there were normal and usual advertising methods, used by manufacturers of such products all over the world. We must affirm that we have full confidence in the ethical basis of our action."[23] From then on, Nestle's inability or unwillingness to recognize any fault on the company's part became one of the battle cries of the activists' campaign against the company.

Six years later, Nestle was still advocating and justifying its defensive position in the case. In a book entitled *The Infant Formula Controversy — Nestle and The Dilemma of Third World Nutrition* (© 1982, Nestle, S.A.), Nestle summarized its actions in the Berne trial as "our decision to pursue legal action against ADW was probably the single most dramatic defensive gesture the company was to make during the infant formula controversy." The company further believed that it set the tone for Nestle's subsequent encounters with its critics as the campaign spread to other countries. According to Nestle, the company was being slandered and lies were being published against the company's position. To Nestle's management, it was the "only route to vindication of its position."

This trial, in many ways, left a permanent scar on the company's psyche. Since then there has been a constant soul searching for explanations as to what went wrong and what the company should have done differently. Almost nine years after the trial, and soon after the boycott had been terminated, I conducted a series of interviews with various Nestle executives who had been closely involved with the controversy. It soon became apparent that the issue still tormented them. Their explanations reflected, as is often the case, their vantage point, the intensity of their involvement, and the need to justify their behavior and actions both during and following the trial. One thing, however, became apparent that despite all its trials and tribulations, the new — post-WHO marketing code — Nestle philosophy was still quite fragile, and its long-term impact on the corporate culture remains uncertain.

Dr. Carl L. Angst, Nestle's director and general manager, and the man who was the main force in bringing about a change in Nestle's strategy and tactics that eventually led to the termination of the boycott against Nestle, commented:

> Although I was not directly involved in the decision to file the law suit, in my opinion, it was probably a mistake. We were so shocked that we reacted instinctively. Even today I am a bit undecided as to what else we should have done.

Mr. Jacques Paternot, another Nestle executive, discussed the outcome of the Berne trial primarily in terms of tactics leaving the impression that he agreed with the strategy.

> First, I think we picked the wrong lawyer. Second, we should have taken only one criticism and not four and that should have been the title. Third, we didn't

manage to have the right kind of witnesses. . . . we should have brought some ministers of health from certain Third World countries as witnesses. We should have handled the media much better. We were full of respect for the procedure — which called for certain silence while the case was in court. And our opponents didn't. . . . They were much more professional.

Nestle had won the battle, perhaps, but it had certainly lost the war. While the company later admitted that this course of action might not have been the best, it explained the problem in hindsight by taking the high road of self-righteousness and blaming "a new breed of advocates/critics, people who themselves were obviously not too concerned with legal niceties, or were bothered by inaccuracy in their facts."[24]

More than anything else, Nestle — Switzerland's strategy and tactics in responding to its critics during the period immediately following the publication of *The Baby Killer* set the tone of confrontation between Nestle and its critics. Consequently, for a long time to come, Nestle's actions at reconciliation and reaching out to its critics would be viewed with great suspicion, its motives constantly suspect, and the comments and statements of the company's executives questioned for their veracity.

Notes

1. Mike Muller, *The Baby Killer* (London: War on Want, 1975), 2nd edition, p. 2.

2. *PAG Bulletin,* Vol. v, #1, March 1975.

3. Nevin S. Crimshaw, Ph.D., MD., PAG Chairman 1970–1973, Professor of Human Nutrition and Head of Department of Nutrition and Food Science, MIT, Cambridge, November 1974.

4. D.B. Jelliffe and E.F.P. Jelliffe, "The Urban Avalanche and Child Nutrition," *Journal of American Dietary Association* 57 (1970), 114–118.

5. D.B. Jelliffe, "Commerciogenic Malnutrition?," *Nutrition Review* (September 1972), 199–205. (Reprinted from *Food Technology*, 25, (1971) 153–154.

6. *Ibid.*

7. Report of the Bogota Conference, January 8, 1971; Concluding Remarks.

8. *PAG Statement 23*, "Promotion of Special Foods (Infant Formula and Processed Protein Foods) for Vulnerable Groups," November 28, 1973, from *The Infant Formula Controversy — Nestle and the Dilemma of Third World Nutrition*, 1982.

9. *The New Internationalist,* August 1973.

10. Maggie McComas, Geoffrey Fookes and George Taucher, *The Infant Formula Controversy - Nestle and the Dilemma of Third World Nutrition* (Nestle, S.A., Vevey, Switzerland, 1982), p. 9., 26–29; John Dobbing, ed., *Infant Feeding: Anatomy of a Controversy 1973–1984* (New York: Springer-Verlag, 1988).

11. Comments made by Mr. Jacques Paternot, Nestle, S.A. Switzerland, to the author in an interview on September 25, 1983.

12. McComas et al., *op. cit.,* supra note 10, pp. 36–41.

13. *The New Internationalist,* October 1973.

14. *Ibid.*

15. Andrew Chetley, *The Politics of Baby Foods: Successful Challenges to an International Marketing Strategy* (London: Frances Pinter, 1987), p. 44.

16. Maggie M. McComas, "Origins of the Controversy," in John Dobbing, ed., *op. cit.*, supra note 10, pp. 36–38.

17. *Ibid.*, p. 44.

18. Andrew Chetley, *op. cit.*, supra note 15, p. 44.

19. *Ibid.*

20. Chetley, *Ibid.*

21. SAFEP, "Nestle Case Will Not Continue — But Dispute Goes On." Information for the press, #5, mimeo, December 1976, p. A5.

22. *Ibid.*

23. *Ibid.*

24. McComas et al., *op. cit.*, supra note 10, p. 44.

5 THE CONTROVERSY COMES TO THE UNITED STATES

It was a hot summer day in Minneapolis, Minnesota. There were hordes of people enjoying the sun around the lakes of Minnesota on the national holiday of July 4th, 1977. However, the Infant Formula Action Coalition (INFACT), a new organization, had other plans. On this day it announced a consumer boycott of all Nestle products in the United States to protest against that company's infant formula marketing practices in the Third World.

INFACT had carefully orchestrated a set of events surrounding the announcement to garner maximum media attention. The first demonstration procession marched down Church Boulevard on Sunday morning because the churches were involved in the issue. Douglas Johnson, the leader of the marchers, recalls, "each church was leafleted as we went through, we gave a talk and then we stopped by the Governor's mansion and informed him of what the issue was."* The second demonstration took place in front of Nestle's office in Minnesota where the group put up an eight-foot puppet of a bottle, and organized a number of skits and other programs to broaden public awareness of the issues raised by INFACT. The marchers carried a baby coffin and other banners designed for maximum media effect. The first ef-

---

*Interview with the author. Unless otherwise specifically stated, all direct quotes or paraphrased statements of various individuals, cited here and elsewhere in the text, are based on personal interviews or written communications with the author.

59

fort, however, fell short of expectations. The demonstration attracted a little over 100 people. The 103-degree heat did not help either. Doug Johnson blamed the heat for the low turnout. The scant media attention was attributed to local news "because a little girl drowned in the lake. But we got radio coverage and interviews with the media."

INFACT's goal was to advocate a "halt in the unethical and dangerous promotion of infant milk formula in Third World countries through widespread public education and generation of grassroots pressure against the offending corporations." It demanded that Nestle: (1) immediately stop all promotion of Nestle's artificial formula; (2) stop mass media advertising of formula; (3) stop distribution of free samples to hospitals, clinics, and homes of newborns; (4) discontinue Nestle "milk nurses"; (5) stop promotion through the medical profession; and (6) prevent artificial formula foods from getting into the hands of people who do not have the means or facilities to use them safely.[1]

INFACT expected to create increased public awareness of the problem, through protest marches and other related activities, and in the process, to move the issue from the pre-problem to the problem identification stage. This was done through a three-pronged effort that began with the widespread distribution and showing of a film entitled "Bottle Babies." This film linked Nestle infant formula products and bottle-feeding to infant diseases and malnutrition in Third World countries. This effort was reinforced through meetings in local churches, community centers, and college campuses to enlist volunteers, raise funds, and build a network for grassroots activism against infant formula manufacturers — in other words, to create a "movement."

It was not an easy task. Like the industry, the activists also had to develop strategies in an iterative manner, learning and adapting as events constantly unfolded. However, unlike the industry, the activist groups initially did not have any established organizational forms to emulate. Nevertheless, INFACT leaders were perceptive enough to realize that in order to achieve some sort of parity in competing with Nestle for public attention, they must somehow become "larger than life." Taking its lessons from Saul Alinsky's teachings,[2] INFACT, from its very inception, used all the tools of confrontation with a view to keep the issue in the public limelight and give it an international character "in order to fight a transnational corporation."[3]

Goals and Strategies of the Activists

At this juncture, the infant formula controversy was in the closing phase of the pre-problem stage. Therefore, one of the primary goals of the activists was to change the nature of the debate from scientific and medical issues and move it in the public policy arena with emphasis on right and wrong policy and concepts of distributive justice, that is, who deserves what and from whom. Although the "dying infants" of the Third World provided a "powerful visual symbol," that in itself was not enough. Those infants were suffering from a variety of ills, most of which could be laid directly to the state of their abject poverty, social inequities, and, to no less measure, indifferent, inefficient, and corrupt local governments. None of these aspects could be dealt with by the activists. Therefore, the issue had to be defined in a manner that would focus on a culprit and an adversary that could be easily identified and that could be subjected to pressure for gaining visible results. Infant formula producers, and Nestle in particular, fit those specifications.

Contrary to public assertions of the infant formula industry's critics, it was not a mass movement, spontaneously crystallized by public's response to an event or a series of events so horrible or dramatic as to create a massive outrage or urge to take action. Instead, it was a calculated action on the part of a select group of activists who were moved by a problem that they perceived to be particularly onerous. The U.S. public was not overly worked up about either the Third World or infant formula. Nor were the European events pertaining to the Nestle controversy of much public concern. These factors, however, were of immense concern to certain public interest groups and individuals who were involved in Third World development issues and the problems of poor people in those countries. The activists, therefore, concentrated on mobilizing the educated middle class in the United States. The discretionary income of this group offered both a source of monetary support to the movement and potential purchasing power that could be withheld from Nestle's products and hence provide some muscle to the boycott. The critics of the industry were helped in their task because the infant formula issue is laden with emotional and moral symbolism, especially in the context of Third World countries. The sponsorship of religious organizations provided the group with a halo effect and gained instant legitimacy for the boycott's organizers.

From the very early stages of the controversy, INFACT opted for a strategy of domain offense-encroachment. Lacking a solid basis of recognition, institutional history, and financial support, it could not do otherwise. They continuously challenged the very contextual frame within which the companies wanted to discuss the issue. By broadening the scope of the issue, they brought the companies out of the "scientific-factual" discussion arena where their strengths lay and into the sphere of moral context, that is, sales and profits at the expense of infant health and survival. The adroit maneuvering on the part of the activists and an unusual level of rigidity on the part of Nestle and, to a lesser extent, other infant formula manufacturers put the companies on the defensive where they were to lose their initiative for action and would become increasingly defensive. This strategy offered INFACT maximum opportunity to attack Nestle from a variety of angles because it did not have to worry unduly about the cost of failure. That it successfully exploited this strategy is a testimony to the adroitness of its leaders. In this they were also helped by the prevailing environment of rising societal concerns about social issues, on the one hand, and the ineptness of Nestle, on the other hand.

Origins of the Campaign in the United States

Although Nestle alone became the object of the boycott campaign, the activists, notably the religious groups under the auspices of the Interfaith Center on Corporate Responsibility (ICCR), had also been pressing the three major U.S. infant formula manufacturers to curb their marketing and promotion practices in Third World countries. ICCR is a "sponsored-related movement" of the National Council of Churches. The roots of this concern can be traced to their existing long-term concerns for the poor in the Third World. However, it would be too facile to suggest that the infant formula issue emerged as a consequence of careful analysis of church priorities or allocation of limited resources in a manner that world maximize some specified objective or even the welfare of a particular constituency, that is, the poor of the Third World. Instead, a thorough analysis of the events surrounding the risk of the infant formula controversy would suggest that the infant formula issue was initiated, and given focus to, by a handful of individuals who picked the issue because: (1) they believed in its importance from their personal and professional perspective; (2) it satisfied a deep felt need to do something worthwhile on issues dealing with the Third World poor; and (3) it helped them confront the large multinational corporation which many of them believed to be capable of doing immense harm in the Third World. Finally, the issue was selected because of its intense emotional appeal and its potential capacity for mobilizing a large number of people and converting it into a political issue. Perhaps another reason, although not a substantial one, for the early spread of the boycott was the fact that participating in the issue on the part of Americans did not entail any meaningful sacrifice either in financial terms or in foregone pleasure through abstaining from the use of certain products.

To most observers, the infant formula controversy and the international boycott of Nestle are associated with INFACT and its national chairperson, Mr. Douglas A. Johnson. In Western Europe and the United Kingdom, the names most commonly associated with the movement against Nestle, and the drive toward the passage of the WHO Code marketing of breast milk substitutes, are those of Mr. Mike Muller and Mr. Andrew Chetley. However, to those who were intimately involved with the controversy in the United States, the name of Ms. Leah Margulies perhaps evokes amongst the sharpest of reactions.

There is an interesting story about how Ms. Margulies became involved in the infant formula controversy and pursued it against Nestle with such intensity and single-mindedness. It also suggests how "chance events" tend to catalyze certain issues and prompt people to become such forceful agents of change. Prior to coming to New York, Ms. Margulies spent a number of years in New Haven where she pursued studies in Third World development and transnational corporations. In the early 1970s she came to New York and, looking for something to do in her area of interest, landed a job at ICCR developing a program dealing with business, world hunger, and transnational corporations' marketing practices as a means of social change. Ms. Margulies became particularly concerned about the issues of infant mortality in Third World when in 1975, she attended the World Council of Churches meeting in Nairobi, which was the fifth WCC assembly. The central theme at Nairobi was "liberation," and a revolutionary stand was taken against Western philosophy and technology in the Third World.[4] This assembly took a specific stance against some of the operational practices of multinational corporations* in Third World countries. As such, its resolutions became the subject of intense controversy and worldwide debate, especially among conservative religious scholars, political commentators, and business leaders.[5] Upon her return, she set in motion forces that eventually crystallized the controversy in the United States. It was Leah Margulies who gave the issue its early momentum by mobilizing a social and religious constituency behind it. She was instrumental in recruiting Edward Baer, Douglas Johnson, and others to the cause and, along with Doug Johnson, was responsible for implanting what was eventually to become an international cause celebre. For a long time, she was the single most influential force behind the issue at ICCR and NCC.

During the summer of 1975, Ms. Margulies attended a seminar at Columbia University's business school where Mr. Jacques Paternot, a Nestle executive, gave a presentation. According to Ms. Margulies, Paternot's presentation was "full of lies and misstatements." As Ms. Margulies recalls, she asked Mr. Paternot about the lawsuit against Nestle, and he angrily answered that the group had dropped all charges and that we had won and they had lost. This statement was not true because it was made almost a year before the settlement of the case. From this point on, she became very involved in the issue and in Nestle's activities in the marketing of infant formula foods. She asked Mr. Timothy A. Smith, ICCR's executive director and Ms. Patricia Young, one of its board members, to start an investigation of the infant formula issue. They were both quite enthusiastic about it and gave her their blessing to go ahead, provided that she would raise outside

---

*Throughout this book the terms *transnational corporations* and *multinational corporations* are used interchangeably except where they appear as part of a direct quote.

funds to support the project. Thus, what started out as a one person, self-started project became in short order a major endeavor and undertaking, committing the moral authority of the church and its vast organizational resources. The rest, as they say, is history. To the extent that Ms. Margulies' description reflects actually what happened, it is an interesting commentary about the manner in which ICCR and the National Council of Churches determined their social action agenda and the rather haphazard process utilized by the organization's leadership.

ICCR and the U.S.-Based Infant Formula Manufacturers

Although ICCR and INFACT deserve the primary responsibility for creating mass public awareness and social action on the infant formula issue, the issue was first raised by the Consumers Union in a report published in September 1974.[6] The period prior to the 1978 Kennedy Hearing could best be described as the learning period both for ICCR and INFACT, on the one hand, and the companies, on the other hand. The opinions, attitudes, and impressions formed by the two sides during this period would forever influence their mutual trust and behavior toward each other and would have a tremendous impact on their actions through different phases of the controversy. INFACT's Doug Johnson described this period as grassroots brush fire and networking phase.[7]

ICCR's initial efforts with U.S. companies were directed at seeking information about their infant formula marketing practices. In this they had various degrees of success, although none too satisfactory from their perspective. As time passed, the discussions between ICCR and the companies became more hostile and confrontational, and requests for information turned into demands for disclosure.

Ross Laboratories

From the early stages of the controversy, Ross Laboratories, a division of Abbott Laboratories, among all the U.S. companies, responded to the concerns of the industry's critics with the greatest sensitivity. Ross/Abbott, along with Bristol-Meyers, did not use direct consumer advertising as part of their marketing strategy and, therefore, were spared from one of the criticisms of the industry. The company also did not join ICIFI, the industry group, contending that ICIFI's voluntary code was inadequate. Ross Laboratories had developed its own "Code of Marketing Ethics for Developing Countries."[8]

In response to ICCR's inquiries, Ross/Abbott held meetings with the group over an 18-month period and supplied ICCR with some of the information it sought. ICCR, however, was not satisfied and, as a consequence, caused a shareholder resolution to be submitted at the company's annual stockholders' meeting. The resolution received 2 percent of the vote which was not large enough to be resubmitted. However, it did serve the purpose of focusing media and public attention on the issue. The company set up a special office to investigate bottle-feeding abuses in its Third World markets. Furthermore, in March 1977, in discussion with ICCR, Ross Labs agreed to policy changes which were reflected in the company's "Code of Marketing Ethics."[9]

American Home Products

American Home Products (AHP) sold its infant formula products overseas through Wyeth Laboratories, its wholly owned subsidiary. AHP/Wyeth's initial discussion with ICCR resulted in the release of some marketing information, but again ICCR felt it wasn't enough and filed a shareholder resolution to be included in the upcoming proxy statement. However, subsequent discussion led to an agreement, and ICCR withdrew its resolutions. Wyeth agreed to furnish ICCR with the requested information. The company also agreed to send a report to its shareholders about its marketing policies.

Bristol-Myers

Bristol-Myers (B-M) initially declined to cooperate with ICCR or to furnish it with the requested information. Consequently, a number of institutional investors, including such venerable names as the Ford Foundation and the Rockefeller Foundation, joined in April 1975 to support a church-sponsored resolution calling for a report on sales and promotional practices of Bristol-Myers.[10] The company responded by issuing a 19-page report on August 7, 1975, entitled, "The Infant Formula Marketing Practices of Bristol-Myers Company in Countries Outside the United States." ICCR was very unhappy with the statement and called the report an attempt to obfuscate the issue. The tenacity of the ICCR's tactics did not stop there. In December 1975, ICCR member groups, specifically The Sisters of the Precious Blood, refiled a 1976 resolution with B-M that requested the correction of the company's August 1975 report because of its misleading statements. In response B-M refused to engage in any further discussions.

B-M issued a proxy statement in March 1976, claiming that it had been "totally responsive" to the requests of the ICCR in its 1975 and 1976 resolutions. The company also claimed that "infant formula products were neither intended, nor promoted for private purchase where chronic poverty or ignorance could lead to product misuse or harmful effects."[11] Church groups and other ICCR supporters were shocked and outraged by these statements. The Sisters of the Precious Blood, feeling sure that these statements were inaccurate, on September 27, 1976, filed a law suit against B-M for its alleged violations of various sections of the Securities and Exchange Act of 1934. The suit alleged that B-M's 1976 Proxy Statement was materially false and misleading in asserting that:

1.   The company (Bristol-Myers) does not sell infant formula products in the least developed countries of the world and has only one-third of its sales in the lower category of developing countries, with more than half of this amount being in the "sick baby" formulas so urgently needed in these countries.

2.   The company's infant formula products are neither intended nor promoted for private purchase where chronic poverty or ignorance could lead to product misuse or harmful effects.

3.   As a matter of policy, the company's infant formula products are marketed through professional medical personnel and not directly to the consumer.[12]

The petitioners sought an injunction ordering the company to resubmit the proposal, with full explanation, at the stockholders' meeting. On May 11, 1977, U.S. District Court Judge Pollack dismissed the case. The court did not find the evidence submitted by the plaintiffs convincing and dismissed it by stating that the "plaintiff has larded the record with a mass of irrelevancies." The judge also ruled that an evaluation of the objective accuracy of the proxy statement regarding the plaintiff's shareholder proposal would be an empty exercise in semantics in the circumstance of the case.[13]

The Sisters filed an appeal stating that the ruling made a mockery of the Securities and Exchange Commission laws. The appeal, however, was withdrawn before it could come up for a hearing. In December 1977, during the pause before active appellate proceedings, each party independently concluded that they shared common goals and that further court proceedings would be counterproductive to their mutual interests. B-M agreed to a voluntary settlement providing for a full report on the issue to be presented in the first 1978 *Quarterly Report,* including a position statement by the Sisters and the Corporation and an opportunity for the Sisters to present their case at the 1978 Corporate Board Meeting. B-M also agreed to revise some of its promotional materials given to doctors, to monitor more closely its marketing and promotional practices in less developed countries; and to take other measures to ensure proper use of its products, including a ban on advertising to the public.

In conclusion, it would appear that ICCR and its supporters had at best achieved mixed results in their dealing with U.S. infant formula companies. Although shareholder proxy resolutions generated sporadic national publicity and greater public awareness, they did not build sustained momentum. The activists' tactics of confrontation did not arouse widespread public outrage because they failed in projecting the companies as evils incarnate. The activities of ICCR and its associates, however, provided the genesis of a new "movement" called the "ethical investor" where institutional investors, especially employee pension funds belonging to religious and public sector employees, foundations, and university endowment funds, sought to use their voting power to nudge companies to modify their behavior in ways that these investors considered more socially responsible.

U.S. infant formula companies were able to contain the damage to their operational freedom. Proxy battles had almost no chance of succeeding because of management's control of the proxy machinery, and lack of support from private-investor driven mutual funds and individual investors. The U.S. companies had demonstrated considerable sophistication in responding to the critics' questions for information and had also shown their agreement with some of the critics' concerns by making changes in their marketing practices and establishing their own marketing codes. These activities, however, did not materially affect their operational results, that is, sales and revenues in those markets.

Nestle Becomes a Target

Nestle, on the other hand, offered an inviting target in the United States on more than one account. The company had already achieved notoriety in Europe, and many people in the United States associated Nestle with all that was objectionable in the marketing of infant formula foods in Third World countries. Nestle was also a foreign company. Although it had some highly successful brand name products in the United States, the company itself was not well known. Nestle did not have a strong public image or corporate identity among large segments of the U.S. population. Therefore, it was easier to build public hostility against the company. Paternot of Nestle–Switzerland thought that in addition to Nestle's being a foreign company, two other factors contributed to Nestle's becoming the target of boycott. Nestle was "the leader in the market," and "our competitors are pharmaceutical companies" which gave them a more positive image of conern for health care and saving lives.

From its inception in the early days of 1977, INFACT had targeted Nestle for special attention. In a reflective article, writing in 1986, INFACT's Johnson stated that the boycott began with a series of intuitions or organizing principles. They were: the need to have the campaign develop through controversy; to internationalize the campaign in order to fight a transnational corporation; to stimulate and free criticism in the Third World from the fear of possible reprisals; to use the U.S. market to mount pressure on the corporation as a whole; to make the churches a legitimate base for the boycott campaign; to focus on organizing the middle class, which is the primary market for Nestle's products and hence its power base; and the need to project winning the boycott and directly saving lives, not just to project education about an issue, as the goals of the campaign.[14]

Unfortunately, these principles or intuitions do not provide convincing logic as to why Nestle was chosen as the target. Many of the principles apply equally to U.S.-based infant formula companies who should have been an even easier target. It is presumptuous to think that less developed countries lacked an adequate international forum to vent their grievances against the transnational corporations. Nor is anyone likely to take seriously the claim of "winning of the boycott and directly saving lives" as the goal of the campaign. The connection between the two is not only "not direct" but is so farfetched that even the staunchest supporters of the boycott would have a difficult time maintaining the pretense. As Doug Johnson himself states, as the campaign progressed the definition of what was meant by "winning" constantly changed and led to some internal conflicts among the activist groups campaigning against Nestle and other infant formula companies.[15]

At this stage of the controversy, the activists had been gaining two types of legitimacy for their actions: intrinsic and functional. By identifying the issue with concepts of morality and justice, they achieved an inherent legitimacy by claiming to be "in the right" and on the side of the poor and the deserving. Moreover, the endorsement of established religious groups with their long history of social action provided them with the wraparound effect of inherent legitimacy. Intrinsic and functional legitimacies, however, cannot build mass movements, much less sustain them. Emotional appeals have a very high decay rate and, after a while, suffer from "compassion exhaustion." INFACT overcame these problems by providing constant stimulation by keeping the controversy going. For the activists, it would not serve any useful purpose to cooperate with Nestle and other companies or to narrow down potential areas of conflict. Instead, every response by the companies would provide opportunities for a further need for explanations, new investigations, charges, interpretations, and calls for action.

Building a broad-based constituency was the next important step if the activists were to create a mass movement based on the infant formula controversy. INFACT and its leadership were successful in creating a broad-based consensus by linking the issue of dying babies with infant formula and stripping it of all its complexities. So defined, it offered ample scope for various groups to be able to rationalize their reasons for participation and become part of a mass movement.

Nestles Goals and Strategies

Nestle's strategies and tactics in the United States could not have been better designed to play into the hands of its adversaries than if the company had deliberately planned to do so. The company was a prisoner of its own value set and operational philosophy. Nestle's value set revolved around conventional business values: a good product, efficiently sold, in every possible market and with flexible marketing and promotional strategies that would adapt to the needs of individual country markets, and by people who were both dedicated to the company and proud of their ability to perform successfully under various operating and competitive conditions. Nestle's management was also insular and looked to its own traditions for guidance. The company jealously guarded its freedom to manage its far-flung worldwide operations as it saw fit as long as they were in harmony with local laws. The preservation of maximum management discretion was one of the core values of the company reinforced by the fact that it was also in harmony with the intellectual and cultural orientation of the Swiss-based management and personal inclination of its then top management.

ICCR's initial contact with Nestle took place in October 1977. At this meeting, Nestle was represented by Geoffrey Fookes from the parent company based in Vevey, Switzerland. Fookes was a veteran of many previous skirmishes with the activists in Europe. He brought with him all the institutional baggage that had so marred Nestle's efforts in Europe when dealing with the company's critics. True to form, Nestle took the position that the concerns of the U.S. critics of infant formula were based on misinformation. Fookes made a detailed and already well-known presentation regarding the scientific and health-related aspects of the controversy. The critics, however, were already versed in the medical argument and instead questioned Nestle about its marketing practices. When this issue was brought to the forum, Fookes replied, "We stopped all advertising in the Third World in 1975." ICCR representatives immediately challenged this statement by producing a study of Nestle's marketing practices in Malaysia where Nestle had been undertaking extensive consumer advertising for its infant formula products in television, radio, and newspapers. Fookes countered by saying that he did not consider Malaysia as a Third World poor country. Above all, Nestle "did not accept the principle of negotiating its marketing policy with the activists."[16] This "contractual legitimacy," which recognizes the opponent with a right to intervene, had been one of the primary goals of the activists that they would constantly seek and fight for until the bitter end. The meeting ended without much resolution. This and similar other responses widened the chasm and distrust that had already existed against Nestle among the leaders of the campaign. Although the two parties were talking, there was no dialogue. With each successive encounter, the relationship between Nestle and INFACT deteriorated.

Initially, Nestle — USA (based in White Plains, New York) tried to respond to the U.S. boycott through public relations. It hired the world's largest public relations firm, Hill & Knowlton, of New York. H&K tried the "truth squad" strategy using a massive information and education campaign including the mailing of "information kit" to 300,000 clergymen in the

United States. This strategy did not succeed, and the ranks of activists continued to swell. Nestle blamed Hill and Knowlton for lack of results and replaced it by the world's second largest public relations firm, Edelman, of Chicago. Edelman viewed the boycott as a tangential and ephemeral issue, and advised Nestle to ignore the problem and to do nothing. This strategy also failed, and the Edelman firm was also let go. Next, the company hired hired two public relations experts, Mr. Bill Brooks from Sterling Drug Company and Mr. Gerry Raffe, to advise them on how to deal with the boycott issue. Raffe had a good feel for the U.S. activist movement. He was also able to develop a good rapport with the U.S. pediatricians and the scientific community. Unfortunately, his tenure with the company did not last very long. The other person, who understood the dynamics of the boycott but also did not stay with the company for too long, was Mr. Henry Cioka, a lawyer in the company's legal department in White Plains. It would appear that Nestle's top managers in the United States were unwilling to consider viewpoints that were different than their own and refused to take actions that did not agree with their own diagnosis of the problem.

Reflecting on Nestle's problems during the early phases of the campaign, Mr. Rafael D. Pagan, Jr., head of the Nestle Coordination Center for Nutrition, stated that Nestle in America had nobody with "any Third World experience in the area of nutrition or food programs. . . . [M]ost of the tactical responses were coming from Switzerland where there was a lack of understanding of the American mentality and the American news media." In dealing with its critics in the United States, the Swiss company continued to use a strategy of domain defense which denied its critics any right to intervene in the company's operational policies in Third World countries. The company felt that it had all the elements of legitimacy in its favor. It had the "intrinsic" legitimacy because it marketed a safe and highly useful product. It also had the functional legitimacy because its marketing practices were not in violation of the laws of the host countries and were considered by the company to be prudent, ethical, and professional. Moreover, its constituency-based legitimacy was affirmed because it was operating in Third World countries at the instigation of host country governments and was selling products that the consumers wanted and were willing to pay for.

Nestle — Switzerland gave even less credence to the strength of its critics in the United States than it did in Europe. In this the company's belief was reinforced by its U.S.-based management. In applying the lessons learned in Europe, Nestle made two changes in its tactics: it was willing to (1) engage in constructive dialogue with its critics; and (2) develop broader coalitions with its U.S. counterparts. However, it resolutely refused to make any changes in its basic strategic stance, that is, to protect all elements of its management freedom at any cost, both from its critics and from its competitors. The cooperation with both groups, appearances notwithstanding, had to be on Nestle's terms.

As events would show, the company persisted on following these strate-gies all through the phases leading up to the enactment of the WHO Code and even sometime after that. During the period 1977–1982, every succes-sive failure would lead the company to resort to even more extremist tactics, in the belief that wrong tactics, rather than inappropriate strategies, were causing the company its reverses. If the critics were counting on Nestle's "bull in the China Shop" approach, they were not disappointed. Their con-frontational tactics were designed to provoke increasingly more strident re-sponses from Nestle's highly abrasive and combative style and thereby pro-vide them with further ammunition to fuel the campaign. In this, they were successful beyond their wildest expectations.

The management of Nestle — U.S. initially reacted to the boycott by calling it an inappropriate strategy. The company argued that Nestle did not sell infant formula in the United States and, therefore, should not be the focus of such a boycott. Doug Johnson responded with a seven-page letter to the president of Nestle in Switzerland where he defended the strategy by arguing that because Nestle — Switzerland refused to recognize the prob-lem, and that this was the way to get the company to hold a dialogue with INFACT. "Nestle's U.S. subsidiary was seen as a 'hand' of the transnational 'body,' the crucial link to the corporate 'head' in Switzerland."[17] The very fact that Nestle thought that such a crude rationale for isolating Nestle — U.S. from the actions of its parent has any merit demonstrates its gross underestimation of the sophistication and expertise on the part of its U.S. adversaries.

In October 1977, Nestle's senior managers from Vevey and White Plains met with members of INFACT, ICCR, and the Ford Foundation. Nestle hoped to resolve the boycott by providing information in a film entitled, "Feeding Babies — A Shared Responsibility." INFACT found the presen-tation informative but wanted to debate the company's marketing practices in less developed countries (LDCs). Nestle's management maintained that promotion was an integral part of education in the proper use of its products. Both sides agreed to continue dialogue.

INFACT held a national conference in November 1977, drawing repre-sentatives from the medical profession, churches, and hunger organizations. The meeting concluded by enlarging the scope of the boycott to the entire United States. A clearinghouse was to be established in Minneapolis, Min-nesota, for coordination and informational purposes; group support would be enlisted to assist with legislative work and legal actions. INFACT would broaden its support network by seeking endorsements from a variety of or-ganizations, including those from the religious, educational, community and health environments, and other activist issue-related constituencies. Media events were organized and month-long coverage began. The Canadian Broadcasting Corporation aired a documentary, "The Formula Factory," in Jamaica. The film exposed violations of government policy by infant formula companies in that country. *Mother Jones* magazine published a major article in its December 1977 issue on the bottle-feeding problem.

A second meeting was held at the behest of Nestle between the company and INFACT on February 14, 1978. INFACT assured Nestle that the boycott would continue until Nestle changed its marketing practices. Nestle released a statement reiterating its basic philosophy and called the boycott an "irrational action."[18] The campaign gathered further momentum on April 13, 1978, when INFACT organized "Infant Formula Day" and held demonstrations at various Nestle facilities and retail establishments throughout the country. To put further pressure on Nestle, local groups across the country sponsored events such as the Boston Nestea Party, demonstrations at Nestle U.S. headquarters in White Plains, New York and letter-writing campaigns to American formula companies and Congressmen. Later in 1978, the boycott with the slogan "Crunch Nestle Quick," was furthered by demonstrations, fasts, leafletting, and other public events, to pressure the corporation. At stake was Nestle's billion dollar market in the United States. Nestle denied that it was adversely affected by the boycott events. Nevertheless, the company reacted by hiring a public relations firm and stepping up its external communications effort. They also participated in debates.

Some movement also occurred on the political front. At the instigation of Congressman Michael Harrington (D. — Mass.), U.S. Congress added an amendment to the International Development and Food Assistance Act of 1977 which required the U.S. Agency for International Development (AID) to develop "a strategy for programs of nutrition and health improvements for mothers and children, including breastfeeding." The report accompanying the amendment also called for the infant formula companies to assume greater responsibility for marketing their products in developing nations.[19]

The combined effect of all these activities, however, was still not enough to propel the issue into national consciousness and provide it with a sustained momentum. The activists needed a national forum that could provide them with the right kind of controlled environment within which to frame the issue, identify the villains and the victims, attract media attention and mobilize public opinion, and above all create a legitimacy for the activists' cause and build a constituency. Enter the uniquely American institution, the Congressional Hearings. The resultant success of the infant formula critics in persuading Senator Kennedy to hold a hearing on the issue was perhaps one of the most critical events that influenced the direction of debate and action in the infant formula controversy.

Notes

1. Nestle and the Infant Food Controversy, A (Revised), School of Business Administration, London, Ontario, Canada, 1981, p. 18. These demands were also publicized through

a mass distribution by INFACT. The four-page letter appears on Appendix A in this case study.

2. S.D. Alinsky, *Rules for Radicals* (New York: Vintage Books, 1971); and S.D. Alinsky, *Reveille for Radicals* (New York: Vintage Books, 1979). For a more contemporary treatment and analysis of Alinsky's work, see: Sanford D. Horwitt, *Let Them Call Me Rebel: Saul Alinsky — His Life and Legacy* (New York: Random House, 1991).

3. Douglas A. Johnson, "Confronting Corporate Power: Strategies and Phases of the Nestle Boycott," in James E. Post, ed., *Research in Corporate Social Performance and Policy*, Vol. 8 (Greenwich, Conn.: Jai Press, 1986), p. 329.

4. *Structures of Injustice and Struggles for Liberation: A Report From Nairobi Assembly of the World Council of Churches, 1975.* (Geneva: World Council of Churches, 1975). For a critique of this report see Ernest W. Lefever, *Amsterdam to Nairobi: The World Council of Churches and the Third World* (Washington, D.C.: Ethics and Public Policy Center, 1979).

5. Ernest W. Lefever, *Amsterdam to Nairobi: The World Council of Churches and the Third World* (Washington, D.C.: Ethics and Public Policy Center, 1979).

6. Robert J. Ledogar, *Hungry for Profits: U.S. Food and Drug Multinationals in Latin America* (New York: IDOC/North America, 1975), ch. 9. "Formula for Malnutrition," pp. 111–126. The Consumer Unions editorial based on the report appeared in its magazine in September 1974.

7. Douglas A. Johnson, "Confronting Corporate Power," *op. cit.*, pp. 312–334.

8. U.S. Senate, *Marketing and Promotion of Infant Formula in the Developing Countries, 1978.* Hearings before the Subcommittee on Health and Scientific Research of the Committee on Human Resources, U.S. Senate, 95th Congress, Second Session, on Examination of the Advertising, Marketing, Promotion, and Use of Infant Formula in Developing Nations, May 23, 1978, pp. 204–207.

9. Paul M. Minus, "A Background Paper on the Infant Formula Controversy," United Methodist Church, Dayton, Ohio, September 17, 1980, pp. 14–15.

10. *Ibid,* p. 14.

11. *Ibid.*, pp. 14–15.

12. "Marketing of Infant Formula Goods in Less Developed Countries," in S. Prakash Sethi, *Promises of the Good Life* (Homewood, Ill.: Irwin, 1979), p. 371.

13. *Sisters of the Precious Blood v. Bristol-Myers Co.,* 76 Cir 1734 (MP) vs. District of New York, "Reply Memorandum of Defendant Bristol-Myers Co. in Support of its Motion for Summary Judgment," pp. 15–18, cited in Sethi, *Promises of the Good Life, op. cit.,* pp. 386–389.

14. Douglas A. Johnson, "Confronting Corporate Power," *op. cit.*, p. 329.

15. *Ibid.*, p. 330.

16. John Dobbing (ed.), *Infant Feeding: Anatomy of a Controversy 1973–1984* (New York: Spring-Verlag, 1988), p. 65.

17. *Ibid.*, p. 67.

18. Dobbing, *op. cit.*, p. 65.

19. Paul Minus, *op. cit.*, p. 16.

6 THE ACTIVISTS THROW THE GAUNTLET

The Kennedy Hearing and its Aftermath

The date was May 23, 1978. The time, 9:30 A.M. The location was the U.S. Senate. Senator Edward Kennedy was presiding over the Hearing of the Subcommittee on Health and Scientific Research of the Senate Committee on Human Resources.* The first witness was Dr. Oswald Ballarin, Ph.D., chairman and president of Nestle — Brazil, representing the Nestle Company.

> Senator Kennedy. We will be in order now. We want to give the witnesses the attention they deserve.

> Mr. Ballarin. My name is Oswald Ballarin. I am a Brazilian, and chairman of the board of the company that manufactures and sells Nestle products in Brazil.

> Senator Kennedy's invitation to testify here today was directed to the Nestle Co., Inc., of White Plains, N.Y. . . . Since I have more than 50 years of experience in

---

*U.S. Senate, *Marketing and Promotion of Infant Formula in Developing Countries, 1978, Examination of the Advertising, Marketing, Promotion, and Use of Infant Formula in Developing Nations.* Hearings before the Subcommittee on Health and Scientific Research of the Committee on Human Resources, U.S. Senate, 95th Congress, May 23, 1989. All references to this document in the text will be referred to as the Kennedy Hearing or the Hearing, followed by appropriate page numbers.

this field, my friends at White Plains asked me to appear before you to discuss the manufacturing and distribution of infant formula products in developing countries.

I came here, therefore, of my own free will, with the understanding that this committee does not have jurisdiction over me or over the Nestle parent company in Switzerland.

Although the U.S. Nestle Co. does not manufacture or sell any infant food products, it is my understanding that certain groups are boycotting the sale of U.S. Nestle products, such as coffee and chocolate. The boycott is for the avowed purpose of putting pressure on Nestle's Swiss parent company to stop alleged misconduct in the marketing of infant formula in the Third World.

I am aware of the specific charges made by these groups, and can state, based on my personal experience in many developing countries, that they are quite misleading and inaccurate.

The U.S. Nestle Co. has advised me that their research indicates this is actually an indirect attack on the free world's economic system. A worldwide church organization, with the stated purpose of undermining the free enterprise system, is in the forefront of this activity [emphasis added].

Senator Kennedy. Now, you cannot seriously — *(Laughter and applause.)*

Senator Kennedy. We will be in order now, please; we will be in order.

You do not seriously expect us to accept that on face value, after we have heard, as you must have —

Dr. Ballarin. I —

Senator Kennedy. If I can just finish my question — the testimony of probably nine different witnesses — nurses, doctors who have served in the Third World, many of them in some of the most remote areas of the world — who related their own kinds of personal experiences, their own studies, and then listen to a distinguished group of panelists that represent the World Health Organization, . . . that draws attention to these same kinds of conclusions . . . that these groups, the Interfaith Center for Corporate Responsibility, which is sponsored by the National Council of Churches and supported by 14 Protestant denominations, including the Presbyterian Church, the Episcopal Church, the Lutheran Church, the Baptist Church, the Methodist Church, the United Church of Christ, as well as 150 orders of the Roman Catholic Church, that they are involved in some worldwide conspiracy to undermine or attack the free world's economic system?

Senator Chafee. I would just like to join in that, if I may. . . . This is a serious matter, and as the chairman has said, we have had very distinguished people here who indicate a deep concern. To make the charge that the worldwide church organization has the stated purpose of undermining the free enterprise system, just does not advance the cause at all, nor your argument [Kennedy Hearing: 126–128].

However, Ballarin was not about to leave well enough alone. Responding to the remarks made by Senator Kennedy and Senator Chafee, he began to elaborate on the reasoning behind his allegations of a conspiracy on the part of church groups and other activists against the company.

> Dr. Ballarin. I appreciate and thank you for these comments. However, I must say that I was led to them because I was surprised with two things: One, the boycott which is made against one company which does not manufacture these products in the United States; and, second because of the film which has been distributed, under the title "Bottle Babies," to many local churches and schools, where the emotional responses necessary for the boycott attempt are made. . . .

> Senator Kennedy. The only point, since you reminded us at the outset that you are a friend from Brazil, is that the boycott is a recognized tool in a free economic, democratic system, and it is used by our society, and it is not recognized as being a part of an international kind of conspiracy to bring the free world's economic system down. It is a system which has been used, and used quite effectively in many instances, and sometimes it has not been effective.

> Senator Chafee. Dr. Ballarin, I do not understand your objection to a boycott against U.S. Nestle operations; what better way of getting at the Swiss parent company. But let's not debate that now. We are interested in what you have to say. If I were you, I would skip over the part of undermining the world's economic system.

> Dr. Ballarin. Nestle started operations in the Third World nearly 60 years ago with the main purpose of making milk of good quality available wherever it was needed. . . . In those days, bottle feeding was already practiced and was not introduced by the infant food companies. Many mothers bottle fed their babies with a milk-looking fluid obtained by simply extracting flour with water, manioc flour with water, or sometimes with fresh cow's milk of poor quality. . . . But very often, and the case was that children were brought to the hospital, after they had been fed for a long time in a very wrong way, and the results were adverse because of the complete inadequacy of the food both from the nutritional and hygienic standpoint.

> Doctors, therefore — and I am witness of that, in 1942, when I went to the Amazon, and I said, "Now, we can have formula here" — they welcomed the possibility of prescribing safe and nutritious product for babies whose mothers had to supplement or replace breast milk. This is a well-known fact, sir, to which any doctor in those regions can testify [Kennedy Hearing: 128-129].

The hearing had all the high drama of a classical opera in which Nestle would be cast as the villain. It was a role which the company's representatives would help unwittingly in constructing in the first place, and would play most effectively to the standing-room-only audience in the hearing chambers — and to the world-at-large through television and radio broadcasts, and through the print media. At the hearing, it soon became apparent to everyone — even those who were not in on the writing of the script — that Nestle was on the road to creating another major strategic blunder and public relations fiasco in the United States, a blunder of greater magnitude than the one that befell the company not too long ago at the Bernè trial and the ensuing adverse publicity against Nestle in Europe.

The debate on the infant formula controversy had already begun to shift, albeit imperceptibly, from the scientific and technical domain, to the ethical and emotional domain. It was projected to be the fight of the poor against the rich, the big companies' greed, the onslaught of high pressured advertising against the unwary, ill-informed, and largely uneducated people of the Third World; the indifference and disregard on the part of the rich industrialized West, for the lives and health of the poor of Asia, Africa, and Latin America.

The opening dialogue was, however, not the end, but the mere beginning of the black hole that Nestle was to dig for itself.

Senator Kennedy. If I could ask you, what is the extent of the misuse of the formula in that part of the world?

Dr. Ballarin. It is very difficult to measure. There is some misuse, but not as much as has been pointed out here.

Senator Kennedy. Well, tell us what you know about it, or what your information is about the misuse of it. We heard testimony here this morning from people who have been involved. What is your information?

Dr. Ballarin. No, Senator, I have no market survey. However, what I do have — and I can supply it to you — are some of these made by doctors, like Alvarado Santos, who studied the case of Kwashiorkor. And in this thesis, he said they cannot attribute any case of Kwashiorkor to the children who had been bottle fed with formulas.

Senator Kennedy. Why do the witnesses, the distinguished scientists, the World Health Organization all reach different conclusions than you reach? And if you reach a different conclusion, what is your evidence?

Dr. Ballarin. My answer is, first of all, we have to be very cautious in over generalizing facts which occur in some regions . . . [Kennedy Hearing: 129–130].

The discussion then shifted to the role of multinational corporations (MNCs) in developing countries and the responsibility of MNCs to ensure the proper use of their products. Here again Ballarin's answers appeared highly unsatisfactory, and in the context of the hearing, quite damaging to the image of Nestle and that of the infant formula industry. Excerpts from the exchange between Senator Kennedy and Dr. Ballarin follow:

Senator Kennedy. Well, let me ask, just briefly: Would you agree with me that your product should not be used where there is impure water? Yes or no?

Dr. Ballarin. We give all the instructions —

Senator Kennedy. Just answer. What is your position?

Dr. Ballarin. Of course not, but we cannot cope with that.

Senator Kennedy. Of course not. Do you think that your product ought to be used in areas where there is illiteracy, vast illiteracy?

Dr. Ballarin. But that is very difficult to control, Senator, because you go into a region and they are not all literate — there are some who are. How can you control that the product goes to one rather than to the other?

Senator Kennedy. Should an illiterate person use your product?

Dr. Ballarin. Pardon?

Senator Kennedy. Should an illiterate person —

Dr. Ballarin. Of course; they have children, too. But there is one point, Senator, which I should like to point out: In those places where there are high birth rates and you have many children in the same house, these children, anyhow, are infected by poor water, whatever they do, and, that, we cannot — we cannot cope with that.

Senator Kennedy. Well, are you advertising down in those areas?

Dr. Ballarin. No, we do not advertise.

Senator Kennedy. Do you give samples down in those areas?

Dr. Ballarin. We give samples to hospitals when requested and to doctors when requested, either for making tests, as I said in my paper, or else sometimes for their own welfare work.

Senator Kennedy. Well, as I understand what you say, where there is impure water, it should not be used?. . . . Where the people are so poor that they are not, realistically, going to be able to continue to purchase it, which is going to mean that they are going to dilute it to a point, which is going to endanger health, it should not be used?

Dr. Ballarin. Yes.

Senator Kennedy. And my final question is, what do you do, or what do you feel is your corporate responsibility to find out the extent of the use of your product in those circumstances in the developing part of the world? Do you feel that you have any responsibility?

Dr. Ballarin. We cannot have that responsibility, sir. . . . How can I be responsible for the water system? . . . . With your permission, sir, even in the State of Sao Paulo, where we have 10 million people today, a great part of the water system is no good. I cannot help it.

Senator Kennedy. Let me take rural Colombia, 72 percent poor water, what are you distributing down there? Do you think you should be distributing down there?

Dr. Ballarin. Well, that is a difficult question, sir. . . . It is almost philosophical, with your permission, because if we do not distribute the product where we suppose the water is no good, also the persons who have the possibility of having good water will not have access to this product.

Senator Kennedy. Well, I am just wondering what you think your corporation ought to be doing in terms of reviewing, to the extent that it is being used in those areas.

Dr. Ballarin. Well, of course, we can study and we can review.

Senator Kennedy. Well, are you doing that?

Dr. Ballarin. Not yet. We cannot review that; from that standpoint, to be very frank, we cannot do it for the time being.

Senator Chafee. Did you say your corporation does not advertise?

Dr. Ballarin. I was asked if we advertise in the Amazon.

Senator Kennedy. In developing countries; excuse me.

Dr. Ballarin. Of course, we advertise, I understand, according to the computer characteristics of the market. But our investment is not of the type that is going to push the replacement of breast milk.

Senator Chafee. Then you do advertise?

Dr. Ballarin. Yes.

Senator Chafee. But you do not advertise in the Amazon. Maybe there is no way to advertise. (*Laughter.*)

Dr. Ballarin. Well, in the Amazon, you may advertise by radio. We advertise other products, but not infant formula. I think that was the question, unless I misunderstood [Kennedy Hearing: 130–133].

The hearing created a sorry spectacle of a Nestle top executive struggling with his English and ill equipped to handle the fast give-and-take exchange of the hearing. Nestle's performance reflected an almost total misunderstanding and disregard of the American political process, the nuances of the congressional hearing process, the strategies and tactics of the activists, and above all, the role of the news media. Ballarin's statements questioned the motives of the religious institutions and raised the specter of the threat of communism. Apparently, Nestle was oblivious to the fact that these cliches had been long discarded in the United States and did not carry any sway. Ballarin's statements and assertions had the effect of making him and the company the object of public ridicule.

The Role of the Activists Initiating the Hearing

The Kennedy Hearing did not come about as the outcome of a longstanding or ongoing concern on the part of Senator Kennedy or his committee. Instead, it resulted from a highly intensive and concentrated lobbying effort on the part of activist groups. It involved the coalition of ICCR, INFACT, all the church lobbying groups, the food activists, and others concerned with public health and poverty. In Washington, D.C., the National Council of Churches also provided strong support through their lobbying organization.

The activists saw the hearing as the process through which they would be able to heighten public sensitivities and awareness of the issue and place it on this nation's political agenda. As Doug Johnson stated: "[Hearings] build a public record on the issue and bring it to the press's attention. If nothing else, Congress has the capacity to legitimize the issue. . . . what we were anxious to do was to pull the companies in front of the public and get some hard questions addressed to them. We wanted to put them [the companies] on record on what they were and weren't willing to do."* The activists wanted the industry to recognize that they, the activists, had a constituency that must be contended with, and the Kennedy Hearing was the vehicle to accomplish that goal. Leah Margulies spoke about the expectations of the hearing: "We wanted Kennedy to sponsor legislation to restrict overseas marketing of hazardous products. We didn't think that such a legislation would win in Congress, but we wanted it sponsored so as to put it in the public agenda."

A large lobbying effort and a tremendous amount of hard work went into the undertaking. The activists mobilized a constantly enlarging network of volunteers, public interest, and church groups to write to Senator Kennedy urging him to hold a hearing on the subject. The effort also acted as a catalyst toward greater network building because it gave people something concrete to do. Doug Johnson enlisted the support of Senator Dick Clark of Iowa who was chairman of the subcommittee on Africa. The massiveness of the campaign was overwhelming. People were urged to write and otherwise contact their congressmen and senators. The letter writing campaign was not based on standard formal letters that were mass-produced and generated more irritation than empathy from the legislators. Before long, more than 50 letters a day were pouring into Senator Kennedy's office. Doug Johnson also met with Walter Sheridan, the man in charge of hearings in Senator Kennedy's office, to persuade him about the need for such a hearing. Additional formal and informal contacts were made with various members of Kennedy's staff as well as that of the subcommittee on health.

Structure and Content of the Hearing

The hearing was organized in three panels representing three diverse but overlapping perspectives. The lead-off panel consisted of social activists, community, and public health workers. The second panel consisted of researchers and public health officials. The third panel comprised of industry representatives. In all, oral testimony was heard from 16 witnesses of which

---

*Interview with the author. Unless otherwise specifically stated, all direct quotes or paraphrased statements of various people, cited here and elsewhere in the book, are based on taped interviews or written communications with the author.

four were industry representatives. Additional testimony for the record was provided by 18 witnesses.

The tone of the hearing was set by Senator Kennedy in his opening remarks when he stated:

> It is astonishing, and it is an enormous human tragedy, that one-fourth of the people on this earth — 1 billion men, women, and children — have no access to any health care whatsoever. Another billion have only the most rudimentary and ineffective care. In some nations, four out of five persons receive no health care at all throughout their lives.
>
> And it is always the children who suffer most. Their suffering is the least excusable. They are the innocent victims. They are the victims of the negligence and unconcern.
>
> Today, we will focus on one small element of their problems. We will focus on the use of a product intended to nourish life, to enable infants to thrive and grow, and see how it can have the unintended effects of fostering malnutrition and spreading disease. We will focus on the advertising, marketing, promotion, and use of infant formula in developing nations.
>
> Can a product which requires clean water, good sanitation, adequate family income, and a literate parent to follow printed instructions be properly and safely used in areas where water is contaminated, sewage runs in the streets, poverty is severe, and illiteracy is high? Whose responsibility is it to see that the products are properly used — the manufacturer, the health professionals, or the government involved? Whose responsibility is it to control the advertising, marketing, and promotional activities which, in and of themselves, may create a market in spite of public health considerations?
>
> Is it enough to establish a code for product use and disown or turn away from the realities of product use? [Kennedy Hearing: 1–2].

And yet with all the emphasis on the impact of marketing and promotion practices on the sale of infant formula, it is ironical that neither Senator Kennedy nor the activists provided a single witness with expertise in marketing and promotion practices. The lone witness with any direct connection with business and management was Dr. James Post, professor of management at Boston University. However, his area of expertise was law and corporate social responsibility, with no prior experience in international business and no direct teaching and research experience in marketing and its related fields.

To an outside observer, the Kennedy Hearing was an indictment of the infant formula industry, if for no other reasons than by the preponderance of testimony and supporting documents provided by witnesses. Nestle, in particular, bitterly complained about the tenor of the hearing and called them stacked against the industry. The infant formula companies, however, must take equal, if not greater, blame for contributing to this confusion, misunderstanding and "public ignorance." For example, infant formula companies were almost unanimous in their fault findings with research evidence provided by their opponents at the Kennedy Hearing, calling it anecdotal, unscientific, and unreliable. And yet, not a single industry spokesperson admitted to doing any studies to see what proportion of a company's sales, if any, were going to poor people with no proper facilities to prepare and use infant formula in a safe manner.

By custom, copies of testimony by witnesses are submitted to the committee chairman at least 24 hours before the scheduled time of the hearing. The chairman organizes the sequence of testimony and the questioning of witnesses. Various sources report that when Senator Kennedy received the Ballarin statement, he immediately realized its potential for controversy, media attention, and for making political and debating points. Accordingly, he rescheduled the order of witnesses so that Dr. Ballarin would be the lead-off witness in the industry panel that followed the witnesses from the two other panels. In that, his political intuition was amply rewarded.

The hearing did not lack for fireworks. Without exception, the nonindustry spokespersons were critical of the infant formula industry and its marketing and promotional practices in the Third World. Public health officials, pediatricians and other medical doctors, social and rural welfare workers, and community leaders presented horror stories emanating from their personal experience with infants and children suffering from diseases and sickness where their parents were shown to have substituted breastfeeding for one or another form of bottle feeding, or used breast milk substitutes. Similarly, field studies by public health researchers and clinicians purported to show linkages between increased infant sickness and malnutrition and artificial feeding. One of the more dramatic statements of the extent of infant sickness and death appeared in an exchange between Senator Kennedy and Dr. Jelliffe.

> Senator Kennedy. And I understand that you believe that there would be a saving of 10 million infant lives a year with the return of breastfeeding, important relief in terms of economic pressures of some families, and important implications in terms of population control with the return of breastfeeding.

> Dr. Jelliffe. Yes. I think the 10 million is an estimate of the number of cases of marasmus and diarrhea which could be avoided, and of those, many would die [Kennedy Hearing: 81].

This statement was a headline maker, widely and erroneously used by the press. The industry challenged the statement and sought substantiation. Although Dr. Jelliffe eventually backed away from his unequivocal assertion, the critics of the infant formula industry constantly used the number as a "fact" not merely of 10 million cases of infant sickness and death but of 10 million babies dying because of industry's marketing and promotional practices.

The Industry Position — Nestle

There was considerable ambivalence within Nestle as to whether the company should accept Senator Kennedy's invitation to send a representative to testify at the hearing. The factors to be considered were as follows:

1.   Nestle was a Swiss company and was not legally bound to participate. Its American subsidiary, therefore, wanted to decline attendance. However, the company also recognized that Senator Kennedy was a very powerful political figure in the United States and it would not do well to antagonize him. Nestle had planned for substantial expansion of its activities in the United States and was afraid of facing unfriendly congressional inquiries if it decided to expand through major acquisitions or control of one or more American companies. According to Mr. David Guerrant, then president of Nestle — U.S.,

> Even though I was opposed to attending, I got the impression that we should because it might cause more harm by not appearing. Once this was decided, the next most difficult thing was to decide who was going to appear. We wanted an important person to testify at the Hearing. We wanted a man who lived down there and someone who was bright and knowledgeable with experience to represent the Company. That is how Dr. Ballarin was chosen.

2.   Nestle's top management in Switzerland was also concerned that the company's refusal to attend the hearing could be interpreted as a confirmation of the activities for which the company was accused by its critics in the United States who had already launched a boycott against Nestle's products.

3.   Finally, Nestle's management was very mindful of the adverse publicity it received as a consequence of poor public relations strategy it followed pursuant to the publication of *The Baby Killer* and the Bernè trial. The company felt that the Kennedy Hearing would provide it with a more civilized and controlled environment where it could make its case before the American and world public opinion.

There was considerable disagreement among the Nestle executives interviewed by this author as to where and by whom the decisions were made both as to the choice of Dr. Ballarin and the text of his testimony. This is not surprising from hindsight, given the tremendous blunder that the testimony turned out to be. Restructuring of the events based on interviews with a number of Nestle executives both in the United States and Switzerland indicated that the final decision as to Dr. Ballarin was made in Switzerland at the very top level of the company, most probably by Mr. Pierre Leotard-Vogt, chairman of the board, Dr. Arthur Furer, president and chief executive officer, and Mr. Franklin L. Gurley, legal advisor. Nestle — U.S. apparently went along with the decision.

Dr. Thad Jackson, a British doctor who was sent to Nestle — U.S. from the parent company in Switzerland, considered the outcome of Kennedy Hearing for Nestle to be a public disaster.

It provided the most clear cut evidence of the lack of political sophistication toward the American System by a company. It was a lack of understanding of what Hearing was going to be that caused them [Nestle executives] to make serious mistakes. It was viewed as a governmental action — and not a political situation, which of course it was.

According to Paternot:

Nestle felt that it could handle it since as the company had always related well with governments all over the world. And yet, Nestle — U.S. had never maintained a strong Washington presence of its own, or followed events in Congress. Although Nestle — U.S. had recently retained Hill & Knowlton, a public relations firm, to advise the company on public relations, H&K's advice was not sought in the issue of Kennedy Hearing.

There was also considerable "passing of the buck" in regard to Dr. Ballarin's statement. The operating staff at Nestle — Switzerland wanted everyone to believe that the text of the draft was developed and insisted upon by Nestle — U.S., with Nestle — Switzerland merely signing off on it — albeit with some reservations. In a 1988 Nestle-sponsored book, Maggie McComas stated that it was at the "insistence of White Plains management, whose reading of the political mood of the American public at large was taken at face value by headquarters management, the 'exposure' of such anti-capitalist sentiments was to figure large in the Company's statement."[2] Mr. Fookes in an interview insisted that he was strongly opposed to the tone and style of the statement, and made his views known to the senior management. He went so far as to state that he put his views on record as he was afraid that this decision would come to bedevil the company in the future. However, he declined to make available a copy of the memo to this author.

It is, however, inconceivable that Nestle — Switzerland would have gone along with the recommendations of Nestle — U.S. unless the Swiss-based management was in basic agreement with the sentiments expressed in Dr. Ballarin's statement. All of Nestle's actions during *The Baby Killer* incident and the Bernè trial, and scores of other public statements and expressions, would indicate that Nestle's Swiss management regarded its critics as the enemies of capitalism and the private enterprise system. Writing in 1988, Maggie McComas stated that Nestle saw the U.S. activists as unequivocal anti-capitalists, a point that "management both in White Plains and in Switzerland thought worth emphasizing."[3]

Through a cross-checking of information gathered through various sources, it would appear that Ballarin had originally drafted his own statement which was primarily devoted to the scientific and health care aspects of infant formula feeding in less developed countries. This statement was rejected by the Nestle people at the company's U.S. headquarters in White Plains, New York. Instead, Ballarin was given a statement and, according to one Nestle executive, was instructed, over his strong objections, to read it at the hearing. This statement was drafted by Mr. Guerrant, president of Nestle — U.S., and Mr. Frank Chiocca, a lawyer with Nestle — U.S. The statement was thoroughly reviewed and revised in Nestle — Switzerland by Paternot and Fookes, the two executives who were heavily involved in the controversy from its very early days.

Mr. Ernest Saunders, who with Dr. Carl Angst, was later to play a major role in initiating the new Nestle strategy following the passage of the WHO Code, reflected on the Kennedy Hearing from the perspective of Nestle — Switzerland. According to Saunders, a statement as important as this one could not have been done without very close scrutiny and clearance at the highest levels of the company. Therefore, the reasons for the failure must be found not so much in the decision-making process but also in the personalities involved. According to Saunders: "Guerrant had a tremendous hands-off approach to the management in Vevey [Nestle — Switzerland]. He felt very strongly about running his own show. He was sponsored by the then company chairman, Mr. Leotard-Vogt, who did not allow anyone to interfere with him."

Saunders described the company's top management at that time as closely knit, inbred, and self-centered.* Added to this was the problem of language that made them somewhat diffident in dealing with the United States. The top management also lacked people with experience in the United States. The only American in the top management group was Frank Gurley, the legal counsel. However, according to Saunders, Gurley may have been an American by the fact of being born in the United States, but he had been in Switzerland for such a long period that he had little understanding of the contemporary American scene.

In recalling the events surrounding Dr. Ballarin's testimony, Dr. Carl Angst stated:

> I was not involved in the decision to send Dr. Ballarin to testify at the Kennedy Hearing. When I found out, I went to the man-in-charge and told him don't do it. Some people accused White Plains [headquarter location of Nestle — U.S.] of having insisted on the statement. I think I know better. Vevey [headquarter location of Nestle — Switzerland] must clearly share the blame for it because responsible people in Vevey saw the statement and approved it.

---

*The top managers of Nestle — Switzerland had come from the German side of Switzerland or had prior work experiences in Germany. Their management style was quite autocratic. A number of European activists interviewed by the author repeatedly alluded to the arrogant nature of Nestle — Switzerland's top management. These activists described Nestle top executives' attitudes toward them as condescending and patronizing.

The first time I saw the statement was on a plane ride to New York. It was in the mail that I was carrying with me on the plane. It was a copy of a letter from New York to Vevey. When I read the statement, I said, this is not possible and must be stopped. I met Guerrant in the evening of my arrival in New York. He told me, "You're too late, it has taken place already. It is just that much water over the dam. It had the approval from the top, but I am not going to name names in Vevey."

Guerrant was livid at the treatment meted out to Ballarin and Nestle at the Kennedy Hearing. He wrote an angry letter to Senator Kennedy on May 26, 1978, chastising him, among other things, for his bias against the infant formula manufacturers.[4] The letter, in part, states:

I am angry, but more important, deeply concerned about the example of our governmental processes exhibited this week by the Human Resources Subcommittee on Health and Scientific Research.

It was the general consensus of several people in the audience that your position toward the manufacturers was "you are guilty until you prove your innocence." Objectivity would have been more becoming, Senator.

Probably, for this gathering, the statement was too strong (though nothing to compare with their theme "Nestle Kills Babies") and should have been more subtle. But the point is well made, and your apparent denial of this possibility concerns me. . . .

As you may know, this whole issue gained its greatest momentum a few years ago in Europe fostered by clearly identified radical leftist groups. Their stated purpose is opposition to capitalism and the free enterprise system. . . . People with far left philosophies are not confined to Europe and are certainly represented in many accepted organizations here and abroad. . . . Associated with the World Council is the National Council of Churches, and one of their units is the Interfaith Center for Corporate Responsibility. . . .

Neither Nestle nor the U.S. companies in this business claim perfection. Companies are comprised of human beings. However, virtually every charge against Nestle has proved to be erroneous. Distorted "facts" and just pure propaganda have been answered by people with undeniable integrity and technical credentials. . . .

Testimony of the U.S. Manufacturers

The representatives of the U.S. infant formula manufacturers had come with their own carefully prepared statements. However, as their testimonies followed that of Dr. Ballarin, they were put on the defensive because of all the commotion caused by the Ballarin testimony. U.S. industry representatives were also defensive in answering some of Senator Kennedy's questions during the hearing. The following exchange between Senator Kennedy and Mr.

Frank A. Sprole, then vice-chairman of Bristol-Myers Co., illustrates the nature of industry responses and the perception of evasiveness they created.

Senator Kennedy. I think that we are trying to get at an understanding of what the corporate responsibilities are in this area; how your own company or corporation is viewing those responsibilities and what they are doing about it. . . .

Mr. Sprole. We believe breast milk is best for the infant, but where it is not appropriate or sufficient, we believe our products are among the finest substitutes or supplements for breast milk anywhere. Breastfeeding is encouraged on product labels and in special pamphlets. Labels contain advisory statements against improper use of the product, and simplified instructions for preparation in both written and graphic form.

Direct advertising to consumers in developing countries is forbidden by company policies, as is distribution of free samples to mothers.

We promote our products through the medical and nursing professions. Although many doctors have praised "Mothercraft" nursing services as a valuable adjunct to their work — there has been criticism that these nurses may not always have followed our policies and practices. In 1977, our management decided to embark on a program to discontinue Mothercraft nurses in an orderly business fashion. The first such service was discontinued in December 1977, and at this time, all of our Mothercraft nursing services have been discontinued [Kennedy Hearing: 140–141].*

Senator Kennedy, however, insisted in knowing what B-M and other companies were doing to find out the extent to which their products were improperly used and to prevent such improper use. Mr. Sprole responded:

We believe it is simplistic and dangerous to contend that more breastfeeding and less formula feeding will solve the nutritional and health problems of infants in the developing world. We believe that the effects of poverty — lack of food and safe drinking water, the absence of sanitation and the shortage of health care — are the primary causes of disease and death of infants in the developing world [Kennedy Hearing: 140–141].

In response to similar questions Mr. John R. Stafford, senior vice president, American Home Products [the parent company of Wyeth International], responded that unlike B-M, his company considered Mothercraft nurses to be performing a useful service, and that there were no plans to discontinue them. He also defended his company's policies of free samples to mothers, and distribution of promotional-educational materials to the medical profession and potential users of infant formula foods. He stated:

---

*Mr. Sprole's comments are excerpted from his testimony and are not necessarily presented in the order they were made at the hearing.

As a matter of business practice, our customers tend to be — as defined by our foreign managers, tend to be middle class of those customers and the abject poverty in the world environment are not the customers that we target. They are the ones that cannot afford the product.

Senator Kennedy. You do not target, but you do know what goes to the poor people?

Mr. Stafford. Yes; the product is available in the stores now.

Senator Kennedy. Do you know what percentage does get there or if it is used correctly? Do you have any idea?

Mr. Stafford. Our products are used mostly in the urban areas and not in the rural remote areas.

Senator Kennedy. Would you go into a market area where there was 70 percent impure water, trying to sell your product?

Mr. Stafford. Well, in many of these lesser developed countries, the system of distribution is complex. We sell perhaps in some countries in the Third World only to a distributor, and that distributor, in turn, distributes the product throughout the country. Even where we have our own company, we sell to wholesalers and other large buyers. The subsequent distribution of that product throughout the country, I think, would be very difficult for us to control.

Senator Kennedy. Well, whose responsibility is it? Is it the distributor? I mean, you really do not mind or care what he does with it?

Mr. Stafford. No, We do care. And actually, insofar as the bad water is concerned, the product needs to have boiled water. That is true almost throughout the world. And if the mother follows the instructions which we provide and which we try to make them available in various ways, and uses it properly, it will be safe.

Mr. David Cox, president of the Ross division of Abbott Laboratories, stressed his company's position and policies by stating that his company has evolved two central marketing principles.

1. The selection and use of a formula should involve the intervention of a health care professional.

2. Our promotion should not be directed to the parent. Consistent with these principles, we have published formal marketing guidelines specifically for developing countries which reject the use of mass media advertising — radio, TV, newspapers — and which confine the promotion of our products to the health care profession.

He also went on to say that Ross sales representatives were prohibited from wearing nurses' uniforms and that free samples were distributed only to health care professionals. Mr. Cox also indicated that his company "maintains a close and fruitful relationship with our critics" and the professional health care community in the Third World:

However, I don't wish to leave a false impression that we agree with or accept many of the accusations or charges made against the industry. . . . We also disagree strenuously with critics that promotion to the health care profession in the Third World should be stopped. In our opinion there is no better group to care for sick or malnourished infants [Kennedy Hearing: 192–195].

Aftermath of the Hearing

For the activists, the hearing was a political and media success. According to Leah Margulies and Doug Johnson, the success of the hearing went beyond what they could have imagined and found possible. The critics felt that they gained a great deal in terms of public exposure and credibility. INFACT reported a substantial increase in their funding, volunteers, and support for the Nestle boycott effort. Summarizing his views of the hearing, Doug Johnson stated:

One of the achievements of the Hearing was that we had a record. We had WHO [World Health Organization] testimony in Congress about the impact of infant formula in Third World countries. We had very eloquent statements by JAMA and other health professionals in the U.S. and by Third World health professionals.

The Hearing itself was very energizing. We got a video tape [made] that we sent around to local groups. We got national attention and also got Bill Moyers interested in doing a special documentary on the subject.

For Nestle, the hearing was an unmitigated public relations disaster. Dr. Ballarin felt humiliated and betrayed by the company because he was misled into making certain statements against his better judgment. The episode finally moved top management to confront the reality that something was terribly wrong in the way the company was handling the issues. Mr. Tom Ward, managing partner of Ward, Lazarus, Grow & Cihar, a Washington, D.C., law firm, who did extensive legal work for Nestle and whose opinions were highly respected by top executives of Nestle — Switzerland, commented:

The issue was a new phenomenon in the business world. We did not know what the critics were after and this was history in the making. The Kennedy Hearings were not constructive because they set Nestle apart from other companies and made them vulnerable, while other companies were doing the same or worse. From then on, Nestle drew more fire.

An important element of Nestle's strategy at this point was to become a part of the U.S. infant formula manufacturers and present a joint front against its critics in the United States. The U.S. companies, on the other hand, wanted no part of the limelight that Nestle had brought upon itself. Instead, they preferred to maintain an independent course.

The Issue Moves to WHO

At the conclusion of the hearing, Senator Kennedy committed himself to meet with industry representatives to discuss and resolve the issues raised during the proceedings. Nestle felt that the Kennedy Hearing had the effect of so politicizing the issue that no rational argument could take place. According to Mr. Paternot, "the issue was getting out of hand." Added Mr. Fookes, "Our experience has been that however legitimate we may or may not have felt, or however sound our scientific case was, no one was listening to us. No one would believe us." The company, therefore, resolved to depoliticize the issue.

In a meeting in Senator Kennedy's office following the hearing, Mr. Paternot presented a letter to Senator Kennedy suggesting that the issue be referred to the World Health Organization (WHO) in Geneva. Kennedy, realizing that the issue was not as straightforward as he had first perceived, agreed that a more appropriate formal body was needed to moderate. Consequently, he wrote to the director general of WHO suggesting that that organization sponsor a conference to discuss the infant formula issue and explore the prospect of developing an international code. This conference would eventually take place in the fall of 1979. Nestle had hoped to be in a better position to influence the course of events in an international forum such as a WHO conference. However, this would prove not to be the case. Instead, the conference largely accepted the agenda of the industry's critics and set WHO toward the inexorable path of enacting a marketing code for infant formula foods.

Notes

1. U.S. Senate, *Marketing and Promotion of Infant Formula in Developing Countries, 1978. Examination of the Advertising, Marketing, Promotion, and Use of Infant Formula in Developing Nations.* Hearings before the Subcommittee on Health and Scientific Research of the Committee on Human Resources, U.S. Senate, 95th Congress, May 23, 1989.

2. Maggie M. McComas, "Origins of the Controversy," in John Dobbing (ed.), *Infant Feeding: Anatomy of a Controversy 1973–1984* (New York: Springer-Verlag, 1988), p. 70.

3. *Ibid.*, p. 70.

4. Cited in "Nestle and The Infant Formula Controversy" (A), revised edition, International Management Development Institute (IMEDE), Lausanne, Switzerland (1981).

7 THE DRIVE TOWARD CODE ENACTMENT

The Post-Kennedy Era

The Kennedy Hearings heightened public awareness of the infant formula controversy. The period between the conclusion of the Kennedy Hearings in May 1978 and the enactment of the Code in May 1981 was marked by intense activity in the United States and in Europe. The activists had gained further credibility for their position, and the companies had seen an erosion in theirs. The infant formula controversy had become broader in scope by including the expressed concerns of the activists. From their viewpoint, the issue life cycle had already entered the problem identification stage and was moving toward the remedy and relief stage. They were now poised to build on the momentum already gained and accelerate the process.

Activists' Strategies During the Problem Identification Stage

The activists' strategy during this phase was that of domain offense-encroachment. They had caused a breach in their main opponent's defenses and were now determined to widen this breach. This was a highly critical phase for INFACT because its actions during this period would determine the organization's staying power in the public arena and its viability as a major activist group. It was imperative that INFACT was continually seen as a grassroots organization of concerned people fighting against heavy odds. At the same time, it had to develop a strong organizational structure

93

and core leadership so that it could design and implement strategies without exposing them to endless public discussion and debate. This would be in sharp contrast to the ethos of the movement which was steeped in a consensual, democratic system of decision making where divergent views are respected and participation in the process is noncoercive.

Another sensitive issue for the INFACT leadership had to do with its dependence on the institutions of the organized church. INFACT had gained tremendously from the halo effect from such an association. These religious institutions also provided the movement with a substantial part of financial support, organizational skills, and technical information. Fortunately for INFACT, a large part of this support was based in the program agencies of various church bodies. INFACT's leadership, however, was concerned about the prospect of increased future scrutiny of its goals and actions by the elders of some of the parent churches. It was determined that the organization was recognized not merely as one of the players in the boycott movement, or even as more equal among the equals, but as the sole authoritative spokesperson for *the* movement. In the absence of such a de facto recognition, INFACT was afraid that it might lose control over the strategic direction of the boycott campaign. Such a course would rob INFACT and its leadership of a great deal of its hard-won authority and legitimacy. It might also weaken the terms of any eventual settlement with Nestle because other groups might be more willing to compromise.

The third element of this agenda was INFACT's posture in dealing with Nestle and other infant formula companies. The *objective* of a domain offense-encroachment strategy is to force one's opponents to deal directly with new groups by making them recognize that this group's concerns are henceforth accepted by the public as an integral part of the conflict. Therefore, people advocating those concerns must also become part of the conflict resolution process. The *success* of this strategy, however, depends on the new group's ability to project itself as a *responsible adversary* who can negotiate on equal terms, and when agreements are reached, to deliver on the promises made. INFACT had to demonstrate that it was a mature and disciplined coalition. It also had to project an image of a socially responsible and dedicated group that was less concerned with power and victory, and more motivated by the need to correct a social wrong while recognizing the legitimate concerns of its adversaries and those who otherwise disagreed with its approaches.

Implementing the Strategy of Domain Offense-Encroachment

INFACT's operational tactics had five major components: (1) it must build broader public and political support for the boycott; (2) it should put further pressure on the companies to reveal information about their infant formula marketing practices in Third World countries; (3) it should generate greater public and political support for the enactment of a WHO Code; (4) it should elevate INFACT to the position where it was the only authoritative group with whom Nestle and other companies must negotiate*; (5) it must constantly engage Nestle and other companies in dialogue and negotiations to solidify its claim as the spokesperson for the movement and thereby enhance its negotiational-contractual credibility both within the movement and in the broader public arena.[1]

The Role of Mass Media

The activists had greatly benefitted from the media interest generated during the Kennedy Hearings. They now moved to make the mass media, especially the broadcast media, as "one of them" in the struggle. The objective was to keep the issue alive by constantly creating "events" and controversies that would keep the issue on the front pages of the print media and on broadcast news and put the companies on the defensive, by forcing them to react constantly to outside events. In this they were exceedingly successful both because they handled themselves so well and because the companies, especially Nestle, handled themselves so poorly.

During this phase, one major news event stands out. It shows in sharp contrast the tremendous success that INFACT and its supporters garnered through their adroit use of the mass media. It was the broadcast of a documentary entitled "Into the Mouths of Babes" on July 5, 1978, as part of a television news series *CBS Reports* narrated by Bill Moyers, a highly respected journalist and commentator.[2] Mr. Moyers opened the program with the following comment:

> For years the use of infant formula as a substitute for mother's milk has been taken for granted in Western nations, prompting only an occasional argument over which is better for babies. But now infant formula has gone global. Multinational companies are selling it even in the poorest parts of the world, and the controversy over breast versus bottle has taken on a new, alarming dimension. At issue is whether in the developing nations the widespread sale of infant formula is doing more harm than good.

Through a series of interviews representing both the industry representatives and their critics, including pictures of sick, dying, and malnourished infants, the documentary carried a vivid image of the potential horrors of

---

*Activists had used both INFACT and IBFAN at various times as the official negotiating organization. However, notwithstanding slight differences in their respective leadership, the control of the two organizations was held by the same group of core leaders.

bottle feeding under unhygienic conditions. Moyers suggested that "Infant formula companies try selling the image of the Western baby, well-fed, contented, and thriving." He commented that in the real world of poverty, impure water, and unsanitary conditions, however, this illusion had turned into the reality of infant sickness and death.

Infant formula industry's perspective was presented by Mr. Jack Stafford (vice president of American Home Products), and Mr. Frank Sprole (vice chairman of the board of Bristol-Myers). Both Stafford and Sprole talked about their companies' efforts to minimize the improper and unwarranted use of their products in Third World countries. However, in the end, they largely disclaimed responsibility because most of the conditions surrounding the use of infant formula in Third World countries were beyond their companies' control. This position was similar to the one that the industry took at the Kennedy Hearings and had just as little impact.

> *Jack Stafford:* I'm sure there's no question that from time to time our products, as well as other companies' products, are used with bad water, and that women don't follow the procedures that we want them to, and that they don't boil the water as they should. I'm sure that would happen occasionally.

> *Mr. Sprole:* We can't control the final product getting into the hands of somebody who possibly might misuse it, but we try in every way possible to avoid abuse with our instructions and so forth, and hopefully through the medical profession. But it seems to me the product is there in every area of the world for people who need it, and these are the best infant formula products.

In his concluding remarks, Moyers summarized the problem by indicating that while everybody seems to be blaming everybody else, nothing much was happening and the number of victims continued to increase:

> The babies are the victims. Because no one will assume responsibility for contributing to their plight, no one takes responsibility for ending it. But the companies could insist the formula not be sold where it cannot be properly used. Doctors could end the conflict of interest and the casual distribution of samples. Governments could also put the care of these children first, limiting the importation of costly formulas that families cannot afford. . . . There are answers if someone will act for the children who cannot act for themselves.

Building Support for the Boycott

This documentary was widely shown by INFACT, ICCR, and other industry critics. It became one of the most effective instruments for the activists to raise funds, sign up volunteers, and build further organizational support for the campaign. The activists were also increasing political pressure on the infant formula companies through congressional hearings and other political avenues. For example, in the spring of 1979, Congressman Dellums of California introduced The Infant Nutrition Act (HR4093), which was a bill designed to regulate the sale, distribution, and export of infant formula in and to developing countries. The number of endorsements from church groups and other public and private organizations continued to grow. New endorsements were received from the Presbyterian Church of United States (PCUS), The New York Annual Conference of the United Methodist Church, and from many other churches, unions, groups, and concerned individuals. With broad public support and increased financial resources, the campaign took on a more offensive stance against the companies.

Dialogue with the Companies

INFACT's leadership recognized that it must bring Nestle and other companies to the negotiating table if it was to succeed in resolving the conflict on its terms. However, the companies were vehemently opposed to any negotiations that would give INFACT even greater credibility and clout. Yet they had to be seen as willing to "discuss, inform and explain" their activities to avoid being viewed as obstructionists by the media and public-at-large. From the companies' viewpoint, this communication strategy was an end in itself. The activists, on the other hand, viewed it only as an "interim" tactic. Every meeting and discussion would lead to further meetings and discussions. Every explanation would call for a further questioning that would lead to further explanations. Having once entered into this dialogue-discussion mode, the companies were trapped and could not get out. The activists would largely control both the tone and direction of this dialogue-discussion and thereby outmaneuver the companies in the fight for the hearts and minds of the general public.

One of the important elements of the activists' strategy was to continually use shareholder resolutions as the vehicle for confronting the U.S.-based infant formula manufacturers and keep the issue alive in the press. The companies also began to engage in discussions with various church groups and institutional investors to avoid future proxy resolutions and adverse and unwanted publicity. The process was successful in increasing corporate managements' sensitivities to the perspectives of the critics. The activists gained further experience in dealing with corporate representatives, building internal organizational depth, and broadening their network.

ICCR also engaged Nestle in a series of meetings during this period. The first meeting took place on September 26, 1977, two months after the start of the boycott. This meeting was attended by other church groups including Lutheran Church Women, Clergy and Laity Concerned (CALC), the National Council of Churches (NCC), and representatives of the Ford Foundation. Responding to Nestle's request, a second meeting was held between Nestle (including executives from Nestle — Switzerland), ICCR, and NCC leadership. This meeting was also joined by the representatives of the Rockefeller Foundation. Dr. William Thompson, president of NCC, urged Nestle to take the boycott seriously and to improve its marketing practices. Another meeting took place in August 1978 in Nestle's headquarters in Vevey, Switzerland. For the church leaders, this meeting was quite disheartening. Mr. Arthur Furer, Nestle's managing director, told NCC's Dr. Thompson that he (Furer) was not too concerned about the boycott and did not feel that his company's infant formula marketing practices needed any change. Furer was quite specific in his disagreement on most of the major points of contention between the company and the activists. He emphasized that samples "had a role to play"; mothercraft nurses "contributed to health education"; and advertising was a crucial educational medium.[3] A number of additional meetings between the two parties showed no meaningful progress.

Control of Organization Direction and Implementation Tactics

During this phase, the boycott leadership was confronted with a severe shortage of skilled and dedicated people in its managerial ranks. Teams had to be established to discuss and negotiate with Nestle and the three other U.S.-based infant formula producers. On the one hand, this would offer an opportunity to INFACT to involve other groups and individuals in the negotiating and decision-making process. The risk was a dilution of focus and a dispersion of central direction and authority. The challenge for INFACT was to create an organization that gave a public appearance of a grassroots mass movement but was also tightly controlled by a small coterie of individuals who made all the critical decisions as to campaign strategy and tactics, decisions that were then ratified through ritualistic processes of consensus building and open dialogue. In this they were following the lessons successfully learned from another master organizer, Saul Alinsky.[4] INFACT's leadership solved this problem by ensuring that these sub-groups had constant input and direction from the movement's core group of leaders. Moreover, membership in the sub-groups was chosen from among the "loyal" followers. Those who refused to toe the line were often pressured through group control. Where necessary, the leadership would also resort to public ridicule, character assassination, and threat of media exposure with charges of disloyalty to the cause.

This pattern of leadership, that is, control through insinuation and "exposure" of one's misdeeds, was consistently practiced by the organization's leadership. This approach seemed to have been quite effective during the early stages of the controversy as it invariably involved people in the trenches. However, during later stages of the controversy, it also involved too many people with higher levels of institutional support and individual leadership stature who were less vulnerable to such crude pressure. Unfortunately, the leadership of the boycott movement could not see this difference and continued to use tactics of repudiation against those who chose to question its modus operandi. This factor, or leadership trait, in my opinion, was one of the major reasons why INFACT/INBC/ICCR core operatives lost a great deal of credibility and initiative when it came to final negotiations and termination of the boycott.

Two incidents, one during the early and the other during the later phases of the controversy, illustrate this pattern. The first one involves Sister Marilyn Uline and the other, Father Theodore Purcell.

Sister Marilyn Uline.   Sister Uline belonged to the Dominican Order. Her Order owned stock in Abbott Laboratories. She represented her congregation in a group called The 8th Day Center — which, in turn, staffed The Illinois Committee For Responsible Investment (ICRI), a coalition of local religious congregations affiliated with ICCR. Early in 1976, she was asked by her group to establish contacts with Abbott Laboratories (AL) and its Ross division (the infant formula production sector) in connection with that company's infant formula marketing practices in Third World countries. This was a logical choice since both her congregation and AL's headquarters were located in the Chicago area. To get the process going, Leah Margulies flew from New York to prepare the Chicago group for its meetings with Abbott/Ross representatives. This was the first time Sister Uline had met Leah Margulies, and the meeting left a strong imprint on her memory. She observed*:

> I was taken aback by Leah's predisposition as to what we should expect from our contacts with the Abbott people. Leah said that "we weren't going to let ourselves be sweet talked into anything by Dave Cox [President of Ross Labs]. As a matter of fact we weren't going to let him have the floor because he would talk and monopolize the whole thing."

The next two years saw a process of increased conciliatory dialogue between the Chicago group and Abbott-Ross representatives. At the same time, ICCR's New York office viewed the Chicago group as veering from the national position. There was a growing undertone of friction between the two groups. Here are some excerpts from the minutes of a meeting of the Chicago-based coalition and ICCR/INFACT representatives that took place on November 7, 1978. The meeting was attended by ten people, including Leah Margulies and Doug Johnson.

---

*Interview with the author. Unless otherwise specifically stated, all direct quotes or paraphrased statements of various people, cited here and elsewhere in this chapter, are based on personal on-the-record interviews or written communications with the author.

> . . . Leah [Margulies] then presented her views of Abbott. She termed Abbott as the most "slimy" company, the most difficult to deal with. In her view, Abbott is very adept at taking halfway measures to address the formula promotion problem that look good on paper but really are not very effective.

> . . . Leah continued citing differences between the way she was able to work with the New York groups and her contacts with the Chicago group. Marilyn stated that she saw the history of non-confrontation with Abbott to be a positive factor; we do not have to deal with the residue of bad feeling built up through proxy fights. . . . [It was agreed] that the relationship with ICCR was primarily consult-ative and that people in Chicago . . . should be the principal decision-makers. [Leah saw no problem in that approach but insisted there had to be complete agreement on everything and that it was] she who will be contacted on a nation-wide basis for . . . verification.[5]

Unfortunately, the situation continued to deteriorate. Sister Uline felt that she was viewed with suspicion by people at ICCR. This became evident when she attended the INFACT meeting in October 1979. Her research and data were not looked at seriously. She was seen as being used by the company. For a number of years following this chain of events, she was unable to secure any job dealing with her Bible ministry. She was ostricized because she was perceived to be naive at best and in the pocket of Abbott at worst. According to her information, Tim Smith and others would contact potential employers and discourage them from employing her. She was ultimately re-duced to seeking psychiatric help for depression. After a number of years, she was able to find gainful employment but *outside* her Bible ministry.

Rev. Theodore V. Purcell, S.J..   Late Fr. Purcell was a distinguished Jesuit scholar and a research professor at the Jesuit Center for Social Studies, Georgetown University, Washington, D.C. He had frequently contributed to both religious and business-professional periodicals. He was quite active in the ethical investor movement. As chairman of National Jesuit Advisory Committee on Investor Responsibility (JACIR), Fr. Purcell had taken posi-tions of moderation on many issues where ICCR and certain other church-related organizations had been more confrontational in their approaches. In 1983, Mr. Timothy (Tim) H. Smith, ICCR's executive director, wrote to Fr. Purcell accusing him of being biased and dishonest, and demanding that he should undertake certain specific actions to redeem himself. Given below are some excerpts from this letter:[6]

> Your active involvement in the leadership of IRD [Institute of Religion and De-mocracy] leads me to some unhappy conclusions about your own work and that of JACIR [National Jesuit Advisory Committee on Investor Responsibility].

> Your tradition of encouraging fairness and balance has been sadly betrayed in your IRD involvement and instead a narrow political perspective has emerged.

JACIR's position within the Jesuits, increasingly under question as an authoritative voice of integrity on shareholder resolutions is now open to further question.

How is it that JACIR's position is quoted in the Bristol Myers proxy statement opposing a shareholder resolution on baby formula supported by scores of other church investors? Does this use of the JACIR position indicate that the baby formula line of Ernest Lefever and Herman Nickel is the one that you have been privately promoting within the Society of Jesus?

Likewise, when JACIR under your urging issues critical letters and statements regarding church-sponsored resolutions on South Africa, can this any longer be seen as an objective review of an issue, or is it an instant replay of the IRD philosophy on this topic?

In short, I find your credibility as an objective analyst now open to question as a result of your active involvement in the IRD. There are several things you might consider that would help to reestablish that credibility:

1. Resign from IRD and disassociate yourself from their McCarthyite attacks on national Protestant Church bodies.
2. Declare yourself in an honest and open way in the style of IRD, arguing your case at JACIR in an above-board fashion as being against the social justice programs of the churches.
3. Disqualify yourself from future JACIR activities on the grounds that the Committee deserves balanced reporting which due to your own strong opinions your [sic] are unable to give.

You can see from this letter that your leadership in IRD distresses me greatly. I welcome a clarification of the record from you. Until then, unfortunately, I see your role in JACIR as one of blunting social advocacy by church investors and promoting a biased response from the Jesuits to corporate responsibility. Unless I am corrected, this is the position I shall interpret to all our Roman Catholic members and in particular your Jesuit colleagues who sit on our Board and cooperate in ICCR's work.

Fr. Purcell was not easily intimidated. His response to Tim Smith was equally blunt. Unlike Sister Uline, Fr. Purcell enjoyed leadership stature in his Order, respect among his peers, and had strength of his convictions. He was also willing to stand up to Mr. Smith's crude threats. In his response to Tim Smith, he stated:[7]

You question the good faith of JACIR's Chairman. You demand that he resign from the Institute of Religion and Democracy, or at least castigate it severely. You blame JACIR for Bristol-Myers' 1983 proxy mistake, for which they apologized. You are severely critical of JACIR's position on the infant formula controversy for which the members of JACIR are alleged docilely to follow the "urging" of JACIR's Chairman. You are totally critical of JACIR's positions on South Africa and on other issues as "biased," "blunting social advocacy," no longer "a voice of integrity," "a narrow political perspective," "betrayed," etc.

I know we are both seeking social justice. Clearly, we differ as to the wisest and most effective ways of achieving that social justice. To speak of "splits within the church community" as though the church must speak with one voice on complex socio-economic, ethical questions is to identify revealed religion with social action — something very dangerous for the churches.

Dialogue can be had only between people of good will. I would find it hard to try to clarify the three issues you raise when, with intemperate language, you question my credibility and the groups with which I am associated. Dialogue is seriously impaired by unfair accusations and guilt by association. These destroy the necessary basis of trust for any reasonable discussion.

As you perhaps know, there is a real difference of opinion among some American Jesuits as to what the Society's role should be in certain aspects of the ethical investor movement. I understand the reason for your personal intrusion. However, your interference does seem unconscionable. I would prefer to work out those differences with my fellow Jesuits - ourselves alone. I shall not discuss them here.

A further comment on intrusion: The activity in the ethical investor movement of major, respected institutional investors, such as TIAA-CREF, Ford Foundation, Stanford, the Jesuit Provinces, etc., gives the movement credibility with management and with the general public. For you deliberately to interfere in the activities of such institutional investors seriously damages your personal credibility. . . . The ethical investor movement is a sophisticated and important movement toward the common good, requiring knowledge, good will and mutual trust. I hope that these qualities can be restored in any dialogue we might have in the future.

Nestle's Strategies During the Problem Identification Stage

Nestle's strategy during this phase was that of domain defense. Although it gave the appearance of leaning toward domain expansion, the company was determined to defend its objectives, market position, and operational autonomy. The company continued to define the problem as being still in the pre-problem stage, and geared all its strategies and tactics to ensure that it remained there. Infant formula manufacturers and the activists viewed the problem in starkly different terms. To the companies, the problem of inappropriate use of infant formula was a peripheral issue affecting a tiny minority of consumers, which should not deny the vast majority of consumers the right to use a perfectly safe product. The major problem, and the one deserving everyone's attention, was to improve public health, sanitary conditions, and infant care in these countries. To the critics, the problem of misuse was not the peripheral but the core issue which could be best eliminated by stopping sale of all infant formula products, except in very rare medical circumstances.

Nestle's Swiss management continued to believe that its critics were essentially a small group of ideologically motivated radicals and that their followers were generally a well-meaning but poorly informed group of people. Thus while the company was willing to discuss and explain its activities to any and all responsible groups, it would not yield to coercion or outside pressure from the self-appointed guardians of the welfare of the Third World's poor. In this sense, Nestle was following a more hard-line strategy than other major infant formula manufacturers. Nestle's value set, tradition, and management orientation were inimical to sharing any decision making with outsiders. The company was afraid to set a precedent. Its dominant market position and enormous financial and manpower resources also led the management to believe that it could withstand the critics' onslaught and fight the battle on its terms.

Developing New Strategies and Tactics to Deal with the Company's Critics

Following the debacle at the Kennedy Hearings, Nestle's Swiss management decided to take more direct control of the company's efforts to deal with the boycott issue. Consequently, Mr. Ernest Saunders, a senior vice president, was sent to the United States to gain first-hand perspective on the problem. He had extensive discussions both within the Nestle's U.S. management and also with a number of conservatively oriented public-political affairs operatives, scholars, and journalists, including Mr. Ernest Lefever, the president of the Washington, D.C-based conservative "think tank" Ethics and Public Policy Center, and Mr. Herman Nickel, an editorial writer for the business magazine, *Fortune*.

Saunder's analysis of the issue and his proposed solutions were the subject of a confidential memo to the management. Unfortunately for the company, this memo was leaked to the activists by someone within the company. According to Dr. Carl Angst, Nestle's managing director, "We were shocked that a copy of this memo got into the hands of the activists. We never found out who did it." The resulting adverse publicity was so bad that the memo came to be known as the Nestlegate Memorandum.[8]

The Nestlegate Memorandum

In one sense, the memorandum was a masterpiece of insight and analysis of the infant formula controversy when seen through the eyes of Nestle's Swiss management. The memo did not attempt to deal with the substantive issues raised by the company's critics. Instead, it viewed the problem almost solely as that of fighting adverse publicity, discrediting the activists, and creating credibility for the company. Saunders recommended a set of operational tactics that were designed to execute the strategy of domain defense. The memo called for a "containment of the awareness of the boycott campaign, without being ourselves responsible for escalating awareness levels."

Saunders believed that agencies like USAID, UNICEF, and WHO were leaning sympathetically toward the positions taken by the industry's critics. He viewed them to be generally anti-business. He considered INFACT and IBFAN's "propaganda activity" to court these groups as "undoubtedly a most dangerous development." His concerns, moreover, were not limited to the United States. Instead he was looking at the international dimensions of the infant formula controversy and the activities of groups like IBFAN and IOCU in Third World countries. He asserted that "in view of the overall propaganda campaign now being mounted through IBFAN and the professionalism of the forces involved, it is always possible that we could even win a battle in the U.S. and lose the war as a result of determined pressure on Third World governments and medical authorities."

Saunders' strategy advocated a more aggressive stance on the part of the company in dealing with its critics. This was to be done through third party agents to create a public impression of broader support for Nestle's position and also discredit the activists. The memorandum called for a launching of an expensive and sophisticated public relations campaign to counter the boycott. The company was to develop closer ties with the academic community, conservative elements in the media, including right-wing think-tanks. Unfortunately, Nestle's link with the Mr. Lefever's Ethics and Public Policy Center created the conditions for another major public relations blunder for Nestle: the Lefever Fiasco.

The Role of Mass Media

Nestle's dealings with the U.S. news media reflected its insular perspective and a tunnel vision about the nature of the boycott campaign and the public credibility of its critics. The company seemed to have grossly underestimated the influence of the news media in the United States and seriously erred in developing strategies to deal with it. Thus while the activists successfully courted the media as partners in a common effort, Nestle viewed the media largely as a hostile element that must be controlled. The important elements of Nestle's media plan as outlined in the Nestlegate memorandum were as follows:

- An urgent need to develop an effective counter propaganda operation, with a network of appropriate consultants in key centers, knowledgeable in the tech-

nicalities of infant nutrition in developing countries, and with the appropriate contacts to get articles placed.
- A systematic attempt to reach the grassroots through people who have greater public credibility. These people would be supported with necessary informational materials to answer specific questions pertaining to Nestle.
- The company should not seek business press articles at random without carefully analyzing the direction such articles might take. Nestle must also avoid investigative journalists simply seeking out sensational pieces to further damage the representation of multinational businesses as a whole.

The Lefever Fiasco

The genesis of the Ethics and Public Policy Center's (EPPC) involvement in the infant formula controversy pre-dated the Nestlegate Memorandum. The chronology of events presented here was provided by Dr. Lefever to the U.S. Senate on the occasion of his confirmation hearing to be Assistant Secretary of State for Human Rights and Humanitarian Affairs.[9] Early in 1979, on its own initiative, EPPC decided to undertake a study of the infant formula controversy. EPPC's president, Dr. Lefever, had been an ardent critic of the mainline churches for their left-wing orientation. Between September and November of 1979, EPPC staff collected relevant information about the controversy. Around the same time, Dr. Lefever was contacted by Mr. Groner of Nestle who congratulated him for his book, *Amsterdam to Nairobi: The World Council of Churches and the Third World*.[10] This book was highly critical of WCC's activities in Third World countries. Groner suggested that Lefever visit him in New York, which eventually led to a Nestle contribution of $25,000 to EPPC. Between November 1979 and March 1980, Lefever also contacted other U.S. corporations and sought their financial support for EPPC's activities. Contributions were received from many other companies, including Bristol-Myers, a major U.S.-based infant formula manufacturer.

In October 1979, Mr. Herman Nickel, an editorial writer for *Fortune*, was contacted and he informally agreed to write an article on the subject. Nickel was assured of complete independence in his research and final output. Nickel's article appeared in the June 15, 1980, issue of *Fortune* under the title, "The Corporation Haters." The thrust of the article was that the "spirit of the New Left lives on in an anti-business coalition — sponsored by the National Council of Churches." The article alluded to many examples of anti-business "propaganda" on the part of New Left groups who were being supported by the NCC and its agencies such as the ICCR. Among the examples listed were those of the infant formula and the Nestle boycott campaign of INFACT/ICCR. The article went into great length listing all the sins of omission and commission on the part of INFACT/ICCR. The tone and the conclusion of the article are best captured in Nickel's comment: "The common theme is plain enough for even the slowest learner in the capitalist economic system, profits and social responsibility simply do not mix."

The article created quite a stir both in the activist and the corporate circles. Lefever contacted Nickel, congratulated him on the article, and told him that the Center was considering reprinting the article, to which Nickel agreed. Permission was also received from *Fortune* after payment of an appropriate fee. The Center's reprint included a new foreword by Nickel and published under the new title of "The Crusade Against the Corporation: The Churches and the Nestle Boycott." Both articles expressed similar sentiments, turning the church's support for the Nestle boycott into the "Marxists marching under the banner of Christ." In September 1980, EPPC began a mass-mailing of its promotional fund raising packet to recruit new supporters; it included a fancy reprint of Nickel's article. More than 100,000 copies of the reprint were distributed, many of which were given out by the U.S. companies.

In the ensuing period, Lefever had extensive contacts with Nestle and other U.S. infant formula manufacturers and received additional contributions from them. He also received funding support from many other corporations. Mr. Tom Ward (a Washington, D.C.-based lawyer who represented Nestle in the United States and was a confidant of Nestle's senior management in Switzerland) "saw the article as the first dispassionate study on this issue. The activists and the infant formula companies have their own biases and viewpoints. This article indicates that there are two arguments and two sides to the story. There is a grey area."

On February 20, 1981, President Reagan announced his intention to nominate Dr. Lefever to be the Assistant Secretary of State for Human Rights and Humanitarian Affairs. On May 22, 1981, *Washington Post* published an article entitled "Lefever Formula Role" and suggested that Nestle was battling the boycotters by painting them red. It revealed that Nestle had given the EPPC $25,000 in 1980.[11] On May 28, 1981, *Fortune* issued a statement saying that Nestle's contribution to EPPC voided Nickel's understanding with Lefever.

The ensuing controversy became the focal point of liberal opposition to Lefever's nomination. During his confirmation hearing, Lefever was extensively questioned about his dealings with Herman Nickel and Nestle. Lefever's statements and answers to questions at his confirmation hearings were less than satisfactory. He vehemently denied receiving money from the Nestle corporation, although he later admitted that the center received two payments of $5,000 and $20,000.

In an interview with the author, Tom Ward commented:

This article was not a commissioned article by Nestle. Many companies disseminated the article but Nestle did not. This whole controversy came out because of a political controversy, the Lefever nomination, not out of infant formula. The political objective was not to find out the truth but to defeat the nomination. Lefever is a very honorable man. . . . When you get tied into accusations of improper conduct, there are certain segments of the public that will believe it.

It soon became obvious that the nomination was in trouble. Rather than face the humiliation of rejection, Lefever withdrew his nomination. In the end, Nestle was left with one more public debacle to clear.

Notes

1. See, for example, Douglas A. Johnson, "Confronting Corporate Power: Strategies and Phases of the Nestle Boycott," in James E. Post (ed.), *Research in Corporate Social Performance and Policy,* 8 (Greenwich, CT: JAI Press, 1986), pp. 323–344.

2. Transcript of CBS Reports, Edition Six, Wednesday, July 5, 1978, "Into the Mouths of Babes," produced by Janet Roach.

3. Leah Margulies, "Meetings Between ICCR and the Infant Formula Industry: 1974–1980."

4. S.D. Alinsky, *Rules for Radicals* (New York: Vintage Boos, 1971); and S.D. Alinsky, *Reville for Radicals* (New York: Vintage Books, 1979). For a more contemporary treatment and analysis of Alinsky's work, see: Sanford D. Horwitt, *Let Them Call Me Rebel: Saul Alinsky — His Life and Legacy* (New York: Random House, 1991).

5. 8th Day Center, "Minutes of the Meeting of Chicago-Based Shareholders Concerned About Infant Formula Promotion," November 7, 1978.

6. Letter from Timothy H. Smith, executive director, Interfaith Center on Corporate Responsibility, dated July 26, 1983.

7. Letter from Father Theodore V. Purcell, research professor, Jesuit Center for Social Studies, Georgetown University, Washington, D.C., to Mr. Timothy H. Smith, executive director, Interfaith Center on Corporate Responsibility, New York, dated October 14, 1983.

8. *Nestlegate Memorandum — US Boycott — Conclusions Based on US Visit (August 2–4, 1980).* Released by ICCR in New York.

9. "Nomination of Ernest W. Lefever." Hearings before the Committee on Foreign Relations, U.S. Senate, 97th Congress, First Session, May 18–19, June 4–5, 1981.

10. Ernest W. Lefever, *Amsterdam to Nairobi: The World Council of Churches and the Third World* (Washington, D.C.: Ethics and Public Policy Center, 1979).

11. *Washington Post,* May 22, 1981.

III ISSUES AND INSTITUTIONS

8 HEALTH, MEDICAL, AND SCIENTIFIC ASPECTS OF THE CONTROVERSY

It would be hard to question the need for scientific research and objective data collection as the necessary preconditions for developing sound policy alternatives. The real-world experience, however, makes this ideal all but impossible to achieve. Scientific research involving human subjects and using randomized samples, control groups, and isolation of various factors is extremely difficult, if not impossible: for example, how one might go about assigning infants randomly to breast- or bottle-feeding groups and keep them there when a change for health reasons may be called for; or, similarly, how might one "isolate" the effect of infant formula from such other factors as poverty, unsanitary conditions, impure water, or illiteracy of the parents. Thus, facts are at best approximations or likelihoods of occurrences given the existence of certain environmental factors.

Infant formula manufacturers and their supporters contend that no substantive case exists for relating their marketing practices to either a decline in breastfeeding or an increase in infant mortality and morbidity in less developed countries (LDCs). Some have even argued that most of the criticized industry practices were substantially discarded even before the passage of the WHO Code in May 1981, and that the opponents of the infant formula manufacturers have continued to repeat old charges primarily for political purposes, that is, with a view to regulate the infant formula industry and severely constrain its sales.[1]

Industry's critics, on the other hand, behave as if evidence is overwhelming and the issue is beyond debate. Consider, for example, the following statement by Dr. Stephen C. Joseph, among the industry's most vociferous critics, before a congressional committee in 1981.[2] "Almost 100 million infants are born in the developing world each year. One in ten of these infants do not live to see their first birthday — that comes to 10 million infant deaths annually in the developing world. Half of these deaths — about 5 million annually — are due to the vicious cycle of diarrhea and malnutrition. Of these 5 million deaths, the best available estimates are that up to 1 million deaths are directly attributable to the association of contaminated infant formula with diarrhea and malnutrition."

While the industry seeks specific scientific evidence, the industry's critics reject the absolute need for such findings and regard totally controlled experiments as unfeasible, unnecessary, and, therefore, a tactic used by the infant formula manufacturers to avoid facing the "real" problem. Instead, they offer "experiential" knowledge and eyewitness accounts from the field, and consider them as strong supportive material to supplement their scientific evidence which the industry has criticized as insufficient and poorly developed. Thus, each party is prone to choosing certain scientific facts that lend credence to its view of the world.

In the process of emphasizing extremes, a vast middle ground is lost to inflaming rhetoric with results that are neither enlightening nor conducive to reaching consensus and implementable public policy options. Typical of this approach is an assertion by Dr. J. Dobbing in a Nestle-sponsored book, *Infant Feeding: Anatomy of a Controversy, 1973–1984*, wherein he states that it is not his purpose "to justify those activities of industry which may have been mistaken in the past, but it will seek to point out the errors, mainly of over simplification, in the tactics of industry's critics when recruiting the sympathies of ordinary, concerned and well intentioned citizens to their crusade."[3] He, of course, does not make any attempt to point out either the "errors" or "oversimplifications" employed by the infant formula manufacturers in dealing with the critics and "recruiting sympathies of ordinary, concerned, and well-intentioned citizens" to their viewpoint.

"Much of the confusion in this complex subject," according to Dr. Dobbing, "has been generated by lay activist groups who rely heavily on the quoted opinions of people we may describe as 'expatriate doctors.' "[4] He is equally scornful of his colleagues, accusing them of poor judgment and fuzzy research.

A career in clinical medicine, and especially in clinical pediatrics, attracts some of the most well-intentioned people. . . . However, although such dedication is praise-worthy, indeed necessary there is always a risk that it will tend to obscure judgements which would be better made coolly and without passion. Although it is inevitable that most clinical judgement depends on a scientifically insecure basis of knowledge, at least we should regret our ignorance and make an attempt to evaluate what little evidence there is by means of intellectual appraisal before being dominated by proper humanitarian concern. Nowhere is this attitude more transgressed than in attitudes to the feeding of babies. . . .[5]

Within the framework of this book, it would be impossible to write a scientific treatise exhaustively discussing the medical and health aspects of the infant formula controversy. Our effort would be to provide a reasonable and comprehensible level of discussion with a view to delineating areas of agreement and disagreement prevailing among various groups. Only then can we hope to understand the scientific and medical, economic and financial, ideological and political, sociological and cultural, and emotional bases that underlie various approaches advocated by different groups and individuals.

In dealing with the controversy, I have drawn, to a great extent, from the evidence found in studies and research that have been cited and defended by representatives and supporters of the infant formula manufacturers and their critics.[6] For an evaluation of the differing perspectives on the adequacy and veracity of various scientific studies, our primary source of information has been the 1984 Report of the American Academy of Pediatrics Task Force assessing the scientific evidence relating to infant feeding practices and infant health.*

Dimensions of the Health, Medical, and Scientific Aspects

There is no disagreement between the infant formula manufacturers and their critics that breast milk is the ideal food for infants and must be the preferred choice. They also agree that infant formula preparations are an excellent and necessary substitute for breast milk when mothers, for a variety of reasons, cannot or will not breastfeed their babies. This is, however, the beginning and not the end of the argument. The differences between the two positions assert themselves almost immediately, starting with the conditions under which mothers are unable to breastfeed their babies either totally or partially. It then goes on to the role of the industry in encouraging or contributing to a decline in breastfeeding, and the costs in terms of infant deaths and sickness, including malnutrition, that follow when infant formula is used improperly.

The critics' argument about the infant formula controversy starts with the assertion that human breast milk is the most natural, convenient, and economical food for infants. Except for a tiny minority of mothers, infants can be completely fed by mothers' milk up to the first four to six months of their lives beyond which weaning and other supplementary foods need to be in-

---

*American Academy of Pediatrics, "Report of the Task Force on the Assessment of the Scientific Evidence Relating to Infant-Feeding Practices and Infant Health," *Pediatrics,* Supplement, 74, 4 (October 1984). All references to this report in the text will be cited as The AAP Report, followd by the approrpiate page numbers.

troduced in a child's diet. A decline in breastfeeding contributes to malnutrition and exposes infants to increased incidence of sickness and death.
This is so because human milk substitutes do not possess the same immu-
nological properties as the breast milk at the point in their lives when infants
are most vulnerable to diseases.[8]

Infant formulas, when properly prepared and fed in adequate quantities,
are likely to be safe and nutritious for the infants. They are, however, quite
expensive and generally beyond the reach of most mothers in Third World
countries. Industry's marketing and promotion practices propel mothers to
buy formula for their babies. Unable to afford infant formula in sufficient
quantities, these mothers dilute it, thus contributing to infant malnutrition.
Moreover, poor sanitary conditions and illiteracy prevailing in most of the
Third World countries make it all but impossible for infant formula to be
prepared properly, thereby exposing infants to diseases.

To put it even more succinctly, critics of infant formula industry claim
that there has been a dramatic and precipitous decline in breastfeeding in
Third World countries. Bottle-fed babies in *both* developing and developed
countries have higher incidence of death and disease than breast-fed babies.
Industry promotion practices have had a significant influence on mothers to
move away from an otherwise "perfect" food, and resort to an unnecessary
and expensive product which they can ill afford and should not be using in
the first place. Hence the charge of "commerciogenic malnutrition" leveled
against the infant formula industry by one of its foremost critics, Dr. Derrick
B. Jelliffe.[9] He originally suggested a number of 10.0 million but later stated
that it was only a "symbolic" figure and not a scientific assessment. Dr.
James Grant, executive director of UNICEF, used the lower 1.0 million figure. However, UNICEF also later admitted to this figure as just being an
estimate.[10] Furthermore, the extent of accuracy of each and every aspect of
this statement, and other assertions made above, have been hotly debated
and vigorously challenged by industry representatives and also by a significant body of the scientific community.

The 1979 WHO/UNICEF Background Paper, while strongly stressing the
advantages of breastfeeding and the dangers of infant formula misuse, recognizes that under certain circumstances, infant formula is necessary and
highly desirable. The study, however, goes on to state that "For many other
mothers who choose not to breast-feed, the use of a formula is merely a
convenience. Thus both formulas and milk preparations are essential. However, it has proved very difficult to avoid their excessive and inappropriate
use as breast-milk substitutes where substitution is neither necessary nor
desirable."[11]

Professors Nevin Scrimshaw and Barbara Underwood of the Massachusetts Institute of Technology also emphasize the need for infant formula under certain circumstances and suggest a different approach to the issue of
misuse of supplementary foods. Their approach to correcting the misuse of

complementary foods is two-pronged: (1) to encourage and provide support systems that favor the choice to breastfeed, and (2) where breastfeeding is not chosen, to try to improve the artificial feeding by attention to the quantity, nutrient density, and sanitary characteristics of the food as it is given to the child. Experience with modern infant formula in the industrialized countries demonstrates that when quantity, quality, and sanitation are adequate, the results, as judged by growth, morbidity, and mortality, need not be different from those observed among exclusively breastfed infants.[12]

Industry's critics, however, express tremendous skepticism as to industry's commitment to encouraging breastfeeding. Dr. Jelliffe believes that the present role of the infant food industry in developing countries is overdominant and inappropriate, as conflicts of interest between profit and social or health issues are forced to occur frequently (Kennedy Hearings). INFACT's Doug Johnson and Leah Margulies go even further. While they recognize that "not all malnutrition is caused by bottle-feeding, and not all bottle-feeding is caused by commercial promotion," they argue that:

> Among the several causes for the decline of breastfeeding . . . the promotion of infant formulas is an important contributory cause that must be controlled. . . . even if promotion of infant formula were responsible for, say, no more than 5% of all decisions to abandon breastfeeding in favor of infant formula, this would still constitute a grave problem worth addressing. But since the influence is clearly much greater, our efforts will go towards controlling industry practices which threaten the welfare of innocent children around the world.[13]

Human Milk — The Perfect Food for Infants

The natural superiority of human milk as the preferred food for babies is perhaps the least controversial aspect of the entire infant formula controversy. It is convenient, requires no sterilizing, mixing, measuring, or purchasing. It is the most nutritious product for a baby. The biological mechanism in breastfeeding helps the baby to develop and grow. There is, however, disagreement as to the conditions that could prevent mothers from breastfeeding their babies, or, to use the WHO Code terminology, "babies that have to be fed" with nonhuman or artificial foods: for example, infant formula. Industry critics define these limits in physiological terms only (1 percent of mothers) and also attribute a part of a mother's alleged inadequacy to feed their babies on an industry-supported and -induced sociological environment. However, a review of available scientific data by the *Report of the Task Force of the American Academy of Pediatrics* puts this number at 4 percent. The AAP Report suggests that the worldwide proportion of mothers who cannot breastfeed is unlikely to exceed 10 percent, and concludes that "given adequate instruction, emotional support, and favorable circumstances, 96 percent of new mothers can breastfeed successfully (AAP Report, p. 611). Infant formula industry argues that both these limits are un-realistic and do not take into account many sociological and economic factors that may affect a mother's choice.

Breast milk contains an abundance of nutrients necessary for a healthy baby. Breast milk also has some anti-infection properties that are important. Studies show that mature breast milk contains quantities of enzymes, anti-bodies, and immunizing agents specifically suited to the infant's very vul-nerable digestive track.[14] A review of scientific literature by the AAP Task Force Report supports most of these findings, although with somewhat dif-ferent inference in the case of industrially advanced and developed countries (DCs) than those of developing and less developed countries (LDCs). Ac-cording to the AAP Task Force Report, there is "some evidence of a positive association between the health of an infant born in the last decade in the United States and breast-feeding, but this evidence is not entirely convinc-ing. If there are health benefits associated with breast-feeding in populations with good sanitation, nutrition, and medical care, the benefits are apparently modest" (pp. 580, 619–630). This observation, of course, would not hold true in the case of poor and low-income people and regions in DCs as they would display many of the characteristics that would be similar to those prevailing in LDCs.

Feeding Practices and Infant Mortality

There have been few studies on the effect of feeding practices on infant mortality in Third World countries. The scattered studies that do exist sug-gest that in less developed countries breastfed infants have lower death rates.[15] For example, critics of infant formula industry widely cite a study by Cunningham suggesting that "assuming universal breast-feeding, a saving of 5,000 lives annually is possible in the United States."[16] Cunningham's estimate was based on the difference between then present overall death rates for infants more than one month old in the United States (4 to 5/1,000) and the "best available" rates of around 2/1,000 in certain subpopulations (p. 617). This study has been widely quoted in discussions of breastfeeding versus bottle-feeding. A careful evaluation of Cunningham's research led the AAP Task Force Report to conclude that "it appears unlikely that 5,000 deaths of infants aged 28 days and 11 months could be averted each year if all infants were breast-fed. However, the number of postneonatal deaths at-tributable to causes with a hypothesized association with the method of in-fant feeding is not trivial. If postneonatal deaths and feeding methods are associated, some of these deaths can be prevented" (p. 619).

Dr. Natividad Clavano conducted research for four years in a Philippines hospital and reported on this study before the Kennedy Hearings. He en-couraged breastfeeding and gave babies to their mothers immediately after birth. The results showed an increase in breastfeeding of over 60 percent, a decrease in overall incidence of illness of 56.8 percent, a decrease in mortality of 44.9 percent, a decrease in diarrhea of 77.8 percent, and a decrease in deaths due to blood infections of 86.1 percent. In the case of less developed and developing countries, the AAP Task Force Report concluded that evidence pointed to "a significant beneficial effect of breast feeding on infant survival. . . . The majority of studies of infectious illnesses demonstrated lower rates of gasteroenteritis among breast-fed infants compared with bottle-fed infants." The research findings were less clear with respect to respiratory infection, and several studies found little or no difference.[17]

These studies, however, are seen by some scientists and medical experts as scientifically unreliable. Dr. Dobbing dismisses most of these studies as merely associational. "It takes more than a demonstration that more dying babies are 'bottle-fed' than are breast-fed to show that the relationship is *causal*." He maintains that in order to prove causality, studies must analyze the relative contributory effect of other variables and also show not only the effect of bottle-feeding but, more important, *what is in* the bottle.[18] The impact of breastfeeding on mortality rates also relies on the nutritional quality of substitute methods, the sanitary conditions of the area, and the overall health conditions of the environment.

The need for the scientific robustness of the findings is apparent. However, to carry the argument to the extent done by Dr. Dobbing is specious. While it is true that all nonbreastfed babies are not fed on infant formula, industry has not shown any studies that purport to ascertain the extent to which bottle-fed dying babies were using commercially produced infant formula as opposed to home grown or locally concocted brews. Moreover, who is to say that industry's promotion practices had not created a perception in the minds of poor and illiterate mothers that bottle-feeding has a therapeutic effect even though it does not contain infant formula. Furthermore, where infant formula is inappropriately used in the case of already sick children, it may not change the number of dying, but it certainly makes it more expensive for the poor families.

Other Benefits of Human Milk

Critics of bottle-feeding contend that additional, substantial benefits accrue to the infant, the mother, and the family because of breastfeeding. These include prevention of obesity among breast-fed infants,[19] contraception and child spacing,[20] psychological and emotional bonding between mother and child,[21] and economic and agronomic considerations.[22] A review of scientific literature and the AAP Report, however, suggests that most of these claims are either ill founded or are of dubious value (AAP Report, p. 632).

The AAP Report indicates that larger birth intervals are not connected with either to infant mortality or population growth. Studies show that population with the highest rate of infant mortality are also the populations that usually have a very small proportion of their births in shortest intervals. This is because these same high-risk populations usually have high rates of breastfeeding.[23]

Decline in Breastfeeding

In his book, *The Politics of Baby Foods*, Andrew Chetley states: "A vast upheaval in infant feeding habits has occurred in little more than 100 years. For nearly two million years infants have been successfully breastfed. However, by the middle of the 20th century, more and more infants were being switched to the bottle, filled with specially formulated powdered skim milk preparations."[24] There is strong evidence to indicate a precipitous decline in the number and duration of breastfeeding in many developing as well as developed countries. However, the overall magnitude of the decline remains uncertain. Nor is there a clear, unambiguous linkage between decline in breastfeeding and infant mortality. Indeed, evidence can be found to support a variety of conclusions, often conflicting, as to the relationship between the two. For example, in Malaysia, the percentage of breastfeeding dropped from 89 percent in 1960 to 74 percent in 1974, and in Taiwan from 93 percent in 1966 to 50 percent in 1980. Furthermore, in Taiwan, during 1967–1968 and 1979–1980, the average length of nursing decreased from 13.6 months to 4.4 months, a two-thirds decline. However, as Adelman points out, Taiwan and Malaysia "have infant mortality rates which rank among the lowest in the developing world. Each country's rate is less than half the average for its region, with Taiwan's close to the average for Eastern Europe."[25] Studies conducted by WHO suggest breastfeeding is still almost universal and is practiced for protracted periods in most of Africa and Middle and Western South Asia, while breastfeeding in Eastern South Asia and East Asia vary between higher incidence of breastfeeding prevailing in rural areas and lower frequency and duration in urban areas. In Latin America breastfeeding is more prevalent during the initial periods and declines both in frequency and duration ranging from higher to lower rates between urban and rural regions.[26]

One must, therefore, conclude that notwithstanding contrary assertions and individual country cases, the incidence of breastfeeding in most of the underdeveloped countries continues to remain very high, and by implication, the incidence of bottle-feeding (both infant formula and other local weaning foods) must be quite low. This statement, however, should not be construed to mean that there is indeed no problem of either infant malnutrition or diseases. To the extent that a decline in breastfeeding is associated with the use of infant formula and other breast-milk substitutes, and the potential for their misuse, the problem could still be quite serious for the affected infants. It may not be widespread as is commonly perceived. However, on the other hand, it may be concentrated in narrow pockets of population subgroups or regions.

What these data seem to indicate is that a decline in breastfeeding may to some extent be associated with the process of urbanization and that factors leading to urbanization may also be associated with a decline in breastfeeding. Where urbanization leads to a more affluent population with better facilities, greater availability, and access to public health facilities, and generally higher living standards, the use of infant formula is unlikely to have any ill effects to these populations. However, where the process of urbanization causes certain population groups to live and work in physically unhealthy and economically poor conditions, the use of infant formula is not likely to be risk-free, and factors contributing to the increased use of infant formula also have deleterious effects on infant mortality and sickness.

The Industry's Marketing and Promotion Practices and Their Impact

The role of infant formula manufacturers must be examined within the framework of two sets of interrelated factors: the extent to which industry's marketing and promotion practices contribute to the move away from breastfeeding, and especially by mothers who cannot afford the product and cannot use it properly because of poor hygienic conditions. The combined effect is likely to be both unwarranted malnutrition, and infant disease and deaths.

An illustration of the industry's perspective can be seen in a statement by Dr. Robert C. Gelardi, executive director of the since disbanded the International Council of Infant Food Industries (ICIFI). According to Dr. Gelardi, the primary conclusion to be drawn from a host of studies conducted by the industry and other institutions is that no single cause can be isolated for the decline in breastfeeding but that a variety of factors influence breastfeeding practices. These include, among others: socioeconomic status and education level of mother and father; nutritional and health status of mother; new pregnancy or desire not to become pregnant; nursing problems; maternal concern for insufficient milk supply called the "insufficient milk syndrome"; infant health; maternal tension and anxiety called the "let-down reflex"; local custom, cultural taboos, or practices; absence of family support for the breastfeeding mother; fear of damaging the breast and of mother's figure; embarrassment about exposing the breast; husband's attitude; government programs such as milk and food distribution; birth order of child; attitudes and practices of the health care profession including avail-ability of oral contraceptives and breastfeeding information; and work pat-terns and the availability of time for child care.[27] It should not be surprising that none of the studies alluded to by Dr. Gelardi seemed to have found any relationship between declines in breastfeeding and marketing and promo-tional practices of the infant formula industry.

Critics of the infant formula industry agree to the existence of the multi-plicity of causes for a decline in breastfeeding and also for infant malnutri-tion, sickness, and deaths in less developed countries. However, they also contend that industry practices have significantly contributed toward this trend through their marketing and promotion practices. These practices in-cluded, among others, direct promotion to mothers, consumer advertising, free samples in hospitals, inducive packaging and labeling, promotion to doctors and other health care workers, saleswomen dressed as nurses to "promote" or "educate" mothers of newborn babies in hospitals, and com-mission-based compensation systems. It should be noted here that a great many of these practices have been either discontinued or restricted and mod-ified in less developed countries since the passage of the WHO Code. How-ever, the two sides disagree as to the extent of compliance on the part of various companies. The companies have also refused to comply with the WHO Code in industrially advanced countries, arguing that such a course was unnecessary.

While it is true that one cannot isolate individual causes and their relative contribution to the decline in breastfeeding, the converse is also true: no factor can be said *not* to contribute to this decline either. Therefore, indus-try's role, like that of all other factors, must be viewed inferentially, that is, the logical association that can be hypothesized between a cause and effect, and any partial conclusion that can be drawn from available data. Infant formula companies also argue that their marketing and promotion practices, even before the enactment of the WHO Code, were designed not to create new demand for infant formula, but to try to sell their particular brand *after* a mother or her doctor had decided on the use of a breast-milk substitute either in a primary or in a supplementary mode of infant feeding.

The issue must also be phrased in terms of "avoidable harm." To wit, the industry has followed marketing and promotion practices that have exacer-bated an existing problem of children's diseases by encouraging mothers, either directly or indirectly, to use infant formula under conditions that car-ried a potential risk of increased infant disease and death. Even if one were to concede that only a relatively small percentage of poor families in devel-oping countries are bottle-feeding their infants, our concern thereby is not necessarily lessened. As Carol Adelman points out: "This is particularly so in the case of poor mothers who cannot afford to purchase formula and are likely to use it with dirty water and to keep it unrefrigerated. A contaminated diluted mix can then be fed to infants with serious, sometimes fatal, consequences."[28] Given the enormous size of population in the Third World, even a small percentage can mean large absolute numbers.

The infant formula industry is quite vehement in rejecting the validity of field studies and "experiential" data in suggesting a link between infant formula, bottle-feeding, and infant mortality and sickness. And yet all the leading manufacturers, and the industry's trade association, claim to have undertaken no studies to examine the extent to which their products were being misused. For example, in the 1978 congressional hearings, Senator Kennedy and other committee members repeatedly asked industry spokespersons, including the chief executive officers and other top executives of various infant formula companies, whether they had undertaken any field studies to ascertain if their products were being inappropriately used by poor people in any of their Third World markets. All of the industry representatives admitted that they had indeed not undertaken any such studies. Even if we were to accept the notion that any industry-sponsored study would be viewed with suspicion if it showed infant formula companies in a favorable condition with regard to their marketing and promotional practices, the fact that there was no attempt to undertake any such studies is surprising given the intense criticism to which various companies had been subjected. In the absence of such studies, industry's refrains about the critics' argument lose some of their credibility.

Notes

1. Carol Adelman, "Infant Formula, Science and Politics," *Policy Review* (Winter 1988), 107–126.

2. U.S. Congress, Statement by Dr. Stephen C. Joseph in *Implementation of The World Health Organization (WHO) Code on Infant Formula Marketing Practices*. Hearing before the Subcommittee on International Economic Policy and Trade and on Human Rights and International Organizations of the Committee on Foreign Affairs, 97th Congress, 1st Session, June 16–17, 1981, p. 154.

3. John Dobbing (ed.), *Infant Feeding: Anatomy of a Controversy 1973–1984* (New York: Springer-Verlag, 1984).

4. Dobbing, *Infant Feeding, ibid.*, p. 10.

5. John Dobbing, "Breast is Best - Isn't It?" Paper presented in a Symposium on Health Hazard of Milk, University of Manchester, September 13–14, pp. 1–2.

6. For a sampling of scientific research and writings that are supportive of the viewpoint of the critics of infant formula industry, see: A. Berg, "Industry's Struggle with World Malnutrition," *Harvard Business Review* 40 (1972), 50; Pierre A. Borgoltz, "Economic and Business Aspects of Infant Formula Promotion: Implications for Health Professionals," in D.B. Jelliffe and E.F.P. Jelliffe (eds.), *Advances in International Maternal and Child Health*, Vol. 2 (New York: Oxford University Press, 1982), ch. 12, pp. 158–202; Statement of various medical experts, public health officials, and community workers at the *Kennedy Hearings*; T. Greiner, *The Promotion of Bottle-feeding by Multinational Corporations: How Advertising and the Health Professions Have Contributed,* Cornell International Nutrition Monograph Series No. 2 (Ithaca, N.Y.: Cornell University Publications Program in Inter-

national Nutrition and Development, 1975); D.B. Jelliffe, "Commerciogenic Malnutrition," *Nutrition Review*, 30 (September 1972), 199–205; Derrick B. Jelliffe and E.F. Patrice Jelliffe, "The Volume and Composition of Human Milk in Poorly Nourished Communities: A Review," *The American Journal of Clinical Nutrition*, 31 (March 1978), 492–515; D. Morely, *Pediatric Priorities in the Developing World* (London: Butterworth, 1973); Michael C. Latham, "Infant Feeding in National and International Perspective: An Examination of the Decline in Human Lactation and the Modern Crisis in Infant and Child Feeding Practices," *Annals of the New York Academy of Sciences*, Vol. 300 (November 30, 1977), 197–209; Dana Raphael, "The Role of Breast-Feeding in a Bottle Oriented World," 2, *Food Nutrition* (1973), 121–126; and Joe D. Wray, "Feeding and Survival: Historical and Contemporary Studies of Infant Morbidity and Mortality," Center for Population and Family Health, Columbia University Medical School, New York, unpublished paper (April 1979), pp. 1–45.

For a sampling of research and writings that disagree with and refute the critics' arguments, see: Carol Adelman, "Infant Formula, Science and Politics," *Policy Review*, 23 (Winter 1983), 107–126; Carol Adelman, "Baby Feat; More Newborns Are Surviving Infancy Than Ever Before," *Policy Review*, 29 (Summer 1984), pp. 80–83; F.C. Barros, C.G. Victora, J.P. Vaughan, and P.G. Smith, "Birth Weight and Duration of Breast-Feeding: Are the Beneficial Effects of Human Milk Being Overestimated?" *Pediatrics*, 78 (1986), 656–661; John Dobbing, "Breast is Best — Isn't It?" *op. cit.*, 1984; John Dobbing (ed.), *Maternal Nutrition and Lactation Infertility* (New York: Raven Press, 1985); John Dobbing (ed.), *Infant Feeding: Anatomy of a Controversy 1973–1984* (New York: Springer-Verlag, 1988); Luther P. Gerlach, "The Flea and the Elephant: Infant Formula Controversy," *Society*, 17, 6 (September/October 1980), 51–57; J.M. Laventhal, E.D. Shapiro, C.B. Aten, A.T. Berg, and S.A. Egerter, "Does Breast-Feeding Protect Against Infections in Infants Less Than Three Months of Age?" *Pediatrics*, (1986), 896–903; Nevin S. Scrimshaw and B.S. Underwood, "Timely and Appropriate Complementary Feeding of the Breast-Fed Infant — An Overview," *Food and Nutrition Bulletin*, 12, 2 (April 1980), 19–22; N. Scrimshaw, "Myths and Realities in International Health Planning", *American Journal of Public Health* (August 1974), 792–798; Nevin S. Scrimshaw, "Code Not Cure," *Nutrition Today* (July 1981), 11–15; See also the statements of various industry spokespersons at the Kennedy Hearings.

7. American Academy of Pediatrics, "Report of the Task Force on the Assessment of the Scientific Evidence Relating to Infant-Feeding Practices and Infant Health," *Pediatrics*, Supplement, 74, 4 (October 1984).

8. Andrew Chetley, *The Baby Killer Scandal* (London: War on Want, 1979), p. 36.

9. Jelliffe, "Commerciogenic Malnutrition," *op. cit.*

11. Adelman, "Infant Formula, Science and Politics," *op. cit.*, p. 111.

12. WHO/UNICEF, Joint WHO/UNICEF Meeting on Infant and Young Child Feeding: Background Paper and Themes for Discussion, DOC FHE/ICF/79.3, Geneva, 1979.

13. N.S. Scrimshaw and B.S. Underwood, "Timely and Appropriate Complementary Feeding of the Breast-Feed Infant — An Overview," *The UN University World Hunger Programme Food and Nutrition Bulletin* (April 1980), pp. 20, 21.

14. From the "Prepared Statement" of Douglas Johnson and Leah Margulies, U.S. Congress, "Marketing and Promotion of Infant Formula in Developing Countries" *Hearing Before the Sub-committee on International Economic Policy and Trade of the Committee on Foreign Affairs of the House of Representatives* (Washington, D.C., U.S. Government Printing Office, 1980).

15. G.J. Ebrahim, *Breast Feeding — The Biological Option* (London: MacMillan, 1978).

16. J. Kondel, "Breast-Feeding and Population Growth," *Science* (December, 1977), 1111–1114.

17. A. Cunningham, Congressional Hearing on "Infant Feeding Practices," before the Subcommittee on Domestic Marketing Consumer Relations and Nutrition, Washington, D.C.: U.S. Government Printing Office, June 22, 1988. Cited in Kovar et Al., AAP Task Force Report, p. 617.

18. AAP Task Force Report p. 582. See also: Janie M. Mason, Phillip Nieburg, and James S. Marks, "Mortality and Infectious Disease Associated with Infant-Feeding Practices in Developing Countries," in AAP Task Force Report, *Pediatrics* (October 1984), 702–725.

19. Dobbing, *Infant Feeding, op. cit.*, p. 14.

20. Andrew Chetley, *The Baby Killer Scandal,* p. 26; B. Hall, "Changing Composition of Human Milk and Early Development of an Appetite Control," *Lancet* (April 5, 1975), 779, and AAP Report, pp. 315–316.

21. Statement of Dr. Derrick B. Jelliffe in the Kennedy Hearing, p. 43.

22. D.B. Jelliffe and E.F.P. Jelliffe, *Human Milk in the Modern World* (London: Oxford University Press, 1977), p. 156.

23. Michael Latham, The Kennedy Hearings, pp. 503–515.

24. Dobbing, *"Breast is Best, Isn't It?" op. cit.* See also: R.G. Whitehead (ed.), *Maternal diet, Breast-feeding Capacity and Lactational Infertility,* supplement 6 (New York: U.N. University Food and Nutrition Bulletin, 1983).

25. Andrew Chetley, *The Politics of Baby Foods: Successful Challenges to An International Marketing Strategy* (London: Frances Pinter Publishers, 1986), p. 7.

26. Adelman, "Infant Formula, Science and Politics," *op. cit.,* p. 112.

27. World Health Organization, *Contemporary Patterns of Breast-Feeding: Report on the WHO Collaborative Study on Breast-Feeding,* (Geneva: WHO, 1981); B. Ferry, *World Fertility Survey Comparative Studies, Cross National Summaries No. 13* (Voorburg, The Netherlands: International Statistical Institute, May 1981).

28. Robert C. Gelardi, "The Infant Formula Issue: A Story in Simplification and Escalation," *Nutrition Today* (September/October 1981), 29.

29. Adelman, "Infant Formula, Science and Politics," *op. cit.,* p. 113.

9 WORLDWIDE INFANT FORMULA SALES, MARKETS, AND INDUSTRY STRUCTURE

A corporation's response to the external environment is conditioned by a variety of factors. One of the most important of these factors is the way an industry is structured: the extent of concentration in both global and individual markets, the ease of entry into and exit from individual country markets, the composition of competitors in terms of their investment and market objectives, and their propensity to take risk. Industry structure influences both the intensity and mode of competition and, through it, market stability and corporate profitability. The presence of a dominant firm influences the types of options available to local governmental authorities for regulating the activities of various firms in a particular industry.[1]

The response of Nestle and other infant formula manufacturers to global criticism and demand for changes in their marketing practices must be understood within the framework of market demand, industry structure, relative market position of individual companies in different countries, and the nature of government regulation prevailing in those countries. Another important factor is the perception of each company's management as to the nature and extent of external threats to its market position and profitability, management's view of its ability to respond, and the value-orientation of the firm's top management about the preferred modes of response. Unfortunately, these factors are poorly understood by corporate critics. The important point to remember is that while internal corporate values condition management's responses to the external environment as the corporate critics claim, they are also influenced, to no lesser extent, by industry structure and market competition. It is, therefore, important that we understand the nature of infant formula industry structure and relative market positions of its major firms, in order to analyze the adequacy of individual company responses to external pressures within the real and perceived market constraints on their behavior.

Worldwide Sales and Relative Market Shares of Infant Formula Foods

The industry structure, comprised of major multinational infant formula manufacturers, displays the classic form of an oligopolistic industry in the mature stage of its life cycle. Although there are more than 30 companies engaged in the manufacture and sale of infant formula foods, the top four companies account for more than two-thirds of total worldwide sales. The top seller in the world markets is Nestle, S.A., of Switzerland, followed by three U.S.-based multinational corporations: Ross Laboratories, a division of Abbott Laboratories; Wyeth-Ayerst, a division of American Home Products; and, Mead Johnson, a subsidiary of Bristol-Myers Squibb. The oligopolistic structure of the market has considerable influence on the marketing and promotional practices of participating companies. The dominant firms are quite likely to increase their promotional activities and to match their low introductory prices, to deter a new competitor from establishing a foothold. Similarly, established firms tend to avoid price competition among themselves because lower prices by one firm are invariably matched almost immediately by other competitors, thereby eroding profit margins for all firms. Instead, they preserve and expand their market share by emphasizing product differentiation through brand promotion, control of distribution channels, and other nonprice competition strategies.

Our analysis of the infant formula industry suffers from a lack of reliable information on its market size, growth, and share of competing firms within the industry. Industry representatives have constantly asserted that comparable sales or market share data are not available, and, in any case, they do not collect them.*

1. Companies justify their reluctance to provide the desired information on grounds of corporate policy and competitive considerations. They also suggest that estimating global demand, worldwide sales, and relative market shares are beset by so many methodological and data collection problems that they make such estimates highly suspect and grossly unreliable. While these arguments are understandable, they are not totally persuasive. For

---

*See the statements of various industry spokespersons at the Kennedy Hearings. Similar assertions were also made to the author in personal interviews.

example, the United States is one of the most competitive markets in the world for a large number of products and services. And yet, in this market, most companies in a variety of industries voluntarily cooperate with industry groups to collect and disseminate industrywide data without any apparent adverse effect on their competitive positions. Where industrywide data collection is not practiced, there are private companies — for example, Nielsen — that collect such data through nationwide sample store surveys and make it available to their clients. Similar services are also available in most other industrialized countries and can be purchased by subscribing to these services.

Even where *real* market share data are not available, companies must make reasonable estimates of changes in relative market shares to assess the effectiveness of their marketing strategies. One approach is for the companies to measure percentage changes in their own sales between two points in time. These changes can then be used to estimate total sales and relative market shares based on historical trends after making adjustments for temporary market aberrations. To the best of this author's knowledge, no infant formula manufacturer has publicly disclosed its own country-by-country sales or percentage changes in its sales in different markets over a given time period.

2. Another difficulty cited in estimating total demand and market share is that of appropriate definition: what constitutes infant formula foods, which regions or countries should be considered less developed, and so on. Should Third World include all countries located in certain geographical regions, or only those countries that would meet some criteria of development based on a measure of gross national product or per capita income? For example, while industry critics define developing countries to comprise all of the Third World, many companies, including Nestle, define them more narrowly and exclude such countries as Hong Kong, Singapore, Taiwan, and South Korea, which they consider to be developed nations.*

3. A third issue involves the problem of locally made breast-milk substitutes and whether they can all be classified as infant formula. Another relevant issue is what should be considered breast-milk substitutes, that is, should one include only those products that are *marketed* as infant formula or all those products that are *used* as infant formula? The latter category would include, for example, Cerelac, a Nestle brand that is promoted as infant weaning food and is widely used as an infant food supplement. The internationally accepted definition of infant formula, according to FAO/WHO Codex Alimentarious, does *not* classify infant weaning foods/supple-

---

*Comments made to the author by Geoffrey Fookes of Nestle, S.A. — Switzerland. Unless otherwise specifically stated, all direct and paraphrased quotes attributed to various people in the text are based on personal interviews or written communications with the author.

ments as infant formula. Its inclusion in the infant formula category would considerably raise the estimate of total worldwide market size and sales. Moreover, broadening the category of infant formula would also require inclusion of all breast-milk substitutes — for instance, sweetened, condensed, evaporated milks, as well as fresh milks and other locally made gruels that are fed to infants within the first four to six months of their lives.

4. Major infant formula manufacturers contend that Third World countries have fewer, if any, data collection services. Estimating sales and market shares for infant formula foods in Third World countries are also beset by a number of special problems. Fluctuating exchange rates of local currency against the U.S. dollar may artificially inflate or deflate sales figures when expressed in dollars, without in any way affecting unit sales or underlying potential demand. In times of foreign exchange shortages, a country may abruptly restrict imports of infant formula foods, thereby depressing sales. Alternately, a country may receive a large supply of infant formula under various kinds of foreign aid programs from industrialized nations which may adversely affect the commercial part of infant formula demand. Finally, in countries where governments act as sole buying agencies through the tender process, a change in government's selection of vendors may drastically alter relative market shares.

While all these arguments point to the difficulties in making good estimates of total sales and relative market shares, they do not obviate their necessity. These problems are not unique to infant formula but are common to most international trade involving Third World countries. Multinational corporations are able to devise estimation techniques to generate the necessary information and market intelligence. Moreover, a reasonable estimate of total industry sales and relative market shares is important to assess the veracity of companies' claims as to their marketing practices, and the accuracy of the critics' charges as to the companies' abuse of such practices. One would have to know the increase or decrease in total sales and relative market shares to assess the impact of different levels of marketing expenditures as well as changes in relative emphasis placed by individual companies on different elements of the marketing mix: for example, media advertising versus point of purchase displays, price promotions versus give-aways, impact of an increase/decrease in free hospital supplies and discharge packs on total sales, and so on. In oligopolistic market structures, major competitors make it their business to know each other's pricing and promotion strategies, profit margins, and market penetration. Otherwise, how would they devise their own marketing strategies to forestall competitive attacks on their market position?

It is also suggested that in most Third World countries, infant formula products are sold largely through independent middlemen who devise their own pricing, distribution, and promotion strategies. In the real world, these small businessmen depend for their livelihood on receiving supplies from the major companies. They also receive numerous support services, different types of financial incentives, such as volume discounts, to promote particular products and brands. They would flout the "directions" of their suppliers at extreme peril to them, a highly unlikely scenario. Infant formula manufacturers cannot have it both ways. If they have such little control over their distribution system, then they cannot assert that their products are not sold to poor people or in areas where appropriate hygienic conditions are not available. To make such an assertion would require either good knowledge or a measure of control over one's distribution channels. Otherwise, such assertions cannot be taken at face value.

It is highly unusual, if not incomprehensible, that these major companies had not done any studies to see who was buying their products and how those products were used. The entire basis of developing a marketing and promotional strategy is to identify potential consumers, determine their needs and preferences, and provide a product that meets those needs. It is not enough to assert, as the companies do, that their products are intended solely for mothers who need them either for biological or other reasons. They must also demonstrate, either through an analysis of sales or end-use data, that this is indeed the case. While we must be willing to accept imperfect but "good enough" research findings, a total lack of any reported research on the part of infant formula companies is hard to explain and justify.

This leads us to one inescapable conclusion. To wit, infant formula sales must be so highly profitable that companies are afraid to disclose these figures. Absolute levels of high profits and a higher rate of profit on sales, especially in Third World countries, would make it difficult for the companies to make credible assertions about not using high-pressure sales tactics. A high rate of profit may tempt local governments to impose higher taxes. It may also provide corporate critics with additional ammunition to accuse the companies of profiteering and to show that their sales are driven by greed.*

Another supportive argument in favor of the high profit hypothesis is the ferocity and tenacity with which companies have fought their critics and each other to hold on to their markets despite tremendous adverse public opinion and enormous demands on their resources, including top management time, to fend off their critics. These resources are only possible through the existence of strategic slack borne out of above normal return on sales and investment in these products and markets. Thus, despite enormous

---

*Anecdotal evidence collected by the author during the course of writing this book lends credence to this notion. Talks with various mid-level executives in the United States and Western Europe suggest that infant formula products are indeed highly profitable. The retail price of major brands is estimated to be 4.5 to 5 times the cost of manufacture and gross profit margins can be as high as 50 percent.

pressure, no major infant formula manufacturer has ever walked away from any of its significant markets. And Nestle, which had remained out of the U.S. infant formula market for most of its corporate history, ventured into this market for the first time in 1988. The fact that this entry has been attempted in the face of already entrenched and formidable competitors, and extremely high entry barriers, only serves to reinforce the point.

Infant Formula Foods: The Antecedents

The rapid growth of the modern international market for infant formula is a post-World War II phenomenon. Although a number of food companies had sold breast-milk substitutes in Western Europe before that time, many of these products were made of evaporated milk or powdered milk and were not considered nutritionally equivalent to human milk as are formulas. As prosperity returned to Europe and multinational firms expanded operations in Africa, South America, and the Far East, infant formula became the "food of choice" for the children of expatriate Americans and West Europeans.

Infant formula producers can be divided into two groups or industries: pharmaceutical/health care and food processing. Of the four major infant formula manufacturers that are the focus of this enquiry, Nestle is generally regarded as the premier company in the food-processing category, followed closely by Borden. The remaining three companies, all of them U.S.-based, belong to the pharmaceutical/health care category.[2] A general description of the four companies' major markets and primary brand names appears in Table 9-1.

In the United States, the principal sellers of infant formula were founded after medical researchers produced an infant food substitute for mother's milk. By the late 1920s, Ross Laboratories, Mead Johnson, and Simulated Milk Adaptation (SMA) were in the business of producing and selling humanized infant formula. Through mergers and acquisitions, these firms eventually became part of large integrated pharmaceutical firms. During the 1960s, a number of special "sick-baby" formulas were produced by different companies for children with special dietary and health requirements. This was true for the companies belonging to both the pharmaceutical/health and food processing groups. While the sick-baby segment of the market is insignificant in comparison to the well-baby segment (perhaps 2 percent of total sales volume), the existence of such specialized products is attributable to the pharmaceutical orientation of one segment of the industry and the research emphasis of both segments.

The Swiss-based Nestle, and Borden of USA, began their business in the sweetened and condensed milk products in the 1860s. Between 1890 to the end of World War II, Nestle's business in the United States was dominated

Table 9–1.   Infant formula: manufacturers' market orientation

Company name:	Nestle	Abbott (Ross)	American Home Products (Wyeth)	Bristol-Myers Squibb (Mead Johnson)
Industry orientation:	Food products	Pharmaceutical -health care	Pharmaceutical -health care	Pharmaceutical -health care
Major brand names:	Nan Lactogen Cerelac Nestogen	Similac Isomil Alimentum	SMA S-26	ENFALAC ENFAMIL
Major markets:	France Germany Australia Brazil	U.S. S. Africa Malaysia Colombia	U.K. France	U.S. Canada Australia
Major LDC markets:	Most LDC regions Africa	Africa & Latin America Middle East	Southeast Asia Latin American (such as Peru and Venezuela)	Caribbean Central America S.E. Asia

Notes: 1. Information adopted from miscellaneous sources referred in text.
2. Nestle did not market infant formula products in the United States until 1988.

by dairy and dietetic infant food products. As medical research indicated that humanized infant formulas, that is, especially modified infant formulas, were nutritionally superior to canned milk for newborns, the food companies sought to retain their share of the infant food market by introducing infant formula products. In the United States, sales of infant formula products rose sharply after World War II and hit a peak in the late 1950s coinciding with the postwar baby boom (there were 4.3 million births in developed countries in 1957). Breastfeeding halved during the baby boom period between 1946 to 1956, dropping to 25 percent at hospital discharge in 1967.[3] Birth rates in industrialized countries also began declining by 1967. The maturation of the U.S. markets spurred the U.S. infant formula companies to make more energetic efforts to expand their sales abroad.

This period of high market growth is identified with the use of many of the mass marketing techniques (including mass media consumer advertising). Infant formula sales expanded through heavy consumer advertising, with special reliance on mass media such as newspapers, radio, and television. Brand identification was cultivated through advertising, with selective use of product promotions and competitive pricing to maintain brand loyalty and market share.[4]

Estimates of Worldwide Sales

In the absence of industry-provided estimates of infant formula sales, industry critics have made their own estimates. Andy Chetley, one of the oldest and most vocal critics, estimated the industry's 1983 worldwide sales at $3.3 billion.[5] This figure assumes a 10 percent annual growth rate from 1979 estimates of industry sales suggested by Borgoltz.[6] If the same trend is assumed to continue, the 1990 worldwide infant formula sales would approximate $6.5 billion. These estimates are, however, subject to gross error. There is no explanation as to the reasons for assuming a 10 percent growth rate. Worst of all, the base point data used by Mr. Chetley, that is, Borgoltz, was itself compiled from a variety of sources with different degrees of source credibility. Furthermore, the data sources were not mutually compatible; the base-year chosen was different for different countries; and the data suffered from serious problems of aggregation. Other recent estimates of total global sales developed by the activists are based on the assumption that infant formula market in the developing countries would grow at an annual rate of between 10 to 15 percent. At 15 percent annual growth rate, the global market would double every five years which, under the best of circumstances, is an unlikely prospect.

Although precise figures are not available, some estimates of total global sales of infant formula can be made from publicly available data. Abbott Laboratories, parent of Ross Laboratories, disclosed in its 1990 Annual Report that its worldwide sales of infant formula were $1,060 million. According to market estimates, Abbott sells about 80 percent of its infant formula in the United States and the balance in foreign markets, and is believed to hold 50 percent share of the U.S. market.[7] Based on these ratios, Abbott's 1990 sales of infant formula in the United States approximated $850 million, 50 percent of the estimated total U.S. infant formula market of $1,700 million. A spokesperson of a major European manufacturer estimated 1990 sales of infant formula in Europe to be around $1,000 million.

Estimates of infant formula sales in the Third World are more difficult to determine. According to a Nestle spokesperson, that company's Third World sales of infant formula represent less than 2 percent of its annual sales. Based on the 1990 annual worldwide sales of $29.4 billion,[8] Nestle's Third World sales in 1990 would amount to $460 million. There is also common agreement that Nestle accounts for over 40 percent of all Third World infant formula sales. This would put the total 1990 Third World sale of major brand infant formula products at approximately $1,150 million.

Adding the above estimated market data for the United States and the rest of the world, we would estimate the global infant formula sales at about $3.9 billion, with the following geographic breakdown:

United States	$1,700 million
Europe	$1,000 million
Developing countries	$1,150 million
Total world market	$3,850 million

These market estimates relate only to worldwide sales of infant formula of major multinational companies. In addition to these companies, there are also numerous domestic producers who sell their products locally and have significant share of the indigenous market. All these figures, however, must be interpreted with a great deal of caution. Although their logic can be defended, they are nevertheless estimates and incorporate a certain measure of educated guesswork. They cannot provide answers at the micro level, and if used indiscriminately, could prove to be misleading. For example, these numbers *do not* provide us with any idea as to exactly which infants are being fed with infant formula. Therefore, even a much lower percentage of infants being bottle-fed may be cause for alarm if those infants came from families who cannot and should not be using infant formula.

Future Growth

Most estimates of worldwide infant formula market are based on the assumption that future growth would come from the developing countries where the need for breast-milk supplement is considered significant. According to industry representatives, anywhere between 5 percent to 40 percent of mothers in developing countries will need infant formula for all or part of their infants' needs during the first six months after birth. Included in this estimate are mothers in the privileged class, working mothers, mothers who lack sufficient milk, and mothers physiologically incapable of breastfeeding. The extent of need indicates the existence of "potential" demand as opposed to "real" demand, that is, demand backed by consumers' willingness and ability to pay.

We estimate the total worldwide sale of infant formula to grow at an annual rate of approximately 5 percent; between 3 percent and 5 percent in industrialized countries and between 7 percent and 8 percent in developing countries. The largest growth in absolute terms would come primarily from the industrialized countries, sparked by a trend toward dual-career families and single parents, higher income, and a tendency, already discernible in the United States, of using infant formula as infant food supplement in place of cow's milk and for longer periods than previously practiced and extending its use amongst elderly and hospitalized people. Thus an increase in infant formula sales would most likely accompany an increase in breastfeeding by mothers — albeit for their infants' partial needs. This trend is already discernible. The domestic U.S. baby food industry is increasingly stressing nutrition and single-serving convenience in its product offerings. Gerber, which claims to have over 71 percent of market share, has targeted some products for adults. Beech-Nut Nutrition Corporation has introduced its Stages line of baby food, which is designed to change as the baby grows. H.J. Heinz Co. has introduced a Beginner Foods line as a natural introduction to solid foods. The infant formula product category also should increase by 8 percent or 9 percent during the next few years due to greater numbers of working mothers.[9]

Among the developing countries, the highest growth rate would most likely come from rapidly industrializing countries such as Singapore, Hong Kong, South Korea, Taiwan, Thailand, and, to a lesser extent, countries of Eastern Europe, and countries like Brazil and India, as they move toward greater industrialization and urbanization. The lowest growth rate perhaps will be recorded in most of the remaining Third World countries in Latin America, Asia, and Africa where prospects of improvement in personal incomes and standard of living remain depressingly low.[10]

The Oligopolistic Industry Structure and Its Impact on Growth in Relative Market Shares

Given the growth in the infant formula market in Third World countries, one would expect some new producers to enter this growing and profitable market. A survey of the industry shows that no new producer entered the market during the past 10 years. Thus the WHO Code has had the perverse effect of raising entry barriers to new competitors who might have offered lower prices or better products without necessarily reducing the demand for infant formula. This state of affairs should not be surprising given the oligopolistic nature of the industry structure and the presence of two or three dominant firms in most major markets. A vivid example of this state of affairs can be found in the United States where Nestle's entry into the infant formula market in 1988 has been less than successful.

The world market is still dominated by the four major multinational companies: Nestle, Abbott Laboratories, American Home Products, and Bristol-Myers Squibb. Within Europe, Nestle, Milupa of Germany, and Nutricia of Holland control 60 percent of the market. The only change visible in the marketplace has been intense competition among the existing producers to increase their market share and the growth of some local producers in countries such as India. The Japanese producers, supported by their government, have increased their market share in some developing countries. According to industry sources, activists, unofficial comments from some of the Third World governments' spokespersons, and even local producers in those countries, Japanese producers have stepped up their promotional efforts and have been aggressively marketing their infant formula brands in many countries in the Middle East, Far East, and Southeast Asia. For example, in just a few years, the Japanese companies have increased their market share in Pakistan from zero to 30 percent and have also recorded substantial gains in market share in other countries such as Egypt, Malaysia, and Sri Lanka.[11] Japanese producers and Glaxo of England, combined with three U.S. manufacturers and Nestle of Switzerland, control almost 75 percent of the world's infant formula market. Moreover, they are estimated to serve up to 90 percent of the market demand in countries which they serve, including their home markets.[12] In their own country, the Japanese companies have been very aggressive promoters of infant formula. For example, in Japan, infant formula continues to be promoted directly to consumers through mass advertising. Also, in-store promotions are used to increase sales and to induce buyers to switch brands. It should be noted here that Japan was one of only three countries that abstained from voting on the passage of the WHO Code.

Notes

1. R.E. Caves and M.E. Porter, "Market Structure, Oligopoly, and Stability of Market Shares," *The Journal of Industrial Economics,* 26 (1978), 289–313.

2. S. Prakash Sethi and James E. Post, "The Marketing of Infant Formula in Less Developed Countries: Public Consequences of Private Actions," *California Management Review* (Summer, 1979), 35–48. See also James E. Post, "Testimony," U.S. Senate, "Marketing and Promotion of Infant Formula in the Developing Nations, 1978" Hearings before the

Subcommittee on Health and Scientific Research of the Committee on Human Resources, 95th Congress, 2nd Session, May 23, 1978, pp. 120.

3. M. Minchin, *Breast-feeding Matters* (Sydney, Australia: George Allen and Unwin, 1985).

4. Andrew Chetley, *The Politics of Baby Foods: Successful Challenges to an International Marketing Strategy* (London: Francis Pinter Publishers, 1986), pp. 18–38.

5. *Ibid.*

6. Pierre A. Borgoltz, "Economic and Business Aspects of Infant Formula Promotion: Implications for Health Professionals," in D.B. Jelliffe and E.F.P. Jelliffe (eds.), *Advances in International Maternal and Child Health,* Vol. 2 (New York: Oxford University Press, 1982), ch. 12, pp. 158–202. Also cited in Chetley, *op. cit.,* supra note 4.

7. J. France, "Abbott Laboratories, Inc., Company Report No. 817163, July 21, 1988" (New York: Smith Barney Upham & Co., 1988).

8. "The International 500: The Fortune's Directory of Largest Industrial Corporations Outside the U.S.," *Fortune* (August 19, 1985), 182–201. Nestle's 1984 *Annual Report* records its worldwide sales at Sw. Fr. 31,141 million. The exchange rate between the two figures is, therefore, calculated to be $1.00 = Sw. Fr. 2.35.

9. *Advertising Age,* Vol. 2, No. 42 (October 3, 1988), S2,4.

10. For a discussion of difficult socioeconomic conditions prevailing in Latin America and Africa, see Julio H. Cole, "Bolivia's 'Right' Not Likely to Endorse the Free Market," *The Wall Street Journal* (July 19, 1985), 21; and Lee Lescaze and Steve Mufson, "Angry New Leaders in Africa Are Trying To Right Past Wrongs," *The Wall Street Journal* (July 18, 1985), 1, 15.

11. Even as far back as 1984, industry critics were expressing increasing concern about the aggressive expansion efforts of the Japanese infant producers in Third World countries. See, for example, "Statement of Douglas Johnson, National Chairperson, Infant Formula Action Coalition (INFACT), and Lisa Woodburn, European Coordinator, International Nestle Boycott Committee," Press Conference, Nestle Coordination Center for Nutrition, Inc., Washington, D.C., October 4, 1984.

12. "Nestle Crunch," Editorial Comment, *Barron's* (July 16, 1979), 7. See also Borgoltz (1982), *op. cit.,* supra note 6, p. 163.

10 THE INDUSTRY AND MAJOR MANUFACTURERS INVOLVED IN THE CONTROVERSY

The four major industry players involved in the infant formula controversy were Nestle, S.A. — Switzerland, and Abbott Laboratories, Bristol-Myers, and American Home Products, all based in the United States. The response of these four companies to the infant formula controversy and to the industry's critics varied considerably from each other. We now turn our attention to a discussion of the corporate persona of these companies with a view to understanding their culture, personalities, and modus operandi. It should also suggest some explanation as to why different companies diverged from each other in responding to external pressures. Furthermore, we may gain insight as to the alternative approaches that might evoke more proactive responses from the companies to changing societal expectations. It should help us in developing more effective approaches that companies can use in creating more flexible and adaptive organizations. Finally, we shall discuss the role played by the industry groups, International Council of Infant Food Industries (ICIFI), and its successor organization, the International Association of Infant Food Manufacturers (IFM).

Nestle, S.A.

The Switzerland-based Nestle, S.A., is one of the world's largest industrial companies, ranking 26th on *Fortune*'s 1990 list of 500 largest non-U.S. companies.[1] In 1990 its revenues and profits amounted to $29.4 billion and $1.46

billion, respectively. Nestle is a truly global corporation with manufacturing and trading facilities in over 60 countries and employing almost 197,000 people worldwide. Although Nestle operates in all five continents, Western Europe and North America account for over 70 percent of its global sales (45.6 percent in Western Europe and 26.6 percent in North America).[2] The company has a highly diversified product line. Over 80 percent of its sales come from food products, including drinks (24.7 percent), cereals, milks and dietetic products (20.0 percent), chocolates and confectionery products (15.3 percent), culinary products (12.4 percent), and frozen food/ice cream (10.8 percent). The balance is contributed by nonfood products.

Under managing director Helmet Maucher, Nestle has been expanding aggressively in Europe in anticipation of the Economic Community (EC) 1992. In 1988, Nestle made a hostile bid for the British chocolate company Rowntree Plc. after Jacobs Suchard, A.G., the other big Swiss *chocolatier,* bought 14.9 percent of Rowntree. Nestle ultimately paid over $4.5 billion for Rowntree and acquired the Italian pasta maker Buitoni-Perugina SpA for $1.3 billion.[3] Nestle is also forging international partnerships to develop new product lines and explore new markets. In 1989, it entered into a 50–50 joint venture with General Mills to market ready-to-eat cereals in all areas outside the United States and Canada. The company has signed a 10-year licensing agreement with Walt Disney Co., which gives Nestle the sole right to use Disney characters in marketing its products.[4] In 1990, Nestle and Coca Cola Co. formed a joint venture to market ready-to-drink coffees and teas under the Nescafe and Nestle brands.[5]

Nestle is a major presence in the Third World. Latin America and Asia account for about 20 percent of Nestle's total worldwide sales.[6] In the United States, Nestle's long-term strategy calls for its U.S. operations to contribute about 50 percent to its worldwide revenues. Rather than making greenfield investments, Nestle has grown through acquisitions of existing companies in the United States. Among some of its major recent acquisitions are Alcon (1977), Beech-Nut (1979), and Carnation, Hills Brothers, and MJB (1985).

Infant Formula Sales

Nestle is the biggest marketer of infant formula worldwide and a market leader in large parts of the Third World. The company does not disclose its worldwide sales of infant formula products. These sales are included in Nestle's cereals, milks, and dietetic products division which accounts for 20 percent of the company's total sales. Until 1988, the company did not market infant formula in the United States. However, its recent entry in the U.S. market has been full of controversy because of its product-related claims and direct consumer advertising. Estimates of Nestle's worldwide sales of infant formula range between $400 and $600 million, representing between 2 percent and 3 percent of the company's total sales.

Corporate Culture

"From its inception, Nestle has been both exceptionally Swiss in character and exceptionally international."[7] The small size of the home market makes it imperative that Swiss companies seek overseas markets, and Nestle was no exception. Nestle had long been one of the most multinational of all multinational companies. The company is very proud of its history and accomplishments in the Swiss–German tradition of its founders. By tradition, top management has been concentrated on the German side of Swiss managers. Nestle is also characterized as having a "strong Swiss personality." The company still keeps its headquarters in Vevey, a provincial city on Lake Geneva.

Nestle emphasizes traditional values of respect for authority and technical competence. Loyalty is highly prized, and the company makes every effort to take care of its own. Employee turnover is low, especially among its professional/managerial group. Top Nestle managers are expected to have both broad administrative experience and a high level of linguistic skills. At its headquarters in Vevey, Nestle uses four working languages, German, French, English, and Spanish, while in overseas markets, there is a preference to use local language(s). A manager who has lived up to these demands in terms of experience and skill is referred to as a real "Nestle Man," a high accolade. Foreign nationals have always had an important role in Nestle's marketing efforts, whether those countries were in Europe, Africa, Southern Asia, or Latin America. There is a strong non-Swiss presence among junior and middle-level executives at Nestle's headquarters where foreign nationals are routinely brought in on a rotational basis. Upper management echelons, however, are mostly peopled by European nationals.

Organizational Structure

Nestle is a management-controlled company with an operating philosophy characterized by strong central financial control. Its organization is hierarchical with clearly established rules and procedures. However, within those organizational boundaries, individual Nestle employees have considerable freedom of operations. Nestle's headquarter in Vevey is known as "the Center." It consists of a managing director (MD) and eight departments reporting to the MD. These departments are planning, organization/personnel, public relations, legal, manufacturing, finance & control, marketing, and research and development (R&D). Each region is headed by a regional manager (RM). There are regional managers for Northern Europe, Southern Europe, Latin America, the Far East, and Africa. Each individual country's operation is headed by a country manager (CM) who reports to the regional manager. The only exception to this organizational structure is the United States region which reports directly to the managing director.

With over 95 percent of Nestle's sales coming from outside of Switzerland, subsidiaries exercise substantial operational freedom. Individual country managers, for the most part, operate their subsidiaries as independent profit centers. Accountability is exercised primarily through financial goals and standards. Annual operational budgets are determined through joint consultation with the headquarters. Nestle does not have a standardized worldwide marketing program. Local managers have substantial freedom in their selling and promotional strategies. Prior to 1982, Nestle did not even emphasize its identity with the result that local consumers were often unaware of the Swiss ownership of local Nestle subsidiaries and thought of them as home grown companies.

Unlike marketing, financial management and research effort are centralized at the Center and directed by the people at the headquarters. Centralized research is viewed important both from the point of view of resource concentration and control of proprietary information. The Center develops new products and offers them to foreign subsidiaries. Individual subsidiaries, however, have considerable latitude in terms of introducing those products in their markets.

An important function of the central staff in Vevey is to become a conduit for information exchange between various units of its worldwide operations. The rotational process of managers, combined with frequent stints at the Center, makes most managers known to each other thereby facilitating communication, transfer, and adoption of new ideas. Given the decentralized nature of its management structure, Nestle feels that local managers are best equipped and should be responsible for handling local issues, including dealing with domestic sociopolitical sensitivities. This also protects the Swiss management from any involvement in domestic issues of a foreign country should such revelations prove to be potentially embarrassing. Therefore, for many years, the headquarters in Switzerland did not even have a corporate public affairs office. A high level of "consistency" in handling sensitive local issues, however, is assured because of the strong corporate culture — its intellectual core and value set — and the extent to which responsible managers, across the entire spectrum of the company's operations, are steeped in that culture. Sharing a common core of values, strongly held beliefs, and operating philosophy, these managers respond to external challenge in a manner that is likely to be quite similar, not unlike the behavior of identically cloned cells.

In cases where an incident in one country is likely to affect Nestle's operations in another country, the Center at Vevey assumes the responsibility for coordinating those efforts. However, even here the top management in Vevey is largely guided by the recommendations of its local management. This is especially the case where a foreign subsidiary constitutes a major business and is sufficiently large in size to have adequate staff resources to handle those issues. Nestle followed this pattern in dealing with the infant formula controversy during at least the first two phases of the issue life cycle: the preproblem and problem identification stages. It was primarily during the remedy and relief stage that Nestle came to grips with the fact of altered external environment and developed a new organizational mechanism and response modes to deal with them effectively.

Nestle purports to be quite sensitive to its strong presence in Third World countries and the special obligation it entails for a multinational corporation. The company claimed that it had put much more into the Third World than it had taken, and had published a glossy publication entitled *Nestle In The Developing World* to highlight its contributions. In this publication, the company points to the 36,000 direct jobs it provides, the vital nutrition it delivers, and the fact that the company is certainly an important customer for one-crop economies. According to a Nestle PR publication: "While Nestle is not a philanthropic society, facts and figures clearly prove that the nature of its activities in developing countries is self-evident as a factor that contributes to economic development."[8]

Impact of Corporate Culture and Organizational Structure on Nestle's U.S. Strategy

One can now begin to understand why Nestle had such a problem coping with the infant formula controversy in the United States. Despite the fact that Nestle's top managers had become aware of the serious problem emerging in the United States, they were reluctant to intervene and second-guess the decision of the local managements of one of their most important subsidiaries. The fact that U.S. managers shared a strong "corporate culture" with the Swiss parent also indicated that the two sets of managers shared a philosophical agreement as to the rightness of the company's position. It is, therefore, not surprising that Nestle's strategic and tactical actions during the early stages of the controversy in the United States bore a strong resemblance to the company's posture and tactics in Europe during the events immediately preceding and following the publication of "Nestle Kills Babies" and the Berne trial.

In the case of the United States, the company's problems were further compounded by a relative lack of knowledge on the part of Swiss management of the uniquely American sociopolitical environment. Furthermore, the decentralized, profit-center-oriented organizational structure, caused Nestle — U.S. to be saddled with all the costs of dealing with the infant formula controversy in the United States without at the same time sharing any credit or benefit from infant formula sales worldwide. Thus, in its desire to minimize its financial burden, Nestle — U.S. generally opted for the least cost, short-term strategies. One consequence of this approach was to downplay the long-term importance and implications of the controversy and its potential impact on Nestle's worldwide operations. It was only after the Kennedy Hearings, and a radical and unprecedented change in Nestle's organizational relationship between the U.S. subsidiary and Nestle — Switzerland, that the company developed and implemented a new strategy of dealing with its critics in the United States, which ultimately led to the resolution of the controversy and the termination of the boycott against Nestle.

Abbott Laboratories

Abbott Laboratories (AL) is a leading U.S. pharmaceutical company with worldwide sales of $6.2 billion and net earnings of $965.8 million in 1990.[9] Based on its 1990 global sales, Abbott ranked 82nd among Fortune's list of the 500 largest U.S. industrial corporations, but ranked 23rd in terms of profits. Among U.S. pharmaceutical companies, Abbott ranked 6th both in terms of sales and profits.[10] Abbott has evolved from its original position as a U.S. prescription-pharmaceutical manufacturer into a broad-based health care company serving a worldwide market. Abbott's products fall into two broad categories: pharmaceutical and nutritional products, and hospital and laboratory products, with the two divisions contributing roughly 51 and 49 percent, respectively, to the company's total revenues.

Abbott today markets its products in some 130 countries through affiliates and distributors. International sales are a growing business. During the past five years, AL's international sales have grown at a compound rate of 14 percent, almost doubling from $1.2 billion in 1986 to $2.3 billion in 1990, while domestic sales grew by less than half. International sales, including direct exports from the United States, amounted to $2.3 billion, representing approximately 38 percent of the company's total revenues in 1990. Of these, $1.3 billion or 57 percent of international sales were in Europe, the Mideast, and Africa; 31 percent from the Pacific, Far East, and Canada; and 12 percent from Latin America. Of the total international sales, hospital and laboratory products accounted for 57 percent while pharmaceutical and nutritional products contributed the remaining 43 percent.[11]

Infant Formula Market

AL entered the infant formula market through its acquisition of Ross Laboratories in 1964. Ross Laboratories, now a division of Abbott, is the industry leader in infant formula sales in the United States, accounting for about 50 percent of the U.S. market. The company also has a strong market position in a number of foreign countries. It offers one of the broadest lines of infant formula products in the industry. In 1990, Abbott-Ross had infant formula sales of $1,060 million compared to $986 million in 1988, an increase of almost 8 percent.[12] AL does not disclose the breakdown of its infant formula sales between domestic and international areas. However, it is estimated that Abbott sells about 80 percent of its infant formula in the United States, for an estimated revenue of $850 million.

American Home Products Corporation

American Home Products Corporation (AHP) is a diversified company. With 1990 worldwide sales of over $6.7 billion, it ranked 70th among the Fortune 500 largest U.S. industrial corporations and fourth among U.S. pharmaceutical companies.[13] Unlike Abbott, AHP is a more diversified company, with 55 percent of its annual revenues coming from prescription drugs, 20 percent from over-the-counter (OTC) drugs, 12 percent from medical supplies and diagnostic products, and the remaining 13 percent from food products.[14] AHP's current product mix can be divided into two broad categories: health care and food. Health care products is AHP's main line of business and includes pharmaceuticals, consumer health care products, medical supplies and diagnostic products; it accounted for 86.6 percent of the company's net sales in 1990. AHP's food products group is a major factor in convenience food products, and contributed 13.4 percent to its 1990 total sales.

Overseas markets are an important part of AHP's growth strategy. AHP is positioning itself in key markets through licensing, co-marketing, strategic alliances, and acquisitions. Presently, AHP is concentrating its marketing efforts in Europe and the Americas. In 1990, foreign sales amounted to $2,168 million, representing 32 percent of the company's global revenues. Fifty-two percent of its international sales were in Europe and Africa, and 33 percent were in Canada and Latin America.

Infant Formula Market

Wyeth-Ayerst Laboratories, a wholly owned subsidiary of AHP, is responsible for its worldwide sale of infant formula products. Wyeth-Ayerst supplies only 17 percent of its infant formulas from its U.S. plants to developing countries. The remaining 83 percent is either made locally or is supplied from Wyeth-Ayerst's other international production facilities. Infant formula represents the company's largest single line of business and in 1988 generated an estimated revenue of $370 million.[15] In the U.S. infant formula market, AHP has a relatively small market share compared to Abbott Laboratories and Bristol-Myers Squibb. In the international infant formula market, AHP is the second largest player after Nestle, with strong market positions in the U.K., France, Middle East, and Pacific Rim.

Next to Nestle, critics have regarded AHP as the most recalcitrant and confrontational company. It is the only U.S.-based company that became the target of consumer boycott by the activist groups in 1988 when they charged AHP, along with Nestle, with serious violations of the WHO Code in its Third World marketing of infant formula products. AHP is considered an insular company that avoids public limelight. It is a financially conservative company where management takes pride in its frugal ways. Financial analysts and news media often describe AHP as a "stodgy" corporation with a tradition of tight-fisted management and a disdain for public attention.[16] This low-key conservative approach is also reflected in a subdued corporate style that affects management succession. Mr. Stafford, the current chief executive officer (CEO), joined the firm in 1970 and was trained for the top job by the two previous CEOs who were in charge for over 22 years. The two CEOs, Mr. Laporte and Mr. Culligan, are still with the firm, retain seats on the board of directors, and have offices at the headquarters.

Bristol-Myers Squibb Company

As a multinational health care company, Bristol-Myers Squibb (BMS) produces and markets diversified health care products in over 100 countries around the world. In 1990, its worldwide sales and profits reached $10.3 billion and $1.75 billion respectively.[17] Based on its global sales, the company ranks 46th among Fortune's list of the 500 largest U.S. industrial corporations. Among the U.S. pharmaceutical companies, it ranks 2nd, behind Johnson & Johnson.[18] In October 1989 Bristol-Myers Company merged with Squibb Corporation to become Bristol-Myers Squibb Company. In 1990, BMS's four core businesses contributed to the company's sales and profits in the following proportions: pharmaceutical and nutritional, 51 percent and 59 percent; medical devices, 14 percent and 13 percent; and consumer products, 35 percent and 28 percent.[19]

Foreign business contributes 33 percent to the company's annual sales with Europe, the MidEast, and Africa, accounting for 82 percent of the sales, with the remaining 18 percent coming from the regions of Latin America and the Pacific Rim. BMS's European market is its most profitable. During the last three years, the company almost doubled its profits in that region.[20]

The Infant Formula Market

Mead-Johnson, a subsidiary of BMS, is responsible for marketing infant formula products. In the U.S. infant formula market, BMS currently holds about 36 percent market share, accounting for over $600 million in annual sales. In 1989, BMS entered into an agreement with Gerber Products Company to market Gerber Baby Formula. This product is being sold primarily in stores rather than through pharmacies and is marketed directly to consumers through mass advertising. BMS holds about 40 percent market share in Canada. Worldwide it generates an estimated $170 million of its sales from the non-U.S. markets. The company, however, is not a significant player in Europe and Japan.

Industrywide Institutions

A variety of considerations influence the structure of industrywide coalitions; these are termed interorganizational relationships, or IORs in management literature. These coalitions or cooperative relationships can be informal, private, and ad hoc consultative arrangements among company representatives on specific issues and challenges as they emerge from time to time. Alternately, cooperation may take place through more formal, interorganizational bodies such as the industry trade associations. The dynamics of creation, operation, and success of these formal organisms can offer tremendous insights into the intraindustry power play; the conflicting interests that must be reconciled in order to develop common response strategies; the role of the dominant player or players; and the maneuvering for competitive advantage against each other and also against the industry's critics.

The primary purpose of IORs is twofold: Firms enter into interorganizational relationships to reduce uncertainty in their external environment and to improve the outcome probabilities of their strategic choices. One noted scholar of industrywide coalitions suggest six contingencies that determine IORs across organizations, settings, and linkages. They are: necessity, that is, IORs are required by legal or regulatory mandates; asymmetry, that is, IOR linkages have the potential for increasing an organization's market power or resource control; reciprocity, where mutual cooperation leads to greater benefits for all participants; efficiency, where IORs generate greater productivity; stability, where IORs lead to greater predictability of the external environment or reduce the volatility of external environment; and legitimacy, where IORs shelter individual organizations from external environmental pressures through association/affiliation with other organizations with greater societal acceptance and legitimacy.[21]

Another important factor in the success or failure of IORs lies in the industry structure. In general, stable industries with mature firms and industries that are dominated by fewer firms display strong industrywide coalitions. Fragmented industries offer a different kind of challenge to developing interorganizational relationships that may be quite weak. Industries are fragmented because of the inherent nature of the product or service they offer: for example, unique service, specialized niche, and so on. Alternately, an industry may be in an early stage of development, allowing for widely divergent approaches to product design, production process, and marketing strategies.[22] In the former case, IORs serve both a "common front" function and a socialization function. In the latter case, industrywide coalitions more often tend to be multiple and ad hoc in character designed to achieve narrowly defined goals: for example, resource use efficiencies.

In this chapter, we will address ourselves to the two industrywide coalitions of the infant formula manufacturers: International Association of Infant Food Industries (ICIFI) and International Coalition of Infant Food Manufacturers (IFM). In particular, we shall analyze their rationale for developing IORs, their modus operandi, and the relative success or failure of these organizations in defining and achieving industrywide goals.

ICIFI

The International Council of Infant Food Industries (ICIFI) was formally established in 1975 with headquarters in Zurich, Switzerland. The timing and circumstances of ICIFI's formation were interestingly coincidental. The formal announcement came two days before the start of the Berne trial of Nestle's libel suit against the Third World Action Group (TWAG). The Council was initially composed of eight companies: three from Europe (Nestle, Cow & Gate, the major UK producer, and Dumex, a Danish firm); four from Japan (Meiji, Morinaga, Snow Brand, and Wakodo) and one from the United States (Wyeth Laboratories, the U.S. subsidiary of American Home Products). In 1980, ICIFI's membership increased to 14 companies with all six new members coming from Europe. These 14 members represented roughly 50 percent of the infant formula market in Organization for Economic Co-Operation and Development (OECD) nations and over 85 percent market in developing countries.[23]

There was a growing awareness of the worldwide decline in breastfeeding and the alleged high incidence of infant mortality among bottle-fed babies in the Third World countries. The stimulus for the original establishment of ICIFI came during the meetings of the Protein Advisory Group (PAG). At the meeting in Singapore in November 1974, government representatives, health professionals, and industry executives first discussed the notion of forming industry councils and national industry councils to act as a forum for the discussion of infant feeding problems. However, after informal meetings, industry representatives decided to establish a council composed solely of infant food companies. When the industry announced the formation of ICIFI, it also simultaneously issued a code of ethics providing the guidelines to infant formula companies to self-regulate their practices in advertising, product information, and advisory services. Compared to the United States, Europe's anti-trust laws are less restrictive and allow for industrywide associations to be more inclusive in the scope of their collective activities than would have been possible in the United States.

An important element of the strategy of Nestle's critics was to isolate the company and make it a focal point of their campaign. Therefore, Nestle wanted to broaden the fight against its critics by making it instead an industrywide problem. This issue, however, had to be defined in Nestle's terms. The company failed to achieve that objective in the United States during the Kennedy Hearings when, despite its strenuous efforts, the U.S. infant formula manufacturers would not identify themselves with Nestle especially as far as that company's strategies and tactics for confronting the critics were concerned. Nestle was, therefore, determined to shape a new organization to conform to its agenda and endorse its strategies for dealing with the industry's critics. From the start, Nestle was the motivating force behind the formation of ICIFI. And in Europe, it had the economic power and political connections to flex its muscle.

ICIFI, however, failed to create a joint industry front. Although its membership included most of the major European and Japanese infant formula manufacturers, the other two major U.S. infant formula producers, namely, Ross Laboratories (a subsidiary of Abbott Laboratories) and Bristol-Myers, declined to join the new group. The two companies disagreed with some of the provisions of the model code and the absence of any formal enforcement procedures. A spokesperson for Abbott Laboratories stated:

> Our company decided not to join ICIFI because the organization is not prepared to go far enough in answering this legitimate criticism of our industry. We feel that for Abbott/Ross to identify with this organization and its code would limit our ability to speak on the important issues.*

Nestle's executives, and in particular Mr. Ernest W. Saunders,† who was then head of Nestle's Infant Foods and Dietetics Products Division, were more cynical of this explanation. According to Mr. Saunders, it was easy for Abbott and Bristol-Myers to seek elimination of direct consumer advertising. The two companies' marketing strategies put primary emphasis on

---

*Interview with the author. Unless otherwise specifically stated, all direct quotes or paraphrased statements attributed to various spokespersons are based on personal comments, taped interviews or written communications with the author.

†Mr. Saunders left Nestle in 1981 to become the chief executive officer of Guinness in London. Based in the United Kingdom, Guinness is one of the world's major producers of beer and distilled spirits. In October of 1987, he was indicted on 37 counts of illegal activities connected with Guinness' acquisition of Distillers Co. in a hostile takeover. Mr. Saunders was convicted and sentenced to a five-year prison term. He served part of his sentence and was granted early release for reasons of poor health. At the time of Mr. Saunder's indictment, two members of Guiness' board of directors were also implicated in the illegal activities connected with the Guinness-Distillers merger. They were: Mr. Thomas Ward, a Washington, D.C.-based attorney, and Mr. Arthur Furer, Chairman of Bank Leu in Switzerland. Mr. Furer was the CEO and chairman of Nestle-Switzerland between 1981–1984. Mr. Ward had been a long time legal advisor to Nestle and had handled some of Nestle's affairs in Washington, D.C.

health care professionals and health care facilities in their advertising and other promotional activities. Restricting consumer advertising would not impose any sacrifices on them. Nestle and many other infant formula manufacturers, including U.S.-based Wyeth, on the other hand, put relatively greater emphasis on direct consumer advertising in their marketing strategies. Thus restricting direct consumer advertising, without limiting other forms of promotional activities, would give an unfair competitive advantage to Abbott and Bristol-Myers. Saunders also commented that Mr. David Cox, president of Ross Laboratories, wanted to be the president of ICIFI. Since he did not get his way, he found it easy to remain outside ICIFI.

The new organization was designed to achieve two purposes: (1) to provide a mechanism for industrywide cooperation and develop cohesive responses to industry's critics; and (2) to take steps toward self-regulation through the creation of a code of ethics for proper marketing and promotion of infant formula foods. Unfortunately, ICIFI turned out to be a poor vehicle for achieving either of the two objectives. From the very start, it was marred with internal dissent about its leadership, modus operandi, and organizational goals. Furthermore, the industry's critics viewed ICIFI not so much as an effort at "putting the industry's house in order," but as a device by the industry to fight the enactment of an effective international code of marketing for infant formula.

ICIFI's Model Code

Subsequent to the WHO/UNICEF-sponsored meeting in October 1979, ICIFI developed a national code of marketing in developing countries. It was allegedly based on the statements and recommendations adopted by the WHO/UNICEF Meeting on Infant and Young Child Feeding held in Geneva in the same month.[24] However, industry's critics viewed it as seriously flawed and at significant variance with the World Health Assembly (WHA) mandate as to its scope and particularly as to its implementation provisions. The ICIFI code required for the member companies to assume responsibility for encouraging breastfeeding. Furthermore, milk nurses were to be paid on a strict salary basis, be professionally trained, and wear company uniforms. Product labels should indicate breast milk as the best infant food. Greater emphasis was to be placed on informing mothers of the correct means of preparing infant formula and of the dangers of dilution or using polluted water. Mothers were to be contacted or provided free samples only through appropriate medical personnel.

Unfortunately, the ICIFI code contained no restrictions on existing promotional strategies; did not rule out mass-media advertising, public promotion, distribution of free samples, or contact with mothers or promotion by health workers. It merely allowed those practices to continue as long as advertising *mentioned* that breastfeeding is the best possible solution or the "first choice" for the nutrition of infants.[25]

ICIFI also presented itself as the monitoring agency for member companies' efforts at code compliance and their public disclosure. Nevertheless, each individual member company was responsible voluntarily to comply with the industry code. ICIFI also lacked any enforcement mechanism. Nor did it have or allocate enough financial resources to fulfill its purported responsibilities. It seemed more designed to appease the industry's critics rather than make way for a genuine reform. And the critics were not mollified. ICIFI's monitoring efforts appeared to be toothless. Its only sanction was to cancel a company's membership, a highly unlikely event. To many of Nestle's critics, and even some within the industry, ICIFI gave the appearance of being a vehicle for shielding Nestle from its critics. As later events would show, ICIFI was indeed dominated by Nestle executives, and Nestle's views held dominance in ICIFI's deliberations and public utterances.

The content and timing of the code was severely criticized by industry critics. Although *The Lancet,* a prestigious medical journal, welcomed the code, it also had some misgivings. Others, however, were not so charitable. The critics accused the industry for its failure to recognize the inherent conflict between profit making and public health, and suggested that industry's actions spoke louder than words.[26] For example, the PAG in January 1976 stated that the code pledges do not go far enough and, as they now stand, pose a danger in that they provide for interpretations that are in contradiction to the spirit of the code. The PAG refused to endorse the ICIFI code on the ground that it was weak and needed substantial changes.

The ICIFI code was also considered inadequate by two of the largest U.S. manufacturers, Abbott Laboratories and Bristol-Myers Squibb. Abbott had reservations about code provisions that did not specifically rule out the use of mass media advertising for infant formula. These two U.S. manufacturers instead chose to adopt their own stricter self-regulatory codes forbidding advertising through mass media.

ICIFI Disbanded

The short but tortuous life of ICIFI abruptly ended soon after the passage of the WHO Code. To the world-at-large, ICIFI was closely identified with the industry's bitter but unsuccessful fight against the passage of the WHO Code. ICIFI was also criticized for the high-pressure tactics that it allegedly used during the WHA debates on the code and the industry's efforts to persuade delegates from many Third World countries to modify the code provisions more to the industry's liking. The internal dissention within ICIFI, and lack of credibility in the broader political community, made it all but impossible for ICIFI to continue working as the combined voice of the industry. This lack of both internal and external support contributed to ICIFI's failure to earn the status of nongovernmental organization (NGO) with WHO. Consequently, in 1983 the ICIFI membership decided to disband the organization. It was succeeded by another industry organization called the International Association of Infant Food Manufacturers (IFM).

IFM

In February 1984 the International Association of Infant Food Manufacturers (IFM) was founded, with its headquarters in Paris, France. IFM membership consists of infant formula manufacturers as full members and manufacturers of feeding bottles as associate members. IFM has 33 national and international member companies, 27 as full members, and 6 as associate members, from 17 nations. With the exception of Jl. Kusumanegara of Indonesia and Maeil Dairy Industry of South Korea, all member companies are incorporated in the Organization for Economic Co-operation and Development (OECD) group of nations. The range of products covered include infant formulas, followup formulas, processed cereal-based weaning foods, sterilized or dehydrated baby foods, fruit and vegetable juices, and dietary products for infants and young children suffering from metabolic or nutritional problems, such as allergies, gastrointestinal problems, hereditary diseases, and so on.

Among the U.S.-based companies, American Home Products and Bristol-Myers Squibb are members of IFM while Abbott Laboratories is not. As in the case of ICIFI, Abbott Laboratories declined to join IFM because it felt that IFM did not go far enough in creating more stringent promotion and marketing standards for member companies. More recently, Nutricia, a Netherlands-based manufacturer of infant formula products also withdrew its membership from IFM despite the fact that one of its executives was immediate past president of IFM. According to a company spokesperson, the company felt that it could not abide by IFM's acceptance of mass advertising of infant formula products. However, according to other sources, Nutricia had made a recent acquisition in the United States and was afraid of adverse public scrutiny in the United States because of its IFM membership.

IFM is a member of International Society of Dietetic Industries (ISDI), which has nongovernmental organization (NGO) status with WHO. Through ISDI, IFM has access to the United Nations and its specialized agencies, and can represent its views and comments on relevant issues to these organizations. ISDI is an international federation of industry associations of manufacturers of foods for special dietary needs of different groups of people, including infants and children, the elderly, and people suffering from metabolic disorders, nutritional deficiency, or others requiring especially adapted foods.

Since its formation, IFM has attempted to keep a low public profile. The organization certainly is not as aggressive and confrontational in its dealings with the industry's critics as was ICIFI, its predecessor. IFM executives also maintain that Nestle does not exert undue influence on the organization's policies and programs. Nevertheless, interviews with executives of other member companies and the industry's critics would suggest that Nestle played a significant role in IFM's affairs and that it was highly unlikely that IFM would take a policy position that would be unacceptable to Nestle.

IFM's Objectives and Primary Activities

IFM's objectives include development of common industry policies relating to composition, utilization, labeling, packaging, and marketing of infant and young children foods; the organization promotes high ethical standards for the marketing of infant foods. It deals with issues of specific interest to the infant food industry; represents industry interests before WHO, FAO, and UNICEF; provides policy guidance and technical and scientific expertise to member companies and industry associations; and collects and disseminates information pertaining to IFM members and their activities in the marketing of infant foods.[27] IFM's posture toward the WHO Code and compliance mode does not differ significantly from that of ICIFI. Its members accept the aims and principles of the WHO Code, but have taken the position that the WHO Code applies only to Third World countries even though no such distinction is recognized in the code. Code compliance by member firms is also voluntary. Where Third World country codes or regulations are at variance with the WHO Code members, member companies comply with the local codes.

IFM allows its members to donate supplies of infant formula to hospitals and other institutions in developing countries for infants who have to be fed on breast-milk substitutes. These donations are given only on the advice of health workers who determine such needs. Given the importance of free supplies in the promotion and sale of infant formula, it is not surprising that this issue continues to be one of the major areas of contention between infant formula manufacturers and the industry's critics.

Code Monitoring.   In practice, individual IFM members are responsible to comply voluntarily with the provisions of the WHO Code and to monitor their own marketing practices in developing countries. Individual members are urged to help local governments, when requested, in formulating local guidelines for marketing practices consistent with the code. In a process similar to ICIFI, IFM undertakes to receive complaints concerning code violations by member companies. This formal complaint procedure was instituted in 1987.

In October 1989 IFM decided to appoint an ombudsman to provide an independent arbitration in cases where dispute or disagreement could not be resolved through its existing procedures. The ombudsman's tasks are to define the differences of opinions that require arbitration; to consult with the parties concerned (complainant and manufacturer) in an attempt to reach an understanding; where a consensus cannot be reached, to draw the attention of the health authorities of the country concerned so that a decision can be taken by the authorities; and to publish an annual report of its activities. The ombudsman is free to consult with appropriate nongovernmental organizations and professional groups, among others, in carrying out this mission.[28]

The process appears more impressive than it actually is in practice. The ombudsman is appointed by IFM members without any input from the industry's critics. The real problem lies not with egregious and provocative violations of the code. Instead, it is the cumulative effect of a multitude of infractions, each one quite small in its own right, but whose combined effect could be quite significant. The ombudsman has no independent resources or staff to initiate and carry out its own investigations. Furthermore, neither the ombudsman nor the IFM has any enforcement powers to ensure compliance from recalcitrant companies.

Notes

1. *Fortune,* "The Global 500" (July 30, 1990).

2. Nestle S.A., *Annual Report, 1989.*

3. Mark Maremont and John Templeman, "How Much Chocolate Can The Nestle Devour?" *Business Week* (May 9, 1988), 64.

4. *Advertising Age* (December 4, 1989), 1, 52.

5. *Advertising Age* (December 17, 1989), 31.

6. George Melloan, "Nestle Courts the LDC Middle Class," *The Wall Street Journal* (June 4, 1990), A13.

7. James E. Post, Stanford University, Case No. S-BPP-5A, Nestle Boycott (A to E), 1981, 4(A).

8. International Management Development Institute, Case No. 9–81-A006, OIE-51, "Nestle and the Infant Food Controversy (A & B)," 1981, 2.

9. Abbott Laboratories, *1990 Annual Report.*

10. Fortune, *The Fortune 500 — The Largest U.S. Industrial Corporations* (April 22, 1991), 288, 324.

11. *Ibid.*

12. *Ibid.* Also, see Abbott Laboratories 1990 Annual Report.

13. Fortune, *The Fortune 500 — The Largest U.S. Industrial Corporations* (April 22, 1991), 288, 324.

14. American Home Products Corporation, *1990 Annual Report.*

15. First Boston Corporation, *Report No. 813046* (June 3, 1989).

16. *The New York Times,* Business Section, Section 4 (February 1988), 1.

17. Bristol-Myers Squibb Company, *Annual Report 1990.*

18. Fortune, *The Fortune 500 — The Largest U.S. Industrial Corporations* (April 22, 1991), 286, 324.

19. Bristol-Myers Squibb Company, *1990 Annual Report.*

20. *Ibid.*

21. Christine Oliver, "Determinants of Interorganizational Relationships: Integration and Future Directions," *Academy of Management Review,* 15, 2 (April 1990), 241–265. This article contains an excellent review of pertinent literature in interorganizational relationships. See also, Rudi Bresser and Johannes E. Harl, "Collective Strategy: Vice or Virtue?" *Academy of Management Review,* 11, 2 (April 1986), 408–427.

22. Marc J. Dollinger, "The Evolution of Collective Strategies in Fragmented Industries," *Academy of Management Review,* 15, 2 (November 1990), 266–285.

23. The 14 companies involved were: BSN Gervais Danone S.A., France; Coop. Condensfabriek Friesland, Netherlands; Cow & Gate Ltd., Great Britain; Dumex Ltd., Denmark; Holland Canned Milk, Netherlands; Leo de Winter Co. N.V., Netherlands; Lijempf International B.V., Netherlands; Meiji Milk Products Co., Ltd., Japan; Morinaga Milk Industry Co., Ltd., Japan; Nestle Nutrition S.A., Switzerland; Nutricia Nederland B.V., Netherlands; Snow Brand Milk Products Co. Ltd., Japan; Wakodo Co., Ltd., Japan; and, Wyeth International Limited, USA. Source: International Council of Infant Food Industries, *Objectives, History and Activities* (Summer 1980).

24. WHO/UNICEF, "Infant and Young Child Feeding," Geneva (October 1979) p. 41.

25. ICIFI, *Code of Ethics and Professional Standards for Advertising, Product Information and Advisory Services for Breast Milk Substitutes,* Zurich, 1975 (amended 1976).

26. "Infant Food Industry," *The Lancet,* editorial (June 10, 1978), p. 1240.

27. International Association of Infant Food Manufacturers (IFM), *Statutes,* Article 2: Objectives (Paris, France), undated.

28. International Association of Infant Food Manufacturers (IFM), *Summary Report on Complaints Relating to Marketing Practices of Infant Formula. Period from 1 November to October 1987, 1988, 1989 and 1990,* 75001 Paris.

11 MAJOR RELIGIOUS AND ACTIVIST GROUPS INVOLVED IN THE CONTROVERSY

Several organizations played key roles in making the infant formula controversy into a national and international cause celebre. Although the early seeds of the infant formula controversy were planted in Europe, the movement was initiated in the United States by the Interfaith Center on Corporate Responsibility (ICCR) and subsequently fostered and managed by the Infant Formula Action Coalition (INFACT). During the period spanning between 1978–1984 when the public awareness and involvement in the infant formula controversy were at their peak, a great many activist groups were involved both in the United States and abroad. They ranged all over the spectrum in terms of their political and ideological orientation, religious beliefs, understanding of the issues, financial resources, and intensity of commitment. They also included groups from many walks of life: health care, education, public services, groups concerned with Third World issues, as well as those involved with the poor and disenfranchised in the United States, to name a few.

It would be extremely difficult, however, to provide a reasonably accurate measure as to the number of people or groups who were actively engaged in some facet of the Nestle boycott or other anti-infant formula campaigns. Since these groups generally required no formal membership or listing, any number of people could start any number of groups (including in theory a group with only one member).

It was also in the interest of the boycott movement to project as broad a level of support as possible and thereby suggest greater legitimacy for its actions. This was indeed a calculated part of the activists' strategy of domain offense in the early stages of the campaign and that of boundary expansion during the problem identification and remedy and relief stages of the issue life cycle. Doug Johnson, the national chairperson and executive director of INFACT, defined seven phases of the boycott. He referred to the objectives of the early phases as: making the infant formula controversy, embodied by Nestle and its actions, a legitimate issue in the eyes of an educated, grass-roots base of support; converting local endorsements of the boycott into national support in preparation for the International Meeting on Infant and Young Child Feeding; and developing a specific international marketing code for breastmilk substitutes, and compelling Nestle, through pressure from consumer groups around the world, to implement such a code.[1] The fact that there was widespread public and news media antipathy to the industry's po-sition also helped the activists' efforts in projecting a larger-than-life image of the magnitude of public support for their cause.

Notwithstanding the large numbers and highly amorphous character of the groups involved in the boycott movement, the nerve center of the strat-egy remained with INFACT and was concentrated in the hands of a small coterie of committed leaders with a well-developed understanding of organ-izing and managing mass movements. They were successful at creating two apparently contradictory public personae for themselves. One, they were the money-short, unsophisticated volunteers who were fighting the greedy and uncaring corporate behemoths. Two, they were the disciplined organiz-ers who could effectively control and direct a large number of diverse vol-untary groups and mold them into a cohesive force of public advocacy. It is a testimony to their strong strategic sense and tactical competence that they succeeded in achieving these twin objectives. It also demonstrated the rel-ative crudeness of the industry's response patterns, which lacked similar skills in exploiting their own strategic advantage in the marketplace of public opinion. However, the relative strengths and weaknesses of the two groups weakened as the issue moved to the remedy and relief and prevention stages. In the subsequent stages, the companies were able to capitalize on their learning experience and gained greater momentum through mobilization of substantial organizational and financial resources. The activists, however, failed to build on their earlier momentum and thereby lost their earlier tac-tical advantage. The fact that they lacked sufficient organizational resources also contributed to their problems. Thus the strategies and tactics employed by the opposing sides in the infant formula controversy offer ample lessons for corporations and public advocacy groups to emulate.

The primary focus of our enquiry in this chapter will be the two major groups, ICCR and INFACT. To be sure, there were a number of other groups that were either sponsored or co-sponsored by INFACT to direct and coor-dinate certain facets of the campaign. In addition, there were other groups, more active outside the United States, that worked independently but in harmony with the INFACT/ICCR coalition. They pursued commonly shared goals but with differing strategies and tactics. Many of these groups were also tied together through cross-holding of leadership positions. The most notable of these was International Baby Food Action Network (IBFAN), which, along with the International Organization of Consumers Unions (IOCU), shouldered the major responsibility for coordinating the activists' campaign toward the passage of the code at the World Health Organization (WHO) in Geneva. Other national and international groups included Baby Milk Action Coalition (BMAC) and Oxfam — both based in the United Kingdom, Third World First (3W1), and the Geneva Infant Feeding Association (GIFA).

ICCR

More than any other group, Interfaith Center on Corporate Responsibility (ICCR) symbolizes church activism in the economic arena in the United States. ICCR acts as the research and consulting arm for member church groups. It acts as the catalyst in selecting social issues, mobilizing the body politic, and developing action strategies. Under the leadership of its longtime executive director, Mr. Timothy (Tim) H. Smith, ICCR has become one of the major forces of social activism exerting pressure on large corporations to modify their policies and operational practices, in their domestic and international operations, in a manner that takes into account the interests of affected communities and the public-at-large.

ICCR started out as an organ of the National Council of Churches. However, in 1984 it became an independent, nonprofit, tax-exempt organization. In part, the change in affiliation was a response to its critics who had argued that ICCR did not represent the broader religious community while it purported to speak for it. Moreover, ICCR's governance process did not provide for a systematic incorporation of the voices of either the laity or clergy of various denominational bodies. There was also a desire to become more independent of the hierarchical leadership of various denominations who were not quite comfortable with some of the issues selected by ICCR or with its manner of advocacy.

Antecedents and Growth

In 1954, The National Council of Churches (NCC) went on record as working against those forms of economic injustice that are expressed through racial discrimination. It was also on record in support of equal employment opportunity for all, use of nonviolent demonstrations to secure social justice, the elimination of segregation in education, and the prevention of discrimination in housing. NCC also recognized that the churches' own purchases must be based on other than strictly economic criteria.[2] To accommodate its program agenda, in the late 1960s NCC established the Interfaith Committee on Social Responsibility, or CIC. By 1970, CIC was conducting research on church investments and their ethical implications. CIC also monitored corporate behavior and published its analysis in a monthly bulletin called *The Corporate Examiner.* By 1973, the CIC and the Interfaith Committee on Social Responsibility and Investments were coordinating church-related shareowner campaigns.[3] Eventually these agencies, both located at the Interchurch Center in New York City, merged to become a working coalition of churches related to the National Council of Churches.

Organizational Structure and Operational Procedures

ICCR's style of operation is not generally well understood. It owns no stock, files no shareholder resolutions, and takes no positions. Group members send representatives to ICCR working groups to discuss issues of mutual concern and possible approaches for tackling them. On the basis of these discussions, ICCR prepares shareholder resolutions and assists in arranging delegations to discuss or negotiate with management, in the solicitation of proxy support for resolutions or the coordination of presentations at annual meetings of shareholders.[4] In practice, however, ICCR's executives and staff take the lead in setting priorities and initiating action. This is not surprising given the fact of their experience and control of information. Moreover, in most cases, ICCR's agenda tends to be similar to the agendas of the more activist elements of the member groups who invariably represent their institutions in the ICCR deliberative processes.

ICCR has an independent governing board composed of representatives of its members. ICCR's decision-making process differs from corporate decision-making in that there is no clearcut authority at the top. The functions of the executive director include generating policy initiatives, coordinating all staff work, and assisting the governing board. Tim Smith's role in the direction of ICCR cannot be overemphasized. To ICCR's supporters and admirers, Tim Smith is an intelligent, articulate, and dedicated advocate of causes advanced through a church-related organization. However, to his opponents, Tim Smith personifies the aggressive, often abrasive, generally self-righteous religious activist who would not be averse to twisting the truth or using deceptive and unseemly tactics — charges that social activists level against their corporate opponents — to achieve a given end. Nevertheless,

his experience in corporate campaigns, his strategic skills, assertive personality, and ability to deal with external constituencies and the news media
have made him a strong leader and a formidable adversary.

ICCR has been criticized — along with some of the major denominations
considered active in the corporate social responsibility movement — for
purporting to speak on behalf of the church and its membership, when in
fact this representation cannot be supported on factual grounds. It is argued
that church membership does not support its leadership's involvement in the
corporate social responsibility movement. The second issue is related to the
organizations for whom ICCR acts as the spokesperson on social issues.
ICCR counts among its members more than 200 Protestant and Catholic organizations, thereby creating the image of a broad-based level of support.
This impression is further strengthened by the public statements of ICCR
members that do not always specify the particular nature of their membership. The reality of ICCR representation, however, may be far more modest
than the organization claims, and its representational character far more
complex and less invidious than its critics imply. Notwithstanding, ICCR is
widely recognized and accepted, both within the church establishment and
by the outside world, as one of the most potent voices of the church, and an
important advocacy group, on economic issues in the United States.

ICCR in Action — The Infant Formula Controversy

Strange as it may seem, ICCR's involvement in the infant formula controversy did not come about as a consequence of careful deliberations by ICCR
leadership or extensive study and analysis on the part of ICCR staff. Instead, ICCR's involvement was primarily the result of the activities and
commitment of two or three people who, with the help and encouragement
of ICCR's director, Tim Smith, succeeded in raising it to a high level of
institutional priority within ICCR and the National Council of Churches
(NCC).

In terms of the ICCR's involvement in the infant formula controversy,
Ms. Leah Margulies played perhaps the most critical role. She was the single
most effective force behind the issue at ICCR and NCC. If Ms. Margulies
were not there, one would have to invent her for the issue to remain viable.
A diminutive person, Ms. Margulies appears to be shy and diffident. To her
admirers and supporters, she is dedicated and committed, and has a clear
vision of her goals. To her detractors, however, she is dogmatic, ideologically anti-business, ruthless, and vindictive against those — in either
camp — who might disagree with her, and has little regard for niceties of
means in order to achieve her ends. Her means are those of a street fighter.
In her dealings with corporate executives she is not beyond using surprise

attacks or creating contrived events to create negative publicity for her adversaries.* As she has stated: "I have been accused of taking a high moral tone in my dealings with the corporations. But what is wrong with taking the high road when the lives of millions of children are involved and when you know that corporations are saying one thing to us while they are doing another thing in the field?"†

INFACT

The Infant Formula Action Coalition (INFACT) was formed in January 1977 in Minneapolis, Minnesota, as a citizens action group. Its beginning was quite modest. However, it burst on the national scene on July 4, 1977, when it launched a boycott against Nestle and invited other groups and individuals from across the country to join them in this effort. The prime architects of this group, in the early stages, were Ms. Leah Margulies and Mr. Doug Johnson. However, during its later stages, Doug Johnson became the driving force behind INFACT and shaped the organization and its modus operandi to his will and vision.

Doug Johnson graduated from Midwestern Presbyterian College and studied international law. He actively participated in the anti-war movement in 1967 and graduated from St. Thomas in Minneapolis, Minnesota. In July 1973, he became the director of the Third World Institute located at the University of Minnesota campus in Minneapolis, and later the president of INFACT. Doug Johnson recalled prior informal meetings with Leah Margulies, Mark Ritchie, and Dick Fernandez with the intent of raising interest in forming INFACT. Their first meeting was held in a private home in Brooklyn, New York, among a handful of people, all veterans of other social movements and public advocacy campaigns. It was here that the broad outline of the initial campaign was developed. A major objective of this meeting was to get recruits to form some kind of grassroots program to get the campaign against Nestle started.[5] In the early stages of the controversy, INFACT played a somewhat secondary role to ICCR in that it was the "street action" agent provocateur while ICCR acted as the "brains" of the movement, and provided the necessary financial and organization resources. Even more important, ICCR enabled INFACT to use the church's imprimatur to gain le-

---

*An insight into the working of ICCR and the role of Leah Margulies both as a charismatic leader and a "take no prisoners" adversary can be seen during various facets of the controversy as detailed in different chapters of this book.
†Interview with the author. Unless otherwise specifically stated, all direct quotes and paraphrased comments are based on personal on-the-record taped interviews or written communications with the author.

gitimacy and recruit a large number of volunteers without which the movement would have been still-born.

Nevertheless, both Ms. Margulies and Mr. Johnson viewed church affiliation and support in strictly tactical terms to be exploited when it served their purpose, but discarded when such an association became restrictive and burdensome from the perspective of pursuing particular strategies and tactics. In addition, uncertain financial resources exerted intense pressure for short-run survival in INFACT's leadership at the risk of sacrificing long-term goals and thereby obliging them to continue to work within the financially strong umbrella of religious institutions and their program agencies. Nevertheless, INFACT leaders constantly strove, and eventually succeeded, in becoming independent of these church-related groups which later played a largely supportive role in the infant formula controversy. This was necessary if INFACT was to have an independent identity, thereby giving its leaders the freedom to pursue strategies and tactics that were more confrontational in nature. In Doug Johnson's words, a campaign power base, to have significant impact, must be "relatively unsusceptible to the tactics available to the industry" and that a network model of campaigns has limitations compared to an organization model because it "tends to welcome many groups into its sphere, thus diluting its focus and decision-making system."[6]

Many church leaders, however, preferred to use more conciliatory approaches in dealing with the infant formula companies. They also looked askance at the veracity of INFACT's allegations and assertions. Events would show that while INFACT's leadership was able to chart an independent course during the later stages of the controversy, it was also considerably weakened because of the mediating role played by the United Methodist Church in bringing about the termination of the boycott against Nestle. In terms of its strategies and tactics, the anti-infant formula campaign largely reflected the vision and attitude of its leaders. Therefore, INFACT cannot be disassociated from the personalities if its two main founders, Ms. Leah Margulies and Mr. Doug Johnson.

INFACT — Strategic Stages

Like ICCR, INFACT also operated as a coalition of many diverse groups representing distinct viewpoints and constituencies, concentrating on students, churches, women's groups, and different college/varsity associations. The organization, in theory, worked as a participative and consultative coalition. However, it was Doug Johnson who shaped the organization into a well-oiled fighting machine. The organization's grassroots network began with local church-related hunger organizations and members of the National Coalition for Development Action. Its initial program was to support the

U.S. churches' institutional confrontation with U.S. companies. But soon afterwards, it became evident that a strategic campaign would have to be launched against Nestle in order to achieve further results with the American companies.

Early efforts were concentrated on "street action" and "spreading the word" through small meetings sponsored by sympathetic friends and well-wishers under various institutional settings, such as churches and universities. INFACT, in order to make its movement more popular at the grassroots level and to spread it across the nation, used these groups very effectively. The effort was designed to: (1) gain media coverage and raise public consciousness; (2) recruit volunteers and create local groups in all parts of the country; (3) raise funds; and (4) create name recognition for INFACT and its leadership and thereby give them leverage in dealing with their corporate opponents. Grassroots activities took all imaginable forms. For example, INFACT days were organized at different places in the United States. There were boycotts against Stouffer hotels in Washington, D.C., and Chicago, Illinois. Some groups engaged in more confrontational activities. For example, at one INFACT day celebration, several Los Angeles area colleges and churches organized an extensive leaflet campaign at local shopping centers. Spanish-translated leaflets were also distributed for Spanish-speaking people. In Philadelphia, there was picketing in front of a Stouffer's restaurant. INFACT also used college students to create high-profile events among the young, such as swim-a-thons, rallies with leafletting campaigns and marches to local post offices to mail protest postcards to Nestle.

The strategies of INFACT from late 1979 to May 1981 concentrated on internationalization of the boycott movement and code development. The objectives were to: (1) secure a strong and specific international code that could define safe marketing practices for Nestle and the industry; (2) build effective working ties with consumer organizations in other countries; and (3) place Nestle in a position that would force it to accept and implement the international code.[7] While these strategies were the overlying objectives, a wide variety of activity was still being undertaken by local INFACT groups. The June 1980 INFACT update report from Denver and Toronto included the following:

> With shouts of "One, Two, Three, Four, Babies Are Dying Don't Go In The Door!", 60 mothers, fathers, grandmothers, children and other supporters converged on Stouffers/Top of the Rockies restaurant in downtown Denver on May 11. They had come to show support for the plight of Third World mothers and to try to convince the customers of Top of the Rockies to join them by not going inside. Despite the rain and cool temperatures, the enthusiasm was high and was recorded by local television news coverage.[8]

According to Doug Johnson,[9] the next phase of INFACT lasted from June 1981 to March 1982. The objectives for this phase were: (1) to build INFACT through greater participation of countries and organizations; (2) to implement the international code as national legislation; (3) to internationalize the Nestle boycott, thereby increasing the costs of noncompliance; and, (4) to increase the direct action and pressure of the boycott.

Between March 1982 and January 1983, the strategy of INFACT became highly defensive: (1) to hold the boycott coalition together through a demand for coordinated and complete negotiations while (2) searching for an effective boycott offensive strategy.[10] The reason for the defensive posture of the boycott was a critically changed condition: Nestle announced that it would abide by the International Code of Marketing in developing countries, and issued a set of instructions to its marketers on how that was to be accomplished. This announcement confused the public; it was also backed up by a sophisticated divide-and-rule counter-boycott strategy that took the boycott leadership by surprise. With no clear offensive of its own, the boycott fell into a defensive posture. Valuable leadership time was taken up with endorsing organizations, to hold them in the boycott coalition. New information about Nestle's structure and training about boycotts indicated that an effective boycott needed a strong grassroots component to have an economic effect; but internal conflicts prevented a full consensus from supporting the boycott's view. INFACT pushed forward a poorly conceived organizing drive to fill an emergency need. It failed, leaving the organization demoralized and heavily in debt. Support from international colleagues helped regain flexibility while INFACT repositioned for a new offensive, which was launched in January 1983 and spanned a year.

The objectives of this phase were to: (1) reduce the sales of Nestle's most important product in the United States and Canada — Taster's Choice coffee; (2) deepen the grassroots boycott in key market areas through a new organizing model; (3) recruit and train new grassroots leadership to extend the model to other market areas; and (4) further diffuse Nestle's anti-Boycott resources through increased international boycott activity.[11] While Nestle concentrated its attention on church leadership, INFACT launched a new organizing drive in its original constituency — the grassroots — emerging at the end of October with two new organizing centers and hundreds of new volunteers pushing to remove Nestle's most important product (Taster's Choice coffee) from supermarkets' shelves.

Infact Update

The organization's newsletter became an important vehicle to provide bonding among various groups involved in INFACT activities, to proselytize and bring in new volunteers, to raise funds, and to provide materials and information to grassroots organizations in their campaign against Nestle and other infant formula companies. A content analysis of *INFACT Update* suggests that during 1978, almost 50 percent of the space was allocated to disseminating information about INFACT followed by reporting on domestic and international activist groups, Nestle, U.S.-based infant formula producers and WHO-UNICEF. During 1979 and 1980 the focus shifted whereby increasingly greater space was allocated to Nestle and infant formula marketing practices in Third World countries. In subsequent years, the focus shifted to WHO-UNICEF and the code deliberations, with continuing emphasis on Nestle and other companies' recalcitrance in curbing their promotion and sale of infant formula in Third World countries. The newsletter also began to play up the successes and victories of INFACT and its allies in the boycott movement. At the same time, the *INFACT Update* continuously appealed in every issue for a membership drive and fund raising.

Sources of Financial Support and Expenditures

Notwithstanding the membership character of INFACT, a majority of its funds were raised through grants and fund-raising activities with very little money coming from members. For example, in 1981 INFACT raised a total of $380,000 of which $348,000, or 92 percent, came from contributions and grants with membership dues accounting for a little over 1 percent. In the same year, INFACT spent over $264,000 (69 percent) in public education and $76,000 (20 percent) in fund raising. It should also be noted that the public education category included services of consultants which accounted for 53 percent of all expenditure in this category. These expenditures more than doubled between 1980–1981, increasing from $64,000 to $140,000. INFACT also reported that in its direct-mail fund-raising campaigns, it received less than 30 cents for every dollar raised, with the remainder going to direct-mail fund-raising companies.

International Baby Food Action Network (IBFAN)

The International Baby Food Action Network (IBFAN) was formed in October 1979, the day after the World Health Organization (WHO)/UNICEF Meeting on Infant and Young Child Feeding in Geneva, Switzerland. It is a worldwide network of groups and individuals actively involved in infant feeding issues. The initial objectives of the group were to promote breastfeeding and the status of women, and to control the marketing of artificial infant milks and feeding products. Participation of nongovernmental organizations as well as cooperation among citizens' groups were essential for the group's effective operations. Between 1979 and 1982, groups participating in IBFAN investigated the marketing practices of the infant food industry; played an active part in drafting a WHO/UNICEF International Code of

Marketing of Breastmilk Substitutes; and initiated campaigns to promote breastfeeding in their countries. By 1981, the number of participating groups, according to IBFAN, grew from six to over 81.

With the successful adoption of the WHO/UNICEF Code in May 1981, IBFAN initiated a new phase of activity. Citizen groups began strong efforts within their countries to press for national legislation toward implementing the WHO Code provisions. However, as we shall see, IBFAN, and for that matter the entire anti-formula movement, was singularly unsuccessful in getting various national governments to pay more than lip service to enacting the code into national legislation. Third World countries, including those most vociferous in their opposition to the infant formula companies during the WHO debate, were equally conspicuous by their lack of action.* This was especially true for countries like India, that had a substantial indigenous infant formula industry. In fact, through a tacit understanding among both the activist groups and the WHO/UNICEF, there was no effort to put pressure on Third World countries to follow their words with deeds. It is apparent that publicizing these countries' inaction would seriously undermine an important rationale for the anti-infant formula campaign. Equally important, it would cause serious erosion into the legitimacy of the movement itself.

IBFAN and other activist groups therefore focused their attention on the code violations by the companies. IBFAN urged various regional and national groups to report on the violations of the code by companies in their areas. The response was overwhelming. According to IBFAN reports, in 1982 a total of 14,985,160 violations of the WHO/UNICEF International Code of Marketing of Breastmilk Substitutes occurred in 50 countries and involved 83 companies. There is no way to check the accuracy of the number or the substance of the complaints reported to IBFAN. The organization was accused by the companies, and even some independent observers, of gross exaggeration and propaganda grandstanding. For example, it was found that a "billboard" or an "advertisement insert" was counted as multiple (in the hundreds of thousands) violations because of the projected viewership of the billboard or ad insert.

INBC

The International Nestle Boycott Committee (INBC) was set up in 1979 to act as the representative for the various boycotting organizations in negoti-

---

*For a detailed discussion of the inaction of various countries in converting the Code into national legislation, see Chapter 19, "The Lessons of Accountability — Third World Governments: Expectations and Performance — WHO: Non-Existent Monitoring."

ations with Nestle. This collective presented a stronger, more unified front to Nestle than the individual organizations could hope to bring to the negotiation process, thereby allowing an intensification of the boycott and ensuring its prolongation. In the latter stages of the boycott, INBC played an important role as the umbrella organization to hold the troops together, coordinate the activities, and often smooth over the personal and institutional frictions between the U.S. groups and those based in Europe.

ACA

Action for Corporate Accountability (ACA), also referred to as ACTION, is a Minneapolis-based advocacy group that was formed early in 1986 as the U.S. member organization of IBFAN. In reality, it is a successor organization of INFACT. ACA's organizers are largely drawn from the former founders of INFACT, with Doug Johnson serving as the new group's chairman. As the public interest in the infant formula campaign waned after termination of the boycott, INFACT sought new territories to cultivate. Consequently, INFACT shifted its agenda and launched a campaign, among others, against the production and promotion of nuclear weapons.

Therefore, it was decided that a new organization should be created to redirect energies to the continued campaign against the infant formula companies for their alleged foot-dragging in implementing the code throughout the world and for their repeated violations of the code in different parts of the world. Hence, ACA was founded by the top leaders of INFACT and other veterans of the Nestle boycott campaign. ACA is now a sister organization of INFACT; both groups continue to pursue distinct but parallel goals and reveal a common heritage.

ACA works through the IBFAN network of organizations, represented in over 60 countries, to promote and protect breastfeeding as a means of improving infant health. Their methods include a program of consumer activism, such as boycotts, and a program of research and education, targeting infant formula marketing and hospital practices. Still seeking support from grassroots sources around the country, ACA looks to national church organizations, medical professionals, labor advocates, and concerned individuals for patronage and sustenance. Monitoring of the marketing practices of infant food manufacturers is now the domain of ACA.

On October 15, 1988, on the occasion of World Food Day, ACA announced the resumption of the Nestle boycott and a new boycott of American Home Products (AHP). ACA officials claimed that through monitoring marketing practices in 42 countries, it found evidence of Nestle's dumping large quantities of infant formula on Third World hospitals and thus violating the WHO Code. The Church of England endorsed the boycott on July 15, 1991, by boycotting Nescafe. According to ACA, this second Nestle boycott is now in effect in 12 countries. However, ACA's new action has not evoked much public interest or news media attention in the United States. To date, no major church group has joined the new boycott.

Notes

1. See Douglas A. Johnson, "Confronting Corporate Power: Strategies and Phases of The Nestle Boycott," in James E. Post and Lee E. Preston (eds.), *Research in Corporate Social Performance and Policy,* Vol. 8 (Greenwich, Conn: JAI Press, 1986), 323–344.

2. Paul Minus, *A Background Paper on the Infant Formula Controversy: Prepared for the United Methodist Task Force on Infant Formula* (Dayton, Oh: United Methodist Church, September 17, 1980), p. 44.

3. *INFACT Update,* April 1987.

4. *Ibid.*

5. Johnson, *op. cit.,* supra note 1.

6. *Ibid.*

7. *Ibid.*

8. *INFACT Update,* June 1980.

9. Johnson, *op. cit.,* supra note 1.

10. *Ibid.*

11. *Ibid.*

IV ESCALATION OF THE CONFLICT

12 WHO's INVOLVEMENT IN THE CONTROVERSY

An important outcome of the Kennedy Hearings was to shift the locus of policy action in the infant formula controversy to the World Health Organization (WHO) in Geneva. The first step by the WHO was to co-sponsor, with UNICEF, an international meeting on Infant and Young Child Feeding in Geneva, Switzerland, on October 9–12, 1979. The objective of the meeting was to stimulate discussion among participants leading to "affirmative actions to be implemented" for improving infant malnutrition and mortality.[1]

The October 1979 meeting was unprecedented in many respects. It set in motion a chain of events that was to influence all subsequent actions pertaining to the infant formula controversy. The process led to the eventual adoption of a Code of International Marketing of Breast Milk Substitutes in May 1981 and an agreement on the interpretation of its key provisions in April 1984. Second, the meeting involved the WHO for the first time in a regulatory mode. This was quite distinct from its normal scientific, technical, and program-oriented activities. Third, the meeting emphasized the issue of corporate social accountability of multinational corporations. This topic had become a key focus of the United Nations in its efforts to build an economic bridge between developed and developing nations.

Antecedents to the October 1979 Meeting

The WHO-UNICEF meeting resulted from a confluence of events. The political pressure came from Senator Kennedy and was reinforced by Nestle and ICIFI. The industry, and in particular Nestle, had actively pushed for WHO involvement, hoping to shift the balance of public opinion and the terms of the debate on the infant formula controversy away from the industry's critics. At that time, WHO had a reputation of being the least politicized institution of the United Nations. Another motivation for Nestle to take the issue to WHO was that Dr. Stanislas Flasche, then deputy director general of WHO, who was about to retire, had contacted Mr. Ernest Saunders of Nestle and a few other people, offering his services to the industry. According to Saunders,* Dr. Flasche had "felt that his understanding of the way that WHO works in Geneva could not only help ICIFI but that he would be able to bring the two sides together informally so as to reach some sort of understanding that would aid the whole process."†

The industry critics were initially not interested in getting involved with the WHO process. They were skeptical of the industry's motives. "The industry had leaped to it so quickly," observed Doug Johnson. "Nestle in particular had spent a year and a half going around and telling people that it's not necessary to boycott us anymore because we are going to this meeting; we welcome it; and we will abide by any recommendations that come out of this meeting." As the planning for the meeting progressed and its dimensions became clearer, the schism between the activists and industry widened. By August 1979, according to the activists, "Nestle had backtracked from its original promise and instead suggested that it will abide by only those recommendations that are accepted by national governments."

Upon accepting Senator Kennedy's suggestion, WHO asked UNICEF to join it in dealing with the infant formula issue. Public health had become a major international issue in terms of Third World development and had assumed a high political profile. Furthermore, 1979 was The Year of the Child, and WHO/UNICEF were planning to have some kind of a meeting. Both Dr. Halfdan Mahler, director general of WHO, and Mr. Henry R. Labouisse, executive director of UNICEF, were anxious to demonstrate a more activist stance toward infant nutrition and health. Although the World Health Assembly (WHA) had already passed two resolutions in 1974 and 1978, there was very little action. Few, if any, governments had taken them seriously.

Organization and Structure of the Meeting

As a first step, the staffs of WHO/UNICEF prepared a background paper which summarized the then state of knowledge on infant feeding practices

---

*Unless otherwise specifically stated, all direct quotes or paraphrased statements attributed to various people are based on personal on-the-record interviews or written communications to the author.
†Dr. Flasche was appointed the executive director of ICIFI before WHO had acceded to Senator Kennedy's request.

prevalent in the world. It identified five major themes for discussion at the meeting: (1) encouragment and support of breastfeeding; (2) promotion and support of appropriate weaning practices; (3) information, education, communication, and training; (4) health and social status of women in relation to infant and young child feeding; and (5) appropriate marketing and distribution of breast-milk substitutes. Nestle and ICIFI were not happy because they saw the document as seriously flawed in that it essentially reiterated the critics' assertions and claims.[2] They also disapproved of WHO/UNICEF ground rules for the meeting to the effect that this briefing document would form the basic agenda of the meeting and that no other papers, reflecting different perspectives, were to be distributed by any group or participant at the meeting.

The next step was to develop a list of participants who would be invited to the meeting. The secretariat staff sought the assistance of ICCR in identifying various nongovernmental organizations (NGOs) who were active in the infant formula controversy and should be invited to the meeting. The industry representatives were upset at the invitation to the activists who "were given full status and full participation rights at that meeting at the same level as industry and government in terms of speaking" and voting rights. Nestle strenuously objected to the inclusion of certain members of ICCR and INFACT in particular. The company was playing hardball. Literally days before the start of the meeting, ICIFI and Nestle visited WHO and threatened to withdraw if certain ICCR-INFACT members were invited to the meeting. It would appear as if the WHO staff were treating the activists as the insiders. They were able to talk directly with the (WHO) staff; they were able to have continued and open access; they knew at every stage of development what the arguments were from various sides and they could work to shape the code.

Unfortunately, the company had grossly overestimated its capacity to influence the course of events. In part, it was due to its lack of experience and knowledge about the decision-making processes at WHO. Reflecting on the WHO meeting, a Nestle executive, Jack Mongoven, vice president of NCCN, was later to observe that the company was totally unprepared for the meeting in terms of its understanding of the organizational dynamics at WHO and its secretariat. "Nestle had never spent much time worrying about the U.N. They knew that WHO was located down at Lake Geneva. But that's about all that they did know." They did not understand the politics of it. As a consequence, they were badly outmaneuvered by the activists at every turn of the proceedings. According to one industry critic, "The aggressive stance of ICIFI and Nestle had the reverse effect than was intended. A large part of WHO and UNICEF's scientific staff found itself in sympathy with the critics' viewpoint and developed a code which the industry considered unacceptable, and in the process WHO itself became more politicized.

The final composition of the meeting included 152 invited delegates comprised of: member governments, 57; U.N. agencies, 16; nongovernmental organizations (NGOs), 28; infant formula industry, 26; professional experts, 22; and intergovernmental organizations, 3. In addition, 53 staff members, 45 from WHO and 8 from UNICEF, participated in the meeting. ICCR and INFACT each had two invited delegates: Ms. Leah Margulies and Ms. Patricia Young represented ICCR, while INFACT was represented by Mr. Douglas A. Johnson and Ms. Shirley Powell. The NGO delegates even included one of Nestle's earliest nemeses, Arbeitsgruppe Dritte Welt (Third World Working Group — ADW).

Lobbying Before the Meeting

Although the WHO protocol of the meeting had barred distribution of any papers by the participating groups during the meeting, this protocol was flouted both by the activists and the ICIFI. ICIFI prepared its own document offering a point-by-point critique of the WHO briefing paper. Other papers were produced by individual companies. On the day before the start of the meeting, ICIFI held a press conference and distributed its document to the press and the delegates. This effort, no doubt, alienated the WHO/UNICEF staff.

In response to ICIFI, the activists also organized a parallel event. They held an information day in order to get some access to the press. This briefing session was jointly sponsored by INFACT and ICCR at the premises of Christian Medical Commission in Geneva. WHO/UNICEF felt that this was a breach of the protocol and tried to stop the event. It even asked the delegates not to attend the activists' briefing session. The briefing session, however, did take place. According to Leah Margulies, "We didn't think there were any ground rules. We were just doing what we knew how to do best which was to organize public opinion. As far as we were concerned, we were coming to Switzerland, Nestle's home country, we wanted to generate support for the boycott in Switzerland and we wanted to mobilize public support for whatever was going to happen at WHO. It wasn't a mystery. It was what we did everywhere we went."

The industry's efforts at creating a unified position were somewhat hampered by internal dissension among members as to strategy and tactics. Nestle was active in staking out a position while leaving ICIFI to coalesce and present the industry viewpoint which the company, nevertheless, believed would be to reinforce its own position. However, this was not always possible. ICIFI did not have strong leadership independent of Nestle. Two major U.S. producers, Abbott Laboratories and Bristol-Myers, were not ICIFI members and advocated positions which, in certain important areas, were at variance with those of Nestle and ICIFI. In essence, ICIFI lacked the collective industry wisdom to participate effectively in the meeting and to achieve results for the collective benefit of the industry.

The activists, however, did not suffer from a lack of unity of purpose. They used the occasion to network with national and regional groups. Anwar Fazal, president of International Organization of Consumers' Union (IOCU), played a key role on behalf of the NGOs while Doug Johnson, Leah Margulies, and Andy Chetley forged a coalition to do something internationally that would strengthen the national activity.

The Meeting Format

The meeting was conducted in plenary sessions and five working group sessions. The first plenary session was held on the opening day of the meeting and was attended by all delegates. The remaining three days were devoted to the substantive discussions of the issues in five group meetings organized along the lines of five themes identified by the secretariat. Delegates were asked to list their top one or two choices and were assigned to different working groups based on their preferences. The arrangement, however, turned out to be less than satisfactory as each side tried to load up their delegates in panels they considered important. The activists complained that industry representatives avoided serious discussions of issues that were important to them. "Despite the fact that we felt women's issues were important, they [the industry] only sent one Japanese industry person who spoke no English. We support weaning foods, so they sent two Japanese who spoke no English into the weaning food section and maybe one other person." On the whole, there were very few industry representatives in the four panels, while there were "sixteen male vice presidents in the fifth panel that dealt with the role of marketing and distribution of breast-milk substitutes."

Industry representatives had objected to the activists' inclusion in the marketing group on the grounds that they lacked scientific knowledge and were, therefore, not competent to participate as equal members in a meeting that was supposed to look at scientific issues. However, the activists successfully argued that it was they who were doing field studies and investigations about the impact of industry's marketing practices on infant feeding and nutrition. Consequently, with the support of the WHO secretariat, some of the real heavyweights among the industry's critics also found themselves in the fifth group. They included Doug Johnson and Leah Margulies (ICCR-INFACT), Andy Chetley and John Clark (OXFAM), and Anwar Fazal (IOCU).

The Meeting Dynamics

The makeup of the meeting, consisting of country delegates, professional experts, industry representatives, and activists, made the outcome of the meeting somewhat uncertain. Industry representatives were expecting a meeting where scientific issues would be discussed among professionals, with fine points debated, and a final report prepared incorporating the diversity of opinions and recommendations. The NGOs, however, wanted to go beyond the scientific agenda and instead politicize the meeting by defining a problem, identifying the victim, and pointing a finger at the culprit. In this, they were hugely successful both because they were astute and practiced in the art of confrontational politics and also because industry representatives were unprepared and inexperienced in the new politicized-confrontational environment of WHO.

The first four working groups operated smoothly because of the highly skewed representation on the part of NGOs with a sprinkling of industry representatives. Most of the people in the first four groups were generally agreed on the nature and scope of the issues and the kind of actions they wanted to propose. A large part of the time was devoted to the "fine tuning" of various proposals and learning from each other's perspective.

The fifth working group, however, was full of fireworks; the debate often turned acrimonious. This group was chaired by Dr. Fred Sai, a Ghanian on the staff of WHO's World Hunger Program. Dr. Sai was admired by both the industry representatives and the activists for the impartiality, adroitness, and sense of humor with which he deftly guided the proceedings of the meeting and brought them to successful conclusion. Nevertheless, the meeting did not lack for fireworks, rancor, and often downright rudeness. The first day of the meeting was consumed by jockeying by the opposing groups as they maneuvered to control the discussion agenda. Industry representatives argued that this workshop was not necessary given the existence of PAG 23 and ICIFI's own code. However, since the WHO agenda had already designated this topic as one of the major themes of the conference, the industry representatives insisted on a discussion of definitions of such terms as infant, infant formula, breast-milk substitutes, and so on, in order to create a common basis for further deliberations of substantive issues.

There was equally little progress on the second day when the participants tried to discuss the industry's marketing practices. There was a lot of talking but very little dialogue. The two sides were uninterested in hearing each other out, having decided, and rightly so, that they knew what the other side had to say. The industry representatives hammered on the theme that infant formula was needed, their marketing practices were responsible, and they were being unjustly accused of an irresponsible behavior. When one physician delegate from a Third World country rose to complain about the NGOs' insulting manner toward the medical profession, Ms. Margulies asked to be recognized by the chair to respond. It was a first-rate stage performance. She sprang a surprise at the delegates by bringing out a copy of Abbott Laboratories' sales manual and presented it as "evidence" of that company's aggressive promotion of infant formula in Third World countries. The manual described how to do a sales pitch to the nurses "who are the best sellers and have the most influence with the doctors; how to choose the doctor with the most sales potential." With mock sincerity, she remarked to Dr. Geara, "I am really sorry to disagree with you. I believe the medical professionals are well intentioned. But they don't realize the extent to which they are being manipulated." With that she started to read some sections from the manual and "everybody began to crack up."

During the debate, industry used Nestle's notion of shared responsibility which implied that the feeding of an infant was the joint responsibility of the industry, the doctor, and the government. According to Doug Johnson, "two sections were left out of this shared responsibility. The activists were unwilling to buy this notion because it left out the industry's critics and consumer groups, and, of course, the mother. The industry could not accept this enlarged set of stakeholders and eventually backed away from this line of reasoning. The activists also complained about some of the antics employed by industry representatives to ridicule them and otherwise disrupt their presentations. Industry representatives were supposed to have concerted "bouts of coughing and laughter" when one of their critics was attempting to say something serious. It should be stated, however, that a number of industry representatives, interviewed by the author, who were present at the meeting denied such behavior, calling it unprofessional and uncivilized. However, in the end the activists had more to show for their effort. The final recommendations of the conference, and especially those of working group #5, reflected more of the activists' perspective than they had hoped for. In retrospect, it seems the industry's position was considerably weakened because of internal dissention and inappropriate tactics.

Prior to the start of the meeting, ICIFI members had agreed to speak only through one person, Ian S. Barter, the then president of ICIFI. This was done to avoid the danger of individual members contradicting each other. However, since both Abbott Laboratories and Bristol-Myers were not members of ICIFI, there were in fact three opinions. In particular, Abbott was against mass direct consumer advertising, thereby weakening the position of the industry giant, Nestle, and other companies that used such promotion practices. This situation was further complicated because of differences in opinion as to appropriate tactics. The industry, apparently prodded by Nestle, had decided to take a hard-line, noncompromising position. This tactic, however, backfired "purely as a method of making sure that the companies got the best deal they could under the circumstances where the activists were going for the bull's eye."

The activists also faced a number of problems. A great many of them had met each other face to face prior to the Geneva meeting. However, they quickly developed a collective leadership based on key individuals' skills and assigned specific roles to different people. This collective leadership consisted of Doug Johnson, Leah Margulies, Ed Baer, Andy Chetley, and

Anwar Fazal. At the 1979 meeting, Anwar Fazal worked as a leader and, according to Andy Chetley, "played a significant role in providing leadership during the working group sessions, and in keeping everyone together and focused." Ed, Doug, Leah, and Andy looked after the possibility of organizing the movement on an international level that would strengthen various national movements and would do more than the total of all the national activities.

As a consequence, immediately after the conclusion of the conference, the activists announced the formation of IBFAN (International Baby Food Action Network). The new coalition included, among others, ICCR, INFACT, and IOCU. IBFAN would soon become a potent force in mobilizing the troops during the WHA deliberations and would play a critical role in the passage of the WHO Code. This network soon would be followed by another organization, International Nestle Boycott Committee (INBC), which would coordinate the worldwide boycott action against Nestle.

The activists were also able, to a large measure, to co-opt the WHO secretariat by maintaining a close liaison with the WHO staff. "We basically tried to get a sense of what they [the secretariat] sought to achieve from the meeting, and then work with them." This alignment of goals and rapport among WHO staff and the activists would prove extremely helpful during subsequent WHA debates and secretariat work leading to the enactment of the WHO Code.

Outcome of the Meeting

Except for the marketing working group, there was easy consensus in the other four working groups about their recommendations of what needed to be done by the world community. However, the marketing group did produce a "consensus" report containing some of the major provisions advocated by the industry's critics. The industry's views were included in the following recommendations:

- National governments must ensure the adequate supply and availability of infant food products to those who need them in ways that will not discourage breast-feeding.
- Government mechanisms should be established to ensure public dissemination of accurate information pertaining to maternal, infant, and young child feeding while discouraging inappropriate messages and publicity.
- All countries should adopt strict legal standards for preparation and use of infant formula and weaning foods as recommended by the Codex Alimentarius Committee.

The fifth working group report, however, went a long way in requiring severe restrictions or elimination of certain marketing and promotion practices that were currently used, in varying degrees, by a number of major infant formula producers. In particular, it asserted that a "regulatory action" was needed and that there was an obvious need for a "concerted and coordinated action" to regulate the proper use of breast-milk substitutes on a worldwide basis while recognizing that their actual implementation will vary from country to country. The report recommended that there should be "an international code of marketing of infant formula" and other products used as breast-milk substitutes by both exporting and importing countries. WHO/UNICEF were requested to organize the process, with the involvement of all concerned parties. It was also recommended that such a code should include at least the following points:

1.   There should be no advertising of breast-milk substitutes to the general public, and sales representatives should not contact mothers.

2.   Breastfeeding should be encouraged and supported, and informational literature or labeling should always indicate that breastfeeding is superior.

3.   Clear instructions, particularly on labeling, should be provided for proper use of breast-milk substitutes.

4.   There should be no direct or indirect promotion of breast-milk substitutes through health and health-related services.

5.   Because of the inherent conflict of interest, producers of breastmilk substitutes and of foods used as such should not be involved in any way in the staffing of health services.

6.   Sales bonuses or other incentives should not be applied to sales of breast-milk substitutes.

7.   There should be no promotional sales, and distribution of free samples to the public should be prohibited; samples supplied to physicians should be used strictly for professional examination.

8.   Bottles and teats should not be promoted.

9.   The packaging of industrially processed weaning foods, milk, and cereal products used as weaning foods should be clearly different in appearance from that of breast-milk substitutes.

10.   Whether labeling should contain information on how to use weaning foods as ingredients of breast-milk substitutes should be determined by national health authorities.

Notes

1. WHO/UNICEF, "Meeting on Infant and Young Child Feeding," Part2 — *Themes for Discussion,* p. 32.

2. John Dobbing, ed., *Infant Feeding, Anatomy of a Controversy 1973–1984* (New York: Springer-Verlag, 1988), p. 84.

13 DYNAMICS OF THE PASSAGE OF THE WHO CODE

Interplay Between Institutions and Players

The report of the WHO-UNICEF meeting was followed by a WHA resolution in May 1980.[1] The 33rd WHA resolution #33.32 requested the director-general "to prepare the draft code and submit it to the current [67th] session of the Executive Board with a view to its communication to the Thirty-Fourth World Health Assembly together with proposals for application either as a regulation in the sense of Articles 21 and 22 of the Constitution or in the form of a recommendation under Article 23, and indicating the legal and other consequences of each choice."[2] The resolution in support of the code formulation was unanimous. The passage of the WHA resolution 33.32 and the activities of the U.S. delegation expressed serious concerns about the WHO decision-making process as envisaged in the resolution 33.32. It also showed internal confusion and a lack of clear-cut vision within the U.S. government as to its position with regard to WHO and the infant formula code. Furthermore, this internal confusion — and cross-purposeness between the political and departmental operatives — would persist through the time of the ultimate passage of the code at the WHA's 34th assembly and expose the U.S. government to worldwide criticism for its negative vote on the code.

Prior to the WHA's 33rd session, the U.S. government's Inter Agency Task Force (IATF) — responsible for developing the U.S. position on the infant formula code — had prepared a number of possible amendments to the proposed code. According to Neil A. Boyer, a key member of the U.S.

delegation, "They were instituted by the Carter administration to air those amendments during the assembly session, but not to block the consensus."*
While the assembly was in session, the United States, along with 10 other government representatives, held a behind-the-scenes meeting with Dr. Tejada-de-Rivero, WHO's assistant director-general. They strongly argued in favor of the code being developed by an intergovernmental group of member states instead of the secretariat task force, the implication being that such a process would make it easier to obtain a consensus for approval. Dr. de-Rivero, however, took it as a sign of mistrust in the secretariat and refused to go along. The U.S. leadership of this group, and its opposition to the secretariat's efforts in devising a code, became public knowledge and helped coalesce strong opposition among a majority of the delegates against that position. It was seen as a power play by developing countries and their European allies. It became apparent that any and all U.S. amendments would most likely face an overwhelming defeat.

In another maneuver, which caught the U.S.-led group unprepared, the chairman of the assembly, surprisingly and without any specific request from a member government, called for the assembly vote to authorize the secretariat to go ahead with the process of code development. This move put the U.S. delegation in a quandary. While it had instructions "not to block the consensus," it did not have specific instructions to vote "yes." Since none of the U.S. amendments had ever been debated, only a "No" vote would have been consistent with the stated concerns of the U.S. delegation. However, while the assembly debate was in progress, the U.S. delegation received telephone instructions from Washington to vote "yes." According to Neil Boyer, "Since the basic purpose of the resolution was to authorize WHO to go ahead and to prepare a code, [by our vote] the U.S., more or less agreed that the Secretariat could go ahead and develop the code." The outcome left the United States empty-handed. Although it voted with the majority, no benefits were garnered from doing so. In the minds of other delegates, the secretariat staff, and news media, the United States was seen as opposed not only to the process but to the code itself. The United States did raise some eleventh hour objections about the procedures that WHO would be using in the code development process. However, these were withdrawn upon WHO assurances that extensive consultations among member states and all other interested parties would take place prior to the submission of the code for WHA approval.

---

*Interview with the author. Unless otherwise specifically stated, all direct quotes and paraphrased statements attributed to various people are based on personal on-the-the record interviews or written communications with the author.

Overview of the Code Development Process

WHO's objective for the code was that it should be: *comprehensive enough* to translate the framework of the October Meeting; *general enough* to constitute a useful international instrument common to all countries; *flexible enough* to provide principles and guidelines for countries with different economic, social, and political systems to enable them to develop their own national legislation in this matter; and *effective and clear enough* so as to emphasize the preservation of breastfeeding, and prevent the sale and promotion of breast-milk substitutes and weaning foods so as to discourage breastfeeding.

The WHO-mandated consultative process was quite elaborate. It allowed for all interested parties to provide within a specified period: written analysis, feedback, suggestions, and recommendations; face-to face and formal presentation to the WHO secretariat in Geneva on two separate occasions; formal debate of the code content and its form of adoption by the executive board; and formal debate and comments by the 33rd World Health Assembly to be followed by formal debate and vote by the 34th World Health Assembly.

Notwithstanding the extensive consultative process, the differences between the industry and its critics remained as wide at the end as they were in the beginning. From the start, the "consultative process" became problematic. The WHO drafting group was acting under two important operating assumptions. First, it did not have to account for its procedural actions or provide justification for intermediate decisions. To the WHO staff, consultation literally meant what it said. To wit, they would listen to everyone's opinions. However, there was no requirement for the WHO staff to provide various parties with a systematic analysis of how different code provisions were modified and the internal procedures that were used to iron out differences. Second, it must provide its bosses with a document that was politically palatable and the one that they would want to pass.

Therefore, the organization did what all bureaucratic organizations do; it created shortcuts to limit information inputs, restrict analysis, and increase dependence on individuals and institutions whose views were more in harmony with those of the secretariat staff and also with WHO's political constituency. As it happened, industry representatives were largely on the outs with the secretariat. The industry members, and notably Nestle, had consistently taken hard-line positions against the need for such a code, the scope of its coverage, and magnitude of monitoring and accountability. Industry representatives were also seen as harsh critics of the WHO staff during the October 1979 meeting. Thus, they were in a poor position to build alliances and make friends, which was essentially a political process. Furthermore, the tide of professional and public opinion was running against the industry's viewpoint. The problem of infant formula was being viewed to be far more serious, and the role of industry in contributing to that problem far more substantive, than the industry was willing to accept. The industry critics, naturally enough, were quite supportive of the WHO-UNICEF task force and felt that, except for the industry's obstructionist tactics and some strong arming by the United States government, the code would have been much stronger.

WHO-UNICEF, however, strongly defended the objectivity and impartiality of its information-gathering process and put the blame for the industry's complaints largely at the industry's door. Mr. E.J.R. Hayward — a senior member of UNICEF staff and the one who was intimately involved with the infant formula issue — maintained that the industry as a whole did not have a unified position and at times their individual positions were not easily reconcilable. Moreover, even when those positions could be reconciled, WHO and UNICEF had to consider the views of others (industry critics, member state representatives, experts, and so on). For these reasons, the WHO secretariat could not provide concrete commitment to any single view in the two formal consultations in Geneva or elsewhere. The only assurance that the secretariat could give was that the views of various parties would be taken into consideration.

Code Development — From the First to the Fourth Draft

In all, four drafts were prepared between February 1980 and December 1980 and were circulated for comments to all interested parties. Although subsequent drafts went through significant improvements as to specificity, in terms of substance, they remained essentially unchanged. The first draft code was submitted for comments and consultation in February 1980. It was at best a "talking paper," although it appeared that the secretariat considered it ready for ratification by the WHA in its session in May 1980. Industry members were alarmed both as to its underlying assumptions and its focus for action. They took strong objection to the tone of the draft which appeared to suggest that breast-milk substitutes were the sole cause of all evils. Furthermore, the entire focus of the draft code was on the infant formula industry and its relations with all other constituencies. The first draft code started with eight articles. Five of them covered relations with "public," "mothers," "health care system," "health care personnel," and "company employees." Articles 6 and 7 dealt with "quality" and "procedures," respectively. The last article covering "definitions" addressed 13 terms in an ad hoc manner.

Both the WHO and the industry critics had acknowledged the fact that infant mortality and morbidity were much more serious in the developing countries than in the developed and industrialized countries. With this in mind, the industry had initially supported the notion of two codes. However,

WHO's aversion to a North–South type of polarization inhibited it from considering anything but one single code. Faced with determined and strong opposition from the WHO-UNICEF staff and most other groups, industry representatives reluctantly accepted the notion of a single but flexible code. Nevertheless, they continued to dispute its equal applicability to all countries and under all circumstances.

The first draft's deficiencies and vagueness largely reflected continuing disagreements within the scientific and health care community pertaining to the reasons for decline in breastfeeding and the use of infant formula. They also reflected, in part, a desire by certain groups who would want to use the imprecise language as grounds for future interpretation and expansion of the code's coverage. The subsequent debate on the second through the fourth draft was quite acrimonious. Various articles and paragraphs of the code were contested. Even the legal authority of WHO for getting into the marketing aspects of infant formula was questioned.

How the Code Took Shape — Deliberations of the 67th Executive Board

The code had occupied the attention of the 67th executive board of WHO for two entire sessions. WHO's top leadership was expecting to receive accolades for their work in creating the fourth and final draft. In that they were sorely disappointed. It took several strong appeals and public assurances, and perhaps some private political pressure, to get the draft through the 33rd assembly and move it toward its formal approval to the 34th World Health Assembly.

An analysis of the deliberations of the 67th executive board as it debated the final shape of the code are quite revealing and offer a poignant lesson in the politicization of the WHO's decision making in the infant formula code-making process. It would indeed be a folly to assume that any decision of such international import — no matter what the scientific realm — could ever be devoid of political considerations. In the real world, politics deals with setting priorities and allocating resources. However, politics can easily become an exercise in raw power where different groups harbor deep mutual distrust and where any compromise is viewed as either immoral, illegitimate, or both.

The script for the meeting of the 67th executive board could not have been a more familiar one. There were the "good guys" — the so-called hard-liners — versus the "bad and otherwise uncaring guys" who wanted to consume interminable amounts of time in discussing and examining everything and thereby talking it to death. The "core group" in the 67th executive board consisted of "insiders," the senior secretariat staff, and professionals who were the primary designers of the code. They had the support of the top brass of WHO-UNICEF. They advocated an expeditious passage of the code in its current form because: it had been a very difficult and time-consuming task; it was badly needed to save infant lives; any apparent flaws were minor and would be easily corrected in the field by people of goodwill acting in good faith; and it required patience, prudence, and sound political judgment. Speaking for the hard-liners, Dr. Torbjorn Mork stated that "infant and child-feeding, the shortcomings of which constituted a man-made problem of global proportions, must be seen as an aspect of primary health care and in the perspective of health for all by the year 2000. The need for a code was certain."[4] He also fully endorsed "the procedure by which the draft Code had been elaborated" and rejected "the contention that the question of infant foods was a trade issue beyond the competence of WHO."[5]

The second group around the core could be described as the true believers. For this group, a strong code was an item of faith. This group was to provide unqualified support to the WHO secretariat. The third group included executive board members who supported the core group for reasons of organizational expediency. The fourth group could best be termed as political "coat-tails." For the most part, they took positions that were in accordance with their political coalitions. In the 67th executive board meetings, quite a few of the board members behaved and voted as part of well-known political coalitions. The Scandinavian countries and many European countries exhibited this pattern of behavior. The last group consisted of members who did not belong to a particular group on all issues, but instead were concerned about ensuring greater objectivity in defining the problem and seeking solutions that were both effective and viable.

The hard-liners and their supporters projected the infant formula controversy to be in the remedy and relief stage where immediate action was needed to correct the harm already done and to prevent future harm. This group advocated a solid, inflexible, and nonambiguous code to be adopted in the form of "regulation" in the spirit of articles 21 and 22 of WHO's constitution. And yet this position created a number of seemingly irreconcilable problems for them.

1. It was apparent that given largely dissimilar conditions among developed and developing countries, a single "regulatory code" would have to be extremely strict to meet the worst possible conditions in Third World nations. And yet, such a code would be almost impossible to enact because of stiff opposition from the industrially advanced countries. Recognizing that "a recommendation would have the advantage" of flexibility, the hard-liners insisted that such flexibility be limited to a "trial period with a fixed time limit" and that WHO should be requested "not only to assist" countries with code application "but also to establish an international monitoring system."[6]

2. A weak code would not force many Third World countries to go beyond paying lip service to the need for such a code.

3.   While Third World countries were willing to impose conditions on multinational corporations, they were less willing to impose restrictive conditions on themselves, or to lose their flexibility in offering differential treatment to their domestic producers of infant formula products.

The hard-liners made two strategic decisions that enabled them to get the support of the 67th executive board for the fourth draft code. They would accept the weak form of "recommendation" in the expectation that "moral force of unanimous adoption of the code" would so mobilize the world community and public opinion as to make compliance with the code almost mandatory. Secondly, they would not seek any specific standards of behavior from governments, but instead would urge them to take appropriate measures to encourage breastfeeding and improve infant and child health conditions in their respective countries.

Objective of the Fourth Draft Code

Despite the strong views of the hard-liners and their hold on the 67th executive board, the draft code did not have a smooth sailing. Numerous concerns were expressed by delegates from both developing and developed countries. Among some of the major objections raised about the fourth draft were:

1.   The code development process did not follow the procedures outlined in the report of October 1979 meeting and resolution 33.32 of the World Health Assembly. According to Dr. I. Cornaz of Switzerland, Resolution 33.32 not only called for consultations but that "conclusions had been reached by consensus." Furthermore, she asserted that "these procedures and principles were fully supported by the 33rd WHA, and there was no justification for not using or deviating from those procedures and guidelines."

2.   The aims and principles of the draft code had been shifted away from children's health to marketing of infant formula. The latter should be evaluated in connection with the former.

3.   Issues of quality control of infant foods had not been seriously addressed.

4.   Although the fourth draft referred to "international standards," it was not clear whether "the secretariat had considered that there should be flexibility to take account of circumstances in different areas" of the world.

5.   The modality of reporting, evaluation, and control, "in terms of the Code's functioning and how the results would be reported to the Executive Board and the Health Assembly," were important and would require serious attention.

6.   The secretariat had not provided any answers, despite repeated requests, "for information on the related costs of educational materials and of the programs and who would bear them, and on the opinions yielded by consultation with other organizations concerned with breast-milk substitutes."

7.   The draft code made unrealistic assumptions as to the role of public health workers and infant care that should be available in developing countries without indicating as to how WHO expected "local health authorities to accept such far-reaching responsibilities as outlined in article 6.1" given serious shortage of funds, and lack of administrative infrastructure and health care personnel.[7]

The U.S. representative, Dr. John H. Bryant, expressed his country's commitment to participate in decisions pertaining to the code. However, he also expressed serious reservations along the lines indicated above and stated that in the absence of satisfactory resolution of these differences "the United States Government would certainly wish to participate and would also feel obliged to introduce proposals for change."[8]

The persistent questioning about the definitions of the fourth draft code had put the secretariat on the defensive. At the same time, WHO was receiving a shellacking in the press which had accused the organization of using high-handed procedures and allegations and of demonstrating a lack of appreciation and sensitivity to internal criticism of the code. The stalemate moved Dr. Mahler, the director-general, to rescue the situation by addressing the executive board. He beseeched the board members not to expend too much energy in debates over small points. He was also disappointed that the board "did not see the proposals not as the Secretariat's policy, but as the high degree of participatory democracy for which the Organization had been able to provide a platform in developing protection for children throughout the world." He felt that the "draft international Code was a respectable democratic product, although not entirely perfect in content. However, what the Board should care about was the impact it would have on child health."[9] Apparently, Dr. Mahler's urging carried the day. The board unanimously adopted the fourth draft code and its accompanying resolution which were forwarded to the 34th WHA assembly for its approval.

The Final Vote

No sooner had the executive board endorsed the code than the Reagan Administration in Washington, D.C., indicated that it would vote against the adoption of the code by the WHO assembly. The vote was taken in the WHO assembly's first committee, comprising 105 countries. The vote was 93–3, with 9 nations abstaining. The two negative votes, along with that of the United States, were those of Chad and Bangladesh, but the latter two stated that their negative vote was a mistake, which left the United States as the sole dissenter. Major U.S. allies, voting in favor of the code, nevertheless stated that they would enforce the code in their countries only as far as their national legislation would permit. Among the countries abstaining, Japan was the most notable.[10] Ambassador Gerald B. Helman, in explaining the U.S. position, said that Washington "strongly supports" efforts to promote and protect breastfeeding "as the ideal form of infant nutrition." The United States also recognizes the right of a nation to "ban or regulate the marketing of harmful products." However, he maintained that "the code contains provisions that cause serious and constitutional problems for the U.S. . . . Moreover, we have serious reservations about this organization's (WHO) involvement in commercial codes and that is a central basis for our inability to support this code."[11]

The report of the committee A was presented to the fifteenth plenary meeting of the WHO assembly on May 21, 1981, with 119 members present and voting. The meeting was presided over by Dr. M. Violaki-Paraskeva of Greece who presented Document A34/42 entitled "Draft International Code of Marketing of Breast-Milk Substitutes" for the Assembly's Adoption. Pursuant to Rule 27, the president restricted both the number of delegates who wished to speak on the resolution and also the time allocated to individual speakers. This was not a major issue, however, since the outcome of the discussion was a forgone conclusion.

All the speakers advocated the adoption of the code. Their sentiments, and those of a majority of other delegates, were best summarized by the delegate of Kuwait:

> Madam President, my delegation fully approves the draft Code of Marketing of Breast-Milk Substitutes. We express our sincere thanks to the Director-General, Dr. Mahler, for his considerable and sincere efforts leading to the production of this well-conceived Code. Madam President, the drafting of this Code is an historic event for all the children of the world, and especially those of the developing world. It is the least that this Organization should do to safeguard our children's health. I wonder why any State, least of all one of those we call superpowers, should so blatantly oppose this Code and raise obstacles to our action for the health of our children. This Madam President, is a tragedy that history will record.[12]

The final vote was: numbers present and voting, 119; required majority, 60; in favor, 115; against, 1; abstentions, 3. The sole negative vote was cast by the United States. The three abstentions were Argentina, Japan, and the Republic of Korea.

The Code

The WHO-sponsored code[13] sets out the overarching goals in the global context within which it is to be viewed and implemented. These goals are specified in the preamble of the code as follows. The code:

1. Affirms the global need by stating that every child and every pregnant and lactating woman has a right "to be adequately nourished as a means of attaining and maintaining health"; and recognizes "that infant malnutrition is part of the wider problems of lack of education, poverty, and social injustice."

2. Acknowledges the unequalled superiority of breastfeeding for the healthy growth and development of infants, its significant relationship with child-spacing, and its contribution to primary health care of infants and young children; and recognizes for the first time the need for infant formula by stating that "there is a legitimate market for infant formula and for suitable ingredients from which to prepare it; that all these products should be made accessible to those who need them through commercial and non-commercial distribution systems; and that they should not be marketed or distributed in ways that may interfere with the protection and promotion of breast-feeding."

3. Allocates responsibility for improving infant mortality on various groups. It calls on governments to "undertake [in addition to promoting breastfeeding] a variety of health, nutrition and other social measures to promote healthy growth and development of infants and young children; . . . develop social support systems to protect, facilitate and encourage" breast-feeding; and "create an environment that fosters breast-feeding, provides appropriate family and community support, and protects mothers from factors that inhibit breast-feeding."

4. Affirms that "health care systems, and the health professionals and other health workers serving in them, have an essential role to play in guiding infant feeding practices, encouraging and facilitating breast-feeding, and providing objective and consistent advice to mothers and families about the superior value of breast-feeding, or, where needed, on the proper use of infant formula, whether manufactured industrially or home-prepared."

5. Considers an important and constructive role for manufacturers and distributors "in relation to infant feeding, and in the promotion of the aim of this Code and its proper implementation;" and recognizes explicitly for the first time the role of NGOs and professional groups in formulating global policies and their implementation by suggesting that "families, communities, women's organizations and other nongovernmental organizations have a special role to play in the protection and promotion of breast-feeding and in ensuring the support needed by pregnant women and mothers of infants and young children."

6.   Aims at providing "safe and adequate nutrition to infants by the protection and promotion of breast-feeding and by ensuring the proper use of
breast-milk substitutes when these are necessary on the basis of adequate
information and through appropriate marketing and distribution." The code
attempts to achieve this objective by "codifying the industry's future
"proper" conduct."[14]

7.   Is comprehensive in its scope. It applies to the marketing and distribution practices of the industry relating to breast-milk substitutes, including
infant formula; other milk products, foods, and beverages, including bottle-
fed complementary foods, which can be used either as total or partial substitute for breast milk; feeding bottles and teats. "It also applies to their
quality and availability, and to information concerning their use."[15]

8.   Imposes the following specific restrictions on the normally acceptable marketing and distribution practices of the industry. Although these
provisions are "ambiguous and inconsistent," these are the minimum required standards to be accepted by the industry and all member states.[16]
These code provisions are listed below.[17]

Information and Education

The industry is obliged to provide only "informational and educational materials" to pregnant women and young mothers which should acknowledge
the definite superiority of breast milk over bottle milk, the need for maternal
nutrition for proper and sustained breastfeeding, "the difficulty of reversing
the decision not to breast-feed," social and financial costs of using inappropriate foods, including infant formula and other breast-milk substitutes and
feeding methods. The code specifically prohibits the industry from using a
picture of a healthy baby or any text implying the superiority of bottle feeding over breastfeeding. The code permits the industry and distributors of
breast-milk substitutes to donate, with the prior written approval of local
government, informational and educational materials and equipment only to
the health care system for distribution to pregnant women and young mothers. "Such equipment or materials may bear the donating company's name
or logo, but should not refer to a proprietary product" within the scope of
the code. The code devolves primary responsibility on local governments,
ensuring that families and those involved in the field of infant and young
child nutrition receive "objective and consistent information on infant and
young child feeding."

Promotion and Advertising

The code bars the industry from advertising or other forms of promoting
breast-milk substitutes to the general public, and from gaining market share

by using "point-of-sale advertising," including distribution of free samples at the retail level, special displays, discount coupons, premiums, special sales, loss leaders, and tie-in sales. This provision does not restrict companies from establishing "pricing policies and practices intended to provide products at lower prices on a long-term basis." In order to discourage the use of breast-milk substitutes, the industry and distributors are disallowed from giving, directly or indirectly, free samples of breast-milk substitutes to pregnant women, young mothers, and their families, distributing articles or utensils that may promote the use of breast-milk substitutes; and from making direct or indirect contact of any kind with pregnant women or with mothers of infants and young children.

Role of the Health Care System

The code enjoins the industry from using health care facilities for certain purposes, including promoting infant formula and other products within the scope of the code, displaying placards or posters concerning such products, or for the distribution of materials, or for "using professional service representatives, mothercraft nurses, or similar personnel provided by the industry." However, the code permits that, instead of industry, only health workers or other community workers, if necessary, should demonstrate feeding of infant formula, whether manufactured or home prepared, only to mothers or family members who need to use it. They should be clearly informed of the health hazards of the improper use of infant formula.

The code permits the industry to donate or make low-price sales to institutions or organizations of equipment, materials, and supplies, including infant formula or similar products "whether for use in the institutions or for distribution outside them" but only for infants who have to be fed on those products and not "as a sales inducement." When the donated or low-price supplies are used outside the institutions, these should be distributed by the receiving institution only, which should ensure that enough supplies will be available "as long as the infants concerned need them." The code devolves the primary responsibility on member states to "take appropriate measures to encourage and protect breast-feeding and promote the principles of this Code, and should give appropriate information and advice to health workers in regard to their responsibilities."

Role of Health Workers

The code requires health workers in general to "encourage and protect breast-feeding" and those particularly concerned with maternal and infant nutrition to acquaint themselves "with their responsibilities under the

Code." Manufacturers and distributors should provide health workers only scientific and factual information which "should not imply or create a belief that bottle-feeding is equivalent or superior to breast-feeding."

The industry is barred from offering health workers and their family members, and the latter's acceptance of, any "financial or material inducements" promoting the sale of specified breast-milk substitutes. However, health workers are allowed to accept samples of infant formula and other breast-milk substitutes or materials for their preparation or use only "for the purpose of professional evaluation or research at the institutional level. Any contributions of fellowships, study tours, research grants, or attendance at the professional conferences, or the like" made by the industry or distributors to a health worker must be reported to the affiliate institution both by the recipient and the donor.

Role of Manufacturers' and Distributors' Representatives

The industry and its distributors are prevented from gaining market share by offering incentive bonuses or quotas set specifically for sale of breast-milk substitutes. However, the payment of a bonus is permitted if it is "based on the overall sales by a company of other products marketed by it." The industry representatives are disallowed to "perform educational functions in relation to pregnant women or mothers of young infants and young children." However, they can be "used for other functions by the health care system at the request and written approval of the appropriate authority of the government concerned."

Labeling

The code prescribes that labels on infant formula products "should be designed to provide the necessary information about the appropriate use of the product, and not to discourage breast-feeding." Moreover, labels, either on or within the container, should describe in "a clear, conspicuous, and easily readable and understandable message printed on it" and "in an appropriate language," the important message that breastfeeding is superior to bottle feeding with appropriate warning that its contents should be used only on the advice of a health worker and following the written instructions for its preparation in order to avoid health hazards. Furthermore, labels should not minimize the significance of breastfeeding either by showing a picture of a healthy baby or by using terms like "humanized" or "maternalized," implying that the packaged product is as good as the natural milk. Labels should also describe the contents of the package, its essential ingredients, directions for its use, and storage and health hazards of its improper use.

The labels on food products that can be used with modification as infant formula should carry "warning that the unmodified product should not be the sole source of nourishment of an infant. The code singles out sweetened condensed milk, since it is not considered suitable for infant feeding nor for use as a main ingredient of infant formula, and suggests that its label should not contain purported instructions on how to modify it for that purpose." The labels on all breast-milk substitutes "should also state all the following points: (a) the ingredients used; (b) the composition/analysis of the product; (c) the storage conditions required; and (d) the batch number and the date before which the product is to be consumed, taking into account the climatic and storage conditions of the country concerned."

Implementation and Monitoring

The code provides a three-tier system for its implementation. It devolves the primary responsibility for its implementation on member governments, which should take an appropriate legal or administrative action, giving effect to the principles and aim of the code consistent with their own social and legislative framework. In this process, member governments are encouraged to seek help from WHO, UNICEF, and other agencies of the U.N. system. However, the code is specific that local laws and regulations "should be publicly stated, and should apply on the same basis to all those (local or foreign manufacturers) involved in the manufacture and marketing of products within the scope of this Code."

Member governments are required to inform the director-general of WHO each year on actions taken by them in implementing the code. The code requires WHO, on request, to provide technical assistance to member governments in preparing their legal or administrative response to the code. The industry (manufacturers and distributors), irrespective of any action taken by member states, is responsible "for monitoring their marketing practices conforming to the principles and aim of the Code and for taking steps to ensure that their conduct at every level conforms to them."

Monitoring of the Code

This was the most contentious issue in the code's development. Under Article 7 of the first draft code, WHO/UNICEF were to assume the key responsibility for monitoring the code implementation and for adjudicating in disputes over its interpretation. Supporting these monitoring activities, the draft code had provided the creation of a "Central Office" for WHO/ UNICEF for collecting, archiving, analyzing, and interpreting the necessary data. However, in the final and fourth draft this provision was dropped in favor of the following three-tier monitoring and enforcement system.

The code devolves primary responsibility for monitoring its application on member countries, "acting individually, and collectively through the World Health Organization." The industry is required to police its employees and distributors for any violations of the code and the local laws implementing it.

The code requires that "nongovernmental organizations, professional groups, institutions, and individuals concerned should have the responsibility of drawing the attention of manufacturers or distributors to activities which are incompatible with the principles and aim of this Code, so that appropriate action can be taken. The appropriate governmental authority should also be informed." WHO, based on the information received each year from member states, is required to inform the assembly biennially in even years of the status of country compliance. This provision allows WHO to modify the code and change its scope if warranted by country compliance experience.

While countries are primarily responsible for implementing the code, there is no mechanism for establishing their accountability. In fact, both WHO and activists treat governments with kid gloves while putting considerable pressure on the industry for the code compliance. In the process of establishing the industry accountability, little attention has been paid to verify the extent to which Third World countries have complied with the code.

Notes

1. World Health Assembly Resolution 33.32 (1980).
2. WHO, 67th Executive Board Summary Report (EBSR), p. 306.
3. WHO, WHO/UNICEF Consultation on Development of Drafts International Code Breast-milk Substitutes, Geneva, August 1980, p. 4.
4. WHO, 67th Executive Board Summary Report (EBSR), p. 307.
5. *Ibid.*, p. 307.
6. *Ibid.*
7. 67th EBSR, pp. 311, 313, 317.
8. *Ibid.*, p. 321.
9. *Ibid.*, p. 320.
10. Victor Lucinchi, "U.S. is a Dissenter as U.N. Agency Votes Baby Formula Code," *The New York Times* (May 21, 1981), p. A.1.
11. "Who Approves Limits on Sales of Infant Formula," *The Wall Street Journal* (May 21, 1981), p. 31.
12. World Health Assembly, *Provisional Verbatim Record of the Fifteenth Plenary Meeting* Geneva, May 21, 1981; World Health Organization, Thirty-Fourth World Health Assembly: Resolutions and Decision Annexes, WHA 34/1981/REC/1, Geneva, May 4–22, 1981.
13. World Health Organization, *International Code of Marketing of Breast-Milk Substitutes* (Geneva, 1981).

14. S. Prakash Sethi, Hamid Etmad, K.A.N. Luther, "New Socio-political Forces: The Globalization of Conflict," *The Journal of Business Strategy,* Vol. 6, No. 4 (Spring 1986), 24–31.

15. WHO, *International Code,* supra note 13.

16. WHO, *WHA Resolution 34.22.*

17. WHO, *International Code,* supra note 13.

14 THE SOLE NEGATIVE VOTE BY THE U.S.: THE IMPACT OF IDEOLOGY AND DOMESTIC POLITICS

The sole negative vote cast by the United States was one of the most vivid examples of the ideological bent of the Reagan White House. In its efforts to assert ideological purity, the U.S. government was willing to sacrifice diplomatic niceties and denigrate world opinion. However, the ensuing storm of public criticism — both at home and abroad — found the administration wanting in its capabilities to articulate its position rationally. The rationale cited centered on concerns of the constitutionality of certain code provisions and the appropriateness of a noncommercial body's principal involvement in drafting a commercial code.[1] However, since the code would not affect the marketing of infant formula foods in the United States in any way that was in contravention of U.S. laws any more than in other industrialized countries that chose to vote for the code's adoption, the practical effect of the U.S. vote within the United States was inconsequential. Nor was the U.S. position ideologically pure or historically consistent. Even while the United States was arguing against the WHO vote, it was pursuing foreign policy initiatives that were pragmatically desirable but ideologically ambiguous or even in apparent contravention of U.S. laws and international conventions. To wit, it was during this era that high-ranking U.S. government officials (among them, former assistant secretary of state for Central America, Elliott Abrams), were involved in what later came to be known as the Iran-Contra scandal. The selling of arms to Iran in return for funds destined to support anti-Sandinista activities was in direct defiance of U.S. law, Congress, and public sentiment. Reason lost its moorings under a barrage

of contradictions. Shorn of political relevance, foreign policy considerations, and ideological principles, the negative vote was reduced to an
expression of bravado on the part of the inexperienced. To the world, the
United States appeared like an arrogant bully that was indifferent to the
political sensitivities of the Third World — one who was unwilling to play
ball with its friends and maintain political appearances, and did not care
about infant sickness and mortality in poorer countries.

There was indeed some validity to the U.S. government's arguments
about the flaws in the code. The United States asserted that the code was
unlikely to achieve its stated objectives because it ignored most of the major
causes of infant sickness and death in Third World countries. It was also
aimed in the wrong direction. The primary need was to improve primary
health care, hygiene, and infant nutrition — all of which were grossly ne-
glected in many Third World countries. However, to the rest of the world, a
negative vote without a positive, pro-active alternative was tantamount to
self-serving righteousness. It was a wrong response, even if the reasons had
been right. Unfortunately, in this case, the reasons advanced were equally
wrong, and "real reasons" were simply untenable. The resulting public relations catastrophe inflicted an enormous cost on the respect for the United
States in the court of world opinion.* It would undermine the U.S. efforts
to get other countries to go along with it on other international issues in the
areas of environment, public health, and economic relations.

U.S. Reaction to the 'No' Vote

At home, the vote touched off a widespread and heated response. In the
ensuing public debate, the substantive issues related to the code were all but
overshadowed by the event of the "vote" where friends and foes alike
started to examine the vote itself, to dissect the process that brought it
about, to speculate about the motives of players and decision makers, and,
above all, to cast doubt on the prudence of the procedures, activities, and

---

*It is ironical to note that the Bush Administration opted for a somewhat similar — although
less ideologically rigid — strategy of negative votes and half-hearted cooperation at the 1992
Earth Summit in Rio de Janeiro. The U.S. Administration, as reflected in a strained and split
delegation, was again seen as internally divided and lacking a cohesive environmental policy. The result was that the United State's relatively strong record of environmental protection was easily overshadowed by a negative public perception of its stance at the Rio conference. Once again, the United States stood alone in rejecting a universal code or treaty
aimed at serving obstensibly humane goals; and, again, in an embarrassing leak to the press,
the public was made aware of the last minute pleas to the White House for a reversal of the
vote that went unheeded.

deliberations involved. In short order, hearings were scheduled in the U.S. Congress by the subcommittees on international economic policy and trade, and on the human rights and international organizations of the House Foreign Affairs Committee.[2] The cast of characters was not altogether different from that of the Kennedy Hearings of 1978.* However, unlike the infant formula companies, it was the U.S. government, and more appropriately the Reagan White House, that was in the dock.

In an opening statement, Congressman Don Bonker (D — Washington), chairman of the subcommittee on human rights and international organizations, commented:

> I regret the United States' lone "No" vote at the World Health Assembly on the Code of Marketing of Breastmilk Substitutes. The United Nations is the only truly international forum for addressing issues of global concern, and the work of the U.N. agencies is invaluable in fostering international cooperation and coordination on a worldwide problem such as the infant health issue.

> The inexplicable withdrawal of the United States from the World Health Assembly's unanimous initiative on infant health is but another example of an abdication of U.S. leadership within the agencies of the United Nations. Because of this vote, we may expect the Third World or the Soviet Union to assume a larger leadership role at the World Health Organization — a role that was once exercised by the United States.[3]

In a statement filed by Dr. Derrick Jelliffe as testimony in the hearings, he attests that the code "is not an attack on the free enterprise system" but rather "a series of guidelines for consideration and modification by national governments to prevent well-documented abuses."[4] Similar sentiments were echoed by Congressman Jim Leach of Iowa, in his written statement to the House subcommittee. "I have concluded, as many of my colleagues in the House, that nothing could be more unfortunate than for our country to have come out against 'motherhood' in the Third World countries and for what many perceive — rightly or wrongly — to be nothing less than child killing: all for the sake, we are told, of Madison Avenue free speech and greater corporate profits."[5]

---

*The Kennedy Hearings served as a forum for many of the same activists who later appeared at the WHO Code hearings, including Doug Johnson and Leah Margulies. Dr. Jelliffe made a statement at the Kennedy Hearings as well, in which he asserted that the return to breastfeeding would save 10 million infant lives a year, an estimate on which he later equivocated, but which was used by the media and the activists prodigiously to attack infant formula manufacturers. Many of the same infant formula companies were represented at both hearings, including Nestle, Bristol-Myers, American Home Products, and Abbott Laboratories (represented on both occasions by Ross division president David O. Cox).

In a more dramatic gesture, Dr. Stephen C. Joseph, a senior aide at the United States Agency for International Development (USAID), had resigned from his post soon after the U.S. negative vote, along with Mr. Eugene Babb, another USAID administrator, as a protest against the U.S. position. At the time of the resignation, Dr. Joseph was deputy assistant administrator for human resources, Bureau for Development Support, USAID. In his testimony before the committee, Dr. Joseph expressed strong disagreement with the administration's and infant formula industry's contentions about the flaws in the code with regard to insufficient scientific evidence linking infant formula promotion to increases in illness and death among infants. And contrary to the infant formula industry's position, he strongly defended the need for the code to be implemented universally, that is, in industrialized countries, including the United States, and in the Third World. Moreover, he refused to backtrack from the estimate of 1 million infant deaths per year being "directly" associated with contaminated bottle feeding, arguing that there was sufficient scientific evidence to justify its credibility.

Dr. Joseph was contemptuous of the administration's argument that the code represented a conflict between "free enterprise versus government regulation." He asserted the code set "no dangerous precedents" and involved "no First Amendment rights or anti-trust positions."[6] Dr. Joseph also believed that the vote, which was designed to help the U.S. infant formula industry, would instead harm the industry's interests in foreign markets. This view was reinforced by the testimony of Dr. Carl E. Taylor, a widely recognized expert in infant health and nutrition:

> The feedback that I am getting from friends in developing countries is that the lonely U.S. vote will probably have an unexpected backlash which may support the underlying purpose of the Code. If the Code had passed quietly and unanimously, most countries would probably not have bothered to make the changes in national laws or regulations that are needed to give it binding force.[7]

Dr. Joseph recommended that Congress take specific steps to contain and reverse the damage done by the U.S. vote at WHO. These steps included: the congressional disapproval of the U.S. vote; strong USAID support for the promotion of breastfeeding in those countries that choose to implement the code; a watchdog effort to bring pressure on the administration and industry to prevent them from pressuring WHO and UNICEF to weaken support for the code; and a furthering of public debate on the health and scientific merits of the issue.

It was not surprising that the administration sought to downplay the impact of Dr. Joseph's resignation and that of Mr. Eugene Babb. Questions were raised about their motives, integrity, and even scientific competence and expertise to speak on the issues. Rumors and innuendo circulated that both Joseph and Babb may have had more personal reasons to resign pertaining to concerns about their careers within USAID.

The critics of the infant formula industry were unequivocal in their condemnation of the U.S. vote. In addition to the strategic concerns of U.S. prestige and power in international organizations, they faulted the U.S. vote on ethical and moral grounds. According to Doug Johnson:

> The United States puzzled friend and foe alike in its refusal to uphold universally held ethical responsibilities to protect the lives of children. The vote in Geneva against the WHO code leaves the American people and the world community with a terrible ambiguity. If the United States were concerned solely with legal and constitutional issues, why did it fail to publicly affirm the existence of a danger related to infant formula marketing? Why did it allow issues not related to the clear-cut health concerns to dominate both the decision and the explanation for it? Is the United States willing to support any limits on private industry to protect the public health? If infants do not deserve this special consideration, who does? And does the right to commercial free speech supersede the right to life itself?[8]

Doug Johnson also stated that in the three-week period after the U.S. vote, his organization had collected more than 16,000 news articles, editorials, and op-ed pieces from all across the United States — an overwhelming majority of which were strongly critical of the U.S. vote — and that their coverage of world press shared even greater criticism of the U.S. vote. Johnson also indicated his support for Dr. Joseph's recommendation for action and added that the United States should communicate to the industry in no uncertain terms that U.S. personnel and resources would not be used to interfere with the code's implementation and, [that the U.S.] expects the industry to abide by the code in nations that voted for it at the assembly.

Leah Margulies of the Interfaith Center on Corporate Responsibility (ICCR) struck a similar chord when she testified that, as a result of the U.S. "no" vote in Geneva, "Some U.S. citizens at the U.S. mission in Geneva were so upset about the U.S. vote and its close association with industry that they began wearing black armbands in silent protest." She also asked for remedial action in even stronger terms than Johnson when she called for the United States to "reverse its position on this code, so inform the WHO and UNICEF, and notify industry that this government expects compliance with the code."[9]

The Administration's Response

The administration, responding to its critics, provided a somewhat cryptic rationale for its negative vote. The spokesperson, Ms. Elinor G. Constable, deputy assistant secretary for international finance and development, Bureau of Economic and Business Affairs, Department of State, tried to allay the critics' fears by providing the following explanation: (1) the circumstances surrounding the U.S. vote are exaggerated, and the vote has not tarnished the U.S.–WHO relationship; (2) the United States continues to support its health-related activities and programs through different agencies, and the U.S.'s negative vote carries no negative connotations in U.S.-originated foreign relations and activities; (3) the U.S. vote did not harm U.S. foreign relations, and other countries understand the United States' position very well. In fact, the United States may have developed some "specific Foreign Relation values" by voting negatively;

> I believe that our explanations about the unacceptability of many provisions of the Code within the legal, social, and economic context of the United States are understood by most of these officials. In fact, the United States stands to gain respect for having the courage — on a well-publicized and controversial issue — to stand alone and say what it believes.

> Further, in relation to the development of new codes in the United Nations system, we think that our vote will have specific foreign relations value. Up until the adoption of the WHO infant formula code, there had never been an international code dealing with the marketing of a specific product. It is a troubling development.[10]

and (4) the *difficulties* and *deficiencies* inherent in the code itself, and the process by which it was developed, could not justify any other position but a negative vote. These difficulties and deficiencies covered a very wide range and, among other things, they included that the WHO is not a regulatory agency, WHO was not the correct forum, the code was not applicable to the United States, the procedures used in developing the code did not meet U.S. approval, and the code is/was too specific and not internally coherent — some sections contradict each other and hence require improvement. In a similar vein, Dr. Edward N. Brandt, Jr., assistant secretary for health, Department of Health and Human Services, stated: "We voted against the Code because it raised significant legal and constitutional questions, and because it would establish a precedent for the World Health Organization as an international regulatory body."[11]

The U.S. Institutional Structure and Decision-Making Process

The negative vote also led to considerable questioning as to the deliberative and decision-making processes that were used within the U.S. government to formulate this company's position with regard to the WHO vote. The final vote was criticized for being politically motivated. It was a stark reminder of the pro-industry bias of the Reagan White House and the influence of industry lobbying on such a decision. The deliberative process was faulted from the very start for its cumbersome structure, conflicting constituencies and perspectives, and changing personalities. Above all, it lacked a strong sense of what the country stood for (as against the Reagan White House) and the leadership to translate that vision into a coherent policy statement. Thus, the system produced documents that failed to provide policy guidance. Instead, they were reflective of the diverse opinions that prevailed within various agencies. Like the ice cream flavor of the day, they could be used to justify whatever final decision their current political bosses chose to take.

It is important to note that the time period covered by the U.S. decision-making process involved a fundamental shift in the political orientation of the federal government as control of the government changed from the Democratic to the Republican party. The development of the WHO Code covered the time period of about 18 months, coinciding approximately with the final year of the Carter Administration and the first five months of the Reagan Administration. The philosophical differences between the two administrations had an impact on the nature of the U.S. vote on the final WHO Code. The first procedural vote in the 33rd WHA Assembly came during the Carter Administration. Although various U.S. government agencies had expressed similar concerns on the code, the representations of the U.S. delegation at WHO were nevertheless conciliatory. This was shown by the fact that the U.S. delegation, at the last minute and on express instructions from the Carter White House, voted to go along with the 33rd WHA Assembly resolution on the code. The second vote came during the Reagan watch. The new administration came into power with a clear enunciation of a conservative, pro-business, anti-regulation, and anti-U.N. agenda. The WHO vote on the code was to provide some of the young Turks with an opportunity to demonstrate their power and affirm their ideological commitment.

Organizational Structure

Within the federal government, the responsibility for developing the official U.S. position on the WHO Code was placed with an interagency task force (IATF). It was headed by Dr. John H. Bryant, deputy assistant secretary for international health, Department of Health and Human Services (H&HS). He was officially responsible for coordinating and formulating the U.S. position on the WHO Code, and headed the U.S. delegation to the World Health Assembly each year. The IATF consisted of 36 members representing Departments of Agriculture (3), Commerce (5), Health and Human Services (12), and the State Department (16). The State Department not only provided the largest contingent in the IATF; it also had the greatest number of high-ranking officials, including at least two assistant secretaries, one deputy assistant secretary, and a senior official from USAID. IATF's composition reflected the diverse nature of medical opinion and public policy concerns on the issue. There were "the hard liners" who were adamantly opposed to the code and WHO's incursion into the regulatory arena; the moderates preferred accommodations with the world health community; while the code supporters, albeit a small minority of the membership, wanted a "yes" vote on the code.

Within IATF, the decision-making process was simple. Copies of the draft codes were circulated to IATF members for review and comments in writing. These comments were then consolidated into a combined version to be discussed by the senior member of the IATF chaired by Dr. Bryant. This forum was used to iron out interagency differences and to decide on changes in the draft code to be negotiated with the WHO secretariat. IATF also maintained a liaison with the industry and other interested parties to accommodate their viewpoints on the WHO Code.* This informal process allowed various groups within IATF to push for their positions while leaving room for compromises and maintaining the appearance of cohesiveness.

The Reagan White House, however, changed the complexion of the IATF in a number of ways — some quite subtle and some rather confrontational. The hard-liners took the code supporters to task for their lack of scientific expertise, a disregard of vital U.S. interests, pandering to the Third World, and WHO political posturing. Their prime target was the top hierarchy of USAID. According to Dr. Carol Adeleman, one of the hard-liners within USAID, IATF membership was deficient in experts with knowledge of infant nutrition. Even though the ultimate responsibility for formulating the U.S. position rested with the Department of Health and Human Services, the USAID, through its Office of Nutrition headed by Martin J. Forman, played a key role in developing the U.S. position. The apparent lack of intimate expertise on the subject of infant formula in developing countries may have given the USAID a greater influence in shaping the IATF's position that it would otherwise deserve. Dr. Adelman was equally contemptuous of Dr. Joseph's position with regard to the need for the WHO Code and his criticism of the U.S. negative vote. She also questioned the publicly stated motives of his "protest resignation" and that of Mr. Eugene Babb. Dr. Adelman suggested that public health professionals such as Dr. Joseph, a pediatrician with a master's degree in public health, predicated their views on

---

*Comments made by Mr. Neil Boyer, director of health and narcotic programs, Bureau of International Organizations, Department of State. Interview with the author. Unless otherwise specifically stated, all direct quotes and paraphased statements attributed to various people are based on personal on-the-record interviews or written communications with the author.

discrete studies that were nonrepresentative and nonscientific in their approach. Dr. Adelman comments:

> The Office of Nutrition in the U.S. AID was primarily staffed by chemists, sociologists and people with no formal or graduate training in nutrition. Martin J. Forman, Director, Office of Nutrition, USAID, and a member of IATF and the U.S. delegation to World Health Assembly, is a sociologist. There were hardly two nutritionists in the entire USAID. The IATF deliberations lacked the scientific and technical expertise in analyzing infant nutrition problems in the world and "tried to pull nutrition into the center of agriculture, health and economic planning."*

Commenting on the dynamics of IATF, Mr. E. Steven Bauer, then senior vice president of Wyeth Laboratories (now Wyeth-Ayerst Laboratories), a subsidiary of American Home Products, observed that most IATF members were quite neutral and were reluctant to indicate their position on the WHO Code in public. It was interesting to observe "how the non-political appointees took orders from their bosses." There were noticeable differences in basic attitudes between the interagency discussions which the infant formula industry had during the Carter Administration and Reagan Administration. During the Carter Administration, the interagency meetings were attended by 30 to 40 people from the Departments of Commerce, H&HS, and State, and the tone was anti-industry. Reportedly, in one of those interagency meetings during the Carter Administration, there was one State Department employee from the Policy Analysis Group "who was an outright INFACT representative" and "spouted the INFACT argument." During the Reagan Administration, interagency meetings with the industry and other groups were attended by fewer IATF members, and their attitude was more of an understanding than of hostility toward the industry.

The Critical Decision of May 1981

The first U.S. vote at the WHO took place in May 1980 under the Democratic regime of President Jimmy Carter. It was a vote in the 33rd World Health Assembly (WHA) on the procedural issue authorizing the director-general of WHO (commonly referred to as the WHO secretariat) to prepare an international code on marketing of breast milk substitutes. The events leading to the first vote were discussed previously in chapter 13. Although

---

*Dr. Carol Adelman is currently assistant administrator for Bureau for Europe, USAID. She has been one of the most ardent critics of the WHO Code and the standard bearer of hard-line criticism of the code and its supporters. See, for example, "Infant Formula, Science and Politics," *Policy Review* (Winter 1983), 107–126.

the U.S. delegations had consistently raised serious objections to the WHO Code-making process as well as its various provisions, it ended up voting "yes" on the resolution authorizing the WHO secretariat to proceed with code development. The second and more critical vote took place in May 1981 under the Republican regime of President Ronald Reagan. It was a vote in the 34th WHA meeting in Geneva on WHA resolution 34.32, approving the fourth and final draft as an "International Code of Marketing of Breast Milk Substitutes." This was also the first major expression of the new Reagan era as to its attitude toward WHO and other international organizations. The Reagan Administration had almost four months to develop its position. The IATF decision-making process had been slow, and until March 1981, no U.S. position had been developed.

In a memo dated March 12, 1981, to Mr. Elliott Abrams, the newly appointed assistant secretary for international organization at the Department of State, Neil Boyer of IATF stated: "None of the participating agencies had attempted to develop a firm agency (IATF) position for the assembly in May. But some opinions were voiced at the working level."* He further informed Mr. Abrams that the IATF meeting held on March 11, 1981, had taken the following key decision:

> The group decided to convene in formal consultations, apparently with three segments of the private sector: (1) the industry (2) the public interest groups, and (3) health professionals and academics interested in infant nutrition. Sessions of approximately three hours with each will be scheduled for April 2, 3 and 6. Those attending will be urged to direct their presentations to the U.S. position. . . .

As events would later unfold, Elliott Abrams would emerge as the point man for the anti-WHO hawks in the new administration, and a lightning rod for the pro-industry stance. Abrams was often described as brilliant, motivated, ideological, and aggressive. Like many of the other young Turks in the new administration, he was somewhat contemptuous of Congress and strongly advocated a more assertive presidency.† In July 1980, IATF invited

---

*A review of the internal documents pertaining to IATF and the events leading to the final U.S. vote leads this author to conclude that Mr. Boyer played a key role in (1) providing continuity to the IATF deliberations, (2) articulating various viewpoints, and (3) keeping open different policy options. And yet, once the final decision as to the vote was made, he was equally at ease in justifying and defending it as in accordance with the long-held concerns of the U.S. government spanning the administrations of both Carter and Reagan.

†Abrams played an important role in the Iran-Contra affair, and was accused for lying to Congress about shipment of arms to the anti-Sandanista rebels. He recently settled the case by pleading guilty to two misdemeanors of withholding information from Congress, and was sentenced on November 15, 1991, to two years' probation and 100 hours of community service.

all groups to participate in the process of developing a U.S. response to the WHO draft code both through written comments and face-to-face discussions. Furthermore, in order to develop the U.S. position, the IATF had a series of meetings with industry, industry critics, and health professionals between December 1980 and April 1981. Based on its internal discussions and meetings with the nongovernmental organizations, the IATF had developed a "paper" stating both the positive and negative positions that the United States might take on the code. On the positive side, the position paper acknowledged the importance of breastfeeding and the need to promote its use for improving infant nutrition in the developing countries. On the negative side, it emphasized that the United States, being a developed country, would not apply the code within its borders as some of the code provisions were in conflict with the constitutional provisions and social practices of the United States. Furthermore, efforts of the U.N. system in general, and WHO in particular, to regulate the private sector were unacceptable to the United States.

In all, Neil Boyer was to prepare three position papers identifying three U.S. voting options. Although there were no major differences in the three papers, they provided the rationale of all three voting options: "yes," "no," and "abstention."

Infant Formula Industry's Interaction with IATF

Representatives from the infant formula industry had two meetings with IATF. The first meeting was held during the last days of the Carter Administration on December 11, 1980. The second meeting was held on April 2, 1981, in the very early days of the Reagan Administration. It is interesting to note that there was a shift in the infant formula industry position from a grudging support to an outright rejection of the code. In July 1980, when the Carter Administration was developing its position on the second WHO draft, the U.S. industry had communicated a somewhat positive attitude toward the code and had expressed their support of its aims and objectives. For example, in a brief submitted to IATF, David Cox of Ross Laboratories stated:

> Our objective throughout the deliberations on this code should be both to protect and provide for infants. While on the one hand, there is a need to protect the mother and the infant from undue influence on the part of industry or anyone else, there exists at the same time a need to ensure the availability of adequate breast milk substitutes, supplements, and weaning foods, and instructions for their use. These goals are not mutually exclusive, but require that a balance be achieved.
>
> Given different priorities and diversity of needs of the countries of the world any code must be balanced, flexible, devoid of biases and suitable for general appli-

cation. It must be clear and realistic in the principles it sets forth if it is to achieve voluntary acceptance and support from industry, governments, or the health professionals.[12]

In a similar vein, Charles Hagen of American Home Products professed his company's strong commitment to promoting breastfeeding and infant care, and responsible use of marketing and promotional practices in Third World countries. "Our company is not opposed to marketing codes for formula which are suited to the economic, sanitary and cultural situations in particular countries, and we have worked with a number of countries in developing such codes."[13] Wayne Davidson of Bristol-Myers stated that his company was in general agreement with the recommendations concerning marketing of infant formulas which were developed at the October 1979 WHO/UNICEF Meeting on Infant and Young Child Feeding.[14]

By this time, infant formula companies (both in the United States and abroad) were reluctantly coming to the conclusion that passage of a WHO Code was a virtual certainty and that an overt opposition to the passage of the code would most likely worsen the situation. On February 25, 1981, Neil A. Boyer, in his memo to Elliott Abrams, summarized the U.S. infant formula industry position on the code as follows:

> In the end, I suspect the U.S. industry position will be: 1) to acknowledge the inevitability of adoption of a code in May and the fruitlessness of attempting to block it; 2) to acknowledge that any effort to amend the code has a high likelihood of making it worse, and to desist from that pursuit; and 3) to attempt to get the U.S. government to stand up and vote "no" even on the recommendations version, even though the vote would be 154–1, since that could be used as an excuse by the companies for paying no attention to the code.

The new Republican Administration brought forth a new mood in Washington. The U.S. business interests were jubilant, and infant formula manufacturers were no exception. The evidence of a new attitude soon became apparent. In short order, a dramatic change in the industry's previous (pre-election) position was seen. Reportedly, in a series of meetings, the industry charted a new territory, and more importantly, formulated a more concerted strategy for dealing with the new administration, IATF, and WHO. On December 30, 1980, Mr. E. Steven Bauer, then a senior vice president of Wyeth International Limited (division of American Home Products), wrote to Mr. Richard McCall, Assistant Secretary of State, Bureau of International Organization Affairs. Commenting on the fourth draft of the code, he stated:

> We have examined it [the fourth draft] carefully and found it unacceptable for many reasons. It appears that other U.S. companies have reached the same conclusion and so has the International Council of Infant Food Industries. . . . We see the WHO fourth draft code as a regrettable document with an open anti-industry bias. Its primary goal seems to be the imposition of restraints and prohibitions on industry rather than to make positive provisions for the improvement

of infant feeding, including the correct and proper use of modern, scientifically prepared infant formula.[15]

And the comments of other companies were not long in coming. According to Bristol-Myers:

Basically, . . . the final draft code is . . . anti- promotion, anti-competition, and arbitrary, . . . we continue to believe that responsible competition between companies to research, develop, manufacture and promote the safe and appropriate use of nutritionally sound infant formulas results in better products, better information, and better services, all of which provide important benefits to the health care community, to the public, to mothers and to infants. This most fundamental premise is not reflected in WHO's final draft code and its absence is viewed as one of the draft's most serious defects.[16]

The new mood in Washington even emboldened Nestle to weigh in with its advice to the U.S. government. In a letter dated January 27, 1981, Kenneth A. Lazarus, representing Nestle in the United States, wrote to Ambassador Jean Kirkpatrick, the U.S. Ambassador to the United Nations:

Much of the substance of the proposed code is sheer foolishness. For example, it seeks to (a) prohibit advertising of fully legal products; (b) prohibit distribution of infant formula samples to the medical profession; and (c) prohibit employee sales recognition bonuses by infant formula producers. The distinction between "regulations" and "recommendations" is, as a practical matter, an ephemeral one relative to American economic interests. Since a "recommended" code would likely be adopted in much of the Third World, United States companies operating in these countries would be subjected to these regulatory exercises . . . in the process, WHO would be encouraged to take a more expansive role in regulating world markets, creating the specter of an international FTC.[17]

Reportedly, on February 23, 1981, industry representatives met in Washington, D.C., to prepare their strategy for the May meeting of the World Health Assembly. They decided to launch intensive lobbying efforts in Congress. Companies met with their local representatives and senators, key members of the Reagan Administration, including Jean Kirkpatrick, the U.S. Ambassador to the United Nations. Nestle, while not a U.S. company, had many high-level connections in Washington and used them through their lawyers and other contacts.

On March 17, 1981, Elliott Abrams had a meeting with representatives of the U.S. infant formula industry where all the related issues were discussed and various options available to the United States were analyzed. This meeting was followed by another one on April 8, 1981, where IATF formally met with industry representatives. Elliott Abrams was also present at this meeting. Industry representatives urged that the U.S. government cast a "no" vote on the code.

Meanwhile, on March 27, 1981, the U.S. mission to Geneva informed the State Department that the International Council of Infant Food Industries

(ICIFI), which was dominated by Nestle, had reached a consensus agreement in Bangkok in February to the effect that its members would *not* actively oppose the code. ICIFI was reported to have been dismayed about the position taken by the three U.S. companies. In particular, ICIFI was so incensed by Wyeth's overt opposition to the code in concert with the other two companies that it was considering a move to expel Wyeth from ICIFI. On May 7, 1981, the U.S. mission further informed the State Department about a letter sent by ICIFI to all Geneva ambassadors incorporating the following:

> If the World Health Assembly resolution allows governments to retain the necessary flexibility in adapting individual provisions of the code to their own needs, given the wide variations in social, cultural, economic and political situations in different countries, the ICIFI membership will be ready and anxious to cooperate with the governments and with WHO in the translation of any proposed code into relevant national measures the governments shall deem appropriate.[18]

IATF Meeting with Health Care Professionals and NGOs

The health profession community was divided on the issue, although a number of major groups — for example, the American Public Health Association, supported the code. The meeting between IATF and health professionals took place on April 3, 1981. Present at this meeting as well, Mr. Elliott Abrams expressed his skepticism that infant formula was a dangerous drug. He further asserted that no link had yet been established (other than heresay) between infant formula marketing practices and the decline in breast-feeding. Among those questioning the need for a code were: Dr. Geroge C. Graham, director, division of human nutrition, department of international health, John Hopkins University, and Dr. Carl E. Taylor, chairman, department of international health, School of Hygiene and Public Health, Johns Hopkins University. And yet, it was the same Dr. Taylor, who along with four others, sent an "open letter," dated June 2, 1981, after the U.S. vote in Geneva, to Secretary of State, Alexander Haig, to protest that they "were deeply disappointed by the recent U.S. vote to oppose the WHO Code." They "were shocked to be told that the U.S. in supporting its vote is now suggesting that scientific evidence is lacking to relate inappropriate bottle feeding with high levels of infant morbidity and mortality."[19] Representatives from INFACT, ICCR, and other groups met with IATF on April 6, 1981, and strongly urged it to support a "yes" vote on the code. Their arguments focused on three central issues: health concerns; the potential foreign policy fallout in the wake of the vote; and the need of the code for the industry itself. They also attempted to meet with Secretary Schweiker, General Haig, and other top-level government officials, but were turned down.

U.S. Position Takes Shape

Between February and April 1981, the Reagan Administration came under intense pressure from lobbyists representing various interest groups. While the industry pressured the administration to vote "no," the NGOs and critics favored a "yes" vote and had the endorsement of their position from the majority of health professionals. The critics sensed that the industry was making an intense lobbying effort in Washington. They tried to neutralize this effort by exhorting their constituents to press their congressmen, senators, and the Reagan Administration to vote "yes" on the code.

This neutralization effort had some impact on the administration's deliberations. According to a Jack Anderson column appearing in the *Washington Post,* offering a post-WHO Code vote analysis, Elliott Abrams (then Assistant Secretary of State for International Organizations) was sent to Geneva to "persuade Halfdan Mahler, director general of the health organization, to accept two concessions" in return for an abstention vote from the U.S. delegation. These two concessions required that the code be defined as strictly voluntary, and that it apply only to infant formula, not other baby food. However, there was a complication. The bargain struck between Abrams and Mahler, which both parties were anxious to realize, was based on authorization from then U.S. Deputy Secretary of State, William Clark, who was acting secretary in Alexander Haig's absence; but Clark "had not cleared the U.S. position with presidential counselor Ed Meese."[20]

The result was that as late as May 11, 1981, Elliott Abrams had informed Mr. David K. MacDonald of the president's office that "we have reached no conclusion yet as to the position the U.S. delegation will take at the Assembly. We expect to arrive at a final decision within the next few days." And yet on May 15, 1981, Abrams made the U.S. position public through the following press release:

> After very careful consideration of this issue at all levels of the administration and with several agencies, we have determined that the U.S. delegation to the World Health Assembly must cast a negative vote on the draft code of Marketing of Breast-milk Substitutes. Formal announcement of our position will be made next week when the World Health Assembly takes up this issue. This has been a very difficult and highly emotional issue in the United States and in arriving at our decision, we have tried to take into consideration the positive and negative aspects of the draft code in the context of our own social, constitutional and legal systems.

> The code causes us serious problems — both on constitutional and legal grounds and on economic/commercial grounds. . . . Fundamentally, it would be hypocritical for the U.S. to vote in favor of a code which we could or would not wish to implement here. We, therefore, could not recommend its implementation to others.

How this final decision was made is a subject of considerable controversy. According to Neil Boyer, the U.S. delegation had gone to Geneva with an understanding to abstain on the vote. Prior to their departure, there was a high-level meeting consisting of Messrs. Elliott Abrams, assistant secretary, Department of State, Richard S. Schweiker, secretary, Health and Human Services, and top officials from USAID. They required the U.S. delegation to make a very strong statement about the ineffectiveness of the code and to abstain. A series of confidential memos and cables apparently intervened to change the intended vote from one of abstention to "no." The columnist Jack Anderson laid out the pieces of the puzzle:

> On May 1, Meese, Allen and two other members of Reagan's inner circle, Lyn Nofziger and Martin Anderson, sat down to discuss the developments in Geneva. Foggy Bottom officials learned from a National Security Council staffer that the four White House aides "have met and concluded that the U.S. should cast a negative vote on the WHO infant formula code" and that they "are not prepared to abstain even if the two conditions are met."

> What happened was that American formula makers like Bristol-Myers, Abbott Laboratories and American Home Products, had lobbied the administration against the code. They were joined by the Grocery Manufacturers of America, which feared the code might be applied to other baby food despite assurances to the contrary.

> The pressure from the companies apparently swayed the White House. U.S. officials in Geneva were put on hold.[21]

It would seem that the decision to vote "no" was taken only a couple of days before the WHO vote. It was made at the highest level in the White House and was cabled to the U.S. delegation in Geneva. The White House decision to vote "no" was a surprise even to the U.S. delegation itself. However, once the U.S. position on the code was decided, all of the administration's resources were mobilized to rationalize and justify that decision.

Notes

1. U.S. government in Geneva, May 1981.
2. *Implementation of the World Health Organization (WHO) Code on Infant Formula Marketing Practices.* Hearings before the Subcommittee on *International Economic Policy and Trade* and on *Human Rights and International Organizations* of the Committee on *Foreign Affairs,* Ninety-Seventh Congress, first session, June 16 and 17, 1981.
3. *Ibid.,* p. 4.
4. *Ibid.,* p. 173.
5. *Ibid.,* p. 2.
6. *Ibid,* p. 157.
7. *Ibid.,* p.144. At the time of the testimony, Dr. Taylor was chairman, department of international health, School of Hygiene and Public Health, Johns Hopkins University.

8. *Ibid,* p. 104.

9. *Ibid.*, pp. 99, 101.

10. *Ibid.*, p. 6.

11. *Ibid.*, p. 9.

12. Ross Labs, Memorandum to IATF, dated July 9, 1980.

13. *Op. cit.,* Hearings, p. 55.

14. *Ibid.*, p. 42.

15. Letter dated December 30, 1980, from Mr. E. Steven Bauer to Mr. Richard McCall.

16. Letter dated January 13, 1981, from Mr. Gary W. Mize, vice-president of Mead Johnson (Division of Bristol-Myers) to Mr. Richard McCall, Assistant Secretary of State, and an IATF member.

17. Letter dated January 27, 1981, from Kenneth A. Lazarus of Nestle (U.S.A), to Ambassador Jean Kirkpatrick, U.S. Ambassador to the United Nations.

18. Referred to in a letter dated May 7, 1981, from the U.S. mission to the State Department.

19. Letter dated June 2, 1981, to Secretary of State Alexander Haig, signed by Michael C. Latham, M.D., on behalf of himself and four other concerned doctors (i.e., Doris H. Calloway, Ph.D., Derrick B. Jelliffe, M.D., Carl E. Taylor, M.D., and Joseph D. Wray, M.D.).

20. Jack Anderson, "Washington Merry-Go Round: Big Business Pressure Swayed White House on Formula Vote," *The Washington Post* (Tuesday, June 2, 1981).

21. *Ibid.*

V DRIVE TOWARD RESOLUTION OF THE CONFLICT

15 NCCN: NESTLE'S CHANGE IN ORGANIZATIONAL STRUCTURE AND STRATEGIES

Nestle's experience in dealing with its critics, the news media, and the public-at-large, until this time, had been less than successful. This was especially the case in the United States where its critics had been singularly effective in launching a boycott against its products and in isolating the company from the U.S.-based infant formula manufacturers. Even Nestle's endorsement of the code — the first of any major infant formula company — was viewed with skepticism. As we pointed out earlier (in Chapter 10), of the book, Nestle lacked experience in social issues management as well as in integrated corporate management. Its highly decentralized corporate structure, localized profit centers, a deference to subsidiary managers in the areas of public and political affairs, and a strong corporate culture found the company ill prepared to handle sociopolitical issues in one country that would impact its worldwide operations.

Nestle — Switzerland first looked to its U.S. subsidiary located in White Plains, New York, for counsel in dealing with the boycott. Unfortunately, it did not receive any meaningful guidance from White Plains.* According to Saunders, Mr. David Guerrant, head of Nestle's U.S. subsidiary, followed

---

*All references to White Plains mean the head office of Nestle — USA, while references to Vevey mean the world headquarters of Nestle in Switzerland.

an "ostrich policy" toward the boycott issue. "Initially Guerrant thought that this wretched thing [the boycott] would go away. When it became obvious that it was not going to go away, he was dragged into doing something. It was a most uncomfortable situation."* Guerrant was also quite reluctant to get involved in this mess since it was going to affect his management of Nestle's operations in the Western hemisphere. According to Saunders, Guerrant wanted to run his shop without any interference from the head office. "He had the ear of the top man in Vevey." Even when Nestle — Switzerland's staff people offered advice, it was generally disregarded by the Nestle — USA management because (1) it felt capable of handling the situation without any outside advice, and (2) Nestle — Switzerland staff did not carry enough upper level management clout to demand attention from White Plains.

The public affairs staff of Nestle — USA was also not equipped to deal with the boycott issue. It was skillful in marketing and product promotion but lacked experience in dealing with political issues, issues which were "decided in the minds of people as opposed to issues related to the quality of the product." According to Saunders, within the White Plains office, there was "nobody who had any Third World experience in the area of infant nutrition or food programs. Therefore, by default, most of the response was coming from Switzerland which lacked the understanding of the American mentality and the American media." The professional staff at Nestle — Switzerland also lacked experience in developing integrated global public affairs strategies. As Jack Mongoven of NCCN puts it: "There was no one [in the Nestle's worldwide hierarchy] capable of developing comprehensive strategies that would be required to deal with one of the most complex and widespread socio-political problems that the company has ever dealt with."

Initially, Nestle — USA responded to the boycott in the United States with a public relations approach. It hired the world's largest public relations firm, Hill and Knowlton of New York. H&K tried the strategy of "truth squad,"[1] using a massive education campaign including mailing informational kits to over 300,000 clergymen all over the United States. This strategy did not succeed and the ranks of activists continued to swell. Nestle blamed H&K for lack of results and replaced it by the world's second largest public relations firm, Edelman Public Relations Worldwide of Chicago. Edelman viewed the boycott as a tangential and ephemeral issue and advised the company to ignore it and to do nothing. When this strategy also failed, Nestle — USA fired the Edelman firm. At the same time, Guerrant hired an in-house public relations expert, Gerry Raffe. According to knowledgeable

---

*Interview with the author. Unless otherwise specifically stated, all direct quotes and paraphrased statements attributed to various people are based on personal on-the-record interview or written communication with the author.

people within the company, Raffe had an excellent grasp of the American activist movement. He had also developed a good rapport with the U.S. pediatric and scientific community. Unfortunately, his tenure did not last too long. Another important person was Henry Cioka, an attorney in Nestle — USA's legal department. However, his views did not carry the day with the top management either, and he, too, was let go.

By late 1981, Nestle's top management in Switzerland realized that it must make changes in its organizational structure to take more direct control of the sociopolitical situation in the United States as it was affecting the company's worldwide operations. It was, however, easier said than done. Any substantive changes could disrupt an otherwise smoothly running and profitable business operation which the company was extremely reluctant to do both for strategic considerations and because of the personalities involved. It could also be viewed as an expression of lack of confidence in the U.S. management on the part of Nestle — Switzerland. Despite all the public hue and cry, Nestle's global operations had not suffered noticeable loss of revenue. Furthermore, many Nestle executives — both in Switzerland and in a great many Third World countries — viewed the boycott problem only as a minor irritant. They also saw it as primarily a U.S. phenomenon, conveniently forgetting the fact that the controversy originally arose in the United Kingdom and from there spread to Western Europe and the United States. Nevertheless, a continuous deterioration of the situation in the United States could not be avoided. Vevey had to make some structural adjustment in its areas of authority and reporting arrangements with the U.S. subsidiary. The company realized that the United States was the key to most of its problems with the infant formula controversy and that what happened in the United States would affect its worldwide operations.

The first step in this direction was the visit to the United States, in January 1981, by Mr. Ernest Saunders, the British-born manager of Nestle's dietetic foods division.* Saunders quickly became aware that the Nestle boycott in the United States was an absolutely new phenomenon "which could not be handled by a public relations firm, a law firm, or by a special emissary of the parent company. Instead, it must be handled in the United States by someone within the company directly; someone who was knowledgeable about the arena in which we are operating; someone who could stand up and say that if something needed to be corrected, it would indeed be corrected, and here is what we are going to do." He decided that Vevey needed a more direct presence in the United States to receive information

---

*It should be noted here that Saunders was the author of the infamous "Nestlegate memorandum," which labeled the activists as Marxists-radicals and argued in favor of using a front organization of conservative groups as a counterforce to the "left wing" activists' strength in the United States. See Chapter 7.

and advice about the local situation that was unfiltered through Nestle's U.S. subsidiary. This was a sharp break from the Nestle tradition.

Saunders recognized the need for establishing an organizational entity that would be divorced from the day-to-day operations of Nestle — USA and would instead focus almost exclusively on dealing with the boycott issue. It would have a direct line of communication to the top management in Vevey, although the new entity would work in close contact with Nestle — USA. Another factor that facilitated the acceptance of the idea of a new organizational entity was the changes in Nestle's top management in Switzerland. The new managers, notably Mr. Helmut Maucher, Chief Executive Officer, and Dr. Carl Angst, Managing Director, were not burdened with the "carryover baggage" of past activities. They were willing to take the situation "as is" and seek a solution that was divorced from the past and was oriented toward the future. The new organization was to lead Nestle into trying out new strategies and away from its previously unsuccessful approaches. Nestle also needed a "lightning rod" to divert activists' attention from its U.S. subsidiary which could then devote its time and efforts to managing the company's normal commercial operations.

Another factor critical to the success of the new entity would be the choice of the person to head the organization. Saunders, working closely with Tom Ward,* a Washington-based attorney who had represented Nestle for a number of years, identified Rafael D. Pagan, Jr., as the most suitable candidate. Pagan had considerable experience working with large corporations on social issues and was considered an expert in "crisis management." According to Tom Ward,

> Ray was known in important circles as an individual who had a certain understanding of the important and emerging socio-political issues and most specifically of the network of activist groups. This is an element of society with which the corporate world is not sufficiently experienced. Ray also knew the theater in which this drama was taking place to a far more sophisticated degree than we did. Although it is hindsight, Pagan appeared to have tremendous personal respect among a lot of church leaders. He could have walked away with their respect even if they totally disagreed with him. All those factors contributed to Nestle asking him to take on the position.

---

*Tom Ward, managing partner of Ward, Lazarus, Grow & Cihar, a Washington, D.C., law firm, had been handling some of Nestle's legal and lobbying activities in the United States for a long time. He had close ties with and confidence of Nestle's top management in Switzerland. Tom Ward was also a key figure in what came to be known as the "Guinness Affair" in the United Kingdom when he, Ernest Saunders, and a number of other people were charged with criminal violation of U.K.'s securities law. Tom Ward was subsequently cleared of all charges connected with the case. ("The World This Week: Business and Finance," *The Economist*, February 20, 1993, p. 5). See also Chapter 6.

Despite his direct involvement in the development of the concept for NCCN, Pagan did not immediately accept Nestle's offer. He took almost four months to think it over and to negotiate certain preconditions for his acceptance, including:

1.   Direct access to Nestle's top management in Vevey without any intermediary or interference. Having worked in the U.S. corporate environment, Pagan anticipated friction between NCCN and Nestle's White Plains office, which would have liked to have the authority over NCCN without the responsibility for its actions.

2.   a willingness on the part of the company to change and a commitment to a more constructive response to external constituencies.

3.   Assurances that Nestle's research and development activities with regard to infant formula and infant nutrition were sound and that its current and past infant formula marketing practices met acceptable professional and ethical standards.

4.   Assurance that he would have full freedom in selecting his own staff and an independent budget necessary to meet the challenge of NCCN's mission.

NCCN's Mission

Angst considered NCCN's top mission to be the termination of the boycott against Nestle. Saunders and Pagan, however, viewed NCCN's mission in broader terms. They believed that it was equally important that Nestle's top management develop a sensitivity to a changing sociopolitical environment and the impact of public interest groups on business operations. "The real challenge was to change the corporate culture and management mind-set so that there is acceptance of genuine and valid concerns about the company's infant formula marketing practices and that Nestle must take those concerns seriously." The third element of the mission had to do with engendering greater credibility for the company's actions on the part of its critics and other important constituencies in public health, medical-scientific, religious, and academic communities.

Organization of NCCN

NCCN was formally established as a new Nestle subsidiary on August 19, 1981. Pagan was named as NCCN's chairman and chief executive officer. NCCN was in operation prior to the August 19 date, however, sending out memorandums on NCCN letterheads as early as June 26 of that year. Pagan dates its formation back to January, 1981.[2] The establishment of NCCN evoked considerable interest in the news media and also on the part of INFACT and other activist groups. In the press release, Nestle stated:

> A central function of the Center will be to serve as an information source con-
> cerning key issues in nutrition which are of interest to professional and lay publics
> alike. . . . Another important function of the Center . . . will be to coordinate
> Nestle's grants to universities and organizations in the U.S. and developing na-
> tions for research in nutrition and the training of nutrition specialists . . . aimed
> at helping to solve the problems of under-nutrition in the world.[3]

NCCN's press release projected the company as part of the solution rather than the problem. According to Saunders, NCCN was a step in a process that attempted to "get under control and bring into a so-called im-partial forum an issue which looked as if it would escalate into a direct com-petition between a major company and a major group of adversaries with no referees assigned."

INFACT and many other activist groups did not view NCCN as a positive act and instead saw it as one more attempt by Nestle to put pressure on the activists through lobbying and expensive public relations. They reacted to NCCN's formation with cynicism, characterizing NCCN as a public rela-tions arm of Nestle rather than a policy-making instrument dedicated to the provision and dissemination of information on infant nutrition and seeking to resolve problems related to infant health. In an INFACT Update dated September 1981, readers were advised that "Nestle tries to squelch public opposition with extravagant public relations gimmickry." In the same pub-lication, INFACT called NCCN's president, Ray Pagan, a "PR whiz" and a "hired-gun coming from another corporation where he led a vicious attack on the churches' corporate responsibility office, ICCR." This was a refer-ence to Pagan's former employer, Castle and Cook, a large multinational agribusiness corporation with a reputation of playing hardball with the activ-ists. Referring to a "PR Packet" issued by Pagan's office on June 24, 1981, INFACT went on to say that "Pagan . . . with the Nestle mailing . . . goes further than mere attacks on ICCR or INFACT. He tries to undermine the scientific basis of the WHO Code. . . . In addition, Nestle's P.R. think tank is orchestrating radio and TV coverage for the Nestle study, at the same time refusing to debate publicly with the leaders of the Nestle Boycott. The Nes-tle Center also donates large research grants to the scientific community. Nestle knows that no one bites the hand that feeds it."[4]

This last point is underscored in a letter to Vevey from Louis L. Knowles, secretary of INBC, dated August 13, 1981. Mr. Knowles writes, "We are concerned that you may be spending a substantial amount of money to per-suade people that your intentions are good while your practices remain un-changed. Certainly, the creation of the 'Nestle Coordination Center for Nu-trition' in Washington indicates that you are unstinting in your spending on public relations devices in the United States."[5] Yet, in retrospect, it is the

conclusion of Nestle executives, such as Dr. Carl Angst, that NCCN's formation went a long way toward ending the boycott.

The actual structuring of NCCN was the brainchild of a triumvirate consisting of Ernest Saunders and Carl Angst, two senior officers of Nestle, and
Ray Pagan. According to Pagan, "Mr. Saunders made the decision for the
go ahead and Tom Ward and I worked on the development of the concept.
But perhaps the most influential person was Dr. Angst who had the vision
to make the right decision. Angst was the most supportive, and was the
power behind the decision." It was not an easy sell, however. Saunders and
Pagan had to overcome fierce resistance from Nestle — USA as well as the
professional staff of Nestle — Vevey before NCCN could be organized. This
antagonism toward NCCN would persist throughout its entire tenure and
manifest itself in repeated second-guessing during the annual budget process
and during the times when NCCN was making one of its frequent "innovative" and, to the head office staff, "highly risky" proposals. As is wont in
all bureaucracies where loss of power, regardless of its legitimacy, is poorly
received, Nestle — Vevey's professional staff and Nestle — U.S. managers
would constantly interject themselves in NCCN's projects and activities so
as to keep themselves involved without taking responsibility for any adverse
consequences. The fact that many of these proposals were successful and
that NCCN was increasingly gaining the trust of Nestle's top management
in Switzerland made matters only worse.

White Plains was not easily mollified with its projected relations with
NCCN. During a meeting in July 1981, Dave Guerrant, head of Nestle —
USA, insisted that "the boycott had to be his [Guerrant's] responsibility and
therefore (NCCN) would have an "operating responsibility" to him.[6] This
would cause problems and make NCCN difficult to operate even before the
new entity came into existence. Pagan communicated his frustration to
Saunders in a letter dated August 7, 1981: "I find it extraordinarily difficult
to operate effectively in the face of the conflicting signals I and my staff are
receiving from White Plains." It would seem that "operational responsibility" involved micro management of "NCCN's tactics in dealing with the
boycott groups" and directing (read *interfering*) the actions of various
NCCN executives. Pagan acknowledged that under normal circumstances a
structural concept prescribing for dual responsibility to White Plains and
Vevey, as originally suggested by Angst and Guerrant, would have made
good sense. In this case, however, "we are dealing with extremely abnormal
circumstances and with a highly unusual and emotional problem. The boycott movement is guerrilla warfare. It is an international war; its roots are
ideological and political and we are being used as a means to a political end."

NCCN was established as an independent "self-sufficient unit — an or-
gano-modular subsidiary"[7] of Nestle with its headquarters in Washington,
D.C. A great deal of thought and detailed planning went into the conceptual
design of the new entity. Considerations of external perception — political,

public relations, and even psychological — were analyzed. Organizational relationships with other Nestle entities, both in the United States and abroad, were carefully delineated. And the complex web of budgeting, reporting, accountability, and channels of communications, formal and informal, were spun out to provide sufficient redundancies within the structure to accommodate a variety of ambiguities in overlapping authority and responsibility between NCCN, Nestle — USA, and Nestle — Switzerland. Henceforth, NCCN would handle all communications pertaining to the boycott with external constituencies, including the news media, in the United States. In order to cement its working relations with White Plains and to fulfill its own mission effectively, NCCN followed a policy of open communication with White Plains. As Ray Pagan observes, "From day one we kept Guerrant fully informed of everything we were doing and sent White Plains copies of every communication we sent to Vevey and vice versa."

In designing the organization, particular consideration was given to the following:

1.   The organization's name, Nestle Coordination Center for Nutrition, Inc., was designed to convey the impression that the new entity's mandate would be to coordinate Nestle's worldwide efforts in nutrition research. NCCN was given a broader public function than a narrowly defined "anti-boycott" mission. This was done to avoid the charge that Nestle was creating a Washington, D.C.-based lobbying and public relations group to fight the boycott. Furthermore, the establishment of an independent organizational unit responsible for "creative crisis management" in the public policy arena would send a bold signal to the critics about the change in the attitude and behavior of Nestle and its willingness to negotiate with its critics in good faith.

2.   The Washington, D.C., office was located in a prestigious building. Pagan received the title of chairman and chief executive of NCCN. No expense was spared in furnishing the new office with top-of-the-line furniture and equipment. They were all intended to convey the image that the new entity was *not* a small Washington, D.C., office of Nestle's U.S. subsidiary. Instead, it *was* the eyes and ears of Nestle — Switzerland and, therefore, reflected a status commensurate with that affiliation. This was an astute psychological move. In the past, activist groups had refused to negotiate with Nestle — USA, arguing that the subsidiary had no authority to negotiate on behalf of the parent. Thus by indicating that NCCN represented Nestle — Switzerland, Pagan was able to ensure that all contacts by U.S. activists were channeled through NCCN. Existence of a direct channel of communication between NCCN and Nestle — Switzerland would convince the activists that they were dealing with an entity that had the total support of Nestle's top management in Switzerland. Furthermore, he was able to enter into discussions with leaders of major religious groups as the representative of Nestle — Switzerland and was taken seriously by them.

3.   The parent company would also approve NCCN's budget. Thus Pagan was assured of unrestricted access to Nestle's top management in Switzerland, thereby expediting the decision-making process. It was felt that a direct relationship between NCCN and the nutrition end of business in Vevey would convince the activists that Nestle was committed to improving infant nutrition in the Third World. NCCN would be willing and able to provide detailed information about the company's infant formula marketing practices in the Third World.

Staffing the NCCN

Pagan specified a lean and tightly controlled organization "which helped us in carrying out our planned strategies with maximum speed, flexibility, economy of resources and budgetary efficiency. Our budget was result-oriented and we were always able to justify it. We used specialized consultants as needed, and specialized talents from Nestle itself, whenever available." The management team consisted of five professionals. They were a closely knit group of people with backgrounds in science, nutrition, social science, politics, knowledge of the Third World, and public interest groups. Ray Pagan, as chairman and chief executive, was the top strategist. Jack Mongoven, another specialist in social issues management, was also an expert in lobbying, dealing with the federal government and elected officials, and in media relations. Dr. Thad Jackson and Dr. Thelma Jackson were experts in Third World and infant health and nutrition issues. Dr. Niels Christiansen of Sweden was a social scientist with experience in dealing with interest groups and religious communities.

NCCN's Operating Strategies and Tactics

Before formulating a comprehensive action plan, Pagan and his associates undertook a detailed analysis of the situation. "It was like planning for a major combat mission" recalls Jack Mongoven, NCCN's senior vice president. "It included an assessment of field conditions, strengths and weaknesses of our opponents, characteristics of their leaders, our own strengths and weaknesses and how they matched with those of our adversaries." In brief, it was the SWOT analysis (Strengths, Weaknesses, Opportunities, and Threats) familiar to practitioners of business strategy, wherein the internal environment's strengths and weaknesses are factored against the threats and opportunities generated by the external environment.[8] This analysis yielded some interesting insights that formed the basis for NCCN's action plans.

Nestle was dealing with "perceptions and images — not necessarily with facts alone — in a highly emotional and sociopolitically volatile environment. People had inadequate appreciation of and belief in Nestle's corporate philosophy which incorporated a "real living commitment and concern for the health and welfare of the people." Nestle, therefore, must fight "ideas with ideas" and this would require "bold and flexible new approaches that would seize the initiative on the issue." It would also require that Nestle's top management must be willing to take a "higher level of risk in terms of market share losses, top management exposure to news media scrutiny, adverse criticism and occasional public relations mis-steps; and certain tactical retreats in the marketplace of ideas and opinion leaders."

Analysis of critics' anatomy revealed that the core of the boycott movement consisted of a small group of hard-line "professional activists" operating under the umbrella of various church-related organizations. They were generally supported by socially involved clergy and lay persons who were not necessarily informed about the issues but, instead, were motivated to follow the activists' lead because they were morally concerned about the problem of poverty and hunger in the Third World.[9] In the process, NCCN also realized that church-oriented critics were uncomfortable with profit-oriented multinational capitalism — especially as it related to the development process in less dynamic, more traditional societies. Nevertheless, these critics were also willing to work with Nestle on behalf of the world's poor and to see if multinationals were as useful and as caring as Nestle claimed they were.[10] Pagan felt that the pressure of such a large group of well-meaning and sincere people in the religious community offered Nestle the best opportunity for rapprochement with its critics and to seek a constructive solution to the boycott.

Strategic Goals

NCCN's next step was to formulate a set of cohesive goals that Nestle would seek to achieve:

1. The resolution of the boycott would come about through long-term dialogue and one-on-one discussions with the critics. It would not be a question of winning or losing skirmishes but creating a viable solution that would provide all sides with definable and measurable victories. In term of the issue life cycle, Nestle would seek to put the controversy in the prevention stage where blames and mutual recriminations for past actions were avoided. Instead, all energies were directed toward the future. As for its strategic response mode, Nestle would seek an "integrated solution" where it would enter into a partnership with its critics and thereby make them an integral part of the solution. By the same token, activists would be persuaded to view Nestle not simply as part of the problem but also as an inseparable part of any solution to the problem.

2. NCCN would seek to change and reinforce those elements of the

company's corporate culture that would increase its commitment to the process of "social dialogue and action and would broaden its base of corporate social responsibility not in terms of how the company's management has traditionally seen it, but how its many external constituencies perceive it. NCCN would set in motion internal forces that would make increasing public credibility of Nestle as a socially responsible company to be an on-going activity on the part of the company with the demonstrable commitment on the part of its top management. This would involve, among other things, that Nestle would:

- avoid confrontational rhetoric at all costs;
- establish dialogue with the moderate element of the critics;
- seek an increase in public credibility and acceptance of its actions and statements; and
- establish the company's public accountability by accepting the WHO Code as the reference or standard.

Avoiding unproductive shouting matches with the company's critics would lower the confrontation intensity of the controversy. Furthermore, listening to its critics would enable the company to learn about their motives, goals, and strategies underlying the boycott. It would also open the door for the critics to listen to what Nestle had to say. NCCN would thus gain greater flexibility of action in containing the critics' boycott campaign against Nestle.

Controlling the Paper Trail

An important element of NCCN's strategy was to influence, if not control, the informational context within which discussions-negotiations among different groups would proceed from one stage to another. The strategy revolved around producing documents — for example, "talking papers" that would frame the agenda around which discussions would be held; Aide Memoire that would be used to summarize the deliberations of meetings and thereby channel future discussions towards successively narrower issues; and "Memorandum of Understanding" delineating the points of agreements already achieved. By taking initiative in generating these documents, NCCN was able to emphasize issues in a manner important to the company, keep the discussions focused, and make it difficult for the parties to opt out of agreements by resorting to differing interpretations. Mongoven was the mastermind behind this strategy. He observed:

> One element of the strategy to resolve the boycott revolved around the production
> of various documents by NCCN, ranging from the NIFAC Charter to the Mem-

orandum of Understanding, the Aide Memoire, and so forth. It was our concrete and conscious decision at the outset that, in order to overcome our (Nestle's) lack of credibility and the continuing shift of the "facts" by the activists that we would create a "paper trail" by which any objective observer could review our positions and statements against any allegations of the activists and conclude that Nestle was taking the issue quite seriously, doing the right thing and then not lying about it later.

Every document was written so that it could stand alone on the front page of the *Washington Post* and appear to be reasonable and professional to all concerned. In addition, to establish a stark contrast with the wild accusations and flamboyant publications of the activists, every document had to be treated as if it were being issued by the Sacred Rota or the U.S. Supreme Court, even down to the typefaces employed. Keep in mind that one of our key audiences to all these documents were the **reasonable and responsible** clergy.

Communication Strategy

In addition to creating and controlling the paper trail, other important elements of NCCN's media strategy included (1) reaching out to the media in a friendly and constructive manner that would avoid hostile pronouncements; (2) providing a cadre of well-trained and informed spokespersons to discuss issues and present company's viewpoint in all kinds of forums; and (3) reaching out to targeted audiences of special interest groups with communications tailored to meet their specific needs and respond to their particular concerns. The implementational details and the relative effectiveness of this strategy are discussed in the latter part of this chapter as well as in other chapters that follow.

Action Plans

NCCN's managers then turned their attention to the development of detailed implementation plans. As in the case of environmental analysis, these tactical plans were meticulously detailed, divided into various phases, types of actions contemplated, risks of failure and fall-back positions, and time-lines with milestones for achieving various targeted goals. According to Jack Mongoven, "The entire office was lined with pages and pages of charts that were repeatedly changed and discarded as participants constantly challenged various underlying assumptions, types of actions included, and their potential for success. Even now, I am amazed as to how closely we were able to implement our plans and achieve our mission given the extreme uncertainties under which we would have to operate and many of the totally new and highly risky actions that we took in order to reach out to our adversaries and persuade our top management to go along."

Another unintended but highly positive side effect of these strategy meetings, according to Mongoven, was that "they brought us all together and fused us into a strong team with tremendous mutual trust and understanding of individual members' thought processes and professional expertise." According to Thad Jackson, "Pagan's management style encouraged vigorous internal debate about alternative options. He was a visionary and a risk taker. But he never let you lose sight of your long-term goal. He would accept tactical defeats and would give you his support to pursue strategic options. He also would not accept 'no' for an answer. He was like a bull dog who would simply wear you down until you're persuaded to see his logic or were able to persuade him to see yours. But for his tenacity, we would have never been able to take some of the more innovative and highly risky measures, e.g., the establishment of NIFAC, opening dialogue with the Methodists, and getting UNICEF and MTF involved in the negotiations that culminated in the termination of the boycott." As Ray Pagan wryly remarked, "You wouldn't believe the amount of resistance that we encountered within the company — from White Plains and in Vevey. It often paled in comparison to the hostility that we faced from our outside critics." The action plan, as designed by NCCN, had four important phases.

NCCN in Action — Phase I

The first phase of the campaign focused on damage control — containment of the activists' boycott from gaining further momentum. NCCN developed a cadre of reliable and articulate spokespersons and scientists who were experienced in the nutrition-related problems in the Third World. These spokespersons were sent to meet with various church leaders and public interest groups to answer charges and criticism leveled against the company. Based on the information received from the field, Nestle realized for the first time the enormous importance of the influence and support of religious groups to the activists' boycott campaign. It was apparent that the professional leadership of the boycott movement had a very narrow power base but for the fact that they were supported by various institutions of organized church and other mainline religious institutions. The magnitude and accuracy of this information allowed NCCN to develop appropriate response mechanisms. According to Jack Mongoven, "The weakness and the strength of the church institutions are first and foremost that they have a conscience, and that once they know the truth, the pressure on them to act accordingly is very heavy. It is unlike a political opponent who could know the truth and forget it because he/she does not have the same pressure from his/her own conscience. But we felt that as a collective body, religious organizations would be forced to do what was right even when it was not politically advantageous and even if it meant a hardship for them. Because they are committed to doing that which is ethical, they became our best hope."

Thus NCCN would find in religious institutions its potentially most prom- ising groups for cooperation. At the same time, this was a risky strategy. The boycott movement was heavily dependent on the religious institutions for resources and moral legitimacy. They would put up a tenacious fight to protect their support base. The weakness of the INBC-INFACT, however, lied in the fact that they had previously taken this support for granted be- cause they had the sympathy of many a professional staff and they did not face any outside challenges. Thus they were in the enviable position of counting on this support and yet were relatively free to direct the campaign as they saw fit. It was this weakness, and the accompanied arrogance of the INFACT-INBC leadership, that would prove to be their undoing. As NCCN sought out the more moderate elements of the church, the activists bitterly fought all actions by the church leaders to hear Nestle's side of the argu- ment. In the process, they cast aspersions on the character and motives of those very church leaders whose support they sought, alienating them and also raising doubts about their [the critics'] own credibility.

NCCN in Action — Phase II

The second phase of the plan was devoted to more substantive action in wooing the moderate church groups to work with Nestle. This phase lasted from June 1981 to June 1982. In part, this strategy was predicated on the actions taken by certain church groups to independently investigate the is- sues involved in the infant formula controversy. Most notable of these was the United Methodist Church which had earlier established a task force (MTF) in April 1980, to ascertain the facts about Nestle's infant formula marketing and promotion practices and to recommend, by October 1982, to the main body of the Methodist Church whether that denomination should join the boycott.* A number of other Protestant denominations — for ex- ample, the Episcopal Church — had also appointed similar task forces al- though with somewhat different mandates. Another factor in working with moderate church groups was the very large constituency of thoughtful and concerned people among their membership who would be absolutely nec- essary if Nestle were to improve its credibility and at the same time make a dent in the activists' support base.

NCCN decided to zero in on the Methodist Church as its top priority for

---

*The working of the United Methodist Task Force and Nestle's strategies and tactics in dealing with the task force are discussed in detail in Chapter 16. "'Winning the Method- ists' — The Last Major Battleground to Enlist the Religious Community's Support of the Boycott."

reaching out to the moderate elements of the religious community. The Methodists were the largest of the mainline Protestant denominations in the United States. Moreover, as Pagan observed: "Their task force's mandate — which called for independent research and determination of the underlying issues of the boycott — offered us the most promising avenue, although some of the members of the task force were already committed to the boycott." Moreover, the MTF's mandate emphasized working with companies "to initiate and implement constructive, non-adversarial dialogue . . . to help them develop policies that (a) eliminate misuse of the infant formula products . . . and (b) implement their recognition that breast-feeding is the best method of infant feeding for most mothers."[11] Soon after its establishment, MTF, headed by Dr. Philip Wogaman, had issued an invitation to all of the major infant formula companies and their critics to present MTF with their viewpoints and positions on the issue of infant formula marketing practices and its impact on breastfeeding, infant nutrition, and health. Pagan, along with two of his key associates, attended MTF's first meeting and found "that the task force members were highly dedicated and competent people and that overall it was a balanced group. We felt we had a chance to discuss, to act, and to expect a reasonable response and support where it was justified and where we had earned it."

With the passage of the WHO Code in May 1981, Nestle immediately announced that "it supported the aim and principle" of the code and repeated its support a month later in congressional hearings in Washington. The activists rejected the statement, calling it strictly cosmetic and a public relations ploy. Nevertheless, it gave NCCN its first opening to try and seize the moral initiative away from the more radical elements among the activists. This was also the beginning of the ascendancy that NCCN would achieve over its outside critics and detractors within the Nestle's U.S. and Switzerland staff who wanted a total victory over the critics and the leadership of the boycott movement.

The dialogue alone, however, would not be sufficient. MTF demanded that Nestle: (1) accept the WHO Code as the starting and central point in resolving the infant formal controversy; (2) demonstrate its commitment to the code compliance by changing its infant formula marketing and promotion practices; and (3) provide evidence that it was doing so. Having put major emphasis on wooing the Methodists, Nestle could not do otherwise. Thus dealing with the Methodists assumed a momentum of its own. At the same time, MTF demands provided NCCN with additional avenues for putting pressure on Nestle — Switzerland to bring about necessary changes in its marketing practices and to become more open in sharing information with the company's critics and well-meaning and concerned external groups.

Nestle's top management in Vevey had already initiated a new set of marketing instructions for its field personnel. At NCCN's instigation, Nestle's Swiss management took two important steps that would eventually change the context of confrontation between the company and its critics and begin the ending of the boycott. Nestle — using NCCN as a conduit — gave the Methodists sensitive internal documents, at considerable risk of premature disclosure, which helped convince the latter of Nestle's concerns and its efforts to respond to changing conditions in the Third World. Furthermore, with dogged persuasion and cajoling of both sides, Pagan brought Nestle's new CEO, Helmut Maucher, Dr. Carl Angst, executive vice president, and other senior executives to come to the United States for a face-to-face meeting with MTF members in Dayton, Ohio. This meeting swept away most of the hidden antagonism and wariness between the two groups and went a long way toward building mutual trust and respect. The Methodists were now taking the initiative on their own by making suggestions for changes to Nestle and attempting to bring the activists and Nestle to engage in direct dialogue with each other. At their suggestion, Nestle, in March 1982, issued detailed instructions requiring unilateral compliance with the code in Third World countries that, as yet, had no codes of their own. In October, as scheduled, the Methodist task force made its recommendation that the church not join the boycott because it believed that Nestle was determined to resolve critics' legitimate concerns.

During this phase, NCCN also undertook to coordinate the company's research-supported activities in the United States pertaining to Third World health and nutrition. A number of grants were made to various universities, including Harvard, Tulane, University of Texas, and University of North Carolina. NCCN also sponsored a number of symposia in the United States on the problems of infant nutrition. All these activities helped the company in gaining visibility and credibility with the scientific community as a nutrition company which it had lacked under previously uncoordinated arrangements.

By mid-1982, NCCN was also able to put into effect an important communication strategy of reaching out to public interest groups. Formulated in early 1982, the strategy involved setting up a data base of more than 700 organizations nationally that had endorsed the boycott. These groups were to be reached "once Nestle had begun to make solid progress in building credibility" so as to create a feeling of movement which would "prepare boycott endorsers for an ending." According to Mongovern:

> We believe that any resolution [of the boycott] happening abruptly would go unheeded and untrusted by large segments of the boycott movement and that they had to be convinced that responsible people were working with Nestle on this issue and progress was taking place. By mid-1982, we began publishing a newsletter called *Nestle News* which covered Nestle's many constructive efforts in the Third World, but almost always led with a positive story about progress in resolving the boycott issue or partnership with a responsible organization, e.g., the United Methodist Task Force.

NCCN in Action — Phase III

Phase III slightly overlapped with Phase II and lasted from May 1982 to October 1984. During this phase, NCCN was to concentrate on creating the conditions that would bring about the resolution of the boycott. The tactics emphasized were the most appropriate for the remedy and relief stages and laid the foundation for the prevention stage. They included: expanding on the constituencies built during the first two phases; developing mechanisms to meet most of the legitimate and reasonable demands of one's opponents and thereby move from boundary expansion to integrative solution type of strategic response; and creating programs and activities that would move Nestle into the social responsiveness mode wherein the company becomes an integral part of building societal consensus in seeking preventive approaches to inhibit future recurrence of the problem.

One of the most important aspects of NCCN's strategy during this phase — and for that matter, in the entire existence of NCCN — was the creation, in May 1982, of an independent entity called Nestle Infant Formula Audit Commission (NIFAC). Chaired by former Secretary of State and a member of the U.S. Senate, Edmund Muskie, the commission was charged with the responsibility for ensuring compliance by the company's field offices with code provisions and the company's own instructions.* NIFAC was intended to build a foundation of trust and credibility needed for Nestle to help resolve the conflict. This was a deep and bold — as well as a highly risky — thrust that would provide the ingredients for verifying Nestle's claims and thereby answering critics' charges, cause an erosion of the rationale for the boycott, narrow the differences between the opposing groups from broad generalities to specifics of content and process, and bring about the conditions for a satisfactory negotiation of the boycott termination.

This phase also saw a significant shift on the part of important news media in favor of resolving the boycott. For example, *The Washington Post,* one of the major national newspapers that had been supporting the boycott, stated in an editorial that "Nestle had overcome the newspaper's objections to its past practices and that it was time for the boycotters to move on to other issues." In January 1983, a major union supporting the boycott, the American Federation of Teachers, voted to withdraw. The high point of this phase took place in January 1983 when, following intense negotiations and support and encouragement of UNICEF and other well-meaning groups, the

---

*The working of NIFAC, NCCN's rationale in establishing modus operandi in dealing with NIFAC, are discussed in detail in Chapter 17, "Nestle Infant Formula Audit Commission (NIFAC) - A Model for Gaining External Legitimacy for Corporate Actions."

two sides agreed to a "Statement of Understanding" outlining the progress made, the issues that remained unresolved, and the process of their resolution. The critics agreed to suspend the boycott, which became permanent in October 1984.*

NCCN in Action — Phase IV

The post-boycott termination phase was intended to instituionalize the public policy function within Nestle and to internalize into the corporate culture the lessons learned from the infant formula controversy and the boycott. Instead, it was mired in a series of internal controversies and tensions arising from the inevitable questions that arose once the boycott issue had been resolved. On the surface, these concerns pertained to the question of what to do with NCCN and its professional staff and what role they might play in the post-boycott Nestle both in the United States and worldwide. However, beneath the surface, lurked the ever-important issues of authority, accountability, staff and line, and field versus home office. Equally important were the issues of personalities and egos that were slighted and pushed aside during the heat of the controversy but were now back in full force to extract their due from the "new upstarts."

All through the year 1983, when it became apparent that the boycott controversy was nearing resolution, the company's top managers, notably Mr. Maucher and Dr. Angst, began discussions with Ray Pagan about the future of NCCN. Pagan wanted to keep NCCN in its then current form for the foreseeable future, arguing that a great deal more work would need to be done tracking the activists, networks established with various religious organizations needed to be maintained, followup activities were required on the unresolved issues, and a greater understanding must be created among various parts of Nestle's worldwide organization about social issues management. To this end, NCCN's Jack Mongoven conducted a series of training seminars for Nestle executives in Latin America. As an indication of how far the relations had improved between Nestle and its critics, Doug Johnson of INFACT participated as a speaker in some of these seminars. NCCN also argued that Nestle's operations in the United States had significantly increased through expansion and acquisitions, such as that of Carnation. Furthermore, social activism in the United States remained a very potent force, and events in the United States were likely to have a disproportionate effect on Nestle's worldwide operations.

---

*For a discussion of the negotiating process, and the strategies and tactics of the opposing groups leading to the termination of the boycott, see Chapter 18.

Nestle — USA was, however, adamantly opposed to maintaining the status quo. The company had undertaken a series of consolidation moves in its U.S. operations. In September 1984, James Bigger, formerly head of Stouffers, was made president of the entire U.S. operation* According to Jack Mongoven, "Bigger saw no need to keep it going. He frankly thought that the boycott was an irrelevance and they could have gone on without even noticing it." However, Nestle's Swiss managers felt that at least a windup phase was necessary. Moreover, Maucher and Angst wanted to take care of the NCCN folks. In true keeping with Nestle's corporate culture, they felt that Pagan and others at NCCN had done a good job and should be rewarded. Moreover, to the extent possible, they wanted to keep the expertise of these people inside the company. Maucher also agreed that the new Washington office, if it were to take place, would be a considerably scaled-down operation. Maucher was the first German manager of the Swiss company. He was also a line manager with a penchant for details and less patience and tolerance for staff activities. He had already reduced staff activity in Vevey. He had also initiated a move toward greater centralization of the U.S. operations.[18] Therefore, he was inclined to agree with Bigger's ideas about a Washington presence.

As a first step, the life of NCCN was extended for one year with the understanding that a firm decision was to be made by the end of 1985. Pagan was offered a position with Nestle in Switzerland. Mongoven was offered a high-ranking position in Nestle — USA. In addition, he would also act as a consultant to Nestle's operations in the United Kingdom. Other senior NCCN executives were made similar offers.

Ray Pagan did not want to go to Vevey. He felt that if NCCN could not be maintained, he would prefer to remain in Washington and start his own company, taking with him all the NCCN team. Nestle was willing to accommodate Pagan and make suitable arrangements that would let Pagan keep Nestle as a client — at least for a short period of time — while seeking additional clients from among the U.S. and foreign multinational corporations. Dr. Thad Jackson, however, did not want to stay in the United States. He and his wife, Dr. Thelma Jackson, decided to return to the United Kingdom. As the plans for the new company were in process, Dr. Niels Christiansen also decided to go on his own and joined another organization. Eventually, the new organization, Pagan International, was jointly formed by Pagan and

---

*During the first reorganization, Carnation was excepted from consolidation into Nestle — U.S.A. and was instead to report directly to Nestle — Switzerland. This arrangement, however, did not last long, and eventually all of Nestle's operations were brought under the control of one holding company headed by Tim Crow, the CEO of Carnation. For details of Nestle's U.S. organization, see Chapter 20. "Code Compliance by the Infant Formula Industry: The New Nestle — The More Things Change the More They Remain the Same."

Mongoven. Nestle, on its part, agreed to become a client. It also allowed the new organization to keep the old NCCN offices rent-free since Nestle was already obligated to pay the rent under its lease commitments. Pagan International also inherited, free of charge, all the furniture, furnishings, and equipment belonging to NCCN.

Interviews with various company executives would indicate that this parting of ways was less than a totally happy one. There was an inevitable clash of personalities and egos. Pagan could not adjust to the new reality requiring an acceptance of a lower hierarchical status within a large organization where he would be devoting more of his time to ongoing, somewhat routine activities. The company, for obvious reasons, could not maintain a satellite organization with direct links to the head office, and a bypass mechanism from the U.S. managers, when the new realities would not justify such an arrangement. According to many people, including even those who were very close to him, "Pagan had a highly exaggerated sense of his self-worth" and he became obstinate in flaunting it almost to the point of being a caricature. Thus his negotiating posture with the company became very confrontational. "At times, things got so bad that Angst refused to discuss things with Pagan except in the presence of others for fear that Pagan would misrepresent him or misstate any agreements made." At the same time, Nestle felt that Pagan, in his efforts to sign more clients for his new firm, was not devoting enough attention to the Nestle business.

Thad Jackson, who was not involved in the Pagan–Angst negotiations, realized that something was amiss when Nestle approached him in London and asked him to return to the United States to take care of the continuing aspects of the infant formula controversy. Jackson returned to Washington, D.C., in September 1986. He found that Pagan had dropped the ball. NIFAC had become relatively inactive and there had been insufficient followup with the religious groups and inadequate contacts with other activist groups. Initially, he operated out of Carnation's Washington office, using outside consultants when needed. Ultimately, in 1990, when all of Nestle's U.S. operations were consolidated in one group under the charge of Timm Crull, the former CEO of Carnation, the Washington office was made responsible for all public affairs activities of Nestle — USA.*

---

*After a couple of years of successful expansion, Pagan International fell on hard times. While Pagan's success with Nestle made him quite attractive to some companies, at the same time, other companies considered him too controversial. Pagan undertook a number of ambitious global projects — for which there were no clients — hoping to build a client base who would eventually support one or more of those projects. These projects created severe cash drain for the company. They also lacked support from other partners and professional staff of the firm. Thus, rather than capitalize on its strengths, issue-resolution, and public policy arena where it had built a unique niche for itself, the company diversified in a host of unrelated areas that failed to expand the client base or generate additional revenues.

NCCN's Achievements — An Assessment

The most concrete measure of NCCN's success was the termination of the worldwide boycott against Nestle's products. In a short period of three years, the company was able to achieve a remarkable turnaround in the public's perception of Nestle. In many ways, the company was seen to be leading — when compared with other major infant formula manufacturers — the reform process in the marketing and promotion of infant formula products and in implementing the WHO Code in its Third World markets. It accomplished a rapprochement with the activists, built amicable relations with large segments of the religious community, neutralized a largely hostile press, and fostered an external environment where the company's actions and pronouncements were accepted at face value, at a level similar to those of other large, high-profile companies, by the public-at-large and important segments of its varied stakeholders.

The end product — the termination of the boycott — was only the most apparent manifestation of NCCN's success. In that sense, it amply fulfilled the parent company's expectations and prime goal in establishing the new entity. However, as we mentioned in the early part of this chapter, NCCN's executives as well as some of Nestle — Switzerland's top managers saw the role of NCCN in broader terms: to institutionalize and embed the system of public affairs management and corporate social responsiveness within the corporate structure and decision-making processes, on the one hand, and integrate it into the corporate culture, on the other hand. A second issue in terms of assessment has to do with the extent to which new organisms, policies and procedures, and strategies and tactics developed by NCCN in dealing with both its internal and external constituencies lend themselves to be adapted by other companies and industries in similar situations confronting crises of public confidence. This relates, in particular, to: (1) the nature of NCCN as a satellite entity bypassing a formal, already established chain of control within the hierarchy; (2) the creation of an independent monitoring authority to investigate the company; and (3) sharing vast amounts of internal policy and operational documents with external communities and by proxy allowing them to directly influence them in its internal operational and decision-making procedures.

It would also appear that the new firm could not cope with the high life style and accompanied expenses to which erstwhile NCCN executives had become accustomed. There was a falling out between the two partners. Mongoven and two other senior PI executives went out and formed Mongoven, Biscoe & Duchin, Inc., a public affairs consulting company that has offices in Washington, D.C. The new firm has remained focused on the original concept of emphasizing conflict resolution and public policy issues involving major corporations and public interest groups. Pagan International went into bankruptcy and was eventually dissolved.

NCCN As An Operational Entity

It would be hard to argue with the success of NCCN as an operational entity within the narrow confines of its overriding mandate, which was to bring about a termination of the boycott. A purview of the entire history of the infant formula controversy and Nestle's involvement therein leads us to one inescapable conclusion: Nestle could not have achieved its avowed objective in less time or with less disruption to its other activities without the creation of an independent organization such as NCCN that would focus entirely on one issue of major corporate crisis, removed from the normal decentralized organizational structure of the company, and would allow top management of the parent company to focus its energies to this issue in a timely fashion. Only such an independent organization could flirt with potentially risky and bold measures and be able to put them into practice without the necessity of long, drawn-out, internal review processes. The crisis facing the company required (1) top management attention, (2) accurate and timely information, (3) flexible and bold responses, and (4) a willingness to put the company's name and prestige on-the-line to win the confidence of leadership of responsible external constituencies. The organizational structure of NCCN, its direct lines of communication to the parent company, and its highly adaptable and effective leadership made it possible to achieve these goals.

It is, however, in the long-term legacy of NCCN and the extent to which its lessons have been internalized in the company's corporate culture that one finds tremendous cause for concern. An analysis of the events following the termination of the boycott, including the dissolution of the NCCN, and Nestle's activities and organizational changes in effectively institutionalizing the notions of stakeholder management and corporate social responsiveness, would lead one to believe the NCCN's long-term impact on the Nestle's parent and its worldwide operations is likely to be negligible. It is not at all clear that, given another crisis of similar proportions, whether Nestle would respond in a substantively different manner. The best that can be said is that NCCN, as an ad hoc organization, achieved its avowed purpose in handling a unique crisis for the company while insulating its normal operations from severe disruptions in terms of decision-making processes and operational responsibilities of the managers of its far-flung operations.

This pessimistic prognosis points to the extreme difficulty that one faces in bringing about changes in the culture of large, bureaucratic organizations, especially when: (1) the crisis is perceived to be ad hoc, externally inspired, and not endemic to the internal core and working of the corporate entity; (2) the prevailing corporate culture and organizational structures are seen as successful in generating above-average market performance; (3) adverse consequences of normal corporate actions are long term, not easily identified with a particular division or manager, and can be blamed on external forces; (4) changes would disrupt the existing power structure within the established bureaucracies of the organization; and (5) shift in power raises important personality conflicts.

Nestle's organizational structure is hierarchical, with a strong sense of respect for authority; its corporate culture is permeated with an emphasis on technical competence and operational excellence through a set of established rules and procedures. Nestle is a company that is self-assured in its manifest destiny, proud of its traditions, and confident of the soundness of its operational strategies as evident in its long history of successful operations around the world. The company has been extremely successful in adapting to changing economic and market conditions, the forte of decentralized management structure. However, when it comes to changes in its external sociopolitical environment that affects overlapping operational jurisdictions, it is found to be inward-looking and totally unprepared to deal with radical and sudden changes in that environment. Consistent with its hierarchical organization structure and rationalistic corporate culture, Nestle believed that as long as it provides customers with quality products and uses scientific evidence in explaining its market behavior, the rest will take care of itself. Hence, Nestle used a highly legalistic rationalistic/scientific approach in its response to a social issue, which was unprecedented and had become highly emotional and moralistic in tone and had assumed an international dimension. Assured of its superior competence and self-worth, Nestle was condescending and confrontational in its style in dealing with its critics. It projected an aura of obsession with details, using it as a tool for obfuscation. Nestle's strategy of dealing with the infant formula controversy on a rationalistic basis and by professional experts and operational staff turned out to be a dismal failure.

Through NCCN, Nestle's top management was able to create a mechanism of dealing with the infant formula controversy as an ad hoc issue of major crisis proportions which must be dealt with in a unique manner. In large part, this was made possible by a transition in the top management. And yet, as a company, Nestle was unable or unwilling to recognize the fact that the emergence of the issue had just as much to do with the external environment as it had to do with the corporate response patterns.

In part this was due to the personality conflicts and shifting of organizational power that inevitably come about with the diminution of external threat and the need for the company to realign its organizational structure to handle these activities at a lower level of intensity. It is, therefore, not surprising that the moment the boycott issue was over, the future of NCCN was degenerated into petty controversies; the new consolidation of Nestle's U.S. operations reduced the Washington presence to a typical public relations and lobbying operation without the nuances of social issues management that are so inimical to some of the most forward-looking corporations. Pagan had been successful in merging both style and substance of his operations in a manner that served to enhance the status of NCCN in the eyes of the company's critics and thereby pressuring them to deal with the company through this new entity. It also served to shorten the lines of communication and expedite internal decision making. However, Pagan failed to realize the changed nature of the circumstances after the termination of the boycott and was unwilling to give up the expensive and expansive style associated with the old NCCN to conform to the new reality of the NCCN's mandate within the larger organization where style had to be submerged into the substance of a new reality of lower expectations and more routinized work. He could not convince Nestle's management of the need to keep NCCN to its existing level of operational independence. Nor could he see himself working under the authority of Nestle's U.S. managers, realizing quite accurately that his view of the public affairs function would receive a short shrift with the market-driven management that was already smarting from the fact that NCCN had previously had a free hand in its operations and had direct access to the top management in Vevey.

The company also saw the emergence into power of those professionals who had been active in the early stages of the controversy and whose failed policies had led to the new approach manifested in NCCN and its activities. The lessons learned by the company in the process of handling the infant formula controversy — that is, creation of NCCN and NIFAC — dealing with the religious institutions, notably MTF, negotiating with one's critics, and developing strategies of proactive response already seem to have been lost or seriously downplayed. For example, consider the following:

1.   In 1988, Nestle sponsored a book called *Infant Feeding: Anatomy of a Controversy 1973-1984*,[19] This book is a description of the controversy as Nestle saw it and as Nestle would like the world to see it. NCCN had strenuously fought the Nestle-Vevey professional people from publishing an earlier version of this book, contending that it would be viewed as propaganda and, given the environment, its effect would be counterproductive. Clearly, the new version is not intended to convert the nonbelievers or the knowledgeable among the external constituencies to accept Nestle's sanitized version of the events. Nor is the book likely to engage the interested lay readers who would certainly be aware of the prior negative publicity about Nestle. It is not surprising that even now, segments of the U.S. population are unaware that the boycott has been successfully settled. Moreover, there is still a significant residue of hostility toward Nestle among segments of the U.S. population and social activists, including elements of the news media and political constituencies. The only justification one can find for the publication of such a book is to re-write the corporate history for the benefit of corporate "institutional" memory and thereby demonstrate the power of the established bureaucracy within the organization.

2.   In 1988, Carnation Company, a wholly owned subsidiary of Nestle, entered the U.S. infant formula market for the first time by introducing two

infant nutrition products. However, Carnation immediately raised a storm of criticism from the medical community, regulatory agencies, and public interest groups by directly advertising to the consumer in direct contravention of every established marketing practice in the United States. It is as if the company had never heard of the WHO Code or was sensitive to the concerns of the health and medical community about infant formula marketing practices.

3. The NIFAC (Nestle Infant Formula Audit Commission) model has yet to be adopted by any other company in the industry or companies facing similar situations. However, as we have argued elsewhere in this book, the problem lies more in perception than in its implications. The very success of NIFAC and its ultimate dissolution when the boycott was terminated made NIFAC appear to be a mechanism that was "Nestle-specific" and designed by Nestle to address a particular type of problem under a unique set of circumstances. Therefore, its broader implications were unrealized and unappreciated by the larger business community.* This impression may have been further re-enforced by the fact that Nestle was unwilling or unable to persuade the new industry association, International Association of Infant Food Manufacturers (IFM), to institute similar procedures for handling industrywide complaint procedures. Instead, IFM settled for an ombudsman with little power or resources to investigate complaints independently or to enforce compliance on the part of the member companies.

Notes

1. Carolyn A. Campion, "Issue Management: How To Mobilize For An Issue And Manage It," Remarks to the Grocery Manufacturers of America Consumer Affairs Committee, Minneapolis, Minnesota. (Nestle Coordination Center for Nutrition, Washington, D.C.) September 14, 1982, p. 5.

2. R. D. Pagan, Jr., "The Nestle Boycott: Implications for Strategic Business Planning," *Journal of Business Strategy* (Spring 1986) 14.

3. Nestle Coordination Center for Nutrition, "Press Release," Washington D.C., August 19, 1981.

4. INFACT Update, September, 1981. p. 2.

5. Letter dated August 13, 1981, addressed to Mr. Arthur Furer, managing director, Nestle, S.A., from Mr. Louis L. Knowles Secretary, INBC.

6. R.D. Pagan, Jr., *Letter Addressed to Ernest Saunders,* August 7, 1981, pp. 1–2.

7. R. D. Pagan, Jr. "The Nestle Boycott: Implications for Strategic Business Planning," Working Paper #85–02, Baruch College, Center for The Study of Business and Government, New York: 1985, p. 4.

8. See, for example, Thomas L. Wheelen and J. David Hunger, *Strategic Management and Business Policy,* 2nd ed. (Reading, Mass.: Addison-Wesley, 1986), pp. 10, 39, 151.

*For a detailed analysis of the working of NIFAC, see Chapter 17 of this book.

9. R.D. Pagan, Jr., "The Future of Public Relations and the Need for Creative Understanding of the World Around Us," a paper presented at the 35th PRSA National Conference, San Francisco, California, November 8, 1982, pp. 3–4.

10. R. D. Pagan, Jr., *op. cit.*, supra note 2, pp. 12–18.

11. Paul M. Minus, "A Petition to Selected General Conference Delegates," *United Methodist Church* (Dayton, Ohio), April 7, 1980.

12. Nancy Giges and Gay Jervey, "Nestle Ups Ante for Food Mergers," *Advertising Age*, September 10, 1984, p. 1.

13. Graham Turner, "Inside Europe's Giant Companies: Nestle Finds a Better Formula," *Long Range Planning*, 19, 3 (1986), 12–19.

14. John Dobbing, ed. *Infant Feeding: Anatomy of a Controversy 1973–1984* (New York: Springer-Verlag, 1988).

16 "WINNING" THE METHODISTS — THE LAST MAJOR BATTLEGROUND TO ENLIST THE RELIGIOUS COMMUNITY'S SUPPORT FOR THE BOYCOTT

One of the major components of INFACT's strategy to mobilize public opinion against Nestle was to enlist the support of the organized religious community. INFACT had strong ties with ICCR and, through it, with the National Council of Churches (NCC). By 1980, INFACT could claim "hundreds of church groups"* among those who supported its boycott. Nevertheless, INFACT lacked the official support of one of the largest mainline Protestant denominations, the United Methodist Church (UMC), although it had already received formal endorsement of more than 30 annual conferences (state and regional bodies) of UMC, and two of its primary program agencies involved in Third World and poverty-related issues, General Board of Church and Society (GBC&S) and General Board of Global Ministries (GBGM). Therefore, INFACT and its supporters decided to get this endorsement at the UMC's General Conference in 1980. Held once every four years, this general conference acts as the principal legislative body of the church. The activists had, as yet, not succeeded in one of their foremost objective — bringing Nestle to the negotiating table to deal directly with

---

*INFACT's claims as to the number of church groups supporting its boycott have been widely questioned. It would seem that INFACT would count each and every group that advocated support for the boycott in its tally, while in fact most of these groups would belong to far fewer parent organizations. Thus, there was a considerable amount of double and triple counting.

INFACT as the official spokesperson of the boycott movement. It was felt that an endorsement by the UMC would exert strong pressure on Nestle to negotiate with the activists.

Going into the conference, INFACT and its supporters mounted a concerted effort. A defeat at the general conference would be a tremendous psychological setback in addition to a public relations catastrophe. From UMC's viewpoint, however, there was more at stake. To wit, how does UMC as a religious body develop its official position on public policy issues that (1) require the church to take a stand on ethical and social grounds; (2) are contentious both as to end and especially as to means; and (3) in the total scheme of things, must be balanced along with many other issues that are at the core of the church's theological and spiritual concerns?

Drive Toward Gaining Formal Endorsement of UMC

The effort toward UMC's formal recognition of the Nestle boycott was initiated by the legislative committee of GBC&S which by a majority vote decided to introduce a resolution [hereinafter called the majority report] at the general conference. The resolution called for UMC to join the international boycott of Nestle until such time as Nestle improved its infant formula marketing, advertising, and distribution practices in Third World countries. It further recommended that all constituent units of UMC, its program agencies, and their annual conference should cease using Nestle's products and services, including those of its subsidiaries, until the boycott ended.[1]

The general mood at the conference appeared to be in support of the boycott. However, there was some concern within the UMC leadership that a boycott may not be the best approach and that UMC should instead engage in constructive dialogue with Nestle and other companies with a view to resolving the issue. This drive was spearheaded by Dr. Paul Minus, a United Methodist scholar and a church leader. Minus had earlier initiated "a low-key non-confrontational" dialogue with Ross Laboratories which had yielded some useful results.* Encouraged by this experience, Minus and his colleagues had submitted a petition to the 1980 general conference and sent an advance copy to some 20 selected delegates and leadership of the General Council on Ministries (GCOM) for their comments. The petition, while exhorting the church "to pioneer a dialogical role in relation to the infant formula industry," recommended, among other things, that UMC set up "a

---

*Interview with the author. Unless otherwise specifically stated, all direct quotes or paraphrased statements of various people, cited here and elsewhere in this chapter, are based on personal on-the-record interviews or written communications with the author.

committee that shall work on behalf of the United Methodist Church to initiate and implement constructive, non-adversarial dialogue" with four major companies in order "to help them develop policies that (1) eliminate misuse of their infant formula products in poverty areas in this country [United States] and around the world; and (2) implement their recognition that breast-feeding is the best method of infant feeding for most mothers."[2] Minus believed that his approach had a good chance of being accepted if it could be brought to the floor for a vote. Since he was not a delegate to the general conference, he arranged through a delegate to introduce an alternate proposal [hereinafter called the minority report] to the majority report (thus named because it had won majority support in the preliminary screening process).[3]

The floor debate among the some 1,000 delegates was quite vigorous and wide ranging. Advocates of the boycott argued that "the boycott is the only way we can create some substantial change in Nestle's marketing practices."[4] They further asserted that the boycott had been initiated as a last resort and only after negotiations with Nestle had failed. The boycott was focused solely on Nestle because the company controlled over 50 percent of the world's infant formula market. In a further move to retain control of the boycott movement in the hands of the activists, the majority report urged that UMC's "boycott . . . be monitored by the GBGM and the GBC&S which would recommend to GCOM the discontinuance of the boycott at such time as the conditions had been fulfilled."[5]

Opposition to the boycott was also quite varied. A number of delegates opposed the boycott because it was unlikely that most people, even most United Methodists, would abide by the boycott. Concern was also expressed about singling out Nestle for the boycott. Others questioned the accuracy of information provided by the opposing groups.[6] In the end when the minority report was put to vote, it carried by a margin of 112 votes with 510 delegates voting for its acceptance and 398 against.

The Establishment of the Methodist Task Force

The directions of the general conference called for the establishment of a representative task force [hereinafter called the Methodist Task Force or MTF] consisting of persons from the GCOM and the church at-large, nominees of the GBGM and GBC&S, and persons with special expertise on issues pertaining to the infant formula controversy. Both GBGM and GBC&S were under intense pressure to nominate members who were involved in the boycott and, in many cases, held leadership positions within INFACT. They went so far as to ask some of the nominees to withdraw their own nominations should their (the activists') preferred choices not be accepted by the executive committee of GCOM which was responsible for the final selection of the task force membership. The opponents were equally concerned with the composition of the membership. Dr. Minus expressed this concern in a communication to GCOM's general secretary, Norman (Ned) DeWire: "It is impossible for me to overstate the importance of GCOM naming persons to the Task Force who are committed to a new style of dealing with the controversy. So embittered has this matter become that 'constructive dialogue' will not be easy to establish. But it can be done if the Task Force is composed of knowledgeable people with an irenic, determined spirit."

In supporting MTF's establishment, The Right Reverend John M. Allen, presiding bishop of the Episcopal Church, in his letter of February 12, 1981, wrote that "rampant emotionalism, often headlined in the media, has polarized the debate on infant formula rendering constructive dialogue between the participants increasingly impossible." He emphasized the need for the task force to engage in constructive dialogue, warning that "moral indignation is a virtue but never when cloaked in self-righteousness." The final composition of the task force by GCOM reflected a combination of the opposing perspectives with additional members who were not previously directly involved with the issue but added a certain measure of leadership and stature to the task force. MTF consisted of nine members under the chairmanship of Dr. Philip Wogaman, then dean of the Wesley Theological Seminary in Washington, D.C.*

The establishment of MTF turned out to be a fortuitous event. It came into existence at a time when both parties to the dispute were at complete loggerheads. According to Dr. Wogaman, the "boycott movement had reached a point of rudderlessness." The strategy of boycott, instead of being a means to an end, had become an end in itself. INBC considered any moderate position within the churches as a threat to its leadership and would try its best to keep the control of the boycott movement by maintaining a firm (uncompromising) stand on the issue.[7] Nevertheless, the specific life span of the task force to four years, and its avowedly nonconfrontational stance, created certain pressure on INBC while offering an opportunity for Nestle to break out of the stalemate and find a solution to the boycott. An even more important event had been the passage of an infant formula code by WHO in May 1981. There was also a change in Nestle's top management in

---

* The members of the original Task Force were: Ms. Anita Anand, Bishop James Armstrong, Rev. Ignacio Castuera, Dr. Connie Yerwood Conner, M.D., Mrs. Eleanor Conrad, Dr. Robert J. Kegerreis, Rev. Frances B. Manson, Dr. Paul Minus, Dr. Philip J. Wogaman (chairperson), and Dr. Norman E. DeWire as staff. In April 1982, Dr. Connie Yerwood Conner and Bishop James Armstrong resigned from the Task Force (in Bishop Armstrong's case, due to his election to the presidency of the National Council of Churches), and were replaced by Prof. Mildred Randall, a nutritionist and nursing educator at the American University, and Bishop Dale White of New Jersey.

Switzerland, creating opportunities for the company to adopt a new, more flexible approach to the issue.

Reactions of the Boycott Advocates

The activists were not at all happy with the formation of MTF or its composition. They did not view it as a manifestation of the responsibility of the Methodist Church to consider issues in a broader context of the church's overall mission. Instead, they saw MTF in narrow political terms where their opponents seemed to have gained a tactical advantage. The boycott advocates saw the task force as a Johnny–come–lately, created by the UMC "as a kind of judgment upon the boycott . . . that somehow we [MTF] were in a superior moral posture because we were questioning . . . whether a boycott itself was really moral and we were taking the high road." The activists believed that the Task Force, because of its inexperience, would be manipulated, or at least confused and overwhelmed, by Nestle and other infant formula manufacturers. However, Dr. Wogaman observed: "The real issue wasn't whether the company was using us; but whether it was using us to find a way to move into a more responsible relationship with its public, or whether it was using us as a device to maintain the status quo."

Although the activist elements in the UMC, GBC&S, GBGM, and annual conferences were involved in the selection of the task force personnel, all other activist groups (ICCR, INFACT) were ignored. The activists also viewed MTF as a divisive element within the ecumenical movement of the church. According to Doug Johnson:

> Had The Methodist Church joined (the boycott) there would have been a lot less internal problems within the churches as a whole. We would have been able to press the boycott harder. We would have gotten settlement sooner. . . . Because they were out (of the boycott) and because Nestle was stroking them, it took away the will power of the other churches to be seriously involved in the boycott as they should.

On the face of it this is a preposterous statement and would be dismissed for sheer impudence except for its source and the utter conviction with which it was made. Here is a national group of Christians whose members are voting in a democratic forum to evaluate the context and substance of a major social issue on which it was being asked to take a position. Why should the United Methodist Church not have a right to do so? And why should Doug Johnson expect that groups like INFACT be officially consulted about the composition of the task force? The only logical explanation would be to assume that they were the "right" groups. However, to do so would a priori legitimize the correctness of the strategies and tactics of those groups. It would thereby render somewhat irrelevant the very establishment of MTF and its mandate to "fact find" and "engage in constructive dialogue" with the industry.

The activists were also not "impressed" with MTF's composition and considered its members to be poorly informed and not totally unbiased. Doug Johnson characterized Dr. Wogaman as a person with a strong ego, Dr. Robert Kegerreis as an unsympathetic person who had already made up his mind, Dr. James Armstrong with having a cowboy mentality, and, Dr. Minus with ulterior motives because of his close relations with Ross Labs executives. The critics questioned UMC's very rationale for creating the task force and viewed it as a cowardly response to an urgent social problem. In the words of Doug Johnson:

> There is a strong appeal that many people like to have in avoiding confrontation. [These people] portrayed the boycott as being confrontational or being somehow radical and that they were seeking something different. The [United Methodist] church in this case has misunderstood its role as a reconciler. When you are talking about a basic battle for justice, which is what this was, where the two sides are not at all equal, either by their power or their legitimate structure, reconciliation is not the right approach to be used.

The activists viewed the role of religious organizations primarily in narrow operational terms, that is, as associates who would follow their lead and work with them in accomplishing objectives and an agenda as defined by them. They were quite willing to work with the church's subunits as long as they could wrap themselves with the moral authority of the church without at the same time having to subject themselves to some of the other values and processes that the main church bodies would consider important. As Doug Johnson observed at a later date: "We had put a lot of staff time into the MTF because we wanted the United Methodists to join us. Eventually we concluded that we did not get much real activity out of the churches anyway at the grassroots level, unless we organized it. We could organize in The United Methodist Church without the endorsement of the Committee [MTF]."

Reactions of the Infant Formula Producers

Industry representatives expressed cautious acceptance of MTF and felt that it provided a more responsible avenue for initiating and continuing dialogue. Abbott Labs, notably among the American companies, had already had an active program of consultations with religious groups. All the U.S.-based infant formula manufacturers were confronted with shareholder resolutions and other forms of protests under the aegis of ICCR. Nestle also had held a series of meetings and written communications with INBC, ICCR, and INFACT, although neither side considered these to be very fruitful. Nestle's new Washington, D.C.-based office, the Nestle Coordination Center for Nutrition, Inc. (NCCN), welcomed the formation of MTF and saw in it a possible opening to reach out and meet "more responsible" leaders of the religious community. Dr. Carl Angst, executive vice president of Nestle, Switzerland, was later to comment that MTF "was one of the most important steps" in the events leading to the end of the boycott.

MTF in Action: Phase I — April 1980 to July 1982

MTF spent the first 10 months of its existence devoted to "background fact finding" in preparation for substantive dialogue with industry. The task force took cognizance of the fact that INFACT and other activist groups had played a crucial role in raising public consciousness about the severe problems associated with inappropriate use of infant formula products among the poor of the Third World, and the role of infant formula producers' marketing and promotion activities in those countries. The Task Force also believed that "the boycott itself was a major factor in calling an important issue to the world's attention."[8] However, it also realized that the scientific and health-related field evidence was not conclusive on either side, and that otherwise objective information was often exaggerated for its propaganda effect.

At the direction of the executive committee of the GCOM, Dr. Minus prepared a background paper on the infant formula controversy. It was submitted to the task force in September 1980 [hereinafter called the report].[9] This report became the foundation document for MTF to initiate its work. The report did not contain any original research, but instead focused on summarizing critical issues, quality and quantity of available information, points of disagreements, and numerous illustrations of differing perspectives of opposing groups. This process of information gathering also included extensive contacts with activists, industry representatives, scientists and public health officials, and WHO officials, sending draft documents to them for corrections and submissions of additional material.

Most actors involved in the issue reacted positively to the report although both the industry spokespersons and critics took issue with specific aspects of the report. Not surprisingly, the crux of the complaints from the two sides was essentially similar. Typical of the industry's objections were the comments made by American Home Products:

> The background paper attempts to give a balanced picture of the differing positions of the activists and industry members, but the use of the technique of juxtaposing and giving equal weight to material of both sides we feel produces the opposite results. The critics' materials use inflammatory language designed to spur action for boycotting, picketing, fund raising and similar activities. The industry members' materials are designed to convey factual information on such

matters as nutritional composition of various infant feeds, governmental regulations in countries around the world, and the like.[10]

INFACT, while complimenting Dr. Minus "in compiling a wealth of information on what is, indeed, a complex issue," found the sourcebook biased and lacking in essential information. According to Douglas Clement, INFACT's coordinator for international research:

> The paper's design — through its pro-con format, in the choice of language and with leading questions that might be considered inappropriate to a background report — has, we feel, painted a picture of furious and heated battle among biased parties in "a reigning spirit of controversy." Such a picture is not a realistic appraisal of the honest and reasonable work of scientists, business people, health personnel, church members and social justice workers who have devoted considerable energies to this problem over the past decade.[11]

This issue became a major bone of contention. The activists simply would not be bogged down in discussing the minutiae of scientific studies. Doug Johnson informed MTF that there was a consensus among church organizations about the correlation between infant formula and infant malnutrition. Reflecting on his experience with the activists, Dr. Armstrong observed that the only way we could appease them was to accept their information "as is" and not question its veracity. "They wanted us to reject all conflicting information. They were coming to us with a rigid, often unsubstantiated, point of view. Each time they came, as we talked with them, there was a natural tendency to back away simply because of the arrogance and dogmatism that seemed to be a part of their presentation."

Meetings with the Activists and Nestle

MTF held its first meeting in October 13–14, 1980, in Dayton, Ohio. It was primarily organizational in character.* The second meeting was held in February 19–21, 1981, in Washington, D.C. This meeting was devoted to discussions with the activist groups; representatives from GBGM, GBC&S, ICCR, and INFACT met with the task force members. Ms. Margulies discussed at length the arduous and, from her perspective, essentially fruitless process of discussions that had gone between INFACT, ICCR, and Nestle over the preceding three years. She impressed on the task force members that the groups involved in the Nestle boycott had not been obstructive and belligerent in their dealings with Nestle. Instead, their current stance was

---

*MTF would hold a total of 13 meetings in three years between October 1980 and October 1983. They would be supplemented with extensive communications with the activists, infant formula producers, scientists and nutritionists, and public health workers. MTF members would also attend various WHA meetings where the infant formula issue was discussed.

the product of their bitter experience through previous encounters with Nestle. MTF also spoke with three scientists and public health professionals, Dr. Michael Latham (Cornell), and Dr. Barbara Underwood, and Dr. Peter Lamptey (MIT). These scientists had extensive knowledge of the issues involved with infant formula controversy. They essentially summarized and repeated the activists' position on the medical and health aspects of the controversy.

By the end of 1980, it had become apparent that an infant formula code would be passed by the World Health Assembly (WHA) in its May 1981 meeting. MTF would, henceforth, consider it given that all companies must comply with the WHO Code, focus its energies on resolving the differences in the interpretation of the WHO Code provisions among opposing groups, and develop an institutional mechanism that would facilitate monitoring and compliance with the code provisions by the infant formula manufacturers.

MTF had its first formal meeting with Nestle in Indianapolis on June 19, 1981. Nestle was represented by three members of its Washington, D.C., office, Nestle Coordination Center for Nutrition, Inc. (NCCN). They were: Mr. Rafael Pagan, chairman and chief executive officer, Dr. Thad Jackson, and Dr. Niels Christiansen. Nestle's representatives indicated that the company was well sensitized to the infant formula issue and was moving expeditiously to modify company's marketing practices. They asserted that Nestle was already in substantial compliance with the WHO Code through its own marketing code. The company had stopped all mass advertising, eliminated all direct contact with mothers, and had stopped giving free samples directly to mothers. Nestle still had certain difficulties with the WHO Code, particularly with regard to its universal application in all nations. Finally, Nestle's representatives reported their difficulties in establishing communication with INBC and welcomed MTF's initiative in facilitating such a dialogue between the company and the boycotting organizations.

In another visit to Nestle's Vevey office by Phil Wogaman in May 1981 (during his visit to a WHA meeting), Wogaman indicated to Nestle that the United Methodist Church had scheduled their annual meeting at the Stouffer Dayton Plaza Hotel (a Nestle subsidiary), but that they would shift the meeting elsewhere if Nestle indicated its reluctance to support the WHO Code which was to be voted by WHA in May 1981.[12] However, immediately after the passage of the WHO Code, Nestle became the first company to announce its intention to comply with the WHO Code. This commitment was further confirmed by a Nestle representative, Dr. Thad Jackson, in a congressional hearing[13] and also through written assurances to the task force.[14] Based on these assurances, GCOM decided to hold its annual meeting on October 27–31, 1981 at the Dayton Stouffer hotel, as previously scheduled.

MTF met with Doug Johnson, chairperson of INFACT, at its fourth meeting in Dayton, Ohio, on September 25–26, 1981. Johnson informed MTF that the Nestle boycott would continue until the company agreed to comply fully with the WHO Code and to subject its marketing practices to independent public scrutiny. INFACT and INBC had also insisted that the company meet INFACT's four demands prior to the adoption of the WHO Code: Nestle must stop (1) direct advertising of infant formula to customers; (2) direct distribution of free samples to hospitals, clinics and homes of newborns; (3) the use of Company's "milk nurses"; and (4) promotion to the health professions through health care institutions. He further argued that the WHO Code provided only the "minimal threshold" and that their demands of Nestle were only "minimal standards." Responding to MTF's question, Doug Johnson defended the use of emotionally laden graphics in their boycott literature as a legitimate way to enlist grassroot support to their cause. It would seem that rather than holding themselves to a higher standard of ethical and professional behavior, the activists were justifying an equal or even lower standard of ethical behavior on their part because they were fighting for a just and moral cause.

Nestle, however, would not get any reprieve even if it were to meet INFACT's demands. According to Doug Johnson, Nestle would have to individually satisfy the concerns of various member churches, stating that the boycott organization was a "covenant" in which "each member holds onto its own power and responsibility (but) a joint negotiating base with the company. Most of the member churches have their own boycott monitoring team, with the burden of proof being on Nestle."[15] Such an approach would leave INFACT holding all the cards while absolving it of any responsibility for its actions.

This meeting was also the occasion for the second formal dialogue with Nestle representatives that took place on September 25, 1981. NCCN presented to the MTF an "Aide Memoire" detailing the actions that it was taking in implementing the code. The company also provided MTF with information concerning its discussions with a number of countries which were intending to implement the WHO Code with a view to assisting them in clarifying and interpreting various provisions of the WHO Code.[16] In this Aide Memoire, Nestle made a novel suggestion by asking the task force to consider establishing a "hot line" between MTF and Nestle "to serve as a conduit for grievances from members of that church as well as from other groups [in different countries] to the company." Nestle felt that "this procedure would be a first step in establishing a constructive dialogue between the company and its critics to address concrete, definable matters."[17]

MTF Dialogue with the U.S.-Based Companies

The MTF had a series of formal and informal meetings with the three major U.S. infant formula manufacturers: American Home Products (Wyeth Lab), Abbott Laboratories (Ross Lab), and Bristol-Myers (Mead Johnson). The first of the formal meetings was held on June 19–20, 1981, in Indianapolis. It focused on the companies' compliance with the WHO Code. All three companies stated that they had their own marketing codes in place which were self-regulated and self-monitored. The WHO Code provisions were viewed as unacceptable or unrealistic by all three U.S. firms, whose representatives characterized them as either "punitive in nature" and "restrictive in its intent" (David Cox, Tom McCulloch of Abbott Laboratories); "restrictive on marketing" (Steve Bauer of American Home Products), or "defective in prescribing a universal set of values to complex problems" and "restrictive and negative in nature" (Gary Mize of Bristol-Myers). The second major meeting took place in Washington, D.C., on June 23–24, 1982, and evidenced a more open attitude on the part of the three U.S. companies than the prior year's meeting. However, in reviewing their respective internal codes, the companies indicated that there were specific areas in which they intended to follow practices contrary to the WHO Code provisions. These areas dealt primarily with the use of gift samples, sales incentives and bonuses, and the right of companies to deal directly with health professionals.

MTF First Phase Completion — Recommendations to GCOM

Under the general conference directive MTF made an interim report to GCOM in October 1981.[18] It recommended that GCOM accept the code "as the best normative frame of reference for dealing with the marketing of breast-milk substitutes" and "to seek its legal implementation in all countries." The task force found that Nestle had supported the aims and provisions of the code and "has taken positive, concrete steps to assist in the implementation of the code" and that "on the few points where company policy is not currently in total conformity with the detailed recommendations, adjustments are being made voluntarily by the Company and are being implemented as quickly as feasible."[19] Later in July 1982, in response to the 1980 General Conference Directive for Definite Recommendations at the mid-point of the quadrennium, the MTF specifically recommended that The UMC should not join in the boycott. Furthermore, it recommended that GCOM's constituent bodies and program agencies, which were already involved in the boycott, should be asked to reconsider their position.[20]

The task force acknowledged that while a boycott was "morally permissible as a technique to effect change," it should be used with extreme constraint because it was at best a crude instrument. Once initiated on a broad scale, it was not easily modified and controlled by the sponsor. It portrayed the boycotted companies as evil incarnate and others as relatively pure when in fact the reality was usually more ambiguous. A total boycott could hurt many innocent people. A religious institution, such as the United Methodist Church, should be particularly sensitive about its support of a boycott, and such support should be "deliberate, theologically (morally) principled, and subject to its own responsible decision making."[21]

Complete compliance with the WHO Code on the part of American infant formula manufacturers remained a major objective of the Task Force. However, based on the progress that had been since made toward this end, MTF recommended to the GCOM in October of 1982 that dialogue with the U.S. firms should continue, and GCOM approved all the recommendations from MTF.

MTF in Action: Phase II — August 1982 to May 1984

The Task Force's response to Nestle's initiatives was a mixed one. MTF complimented Nestle on its acceptance of the WHO Code and on its assurance to follow "the WHO-Code as a whole, even in those countries not having relevant legislation." Nevertheless, MTF felt that it was not receiving sufficient documentary evidence with respect to Nestle's voluntary compliance. MTF also sought information about Nestle's field organization, and policies and procedures, pertaining to the marketing of infant formula products in various parts of the world. With regard to the hot-line proposal, the MTF refused to accept this responsibility (arrangement) because it was "not sufficiently comprehensive" to address "the overall problem" and because MTF would prefer to establish Nestle's credibility on the issues in dispute before considering the hot-line proposal.[22]

Nestle responded by agreeing to provide MTF with detailed in-house documents concerning all the changes that the company had made or was in the process of making. It was agreed that MTF would use these in-house documents on a strictly confidential basis since their premature release and public disclosure could cause considerable competitive harm to the company. Consequently, between October 1981 and January 1982, Nestle provided MTF with a copy of five sets of documents totaling approximately 300 pages. These documents came to be called the Rainbow Book since different sets of documents were reproduced in different colors to ensure their protected handling. Each set corresponded to the five requests made by MTF for internal documentation. The Rainbow Book put the discussions between MTF and Nestle on a different plateau. By providing MTF with confidential documents, the company was reinforcing its claims of truthfulness with the task force. Although, there was some misuse of the materials by the activists, on the whole, MTF was able to maintain the confidentiality of the materials.

The Dayton Meeting

One of the most critical events in the infant formula/Nestle boycott controversy occurred on February 12, 1982, when Nestle's top management from Vevey met the MTF in Dayton, Ohio. This meeting proved to be the beginning of the end of the Nestle boycott in 1984. NCCN's Pagan had known that Helmut Maucher, chief executive officer, and Dr. Carl Angst, executive vice president of Nestle, S.A., were planning to visit the United States in February 1982, around the same time that UMC was scheduled to have its meeting in Dayton, Ohio. He thought that it would be helpful if they could meet with the MTF during this visit and convince them of Nestle's commitment to the WHO Code. Mr. Pagan called Dr. Angst in Vevey and told him, "I need your help and Mr. Maucher's. Since you are going to be here in the States, I think it will be a tremendous coup if you fly with me to Dayton, Ohio, to meet with the Task Force." It was an indication of the changed environment at Nestle, and the enhanced status of NCCN with the head office, that Carl Angst gave the go-ahead for the meeting.

Such a meeting, however, was fraught with danger. Given the high level of executives involved, a failure could precipitate a crisis of confidence among the parties involved. Nestle's top executives had no prior experience in dealing with their critics in an unstructured, open-ended environment. There was also internal dissention in the company's head office bureaucracy about the desirability of such a meeting. The arrangements for the meeting were extremely detailed, and proceeded with a measure of caution and deliberateness that reminded one of summit meetings between the heads of states. Nestle tried to exclude certain members of the task force from the meeting, believing them to be antagonistic to Nestle. This demand was, however, summarily rejected by the MTF. Nestle also wanted the meeting to be held as a strictly private gathering. There was to be "no press, no activists and no INBC." It was decided to hold the meeting in the home of Ned Dewire, GCOM's general secretary, instead of at the Dayton Motel where the MTF was meeting in the presence of the press and the activists. Ned Dewire recalled amusingly that Nestle people even enquired about the layout of the house, the size and shape of the table around which the two parties would meet, and other protocol issues.

The meeting was scheduled for the afternoon of February 12, 1982. Nestle's representatives included Mr. Helmut Maucher, president and CEO; Dr. Carl Angst, executive vice president; Mr. David Guerrant, president, Nestle USA; and Mr. R.D. Pagan, Jr., president of NCCN. During the plane ride between New York and Dayton, Ohio, Pagan briefed his management, saying, "These people (MTF members) are going to see you. They have certain pre-conceived notions of the Europeans, the Swiss, and the Nestle management. You are going to meet a lot of Mid-Westerners, who have a more open manner of interaction. Let's be as informal and friendly as we can be." Upon arrival at the Dayton airport, the Nestle people went to Ned Dewire's home where they were received by Mrs. Dewire. "She grabbed Angst and Maucher and started showing them around the house. Telling them that the house was designed by Frank Lloyd Wright and who Lloyd Wright was. Maucher went into every room. He looked at the furniture . . . and saw the bathrooms."

MTF people were late by half an hour for their scheduled meeting. According to Dr. Angst, "when they finally arrived, some had a warm, at least kind welcome. Three or four were rather rude." Pagan commented: "I had told Maucher to stay close to Bishop Armstrong. Dr. Angst stick close to Mr. Wogaman. And Guerrant, you stick close to Ned Dewire." However, following the initial introductions, all programmed protocol broke down. There was instant chemistry. Rather than move into a formal setting, they all sat down in the living room and started their dialogue in a relaxed and informal fashion.

The MTF members had asked some very hard questions of Maucher and Angst. Bishop Armstrong said, "We have been very doubtful (of Nestle). We have heard you are committed to the Code, but can you give us some tangible evidence beyond what we have seen?" MTF was in for a surprise. It would appear that Nestle's management was willing to be more proactive than anyone had expected. Ned Dewire recalled: "Maucher said we have a bigger surprise for the Task Force." He disclosed that Nestle had prepared a draft of the instructions for its infant formula marketing personnel worldwide and that the company was going to send a copy of this draft to MTF for its input. Maucher also indicated that Nestle intended to implement its instructions within a short time. This news left everyone elated. The meeting had lasted longer than either side had expected. According to Dr. Angst, "When we left, the goodbye handshakes were friendly and warm, even on the part of one or two MTF members who were cited to me before as being really enemies of Nestle. It was the first thawing action. It greatly influenced us." On their flight back to New York, Maucher said to Pagan, "These are good people. These are not the ugly critics that we were told about." Both Maucher and Angst felt that the MTF had some genuine concerns and wanted to work with Nestle. Carl Angst, commenting on Nestle's marketing instructions said to Pagan: "I will get to Fookes right now to get that document finalized and cleared so it's up to you to get it through to the United Methodists, and get it back to us. Let us get it out to the field as soon as possible. We are committed."

The task force members were equally impressed by the Nestle management. Phil Wogaman characterized the meeting as one at which "from our side, we strongly encouraged them [Nestle management] to have some faith in the negotiation process with their critics" and said of the event "I believe they trusted us, and we trusted them." Jim Armstrong felt that "both Maucher and Angst were willing to move beyond the extreme rigidity of their predecessors" while recognizing that Nestle representatives were "still understandably hesitant to make any sort of commitments, and none were made, but they indicated a willingness to converse."

The activists, however, were not mollified. They were angry at being left out. There was a feeling that MTF was reaching out to Nestle in ways that would compromise the activists' stance on the boycott. It was also felt that Nestle was succeeding in creating divisions within the church community.

Nestle Field Instructions. Within days following the Dayton meeting, Nestle provided MTF with a draft copy of a manual detailing marketing policy instructions to the field that would be in faithful compliance with the WHO Code. In response, MTF suggested that the instruction manual be used as a basis for initiating a serious dialogue with the critics by inviting them to submit questions or objections on Nestle marketing instructions.[23] MTF immediately moved to transmit the Nestle's marketing policy to the leaders of other denominations "to generate advance discussions" as agreed at the Dayton meeting. There was an air of heightened expectations and a sense of optimism that conditions existed that might facilitate a successful resolution of the controversy and an end to the boycott. It was also hoped that the momentum generated by the Nestle announcement could be used "to bring pressure on the other companies" and to "generate a new level of serious dialogue with Nestle."[24]

MTF members Anita Anand and Ignacio Castuera met with members of INBC, ICCR, and UNICEF at a meeting in New York City on March 17, 1982, where Nestle's new document was discussed.[25] It was agreed that the WHO-Code guidelines should stand as the normative frame of reference for resolution of the boycott. Some disagreement centered around the way in which various groups might best disengage from the boycott. Ms. Margulies indicated that it would be important for the termination to occur as a result of actual negotiations in order that the momentum of a victory could be carried over into work with other companies. However, MTF "objected to such an approach because it would be important to avoid a formal win/lose situation." Another denominational representative speculated that a waiting period of six months or so might be needed "to test Nestle's good faith." The task force discussed the Nestle document in its sixth meeting held in Indianapolis on April 2–3, 1982. It reviewed the new Nestle code in detail and instructed Bishop Armstrong to review a number of questions with Nestle in a meeting scheduled for April 16, 1982.[26]

The Indianapolis Meeting

The next crucial step in the negotiation process occurred on November 11, 1982. A meeting of the INBC executive committee was to take place at the Atkinson Hotel in Indianapolis, Indiana. Bishop James Armstrong, aware of the INBC's assembly, set up a 6:30 P.M. dinner meeting between INBC and Nestle at the Indianapolis Athletic Club. Present at this meeting were: Dr. Claire Randall, general secretary of NCC; Dr. Avery Post, president of the United Church of Christ; Mr. William P. Thompson, the stated clerk of the United Presbyterian Church; Mr. Jonathan Churchill, attorney for the INBC; Dr. Carl Angst, executive vice president of Nestle; Mr. Rafael Pagan, president of NCCN, and Bishop James Armstrong, president of the National

Council of Churches. Jim Armstrong recollected driving Bill Thompson and Claire Randall from the dinner back to the Atkinson Hotel. He characterized their attitude as one of "elation"; the meeting was viewed as a "break-through session."

This was not to be, however. No sooner had the participants returned than INBC communications became confrontational and vitriolic. The turn of events was so sharp and unexpected as to make Dr. Armstrong wonder if he had completely misinterpreted the mood of the meeting. The Indianapolis meeting, which had all the seeds of success, ended up in a situation that prolonged the Nestle boycott for another two years. The activists insisted on having their own monitoring mechanism for ensuring Nestle's worldwide compliance with the WHO Code. Carl Angst was surprised at this suggestion of INBC which "displayed a degree of skepticism about the Muskie Commission (NIFAC). . . . I told them everybody wants to have monitoring and all financed by Nestle. Why don't you put some of your people in the Muskie Commission? Then I said, 'It's not my decision, but I shall mention it to Senator Muskie.'" A telegram from Jonathan Churchill to Ray Pagan on December 23 of the same year sheds some light on the points of contention. INBC had become insistent on the inclusion of non-church activists in future meetings with Nestle's senior executives. The activists wanted to match Nestle's team with their slate consisting of Doug Johnson, Leah Margulies, and Ed Baer. This caused a major disagreement between the two parties since Nestle had reiterated its decision not to negotiate with Leah Margulies. The activists resented Nestle's effort to dictate as to who would represent them and interpreted Nestle's behavior "as a stalling technique." In his communications to INBC and other church leaders, Armstrong referred to the agreements that were made in Indianapolis and were now being breached by the Churchill telegram. He felt that the hard-line activists were willing to risk a breakdown in negotiations and to prolong the controversy, in the event that they could not obtain a settlement on their own terms.

The door to discussion between Nestle and the INBC remained only slightly ajar in subsequent months, with much of the dispute centered around the participants and form of the meetings. The activists' attitude toward Nestle became further evident in ICCR's response to Nestle's marketing instructions (the Nestle code). ICCR found them to be grossly inadequate on a number of important issues. According to Phil Wogaman, within a few weeks ICCR's cautious reception (mild criticism) turned into a tirade with ICCR, branding the Nestle code "as fraud." On September 10, 1982, INBC submitted a list of 106 questions to the MTF.[27] Subsequent meetings between MTF, ICCR, and INBC were unproductive. The activists continued to insist that their boycott against Nestle would continue until Nestle had met all conditions listed in INBC boycott criteria. Furthermore, INBC was willing to negotiate with Nestle and had formed a nine-member steering committee as its negotiating arm.[28]

Dialogue With U.S. Infant Formula Companies

An important meeting of MTF with the U.S. companies during this phase took place on September 10–11, 1982, in Arlington, Virginia. It became clear that all three companies, despite their reluctance to endorse the WHO Code in its entirety, had made fundamental changes in their marketing policies and practices, bringing them closer to compliance with the WHO-Code provisions. Both Abbott Labs and Bristol-Myers expressed their dissatisfaction with MTF's February 1982 endorsement of the public advocates' petition, a move they felt hurt MTF's credibility in the eyes of the industry. By April of 1983, it became apparent that the three U.S. companies were unlikely to accept the WHO Code in its entirety.

The pace at which the companies had been moving toward the compliance goal began to slow perceptibly thereafter. Resistance to the WHO Code from all three companies was most notable in regard to policies on samples, supplies, and discharge packs. The MTF was charged with the responsibility of proposing appropriate policy changes to the three companies, with a target date of November 30, 1983, to make such changes effective. Meetings held in the summer of 1983 led to a MTF strategy that concentrated on resolving the controversy first and foremost with Bristol-Myers, the company that was engendering the greatest hope among MTF representatives, and then presenting the remaining two companies with a package that the task force considered defensible.

Final MTF meetings

On April 4–5, 1983, the MTF held its tenth meeting in Washington, D.C. Phil Wogaman reported on his visits to five nations in Africa, including Kenya, Nigeria, Ghana, Zimbabwe, and Liberia, where he had visited hospitals, and met with church representatives and missionaries. He then filed five violations with NIFAC, believing that none was caused by policies approved by Nestle's central office. His positive findings included broad support for breastfeeding, TV spots in Liberia to promote breastfeeding, no formula in Ghana due to that country's poverty, and one hospital where a milk bank had helped create a marked decrease in mortality rates. At the time of this meeting Nestle still felt that dialogue with the INBC was too difficult, if not impossible, because each time some agreement had been reached, INBC "raised the ante" and there could be little dialogue in good faith. For their part the INBC continued to insist that Nestle participate in the "universal application of the WHO code and full implementation."

On June 17–18, 1983, the task force held its 11th meeting in Washington, D.C. Senator Muskie reported on the activities of NIFAC. Also presented were representatives from Bristol Myers and American Home Products who announced their willingness to comply with the WHO Code in developing countries. Announcement was made at this meeting that the Council of Bishops had acted on the recommendations made by the task force in May 1983 and would not join the Nestle boycott. The last (14th) meeting of the MTF was held in Washington, D.C., on October 30–31, 1983, where the task force agreed to the general outline of its recommendation to be made to the 1984 general conference.

The 1984 General Conference

MTF, through GCOM, presented its final report to the general conference in May 1984. It was a story of dedicated people trying to achieve what had seemed at the beginning an almost impossible task. However, through faith, commitment, and perseverance, they had succeeded in their assigned task. Acting for the entire task force, Phil Wogaman made two resolutions recommending that the UMC formally vote to endorse the suspension of the boycott and that the task force should cease to exist. In his remarks to the conference, he observed: "The important change to which I refer is the suspension of the Nestle boycott by the INBC and by the GBGM and GBC&S. This event means that we can all celebrate an important accomplishment together and put the confrontations of the past behind us. . . . This is one of the few times in the United Methodist history when anything of this sort has occurred."

Notes

1. Legislative Committee of GBC&S's "Majority Report."
2. Paul M. Minus, "A Petition to Selected General Conference Delegates," April 7, 1980, pp. 1–2.
3. *Daily Christian Advocate,* April 26, 1980, p. 38.
4. *Ibid.,* p. 39.
5. *Ibid.,* p. 39.
6. *Ibid.,* p. 41.
7. Sixth Task Force Meeting held at Indianapolis, Indiana, on April 2–3, 1982.
8. MTF Report to 1984 General Conference, p. 15.
9. Paul Minus, *A Background Paper on the Infant Formula Controversy: Prepared for the United Methodist Task Force on Infant Formula* (Dayton, Ohio: United Methodist Church, September 17, 1980)."
10. American Home Products, letter dated October 9, 1980, to Dr. Paul Minus.
11. INFACT letter to Dr. Paul Minus dated October 9, 1980.
12. Letter written by Ned DeWire to Tom Lee (general manager, Stouffer's Dayton Plaza Hotel), May 11, 1981.
13. Dr. Jackson, Testimony before the House Subcommittee on International Economic Policy & Trade Committees on Foreign Affairs, June 16, 1981.
14. Press Release by UMC, 601 Riverside Avenue, Dayton, Ohio, undated, p. 1.

15. Infant Formula Task Force of the GCOM, "Minutes," Dayton, Ohio, September 25–26, 1981, p. 3.

16. Nestle Coordination Center for Nutrition, Inc. "*Aide Memoire* to The United Methodist Task Force" (Washington, D.C., September 25, 1981).

17. *Ibid.*

18. Report of the Infant Formula Task Force to the GCOM, October 30, 1981, pp. 11–12.

19. *Ibid.*, p. 10.

20. Infant Formula Task Force of the GCOM, "Second Report to GCOM," July 1982.

21. Report of the Infant Formula Task Force to the GCOM, October 30, 1981, p. 8.

22. Infant Formula Task Force of the GCOM, "Minutes," Dayton, Ohio, September 25–26, 1981.

23. Infant Formula Task Force, "Second Report to GCOM," July, 1982, pp. 4–5.

24. Phil Wogaman, Letter to MTF members and other church leaders, dated March 8, 1982.

25. *Ibid.*

26. Infant Formula Task Force, Minutes of the Meeting, April 2–3, 1982, p. 2.

27. Infant Formula Task Force Report, April 1983, p. 3.

28. Infant Formula Task Force Meeting, January 28–30, 1983, pp. 7–8.

17 NESTLE INFANT FORMULA AUDIT COMMISSION (NIFAC) A NEW MODEL FOR GAINING EXTERNAL LEGITIMACY FOR CORPORATE ACTIONS

On May 3, 1982, Nestle announced the establishment of the Nestle Infant Formula Audit Commission (NIFAC). The new organization was to be chaired by former Senator and Vice Presidential candidate, Mr. Edmund Muskie. Commenting on the rationale for establishing the Commission, Dr. Carl Angst, Nestle's executive vice-president, stated:

> . . . the Muskie Commission plays a vital role in evaluating our policies and in ensuring that our infant formula marketing practices are in conformity with the WHO Code. The Commission also provides a channel of communication with all concerned people through which legitimate questions about our policies can be raised and which guarantees serious consideration of all reasonable criticism.[1]

Antecedents to the Establishment of NIFAC

The creation of NIFAC was an important element in Nestle's strategy to end the boycott. Along with NCCN, NIFAC was to provide an essential structural mooring to the company's strategy in dealing with its critics. It was apparent that the company's substantive efforts in complying with the WHO Code were being dissipated, and the veracity of its communications undermined, because of perceived public distrust in company's motives and actions. Something had to give if the company were to be able to persuade various public interest groups, and especially religious institutions, that its actions in complying with the WHO Code justified a lifting of the boycott.

The resolution of the problem, however, raised a number of thorny issues. Although the company had grudgingly entered the remedy and relief stage of the issue life cycle, it was by no means clear that a change in the company's perception of the infant formula controversy had become rooted in its culture and was widely shared by its management and professional cadres. There was still a strong residue of bitterness and animosity toward the activists, notably the INFACT and ICCR leadership, whom the company's management considered to be irresponsible and unethical. The need for generating greater credibility was critical to the company's strategy of boundary expansion where it sought to involve its critics in mutually supportive arrangements to resolve the problem. The critics, however, were unlikely to accede to such an involvement where "terms of engagement" were defined by the company. And yet, the company was unwilling to yield control of any potential resolution mechanism to its critics, or have the company's actions evaluated by "biased" outsiders. Therefore, it became apparent that for the new strategy to work, the company must seek outside validation of its actions. Furthermore, these outside institutions must be seen as "completely independent" by the public-at-large, and their credibility could not be easily undermined by the company's critics.

Search for Solutions

NCCN executives first approached UNICEF to monitor Nestle's Third World operations. UNICEF's worldwide operations and experience in dealing with the problems of infants and children made the agency uniquely suited to undertake such a task.* It would also be in keeping with the spirit of Article 11.3 of the WHO Code which called for the infant formula manufacturers to undertake measures of independent monitoring of their activities. UNICEF, however, declined, feeling that as a governmental agency, it could not take on the regulatory task of inspecting and verifying the behavior of companies in the private sector. Nor did UNICEF have the resources to investigate what appeared to be hundreds of claims and counter-claims all over the Third World and thereby get embroiled in a politically and emo-

---

*The discussion of Nestle's rationale in creating NIFAC and its operations is based on internal company documents, NIFAC materials, and extensive on-the-record interviews with Nestle and NCCN executives, NIFAC board members, and other people involved in the controversy. Unless otherwise specifically stated, all direct quotes or paraphrased statements attributed to various persons are based on personal, on-the-record interviews or written communications with the author.

tionally charged issue where it ran the serious risk of tarnishing its own reputation.

NCCN next asked the United Methodist Task Force (MTF) which also declined. The issue of whether to support the boycott was already absorbing more time and energy than MTF members had expected. MTF felt that it could not become the official watchdog of a corporation's affairs, a task for which it was totally unequipped. Moreover, such a course of action was outside its mandate and would have been particularly ill advised given the fact that the task force was already under intense pressure from the activists for its allegedly conciliatory stance toward the companies.[2]

NCCN then looked into the possibility of an independent investigator, like an ombudsman or special prosecutor. One person just wasn't feasible, however. The amount of time, energy, and expertise necessary for the job would severely limit the number of eligible candidates. Furthermore, it was believed that an individual, with the prominence and public stature necessary to generate and maintain credibility, would not be able to devote the required amount of time to a single project.

The concept of an independent audit commission evolved over a period of weeks during intensive strategy meetings at the NCCN. It was a unique idea. NCCN had no precedents or prior role models but "we were willing to take a chance," observed Mr. Pagan. It also faced the difficult task of selling the concept both to Nestle's senior executives in Switzerland and to more moderate elements among its critics. The success of such a commission was hardly assured, and the consequences of failure could be quite serious both for the company and for the personal careers of NCCN executives. NCCN, therefore, proceeded very cautiously with the concept. Through extensive internal discussions, it developed a set of conditions that the new entity must meet. It also clarified a set of strategic and tactical objectives that should be achieved through the working of the audit commission.

Discussions with Nestle — Switzerland

NCCN's Pagan had a series of discussions — both in person as well as through formal and informal communications — with Nestle's top management in Vevey. The process was not easy. "We did not simply go to Nestle's top management and present the proposal for a commission suggesting that here is what we should do. We had to prepare them for it.", observed Jack Mongoven, NCCN's senior vice president. NCCN approached Vevey strategically with the NIFAC idea and sold it to them in stages. According to Mongoven, Vevey was "led into it. . . . We knew where we wanted to go, but we thought if we proposed it all at once, there was a high likelihood of it being shot down." Mongoven wrote a series of papers, delivering the concept piecemeal in terms of what resources were needed in order to achieve specific objectives. "In the end, it was Pagan's persuasiveness and the substantiveness of the concept that carried the day."

The issues to be resolved with Nestle — Vevey ran the gamut of major strategy, operational tactics, corporate culture, and the inbred distrust of many Nestle executives toward the company's critics. The corporation would be asked to turn over a great many of its internal documents, a request to which few companies would easily acquiesce. The company felt that given the pervasive anti-business and anti-Nestle climate of public opinion, the cost of such an action might far outweigh any potential benefits. There was no guarantee, or even reasonable certainty, that the project would successfully re-establish Nestle's credibility.* There was also a concern that Nestle might be expected to deliver "too much" in terms of compliance. A large corporation, with worldwide operations and a highly decentralized management system, might face considerable resistance — both formal and informal — in having all of its field offices follow head office instructions. This was especially so because a great many of Nestle's foreign subsidiaries were not persuaded that Nestle indeed had a problem since they did not see any adverse effects of Nestle's U.S. problems in their territories. In any widespread business operation like that of Nestle, by the time the orders of top management filter down to the local level, discrepancies inevitably arise between a company's official policies and their implementation in its far-flung operations. An independent commission might take it upon itself to expand its activities beyond its original mandate. The commission would be operating under intense news media glare and scrutiny by its critics. Therefore, once started, it would be all but impossible for the company to "rein in" the commission regardless of the legitimacy of its position. In addition, not only might the commission find some instances of lapse of control between headquarters and first-line marketing managers; there was also the very real possibility that code infractions might be contrived by some of the more militant activists as media events. Despite these concerns, Nestle's new executive, Dr. Carl Angst, was willing to give the new approach a try. In order to demonstrate NIFAC's independence further, Nestle — Vevey also agreed that NIFAC would be allowed to serve in the same capacity with other companies. However, as it turned out, none of the major U.S. infant formula manufacturers expressed any interest in following such a course of action.

---

*Nestle had already experienced the embarrassing effect of unauthorized public disclosure of the company's internal documents, nicknamed the "Nestlegate" memorandum. It was believed that any large public release of company documents would risk further unauthorized disclosures and might create additional problems for the management. See Chapter 7, "The Drive Toward Code Enactment — The Post Kennedy Era."

Composition of the Audit Commission

A critical issue with regard to the new commission was the selection of its chairman and the composition of the board. It was important that the most visible member, the chairman, be a nationally and internationally recognized statesman whose integrity and stature would be beyond reproach, not only for the benefit of the organizations supporting the boycott but also to assuage the fears of Nestle — Switzerland. The company needed to be assured that the chairman would be strong enough to withstand public pressure from all quarters in the work of the commission. A number of prominent public figures were considered. However, former Secretary of State and U.S. Senator Edmund S. Muskie appeared to be on all the lists prepared by NCCN's managers. Muskie had a well-established reputation for integrity and a commitment to the disadvantaged. He was often called a "man of the people." He was politically astute and had experience in dealing with the press. His other strength was his 22-year career as an elected, as opposed to appointed, official. He was held in high regard by the senators and congressmen of both parties. At the time of the formation of the commission, Muskie was a partner in the law firm of Chadbourne & Parke in Washington, D.C. Accordingly, it was decided that Muskie would be the first one to be approached.

Muskie was amenable to the idea but insisted on a number of conditions. The commission budget and staff had to be independent and under the full control of NIFAC. Daniel J. (Jack) Greenwald III, a staff lawyer and later a partner at Chadbourne & Parke, and Philip Wogaman, chairperson of the United Methodist Task Force (MTF), in effect negotiated the NIFAC charter with Nestle. Their two foremost concerns were the issue of independence and the issue of resources. NIFAC didn't want its hands tied. Muskie also insisted on the right of the Commission to undertake independent investigations and to make public its findings.[3] These findings were to be published in regular quarterly reports without any prior censorship from the company. Nestle, however, would be afforded an opportunity at least a month prior to issuance to prepare comments and respond to issues.* All these conditions were agreed to by the company and incorporated in the legal charter of the Infant Formula Audit Commission. The charter incorporating the commission also set forth in considerable detail the structural and procedural characteristics of the new entity, the scope of its authority and responsibility, and its relationship with its sponsor, Nestle. They provide a useful road map for establishing similar mechanisms by other companies.

---

*During its tenure, NIFAC published 14 reports, issued quarterly through March 1984, and annually beginning in June 1984 through June 1989. The final report covered two years of activity and was published in June 1991.

Salient Features of the Charter Establishing NIFAC

Mission and Authority

The commission's authority is derived from Article 11.3 of the WHO Code. The mission of the board is explained in Article II. It states that:

> The mission of the Commission shall be to apprise the Company of any problems it discovers in the internal investigation and control systems of the company in its application of the WHO or National Codes. It shall answer inquiries from the public, as it deems necessary, regarding Nestle's implementation of the WHO Code or compliance with the applicable National Code.

The sixth article of the charter explains that the responsibility for monitoring compliances with the code lies with the individual countries involved. If at anytime NIFAC and Nestle cannot agree on a point involving marketing practices, the decision of the country involved would be solicited and would be considered binding.

Autonomy of the Commission

Article V of the charter declares, "The Commission shall have full and total control, under the chairman, of the annual budget allocated to it by the Company and shall report quarterly on its management and expenditures under the budget to the Company." This autonomy was achieved through the use of a block grant, the appropriation of which is dictated by the commission itself. In addition, the articles of incorporation give the commission "full power in the management and control of the policies, activities, funds, properties and affairs of the Nestle Infant Formula Audit Commission," including the selection of its own staff. The procedures for drafting quarterly reports are defined and described in the final article of the incorporation papers.

Procedure for Assessing Complaints

The articles of incorporation specifically outline the procedure for registering and processing complaints. All complaints received are first logged in. If the complaint is not within the scope and authority of the commission or does not include sufficient information, then it would be returned to the sender for further documentation. Complaints with enough information for a serious investigation will be forwarded to Nestle for examination and response. Nestle's report will then be studied to see if its handling of the complaint (including any corrective action that might have been taken) conforms to its commitment to the WHO Code. The commission would then write a report describing the complaint and the board's assessment of Nestle's response.

The life of the commission was originally established at 15 months. The additional (fifth) quarter was added to enable NIFAC to respond to the May 1983 WHA meeting. That meeting was to review the code for possible changes. At that point, NIFAC could consult with Nestle in order to extend the life of the commission to perpetuity if it were deemed necessary.

NCCN's Considerations in Establishing NIFAC

NCCN also had certain strategic and tactical considerations that it wanted to accomplish through NIFAC. According to Jack Mongoven, one of the senior executives of NCCN, "Muskie had his own ideas as to the nature and scope of the Commission's activities. However, we had our own ideas as well as to what the Commission should accomplish":

> We wanted the Commission to create processes that would ensure regular communication between it [the Commission], NCCN and Nestle, and the boycotting groups. Specifically, NCCN was seeking: (1) credibility for the Commission and, through it, credibility for the company's performance; (2) formal, regular reporting; (3) a clear-cut process for handling complaints; (4) a well-defined process of communication; and, (5) a clear charter for the commission that would specify its objectives, responsibility, accountability, and relationship with Nestle. Muskie insisted on an absolute commitment in writing from Nestle as to the Commission's designated role.

> NCCN wanted to ensure that there would be a regular "event hook" for the news media which would both direct the media focus to the new commission and put some boundary around the issues that the activists would raise and the manner in which they would be raised and addressed. We also wanted the press to feel that they must check with the new commission in the event the activists were levelling any charges or there were "new" developments in the infant formula controversy.

Once Muskie accepted the chairmanship, he played an important role in the selection of other members. It was decided that, to the extent possible, commission members should represent a cross-section of stakeholders and constituencies involved in the infant formula controversy. Dr. Philip Wogaman, chairperson of MTF, was one of the first choices. He had been invited to join the commission even before Muskie had accepted the chairmanship. Wogaman and Muskie had a couple of meetings during this period "while both of us were weighing whether we should accept the invitation to participate and under what circumstances." Wogaman had gained considerable knowledge about the issue through his work with the United Methodist Task Force. He could also open additional channels of communication and information exchange between the commission, the religious community and other activist groups.

The medical, public health, and scientific communities were represented by four members. Dr. Shelden Margen was director of Public Health and Nutrition Program at the University of California, Berkeley. Dr. Lewis A. Barnes was chairman of the Department of Pediatrics at the University of South Florida College of Medicine in Tampa. Dr. Vijaya L. Melnick was a special assistant for policy and bioethics at the National Institute on Aging, National Institute of Health (NIH), and later a professor of biology and a senior research scholar, Center for Applied and Urban Policy at the University of the District of Columbia. Dr. Omar J. Fareed, a diplomate of the American Board of Internal Medicine, was also a member of the Royal Society of Tropical Medicine and Hygiene.

Two clergymen who were quite active in the boycott were invited to join the Commission. They were Dr. Avery Post of United Church of Christ and Auxiliary Bishop P. Francis Murphy of the Baltimore Catholic Archdiocese. Both of them, however, declined the invitation, yielding to pressure from the more militant elements of the boycott movement who believed that the commission could not be objective in its deliberations. Wogaman observed: "There is no question that Avery Post and Bishop Murphy declined to participate in NIFAC because of pressure placed against them. Others, including myself, were also subjected to great pressure not to participate in NIFAC." According to *INFACT Update*:

> Dr. Avery Post, President of United Church of Christ, in rejecting the Nestle Company's offer to join the Commission, observed that, "it would seem that Nestle's instructions apply to very few of Nestle's major markets." Moreover, "until there are assurances that implementation of the International Code is in force, the Nestle Boycott will continue, and I believe, our constituency will have little confidence in the Nestle Audit Committee."[4]

Bishop Murphy cited similar reasons and also said that "he felt his participation would create serious misunderstandings among members of the International Nestle Boycott Committee and would confuse the boycott supporters."[5]

In lieu of Dr. Avery Post, Dr. Henry W. Andersen was invited and agreed to join. Dr. Andersen was the pastor of the Fairmount Presbyterian Church in Cleveland, Ohio. The second person was Dr. Robert C. Campbell, former general secretary of the American Baptist Churches, one of the largest mainline churches participating in the Nestle boycott. Thus NIFAC started out with eight members at the time of its creation on May 3, 1982. During the course of its organizational work, the commission added three new board members. Dr. Mildred Randall was an associate professor of nursing at the American University, Washington, D.C., and had spent a number of years in Africa and South America doing nutritional research. She was also a member of the United Methodist Task Force. The Most Reverend Ricardo Ramirez, then Catholic Auxiliary Bishop of San Antonio, Texas, also joined the commission. Bishop Ramirez resigned from the commission on October 1, 1982, due to increased responsibilities arising out of his new appointment as full Bishop of Las Cruces, New Mexico. He was replaced by Ms. Fetaui Mata-afa, the widow of the first Prime Minister of Western Samoa, and chairperson of the Pacific Council of Churches. And finally, in June 1984, two new members were added to the slate: Ms. Angela Glover Blackwell, J.D., and Dr. James W. Post. Ms. Blackwell was the managing attorney for San Francisco-based Public Advocates, Inc., a statewide public interest law firm defending the rights of the legally underrepresented in areas of health, education, and employment. Ms. Blackwell later resigned from the Commission, citing pressure of other work. Dr. Post was a professor of management and public policy at Boston University's School of Management. He had been a consultant to WHO, the Population Council, and the Rockefeller Foundation on the impact of multinational business on public health in developing countries. Dr. Post was also actively involved with INFACT. From 1984 until the time of its dissolution in 1991, NIFAC had a total of 11 members.[6] They were Dr. Henry W. Anderson, Dr. Lewis A. Barnes, Dr. Robert C. Campbell, Dr. Omar John Fareed, Dr. Shelden Margen, Ms. Masioto Fetaui Mata-afa, Dr. Vijay Melenick, Mr. Edmund Muskie (chairman), Dr. James W. Post, Dr. Mildred Randall, and Dr. Philip Wogaman.

Public Reaction to NIFAC's Formation

The United Methodist Task Force (MTF) responded positively to NIFAC as a major step by Nestle to back up its stated policies with active monitoring of its behavior. The more radical elements of the boycott movement were not similarly impressed. According to Mr. Jack Greenwald, the critics' view was that "the Commission is like asking the fox to guard the chicken coop." However, Greenwald contended that just the opposite was true. He felt that in this case, Nestle was the proverbial "chicken" and activists were the "fox" since their sympathizers were on the NIFAC board. The issue of the commission's funding and budget was publicly raised on November 11, 1983, at the closing session of the convention of Unda — USA, a national Catholic association of broadcasters and other communicators at the Hollenden House, Cleveland. A member of the audience asked Muskie how he could expect volunteer organizations such as INFACT to compete, in effect, with NIFAC with all Nestle's money and resources behind it. It was at this point that Muskie publicly disclosed that NIFAC's annual budget was approximately $400,000.[7] (This amount, however, was substantially increased in later years). Jack Greenwald, however, dismissed this comparison as somewhat spurious. According to Greenwald, what was *not* disclosed at the press conference was the fact that INFACT was operating on a budget of $500,000 a year. Furthermore, INFACT had access to tremendous volunteer help which, if it were to be paid, would represent additional significant chunks of money.

In the question–answer period after the press conference, reporters repeatedly raised the issue of the possible conflict of interest stemming from Nestle's responsibility for assuming the total cost of NIFAC operations. The compensation Muskie was to receive was of particular interest to the reporters present. Since Muskie, in his role as chairman, would be putting more time in NIFAC than any other member of the commission, he would be paid an unspecified hourly rate commensurate with his normal fee as an attorney. The reporters tried to pin him down as to the exact amount. Since the projected volume of work was as yet undetermined, this was impossible to predict. However, Mr. Muskie pointed out that the NIFAC contract provided for a "cap" on the total annual payment to the law firm for his services. All other members of NIFAC would serve on a voluntary basis and would receive no compensation for their services.[8] According to Wogaman, "Ultimately all members of NIFAC received some compensation for their work, though some dedicated this to particular institutions."[9]

Doug Johnson, national chairperson of INFACT, declared in the May 1982 issue of *INFACT Update* that "an audit committee is a sound concept, but to be satisfactory, there must be a mutual agreement on what is to be audited, who will do the work, and what power they will have to affect company policy. Nestle has been very ambiguous on these issues. They've not even made public where their new marketing instructions are to be applied. We can only hope that a man with Senator Muskie's prestige will prevail upon Nestle to *adopt* the WHO/UNICEF Code [and] fully support the WHO/UNICEF Code."[10] In an interview with the author in May of 1984, Doug Johnson reflected on INFACT's view of NIFAC. He did not think that NIFAC could be truly independent. He went on to assert that NIFAC's members were selected by Nestle. Appointments were predicated on the candidates' alignment with "Nestle's world view." However, a counterpoint to these accusations was made in a letter dated May 14, 1982, from Mr. Fookes to Dr. Avery Post of the United Church of Christ (and member of the INBC), wherein Mr. Fookes stated, "the fact that it [the audit commission] also includes leaders of boycotting churches should put to rest, once and for all, any doubts as to its independence."[11]

Doug Johnson also questioned the overly legal approach embedded in NIFAC as the most appropriate way to resolve the controversy. "Structurally what's wrong with this approach is that it shifts the burden of proof, as if it were a court of law, where Nestle was innocent until proven guilty. Thus the responsibility for establishing violations was unduly placed on those organizations who had the least capacity and the fewest resources to pursue them." Senator Muskie, however, contended that an element of legal approach was one of the strengths of NIFAC.

Although criticized at times, the rule of law played an important role in the Commission's work and its accomplishments. The infant formula controversy raised extremely complex issues on which there was wide disagreement among informed, reasonable individuals. Personal opinions have varied widely (within the Commission and outside it) as to acceptable and harmful infant formula marketing practices. However, notwithstanding its faults, the WHO Code represented the consensus of interested opinion in 1981 about the proper guidelines for marketing breast-milk substitutes, and it remains the only statement of appropriate marketing guidelines that has been accepted by an international body of public health officials, the World Health Assembly.[12]

Charged with examining complaints against Nestle's code violations, the commission could not ignore the code's provisions and substitute its own opinions as a standard for Nestle's behavior. Rather, the commission decided that it had to abide by the "rule of law" and the standard in the complaint process has been the WHO Code, not necessarily what any individual might have personally believed was good. Consequently, the commission was able to minimize its debates about which practices might or might not have an effect on a mother's breastfeeding/bottle-feeding decision or which practices might or might not be beneficial, on balance, for mothers and infants. Instead, the commission could accept the WHO Code as it was passed and could direct its efforts to interpreting the Code and applying its provisions to specific situations.[13]

Edward Baer of ICCR/INFACT saw the Commission as "a very fancy legitimizer of the new Nestle instructions" and felt that dissenters on the board would "have only limited power to have their views considered." Tim Smith, executive director of ICCR, questioned, "Why is the Commission being used by Mr. Pagan to try to stop the boycott in this country?" This question would at best seem rhetorical and at worst irrelevant, since one would expect that the goal of all parties involved would be to create conditions that would lead to the termination of the boycott.

NIFAC in Action — Phase I

No sooner had NIFAC set up shop when it appeared that one of its basic assumptions lacked a solid foundation. Prior to the establishment of NIFAC, there was a common impression — no doubt created by the boycott movement and fostered by the news media — that there were widespread violations of the code on the part of Nestle and other companies. Consequently, NIFAC believed that one of its main tasks would be to receive and investigate complaints against Nestle. In that, NIFAC could not have been more disappointed. Whether it was antipathy toward the commission or difficulty in systematic collection of field reports on the code violations, the fact remained that during the first few months of NIFAC's existence, there was not much new activity on the part of the boycotting groups by way of highlighting Nestle's field operations and the extent of their compliance with the code.

In an effort to "drum up" business, NIFAC even tried to reach out to Nestle's critics. Approximately, 100 copies of the charter and the articles of incorporation were mailed to parties actively involved in the controversy. The situation was best expressed by Mr. Muskie at the press conference on the release of NIFAC's first quarterly report in October 1982 where he expressed the "frustration of the Commission that we are overwhelmed by volumes of Xeroxed, faded, illegible press clippings, charges that have been repeated over and over again over the years. We couldn't possibly untangle that can of worms through any kind of an orderly process."[14]

Perhaps there was a good reason for the activists' lack of response which should have been anticipated by NIFAC. The boycott movement was primarily rooted in the United States and to a minor extent in Western Europe. And yet, the entire field of operations was in Latin America, Asia, and Africa. INFACT/INBC and other surrogate organizations had no field offices. Even International Organization of Consumer Unions' (IOCU) major initiatives came from its headquarters in Kuala Lumpur and were not necessarily driven by their field offices. The movement's organizers were content to collect "complaints" from whatever sources they came. The magnitude and the extent of complaints, therefore, were more a function of the originating agency than the relative scope of the problem or its potential for injury.

NIFAC's structured and legalistic approaches would radically alter the terms of confrontation between the protagonists and shift them in the direction of Nestle. These approaches required the existence of large field networks that would collect and channel information for processing in the investigative-legalistic mode. Such a structural arrangement was particularly suited to Nestle and placed the activists at a relative disadvantage. NIFAC was also consensus driven. Members trusted each other. The focus was on resolving the issues and finding ways to explain and understand differences in members' viewpoints. However, from the critics' viewpoint, the commission's cohesiveness reflected the dominance and control by Mr. Muskie over other commission members.

From the activists' point of view, it was the logic behind the complaints that justified their advocacy. Given the commercial nature of the effort, Nestle and other infant formula manufacturers were bound to take all possible measures to increase sales and profits. Therefore, the number of reported complaints, in and of themselves, were not an adequate measure of the severity of the problem or potential for harm. Instead, they merely reflected the uneven nature of the resources with which the poor of the world and their advocates in the United States had at their disposal to deal with the multinational corporate behemoths. To the activists, this approach was akin to the efforts by Nestle and other infant formula manufacturers during the pre-problem and problem identification stages where industry representatives insisted on describing the issue in narrow scientific and medical terms. The activists, on the other hand, contended that the scientific aspects of the controversy must be interpreted within the broad sociopolitical context where institutional structure, political power, and the voice of the disenfranchised poor must be taken into account in defining the parameters of the problem and crafting approaches to its resolution.

Nestle's critics may have been on weaker ground in terms of the magnitude of code violations on the part of the company, but they were absolutely right in terms of their strategy in dealing with Nestle. The structure within which a problem is defined and the terms of its definition almost invariably provide the specifications under which solutions must be developed and remedial measures carried out. In a long war of attrition, the most useful resources are not necessarily a high level of emotional commitment and creativity to do more with less, which was the strength of the boycott movement, but a system with long staying power that can overwhelm the communication channels with excessive data and procedural technicalities, which is the strength of organized bureaucracies, such as the infant formula manufacturers. Therefore, while Nestle's missteps were based on lack of information as to what the activists had by way of the company's alleged code violations, the activists were equally unprepared in understanding the weakness of their tactical decisions. They failed to foresee the force of events that would gradually shift the issue from a broad sweep of denunciations to the nitty-gritty of specific complaints as the life cycle of the issue moved from the pre-problem and problem identification stages to remedy and relief, and prevention stages. Their tactics and response patterns increasingly became less effective, creating their own credibility gap and also losing momentum. While the activists were able to bring the issue into the problem identification stage despite fierce resistance on the part of the infant formula industry, they were unable to maintain their control over the flow of events. They failed to perceive the changed circumstances that called for an accommodative mode, both in form and in substance. It was a triumph of ego and emotion over logic and rational action. The results were not long in coming. Both the NIFAC and MTF would prove the undoing of the more radical elements of the boycott movement, notably the INFACT leadership, who would see a gradual erosion of their power and control over the direction of the anti-boycott campaign.

NIFAC's Change of Strategy — From Passive Investigator to Proactive Instigator

Rather than remain moribund and mired in the minutiae of handling "complaints," NIFAC decided to expand its mission from that of "managing process" to the one that focused on desired outcomes. This may have been the most thoughtful and effective change in strategy. It would allow board members greater freedom to bring to bear their combined professional expertise on the problem. It also reflected one of the criticisms of the commission, namely, that it was too legalistic in assessing the substance and veracity of individual complaints and was thereby losing sight of the bigger picture.

From Nestle's viewpoint this move could not have been more prescient. At first Nestle was concerned that NIFAC was spreading in all directions, going beyond its mandate and taking on more activities than its board members had time to handle. Nestle's executives were also jittery that their earlier concerns in establishing NIFAC would come true. It was feared that a monitoring agency accountable to no one but itself would become uncontrollable and ineffective and, in the process, would harm Nestle's interests without any commensurate benefits in improving the prospects of terminating the boycott. A third concern was that of costs. NIFAC's budget had started to balloon and was approaching $1.0 million per year, more than twice as high as the initial projections. The reality, however, could not have been more pleasant. Although NIFAC did expand the scope of its activities, thereby escalating its budget, it also filled a vacuum in data collection and information gathering with regard to complaints on Nestle's code violations. The expanded scope of NIFAC's activities included four areas: examination of Nestle's internal marketing instructions; on-site inspections of infant formula usage and Nestle's marketing practices in Third World countries; discussions with WHO to clarify some of the ambiguities in the code; and sponsorship of a Conference on Breast Feeding and Infant Nutrition.

Nestle's Instructions to Field Personnel

One of the most frequently levied criticisms against Nestle was that the company was not truly committed to the WHO Code as reflected in its marketing policies and practices. NIFAC, therefore, decided to review Nestle's instructions to its field personnel. Commission members met with Nestle's top management in Switzerland, held discussions with WHO staff members in Geneva, visited various infant formula plants and facilities, and engaged in discussions with the company's critics and other outside observers. Consequently, NIFAC felt that those instructions needed clarification; in some areas the wording could be stronger and more explicit, and that it was in Nestle's best interest to adapt them accordingly. Nestle accepted NIFAC's recommendations and implemented them in November 1982. This was the first indication that NIFAC's larger role had been accepted by both the external and internal constituencies.[15]

In all, NIFAC made 10 recommendations for changes in the instructions. These were announced at the October 14, 1982, press conference.

1. The instructions were amended to make it clear that they were only

supplemental guidelines for the practical applications of the WHO Code. The code itself took precedence.

2. Independent retailers would be advised not to advertise infant formula at point-of-sale.

3. The revised document applied to all infants, regardless of age. This eliminated the possibility of any allegations that Nestle was attempting to restrict the provisions of the code to infants under four months old.

4. The use of mothercraft nurses was explicitly prohibited.

5. Free or low-cost samples of formula could only be provided to health care workers and only in limited supply.

6. Direct advertising was forbidden, even in the form of educational materials.

7. Generic (nonbrand) promotion of formula was also prohibited.

8. The original instructions had stated that no gifts significant enough to serve as inducement to promote products would be permitted. In order to eliminate any confusion, this provision was dropped, and no gifts of any kind would henceforth be allowed.

9. The lengthy complaint form was abridged to a concise two-page document so as not to discourage people from filing complaints.

10. The guidelines were tightened to insure that no contact between sales representatives and mothers and expectant mothers was acceptable.

Fact Finding Missions

NIFAC board members undertook a series of fact-finding missions to various parts of the Third World to assess for themselves the magnitude of the problem pertaining to the use of infant formula. They included: Dr. Omar Fareed (January–May 1983): Philippines, Singapore, Malaysia, Hong Kong, Trinidad, West Indies; Dr. Mildred Randall (May–July 1983): Mexico, Bangladesh, Somalia, Sri Lanka, Kenya, and South Africa; Dr. Henry Andersen (February 1983): Tanzania, Thailand, Singapore, and Malaysia; Dr. Philip Wogaman (February–March 1983): Liberia, Ghana, Nigeria, Kenya and Zimbabwe; Dr. Robert C. Campbell (May–July 1983): Japan, Hong Kong, Philippines, Thailand, India, Brazil, and Argentina; and Ms. Fetaui Mataafa (April 1983): South Pacific, including Fiji and Tonga. The commission members' findings from these trips were reported in NIFAC's fourth and fifth quarterly reports.[16] Briefly summarized, they found that among the poorest countries — for example, Bangladesh and Somalia — breastfeeding was almost universal. In other countries, such as India and Sri Lanka, local producers and/or governments' own brands accounted for a large market share which, in general, did not comply with the code standards with regard to labeling, and so on. In most markets where Nestle was a major player, the company was taking necessary steps to comply with the code, although in some markets this effort was somewhat slow especially when there were large inventories of existing stock. In many countries — Kenya, for instance — Nestle's efforts in encouraging strict enforcement of the code were looked on with suspicion by the local authorities. NIFAC members also found that Nestle's major international formula competitors generally lagged in code compliance. At least a few competitors were not averse to taking advantage of Nestle's strict compliance by grabbing additional market share. In most countries visited, local authorities, including health care administrators and hospital workers, did not consider infant formula and the boycott to be much of an issue although some of them were critical of infant formula manufacturers' practices, including Nestle's past promotional practices. Another point that was repeatedly voiced by local authorities in a great many countries visited was that they [the local authorities] were aware of the problems associated with the improper and unwarranted use of infant formula, but that they wanted to handle these problems in their own way.

Meeting with WHO

NIFAC found that the code was vague in some parts and was, therefore, difficult to implement. Senator Muskie met with the WHO director general, the assistant director general, and several staff members with a view to obtain their perspective and guidance for those who were responsible for implementing the code.

Conference on Breastfeeding and Infant Nutrition

On June 5–6, 1983, NIFAC sponsored a Conference on Breast-feeding and Infant Nutrition at the University of California at Berkeley. The conference dealt with physiological and ethical aspects of the breast versus bottle debate. The deliberations of the conference showed that there had been no significant change in the views of various groups as to the scientific and health aspects of the controversy. INFACT participants and some other activists also expressed their skepticism as to whether Nestle and NIFAC were committed to the broader issues of promoting breastfeeding and infant nutrition.[17]

NIFAC in Action — Phase II

During the first phase of its operation, NIFAC had earned a level of credibility with a broad spectrum of religious and moderate elements of advocacy groups, news media, and the public-at-large. In part, this resulted from the demonstrable stature of the commission members and their proactive stance in going outside their initial narrow mandate to seek answers to some of the issues raised by Nestle's critics. There was also the fact that NIFAC's existence simply could not be ignored. By not appearing to cooperate with the commission, the activists were put in an indefensible position of being unconstructive and confrontational. The activists also lacked for other, more viable, alternative avenues for action. They had to remain in the limelight and keep the issue on the front burner. They also needed to occupy the high moral ground. It was clearly not possible to sustain a strongly confrontational posture without, at the same time, showing Nestle as the recalcitrant party.

Therefore, in November 1982 INFACT/INBC changed its strategy and decided to make use of the commission's complaint investigation mechanism. Participation in the process would yield the activists a number of tactical advantages. A large number of complaints would suggest widespread code violations on the part of Nestle and would also be seen as evidence of the activists' vast reporting network. A heavy workload of complaint investigation would necessarily slow down the commission's work and open it to charges of foot-dragging. Nestle's responses, where inadequate or evasive, would provide the activists with further opportunities for lodging complaints. And to the extent that Nestle was made to institute changes in its marketing and promotional practices — in response to activists' complaints and NIFAC's recommendations — the goals of the Code would have been advanced.

These were indeed good tactical insights. However, the activists failed to gauge accurately NIFAC's strengths and underestimated its resolve. The structured review process would necessitate gathering substantive information that could be verified. It would also force the activists to "play the game" according to NIFAC's rules and thereby yield tactical advantage to NIFAC. Moreover, Nestle would be able to channel its response to the complaints filed through NIFAC. Thus it would gain tremendous public credibility by the speed and character of response, both controlled by Nestle and tailored to yield maximum tactical and strategic benefits to the company. Nestle was also protected from being broad-sided on the complaint issue, since all complaints were now coming through NIFAC. The process would also act to de-emotionalize the controversy and thereby neutralize the activists' tactic of "a display of moral outrage in the public."

On November 19, 1982, in a formal meeting between INBC-ICCR and NIFAC, the former submitted 60 reports of Nestle's code violations to NIFAC for investigation. This was the first and only formal meeting between NIFAC and the activists.* NIFAC was finally able to act in its pri-

---

*Two more years would elapse before another formal meeting between INBC-ICCR and NIFAC would take place, although on several other occasions one or more INBC representatives met with NIFAC.

mary role, which was the investigation of complaints and "to question both sides and compel them to provide information clarifying the allegations and responding substantively to the positions of the other."[18] The commission members went to extraordinary lengths to investigate the initial set of complaints to avoid any potential criticism for lack of diligence. NIFAC members went so far as to examine *all* of the original supporting documents provided by INFACT-INBC and those attached to Nestle's responses. They often ran to over 100 pages for some complaints and company responses. The process took over four months; by the time of the March 1983 meeting, the investigation process was completed and documentation was sent to those who had registered the allegations.*

The process was not devoid of tension and antagonism, however. Doug Johnson and INFACT were still following their tactic of continuous confrontational dialogue between the opposing groups that would lead to a further exchange of letters and mutual recriminations about each other's intentions and interpretations. While this tactic had been quite successful in the early stages of the controversy in creating a forum for engaging the companies by the activists, in the current circumstances it merely became a delaying tactic and made the activists appear as obstructionists. For example, in discussions between INFACT's Doug Johnson and NIFAC's Mildred Randall, Doug Johnson had agreed to isolate eight violations for priority investigation by NIFAC, out of a total of 60 violations that INFACT had submitted to the commission. INFACT did not provide sufficient information on a number of violations and contended that it would not do so "until the Commission established clear procedures for confidentiality." However, he later expressed his displeasure at Randall when she reported to a joint meeting of the Methodist Task Force and NIFAC that INFACT had withdrawn 52 violations because it was warned that its "credibility would be undermined if the violations would not stand up to scrutiny. All of the violations stand as reported to WHO, the press and to the Commission (NIFAC)." Mildred Randall, in her responding letter of February 25, 1983, indicated to Doug Johnson that he was misinformed about the report to the joint meeting of MTF and NI-FAC. What actually transpired was that:

> . . . as a demonstration of the Commission's goodwill and out of mutual interests, one of the Commission's group expressed appreciation that it is possible to narrow the focus at this time and warned INFACT, as the Commission continually warns itself, that in this process everyone must establish credibility. Statistically speaking, we all stand a better chance of validating all or almost all of 8 alleged viola-

---

*By the time the commission dissolved itself in May 1991, it had reached determination of 315 complaints over a nine-year period. See, Nestle Infant Formula Audit Commission, *Joint Statement by Nestle and the Nestle Infant Formula Audit Commission* (Washington, D.C., June 1991), p. 2.

tions than we do of 60. If the Commission submits in haste many allegations and some of them are disapproved, the Commission's credibility is diminished. If IN-FACT submitted them to the Commission in the first place, INFACT's credibility is also at risk.

By the time the sixth quarterly report was published in January 1984, NIFAC had received 97 complaints. Of these, 88 had been processed, two were still awaiting additional information from the submitting parties, and seven had been dropped altogether because the complainants failed to provide additional needed evidence after more than a year's time.[19] A majority of the complaints (54) came out of Southeast Asia and India. Some were sent from Africa (17), the Caribbean and South America (11), and the remaining 6 were more or less scattered (including one each from Switzerland and from Spain). Twenty-nine countries in all were represented in the reports, out of the 140 countries in which Nestle markets infant formula.

Distribution of free samples and supplies, and promotion and advertising, accounted for 34 complaints each. Another 16 allegations involved labeling. In the area of sampling and supplies, a vast majority of the complaints involved donations of relatively large quantities of infant formula to hospitals for distribution to new mothers. In its response, Nestle admitted that in Indonesia, where most of these complaints originated, its compliance efforts had lagged behind those in other countries. However, by December of 1983, the company had tightened its policy. Henceforth, samples could only be provided for professional evaluation to health care workers in small quantities and only in certain situations, such as a new doctor, a new formula, or a significant reformulation of a current brand. The remaining handful of complaints, in the Far East, the Pacific Rim, and the Caribbean nations, indicated relatively minor infractions that could be explained in terms of individual ignorance, oversight, or indiscretion; they were corrected by the company.

Complaints involving labels concerned cans of formula in local stores with pictures of babies and insufficient health hazard warnings. NIFAC found that in at least one case, the arrival of products with the new labels was delayed by the Nigerian government who, because of unfavorable foreign exchange rates, stopped issuing import licenses. The situation was later remedied with the arrival of new supplies in Nigerian stores. In two cases, reports referred to labels on products that were baby cereals and were not marketed as breast-milk substitutes. The remaining one complaint referred to a Milkmaid Sweetened Condensed Milk label. Nestle contended that Milkmaid was not marketed as an infant food, and, therefore, the company did not include instructions on modifying the product for use as one. Three of the reports mentioned gifts distributed by Nestle in Yemen, Singapore, and Indonesia. The Yemen gift was valued at less than $1.00 and was considered trivial. The other two gifts involved a case of powdered milk for use by hospitals and a nutrition book for use by the hospital staff. Although these gifts had the appearance of being inappropriate, NIFAC agreed with the company's contention that they were inadvertent and were not intended to promote the sale of infant formula products.

Interestingly, one of the hottest issues of the boycott, mothercraft nurses, came up in only one of the reports. The Malaysian complaint alleged that company "nurses" distributed free samples to mothers in the Ng Maternity home in June 1982. Nestle contended that these women were actually "Medical Delegates" whose contact was limited to health professionals and did not extend to patients. NIFAC agreed that there was no proof that mothercraft nurses (as defined by the code) were employed by the company.

In the area of advertising and promotion, a major issue of concern was the continued existence of noncomplying materials, posters, booklets, and pamphlets in hospitals and clinics. NIFAC recommended that Nestle make an effort to track down this outdated literature. While the company recognized the problem, its correction was not easily accomplished. Not only were there a large number of small and off-the-beaten-path clinics that might still have old yellowing posters on their walls; there were also all the patients and visitors who might have taken home educational booklets. Another issue that touched on promotion in a broader sense pertained to lobbying. The company was accused of lobbying against stricter local codes in the Philippines and Sri Lanka. NIFAC found that the company's local subsidiaries were lax in following head office directives and that top management in Switzerland had tightened control and reporting procedures to ensure proper compliance.

NIFAC in Action — Phase III

In the closing months of 1983, NIFAC launched a new project that vastly expanded the commission's scope of activities. Instead of merely investigating complaints, NIFAC decided to undertake its own study of Nestle's marketing practices. This was based on an elaborate 22-page questionnaire covering respondents from 19 developing countries. It was to be an exploratory study to develop an independent sense, from the commission's point of view, of what was actually happening in these countries with regard to Nestle's marketing and promotional practices in the sale of infant formula foods. The original study design contemplated that NIFAC board members would personally visit different countries surveying hospitals and clinics in a number of cities and towns. Unfortunately, for a variety of reasons, most of NIFAC board members could not undertake such an extensive assignment. Instead, the visits were taken, at an enormous cost in terms of legal fees by attorneys from Mr. Muskie's law firm. Two knowledgeable sources put the cost of the Mexico study in the neighborhood of $1.0 million. Their lack of experience in field research, coupled with their lack of knowledge of the medical and health issues pertaining to the infant formula controversy, made their findings of dubious value. After a decent pause, the report was conveniently forgotten.

NIFAC in Action — Phase IV

In January 1984 the boycott against Nestle came to an end. In terminating the boycott, INBC-INFACT recognized the progress made by Nestle in complying with the code, while other companies were lagging. NIFAC had significantly contributed to the conditions — in monitoring Nestle's field performance and in improving its code compliance — that made it possible for the two parties to come together. Although NIFAC "superficially" played only an observational role in the negotiations leading to the termination of the boycott, a number of its members, notably Wogaman, were "in the thick of the diplomacy." The suspension of the boycott would cause a substantial curtailment in the scope and intensity of NIFAC's activities. In part, this resulted from the success that NIFAC had achieved in meeting and expanding on its original mandate in the previous 16 months. Nevertheless, it would be another 7.5 years before NIFAC's mission would finally come to an end and NIFAC would be dissolved.

With the end of the boycott, Nestle issued a Statement of Understanding that left some issues unresolved, particularly with respect to the free supply of breast-milk substitutes. NIFAC continued to act in a monitoring capacity and assisted in clarifying aspects of the code pertaining to the donation of supplies to hospitals. Working with WHO and Nestle, NIFAC helped in WHO's issuance of "Guidelines Concerning the Main Health and Socioeconomic Circumstances in Which Infants Have to Be Fed on Breast-Milk Substitutes" in April of 1986, thus resolving a major area of controversy in Nestle's implementation of the code (i.e., free supplies would be permitted for socioeconomic reasons as well as physiological reasons).

NIFAC also worked closely with UNICEF and the World Health Assembly which culminated in the issuance by WHA, in May 1986, of a resolution urging member states to ensure that small amounts of breast-milk substitutes, needed for the minority of infants who required them in maternity wards and hospitals, be made available through normal procurement channels and not through free or subsidized supplies. During 1986–1990, NIFAC continued in its efforts to urge Nestle to take action on the issue of free and low-cost supplies to hospitals. Notable success was achieved on a country-by-country basis. It also called for mutual cooperation by all concerned parties in improving infant feeding and nutrition in Third World countries. Further efforts in this direction led to extensive meetings between Nestle and

NIFAC and prompted the company to develop a plan of action for infant and young child feeding. The plan set forth Nestle and NIFAC's agreement on a 10-point program to be implemented by Nestle. The program expanded Nestle's commitments beyond the code and sought to promote new cooperative initiatives with the overall objective of terminating all donations of infant formula that may discourage breastfeeding.[20]

During this period, the number of complaints had dramatically declined. In its final Report, NIFAC listed determination of 14 complaints and found that Nestle was generally following its publicly stated commitments with respect to the distribution and promotion of infant formula products. This fact, combined with the appointment in January 1991 of an ombudsman by the International Association of Infant Food Manufacturers (IFM), who would endeavor to settle disputes concerning code violations against IFM members (including Nestle), contributed to the joint decision of Nestle and NIFAC to dissolve the Commission. NIFAC determined that it had completed its mission as stated in its charter, and that mechanisms were established to monitor future code compliance.

NIFAC's Achievements — An Assessment

One would be hard-pressed to overestimate NIFAC's accomplishments. It played a pivotal role in resolving the boycott issue. The commission achieved this by setting standards and procedures — adhered to by all parties — under which Nestle's violations against the code would be investigated and disposed. It was the perfect instrument for Nestle during the remedy and relief stage of the controversy. Moreover, by channeling all issues of remedy and relief through the commission, it would severely limit the future options of the boycotting groups in re-opening the issue and seeking alternative courses of action. Equally important, the commission would set the parameters under which the two sides would negotiate during the prevention stage of the controversy. What started out as an issue defined by Nestle's critics — raised in arenas that were hostile to Nestle's vital interests and its view of the world — ended up becoming an issue that would be defined in extremely narrower terms, processed under bureaucratic and legalistic procedures, and resolved under terms where Nestle, instead of appearing as the offending party, would emerge as a forward-looking, proactive corporation, while the activists were reduced to negotiating the fine points of compliance. Lost in the entire process were the ultimate moral and ethical concerns on the social responsibility of Nestle in particular and multinational corporations in general. Of course, it did not help the activists' cause that most Third World countries were found derelict both in their commitment and actions toward implementing the code. Nor would WHO become more aggressive in seeking the code compliances when its political masters, namely, the member states, were singularly uninterested in doing so.

The commission's work would go a long way toward a de-emotionalization of the issue and a diminution of inflammatory rhetoric. It would thus create a framework and a forum wherein points of disagreements could be narrowly and clearly defined and resolved through discussion and negotiation. Two, it helped Nestle to act expeditiously and substantively in responding to complaints and to NIFAC's suggestions for improvements in the infant formula marketing and promotion practices. The fact that such a feat occurred is all the more remarkable because as an institutional mechanism, NIFAC was totally without precedent, was created under hostile circumstances, and, at least during the early stages of its existence, did not have the whole-hearted support of its sponsors. NIFAC's success is an apt testimony to the strategic genius of its creators, NCCN and Ray Pagan, and to the caliber and commitment of its members who made the new entity work.

The unique conditions that brought the commission into being are being increasingly confronted by other large corporations (notably multinational corporations) in a host of similar and diverse situations where their operations impact other institutions and people who feel unfairly treated in the economic arena and are unable to seek redress within the traditional sociopolitical and legal mechanisms. Therefore, institutions like NIFAC offer alternative avenues and organizational mechanisms within which one might fashion new solutions to emerging problems. Whether NIFAC-like organizations might be more effective without all the legal paraphernalia that came with Muskie's law firm is a moot point. As Thad Jackson commented, "The legal apparatus had its pros and cons and sometimes it got a little pedantic. But at the same time, it probably protected the Commission from getting on shaky ground." Reflecting on his experience with NIFAC, Mr. Muskie observed:

> Companies may have experience in handling controversies in the legal domain, be it in the courts or in the legislature, but in the realm of political and social controversy, a company's ability to respond effectively may be severely limited. The company's credibility and motives may be in question, and no forum may be available, with established procedures and guarantees of due process, to find the truth objectively. The Nestle Infant Formula Audit Commission . . . may serve as a model in handling such controversies.

> The Commission achieved its success in a controversy that was largely outside the legal domain — there were no judges to interpret the law, no police to enforce it, and no legislators to amend it. However, much as Nestle may have been concerned in early 1982 that events were moving out of control, the controversy had not been taken completely from Nestle's control — no lawsuits had been filed requiring Nestle to handle the issue in the courts, and few governments had taken control to impose specific requirements on Nestle, for better or for worse. Thus,

Nestle was able to act, by unilaterally implementing the World Health Organization (WHO) Code and by asking a group of eminent individuals to form an independent audit commission to judge whether Nestle was complying with its publicly stated commitments.[21]

Muskie listed five elements he considered essential to the commission's success. They were: commission's independence, company's commitment, commission's membership, commission's leadership role, and emphasis on the use of legal procedures in the commission's work and deliberation. He believed the Commission's "absolute independence — both actual independence and publicly perceived independence" to be the most important factor. NIFAC was independent both from Nestle and the boycott groups. Although Nestle initiated the new commission and funded its operations, the commission members made the group their own. The commission's legal charter incorporated inviolable legal guarantees of independence that were further reinforced by its right to undertake its own investigation, set its own agenda, develop its own operating procedures, and finally make public its findings. Thus the commission was able to demonstrate repeatedly its independence and objectivity and challenged the critics to judge it by its actions and not by some pre-conceived notions.[22] An equally important factor, from Muskie's perspective, was the commitment of Nestle's top executives in Switzerland to the implementation of the WHO Code. In the absence of such a commitment, NIFAC would have been unable to prompt the company to get into a proactive mode by conforming its policies and practices closer to the standards of the WHO Code and to stricter interpretation of it.

Nevertheless, it is apparent that by taking the initiative in establishing the commission, Nestle was able to specify the "terms of references" within which the commission would operate. Thus, to the extent that broader issues of public policy were addressed, they were biased in favor of Nestle's views of the world. It is true that the commission, on its own initiative, was able to enlarge its mission and thus deal with the underlying issue of infant health and nutrition. However, this cannot always be taken for granted and would necessarily depend, in other instances, on the composition and caliber of board members. Thus, despite its success, the commission created an image that the need for such an institution was "Nestle-specific." This perception is further reinforced by the fact that no other infant formula manufacturer chose to use NIFAC's good offices, nor did they create their own similar organizational entities. It is also interesting that the new industry grouping, International Association of Infant Food Manufacturers (IFM), did not opt for a NIFAC-like mechanism in handling complaints against its member companies, and instead chose to rely on a more controllable form of ombudsman with the mission of a passive recipient of complaints and little authority for enforcement.

Muskie felt it was important that commission members assume a leadership role without becoming "another advocate."[23]He also strongly defended the quasi-judicial character of the commission because it created a common language with which issues could be defined and areas of disagreement delineated, and procedures through which disagreements could be settled. The multiple roles demanded of the commission, he argued, could not otherwise be satisfactorily met. However, he emphasized that all these roles "became necessary because of some aspect of the Nestle problem."[24] For example, the commission became:

- a public auditor, because Nestle was convinced that it would comply with the WHO Code, but it did not have the credibility to convince the public, and the public was acting as policeman and judge;
- an expert body, because many of the key underlying issues were subject to dispute, information gaps were prevalent, and the WHO Code needed reasoned interpretation and application to real-world situations;
- a quasi-judicial body because it had to interpret the code, and because it had to determine whether Nestle had violated the code in specific aspects, by applying the code provisions to specific complaint allegations and defenses; and
- a source of pressure on Nestle personnel in the field to implement company policies and the WHO Code, because Nestle has a decentralized operation in approximately 140 countries and it faced a difficult task in convincing its personnel to abandon well-established and successful marketing practices used by their competitors and to comply instead with a complex set of instructions that placed them at a significant disadvantage in the marketplace.[25]

Thad Jackson categorizes the commission, in hindsight, as an advisory body. If the commission said, "We don't really think what you're doing is right," the company listened.

Muskie also attributes the success of the commission to its members who "were chosen for their independence, objectivity and involvement with the issues. A balance of expertise and backgrounds was sought — religious, medical, ethics, civic — and a balance of personalities was achieved."[26] Strange as it may seem, the commission's board did not have any expert with knowledge and experience in marketing practices either in industrially advanced countries or in developing nations. Nor did the commission have members with in-depth experience in the workings of international business and multinational corporations. One can rationalize the absence of such expertise from Nestle's perspective. The company's prime motivation in establishing the commission was to end the boycott. Nestle could not, therefore, be expected to open the Pandora's box by raising issues that pertained to the nature of the multinational corporation and were embedded in its structure, operational strategies, control mechanisms, and the relative bargaining power it enjoyed in Third World countries as to the autonomy of its operations.

It is not clear why the activists (and these include not only INBC-INFACT but also the more moderate elements in the religious community, notably the United Methodists and their Task Force) would not foresee such a lacunae and pursue this line of enquiry. Such an approach could have provided us with guidelines with applicability to other issues involving similar situations — promotion of tobacco and cigarettes, unhealthy foods, and other items of conspicuous consumption, to name a few. By ignoring the structural and general operational issues, both NIFAC and the activists missed a useful opportunity to explore the prospect of general applicability of the NIFAC model in other situations. In the absence of such an exploration, NIFAC is likely to be viewed by others in very narrow terms, a conclusion that is buttressed by the fact that to date, no other company has sought to emulate Nestle's example.

Notes

1. Nestle Infant Formula Audit Commission, *Press Conference - Transcript of Proceedings*, Washington, D.C., October 13, 1983.

2. For details of Nestle's discussions with the Methodist Task Force on this point, see Chapter 16, " 'Winning the Methodists' — The Last Major Battleground to Enlist the Religious Community's Support for the Boycott."

3. Edmund S. Muskie and Daniel J. Greenwald III, "The Nestle Infant Formula Audit Commission as a Model," *The Journal of Business Strategy* (Spring 1986), 19–23.

4. *INFACT Update*, May 1982.

5. Melinda Gipson, "Muskie Heads Units Formed by Nestle to Monitor Ways it Markets Infant Formula," *Religious News Service*, May 4, 1982, p. 6.

6. Nestle Infant Formula Audit Commission, *Joint Statement by Nestle and the Infant Formula Audit Commission* (Washington, D.C., June 1991), pp. E-1 - E-3.

7. Pauline Thoma, "Muskie Defends Nestle, Panel He Directs," *The Plain Dealer*, November 12, 1983, p. 13-A.

8. Nestle Infant Formula Commission, *Press Conference - Transcript of Proceedings*, Washington, D.C., October 13, 1983.

9. Letter from Wogaman to the author, dated February 25, 1993.

10. Doug Johnson, *INFACT Update*, May 1982.

11. Nestle, S.A., *Letter from Mr. Geoffrey Fookes to Dr. Avery Post* (Vevey, Switzerland), May 14, 1982.

12. Muskie and Greenwald, "The Infant Formula Audit Commission as a Model," supra note 3, p. 22.

13. *Ibid.*

14. Nestle Infant Formula Audit Commission, *First Quarterly Report* (Washington, D.C., October 1982).

15. *Ibid.*

16. Nestle Infant Formula Audit Commission, *Fourth Quarterly Report* (Washington, D.C., July 1983); and *Fifth Quarterly Report*, (Washington, D.C., October 1983).

17. Nestle Infant Formula Audit Commission, *Fourth Quarterly Report* (Washington, D.C., July 1983).

18. Nestle Infant Formula Audit Commission, *Sixth Quarterly Report* (Washington, D.C., January 1984).

19. *Ibid.*

20. Nestle Infant Formula Audit Commission, *Joint Statement by Nestle and the Infant Formula Audit Commission,* supra note 6, pp. E4–E5.

21. Muskie and Greenwald, "The Nestle Infant Formula Audit Commission as a Model," supra note 3, p. 19.

22. *Ibid.*, p. 21.

23. *Ibid.*, p. 22.

24. *Ibid.*, p. 23.

25. *Ibid.*

26. *Ibid.*, p. 22.

18 SETTLEMENT OF THE DISPUTE AND TERMINATION OF THE BOYCOTT

Discussions Between INBC/INFACT and Nestle-UNICEF in the Role of an Honest Broker

On January 26, 1984, the activist groups represented by INBC agreed to suspend their boycott against Nestle. This was done in a jointly held news conference by Nestle and INBC at the NCCN's offices in Washington, D.C. The suspension was made final on October 4, 1984, in Washington, D.C. It was a culmination of the efforts that started immediately after the passage of the WHO Code and subsequent Nestle's commitment to implement the code in its Third World operations. The process of discussions-negotiations,* the external conditions that brought it about, and changes in Nestle's organizational structure, operating practices, attitudes toward its critics, and negotiating tactics, all offer an excellent road map with which to enhance our understanding of how corporations might best work in a proactive mode with their critics in the public policy arena.

---

*It was an unshakable tenet of faith with Nestle that the company would not directly negotiate with its critics. As far as the company was concerned, the word "negotiations" was not part of its lexicon when meeting or dealing with the activists. Hence throughout the entire controversy, Nestle insisted on calling its meetings with the activists as "discussions" while to the rest of the world, they were negotiations by another name. In order to avoid opposing contentions by the two parties, in this chapter we have referred to these contacts as discussions-negotiations.

Antecedents to the Final Discussions-Negotiations

Immediately upon the establishment of NCCN, its chief executive, Ray Pagan decided that a core element of his company's strategy to bring about an end to the boycott would be to create an environment wherein the company and its critics could engage in meaningful discussions to understand each other's concerns and find ways to deal with them.* This was not easily accomplished, however. Both Nestle and INBC viewed each other with extreme suspicion, did not trust the other group's integrity, and felt that discussions would not be conducted in good faith. An even more important issue, from Nestle's viewpoint, was the legitimacy of the activist groups. To wit, who did they stand for; what right did they have to represent the Third World people; and where is the assurance that any agreements made by the company would be honored by the critics?

To the activists, however, the legitimacy and recognition were of paramount importance. It was they who had organized the boycott, mobilized public opinion in the United States against Nestle and other infant formula manufacturers, and provided the major momentum to the nongovernmental organizations (NGOs) at the World Health Assembly that led to the passage of the infant formula code. It was their boycott, and therefore Nestle must negotiate with them on the terms and conditions under which that boycott would be terminated and the process by which Nestle's compliance efforts monitored. A second concern for the INBC leadership was that of maintaining control over their internal constituencies and support groups. They could not be seen giving in to the company or compromising on the basic issue of full compliance with the code throughout the world.

The two positions seemed irreconcilable. The company had realized that it must explore new ways for coping with its critics and for ending the boycott. An important step in that direction had been the establishment of NCCN. Nevertheless, the internal organizational imperatives and personalities involved made it difficult for Nestle's top management to accept the reality of holding face-to-face discussions-negotiations with the activists. Therefore, Nestle — Switzerland gave specific instructions to NCCN's Pagan that he was not to establish any direct contact or initiate direct dialogue with the activists. Thus, during the initial; period of its operations, NCCN focused its attention on establishing relations among the moderate elements of the boycott movement — who may or may not be members of INBC — while avoiding any direct contact with the INBC leadership. Nevertheless,

---

*For a detailed discussion of NCCN's strategies and tactics see Chapter 15, "Nestle Coordination Center for Nutrition, Inc. (NCCN): Nestle's Change in Organizational Structure and Strategies."

Pagan realized that Nestle must eventually deal with the INBC leadership if it wants to make significant progress with even the moderate groups, and especially the religious institutions. An extremely rigid and uncompromising posture toward the leadership of the boycott movement would make the company appear arrogant and exacerbate its already negative public image. It may even have the preverse effect of further unifying the opposing groups under the leadership of INBC. It would also not be in keeping with Nestle's efforts in persuading its critics and the news media that it was a new Nestle — in both style and substance — that the public is looking at in the post-code phase. NCCN was, therefore, determined to find some way of reaching out to its critics and engaging them in a constructive dialogue with the company.

NCCN designed a two-pronged strategy to deal with the situation. The first element of the strategy would be to provide accurate and timely information to important constituencies about what Nestle was doing in implementing the code. This approach should result in enlarging the information base in the public domain on the infant formula controversy, counteract some of the more virulent and allegedly unfounded accusations made by the critics against the company, and induce people to make more informed decisions with regard to their stand on the issue. Such an approach would raise Nestle's public stature and make its pronouncements more credible to the public. Only then Nestle would be able to deal effectively with the leadership of the boycott movement, which it must eventually do. The second component of the strategy was to project NCCN as willing and ready to meet with any and all concerned groups — with the exception of INBC whom NCCN branded as extremist — discuss pertinent issues relating to the infant formula controversy.

MTF — INBC and Nestle — Talks without a Dialogue

Dr. Philip Wogaman of the United Methodist Task Force (MTF) had already taken some tentative steps in arranging face-to-face discussions between INBC and Nestle. Recall that one of MTF's mandates was to bring about a resolution of the controversy by engaging in a constructive dialogue with the infant formula manufacturers (for further details, see Chapter 16). Earlier in July 1981, at his behest, a delegation of INBC had visited Geneva and had a meeting with Nestle's top management, including its chairman Arthur Furer. This meeting turned out to be a disaster. Nestle felt that it was being misrepresented by its critics and reneged on its previous agreement to meet with them. Wogaman, however, remained convinced that only through face-to-face meetings between INBC and Nestle would any progress be possible. Therefore, in August 1981 he persuaded Doug Johnson, head of INBC's steering committee, to meet with Nestle's representatives. Johnson agreed to such a meeting with Nestle (NCCN) with the avowed purpose of educating the members of his (INFACT's) steering committee about Nestle's efforts toward implementing the WHO code. Johnson's action put Pagan in a dilemma. He was under specific instructions from Vevey not to interact with INBC. He also realized that a spurning of MTF initiated dialogue with INBC would risk NCCN's losing the goodwill of the Methodists and thereby endanger the very fragile bond of support that it had built with MTF. Therefore, he agreed to the meeting with the proviso that Nestle would be represented by the company's Washington, D.C.-based lawyer, Tom Ward. Through this astute maneuver, he was able to engage in MTF-sponsored discussions with INBC while at the same time complying with the company's policy proscribing any face-to-face meetings with INBC.

The first meeting between NCCN and INBC was held in September 1981 with Tom Ward representing NCCN and Jonathan Churchill, a lawyer, and Doug Johnson representing INBC. Wogaman (presiding) along with Paul Minus represented MTF, a neutral party. Wogaman recalls with some irony "the truly memorable thing [about this meeting] was that when asked what Nestle would have to do to terminate the boycott neither Johnson nor Churchill had an answer! In effect, they were surprisingly unclear about the fundamental objectives of the boycott!"[1] It was agreed that the discussions would be kept confidential and that all parties would refrain from making any public pronouncements. As a follow up, Nestle submitted to MTF its promised field instructions — statement of policy on March 2–3, 1982. In the previous September, MTF had earlier enquired Nestle as to why the company could not conform to the WHO Code in countries where it felt it could not. The field instructions and statement of policy were in partial response to that query. However, soon thereafter, Nestle cut through all the qualifiers and clarifications with a flat decision to conform to the WHO Code. This outcome was the result of deliberations of the famous "Dayton Meeting" between MTF and Nestle's top brass (see Chapter 16).

The Field Instructions-Policy Statement document was discussed on March 12, 1982, in Louisville, Kentucky, at the Church Unity Meeting where many denominational leaders were present. Wogaman had circulated copies of the Nestle document in advance of the meeting to a number of church leaders prominent in the boycott movement, including Dr. William (Bill) Thompson, moderator of the Presbyterian Church of USA, and Dr. Claire Randall, general secretary of the National Council of Churches.* The reaction to the Nestle document was quite positive. Bill Thompson thought that

---

*For further details of MTF's efforts in bringing together the activists, other church leaders, and Nestle, see Chapter 16; "Winning" the Methodists — The Last Major Battleground to Enlist the Religious Community's Support for the Boycott."

the document was qualitatively better than anything that Nestle had previously done. Claire Randall was equally impressed and encouraged. It was agreed at the Louisville meeting that the denominational leaders could share the Nestle document with their staffs for seeking advice and counsel on a confidential basis. Wogaman also shared the document with Leah Margulies of INFACT-INBC. During their meeting, Margulies expressed some reservations about the Nestle document. However, the same day, during her address to the American Public Health Association, she exhorted the membership to intensify the Nestle boycott.

Wogaman now faced the problem of bringing together Nestle and INBC for a serious discussion of the Nestle document. Curiously, Nestle was no more eager at that time for the meeting than the other side. Wogaman had persuaded Pagan and Geoffrey Fookes (Nestle — Switzerland) for such a meeting with the understanding that this would not constitute negotiations but an opportunity for clarification of their document. The meeting was arranged for March 17, 1982, St. Patrick's Day, in New York City. However, Nestle released its document to the public a day before, on March 16, 1982. Wogaman, who also chaired the March 17 meeting, felt that it achieved its desired purpose. INBC had raised some issues regarding Nestle's field instructions which the company representatives answered. At the conclusion of the meeting, INBC representatives indicated that they had some additional points that needed Nestle's clarification. INBC subsequently submitted a list of some 100 issues for amplification by Nestle.

The Next Phase — From Talks to Dialogue

Following the March 17 meeting, Wogaman started exploring with both parties the possibility for further dialogue. Nestle was willing. INBC, however, objected to MTF's facilitator role and questioned its impartiality. This situation placed MTF in an awkward position. MTF could no longer in good faith press Nestle for further discussions if MTF itself was ruled out of such a discussion. Nestle, however, insisted on MTF's involvement to provide continuity with the past discussions and also to ensure accuracy in the reporting of the proceedings of such meetings.

The process of dialogue had now gathered momentum and acquired a life of its own. Between January 1982 and spring 1983, NCCN and INBC representatives had 13 meetings with MTF being present in almost all the meetings either as the sponsor or as a third party observer. There was also progress in other areas. For example, in February 1982, MTF had a meeting with Nestle's top managers from Switzerland who flew to Dayton, Ohio, to meet with the task force. The meeting turned out to be quite crucial toward building mutual trust between the Methodists and Nestle. It prompted the company to become more proactive in responding to the concerns of its critics through implementing changes in its marketing practices, and motivated MTF to make renewed efforts to bring about a termination of the boycott.

The dialogue, however, could not continue indefinitely without some tangible progress. From the activists' viewpoint, the process was a significant achievement in itself. They stood to gain considerably from prolonging it and thereby creating a de facto investigating and monitoring body over Nestle's compliance efforts. Nestle, on the other hand, did not want to legitimize the process through interminable discussions. The company was determined to move the process in a manner that would focus on successively narrower issues with the objective of resolving the boycott within a reasonable period of time. Through these meetings there emerged two sticking points that would prove to be stumbling blocks to further substantive discussions. NCCN insisted that Leah Margulies would not be acceptable to the company as part of INBC's negotiating team. INBC naturally took umbrage to Nestle's dictating as to who should represent the activists. NCCN also wanted to impose a limit on the length of time this meeting-dialogue process should consume. The company did not want to engage in endless discussions of INBC's 100 issues and thereby get into a quagmire of claims and a counterclaims.

By this time, the external environment was weakening the activists' position. Nestle's willingness to work with MTF, the establishment of NIFAC, and a posture of social responsiveness on the part of the company were being viewed as positive signs that needed a less confrontational response from the activists lest they were seen as confrontational for confrontation's sake. Fissures were also appearing in the INBC support base. Some mainline Protestant churches, notably the Baptist Church, had begun to seriously consider the proposal for pulling out of the boycott. Dr. Robert C. Campbell, head of the Baptist Church and a member of NIFAC, was to have raised the topic at a meeting of the Baptist Church Task Force on Infant Formula in Philadelphia on December 12, 1983. He was, however, outmaneuvered by INBC. The meeting was presented with a letter from a missionary living in Philadelphia to the effect that Dr. Campbell's field visit to that country was cursory and that his finding regarding Nestle's infant formula marketing practices were untenable. Copies of the letter had been distributed to many prominent members of the Baptist Church prior to the task force meeting and without Dr. Campbell's knowledge. A few weeks later, the council had a meeting in which one of the items on its agenda was a resolution suspending the boycott. Dr. William McBeath, executive director of the American Health Association, vice chairperson of INBC, and a member of Baptist Church Task Force on Infant Formula, made an impassioned plea for the continuation of the boycott for a few more months. He also presented the wife of the American clergyman from the Philippines who had written the letter that was previously distributed. The council then decided to table the resolution and reconsider it in February or March 1984. When this incident became public, several Baptist and other senior church leaders, including those of the Brethren Church, expressed their concern and resentment that Dr. Campbell's authority had been deliberately abused and undermined. For a rigidly hierarchical organization, it was a bad and an unacceptable precedent. Consequently, they served notice on Tim Smith of ICCR that something had to be done. This put further pressure on INBC to consider seriously the option of ending the boycott through a negotiated settlement.

Gathering Momentum for Discussions-Negotiations

NCCN's Pagan realized that the time was now right to make a determined push toward settling the boycott. He was convinced that both parties would lose in the event the boycott were to fade slowly away. Under the circumstances, Nestle's victory would not be credible in the eyes of the news media and religious institutions. INBC and its allies must also have some kind of victory in order to leave the battle field without a large residue of hatred and ill will against Nestle. Wogaman also felt that everybody needed a clean ending, particularly the churches. The credibility of the boycott mechanism as a legitimate moral tool was on the line. It was, therefore, highly desirable to end the boycott through a negotiated settlement. Consequently, on November 12-13, 1983, he met with Tim Smith of ICCR and urged him to consider negotiations with Nestle with a view to ending the boycott. He suggested to Tim Smith that INBC should pare down its list of 100+ accusations to three or four key issues and inform Nestle by letter that the boycott could be ended in the event that those issues could be satisfactorily resolved. Tim Smith confined to Wogaman that INBC had already been thinking along similar lines and had indeed narrowed down its list to only four issues. Wogaman further suggested that INBC should not insist on a full-dress meeting but should initiate discussions in an informal manner. Thus no one would be committed to anything until such time when those people, who were doing the informal talking, got close enough where they thought that negotiation should become more formal. Within a few days, he received word from Jonathan Churchill to the effect that ICCR and INBC were favorable to the idea and that he should go ahead and arrange a meeting with Nestle representatives.

Pagan was extremely conscious of the critical nature of these "negotiations to end negotiations." He wanted some tangible, demonstrable, symbolic action on the part of the activists to indicate a change of strategy and attitude on their part. He suggested to Wogaman that for him to convince Nestle — Vevey to engage in serious discussions, INBC would need to "curb its rhetoric and vitriolic attacks on Nestle and give public credit to Nestle for what it has done." A continuation of public condemnation on the part of INBC would "be the kiss of death for any attempt to end this stalemate in a peaceful way." These messages were communicated to INBC. Simultaneously, Pagan asked NCCN's Christiansen to initiate direct, albeit discrete, contacts with Doug Johnson of INBC. The discussions between the two led to a series of mutual understandings. INBC would use a conciliatory tone and a constructive approach in a letter that it planned to send to Nestle — Vevey with regard to INBC's four points. INBC had also scheduled a press conference on December 14, 1983, outside NCCN's offices in Washington, D.C. Pagan had indicated to Wogaman that although he could absorb a token demonstration against Nestle and explain it away to Vevey, a full-blown demonstration would make it all but impossible for him to move the company into direct discussions-negotiations with INBC. A similar point was made by Christiansen in his talks with Doug Johnson. The upshot of all these communications was that the INBC press conference was quite muted in its criticism of Nestle. The demonstrators, numbering no more than 20 people, presented NCCN with a petition in five bundles in a baby carriage. It was the signal that NCCN had been waiting for. Pagan immediately communicated to Vevey and alerted Angst about the letter that he would be receiving from INBC.

The INBC letter to Angst set forth the group's agenda on four issues and asked for discussions with Nestle based on those issues.[2] While the letter's tone was conciliatory and INBC acknowledged Nestle's efforts to comply with various code provisions, the letter also pointed out that INBC had identified "over 2 dozen areas of discrepancy with the WHO/UNICEF Code in letter and spirit, and in terms of effectiveness of implementation. These are the areas which we will continue to raise with Nestle management, WHO and UNICEF and NIFAC, as well as our own constituents. Therefore, we sought to undertake an evaluation of what areas remained that were significant enough to warrant our continued recommendation of the international Nestle boycott." The four major areas of conern identified by INBC were:

1. *Free supplies to hospitals should be limited to mothers with a real need, based on medical criteria.* INBC stated that it "cannot accept the Nestle definition of 'need' in this regard. The policy Nestle proposes would continue the routine distribution of formula in the hospital, and discourage hospitals from beginning effective breast feeding promotion policies. Nestle should restrict its free supplies within the hospital to those children who require it for medical need, or accept the obligation in Article 6.7 to continue to provide free supplies for the term of the child's needs."

2. *All personal gifts to health professionals, regardless of the economic value, should be halted.* The WHO/UNICEF limits the interaction between the infant formula producing companies and health professionals to "scientific and factual information" and prohibits giving gifts. INBC disagreed with Nestle's defense that gifts of calendars, books, and other inexpensive items to doctors were inconsequential.

3. *Information to mothers and health professionals must provide objective and balanced information regarding use and misuse, the benefits and hazards of the product.* The WHO Code provides that manufacturers provide mothers with "educational materials" on all aspects of infant feeding. INBC stressed that "the Code is a testament to the belief that fewer women would so choose to breastfeed, if provided with the information of the real costs in financial terms and to the health and lives of their babies. Without provision of this information, there can be no 'informed consent' by mothers on the choice of a feeding method." Although Nestle emphasized the benefits of breastfeeding in its literature, INBC had yet to identify any Nestle document that forthrightly conceded to doctors of mothers that the (infant formula) products could do harm and should be used only as a last resort.

4. *Provide strong warnings of hazards on the label.* INBC's key objection was to the product labels, believing that it "is the most widespread promotion mechanism measured by volume" to the mothers it reaches. Although Nestle had finally removed infant pictures from its labels, the new label did not meet the spirit of the code. A warning must warn and should "caution those who should not use this product and remind those who must."

Through this letter, INBC also informed Nestle that INBC and INFACT were co-hosting a conference on "International Baby Milk Campaign: Strategies for Action" in Mexico City between February 2–5, 1984. It further suggested that "if Nestle can demonstrate to us adequate progress in these four areas, the INBC is prepared to recommend to the entire conference that the Nestle boycott be suspended worldwide."

Upon receipt of this letter, Geoffrey Fookes of Nestle — Switzerland drafted a reply which in essence reiterated the past. He stated that as Nestle had taken suitable implementation action in those four areas of major concern to INBC, no discussions were warranted between the two parties. Pagan was enraged when he received a copy of the draft letter for his comments. This was precisely the situation that he had anticipated and wanted to avoid. He immediately called Fookes on the phone and "literally pinned him against the wall." Pagan blamed Fookes for his insensitive, reckless, and irresponsible response to a bona fide and conciliatory approach from INBC. He further told him that he would not let Vevey send such a letter to INBC, and should Angst override his recommendation and send the letter to INBC, he [Pagan] would forthwith resign from NCCN. Pagan then called Carl Angst. According to Pagan, Angst was angry because Pagan had given him an ultimatum and had "threatened to pull out." Responding to Pagan's statement that the letter would cause the loss of support from Dr. Campbell and Dr. Wogaman, Angst asked whether Pagan would object to his direct contact with Drs. Campbell and Wogaman. Pagan became incensed and said, "What you are telling me is that you need other witnesses and other evidence before you believe what I am saying. I will let you talk to them, but you must understand how I feel about it."

It is apparent that Angst was caught between two organizational problems: authority and alleged expertise, on the one hand, and personality conflicts, on the other hand. Fookes represented the continuity of infant formula expertise and policy formulation at Vevey. Fookes was also acting as the proxy for headquarters staff and could not be dismissed easily, if for no other reason than to maintain appearance and harmonious relations. Pagan, on the other hand, represented the company's new approach to conflict resolution which had been instituted by Angst himself. Angst also had to exercise a degree of caution as the negotiating process was reaching a critical stage. He was aware of the often bold and risky moves that Pagan was apt to make. He also knew that Pagan, in his determination to see things his way, was prone to creating mini crises and contrived situations so as to get Vevey to go along with his strategic and tactical initiatives. As it happened, both Campbell and Wogaman independently lent support to Pagan's contention. At Angst's direction, Pagan prepared a draft letter. It was a rather brief and cordial response opening the possibility of direct discussions with INBC. Angst approved the letter and it was sent to INBC.

Meanwhile, Christiansen and Johnson continued their meetings. In all five meetings took place between December 14, 1983, and January 8, 1984. These meetings provided NCCN with the first set of unadulterated soundings about the issues and concerns that were on the front burner for the INBC. The upshot of all these meetings, and further contacts between the parties through Wogaman, was the emergence of a consensus that discussions-negotiations between INBC and Nestle would use a format where a third party would act as the mediator/facilitator. Furthermore, the negotiations-discussions would be limited to a predetermined set of issues, that is, INBC's four points, and would not be extended to include other issues not previously agreed on by the two parties. What remained was the selection of the forum, the mediating party, and the format of discussions-negotiations.

Discussion-Negotiation Strategies

A great deal of ground had been covered in narrowing the differences between the two sides. This did not, however, lessen the importance of the final meetings. On the contrary, they assumed an unusually high importance for the simple reason that the outcome of these meetings would define — both for their internal constituencies and the public-at-large — the legitimacy of the basic positions taken by the company and the activists and their conduct during the preceding six years. They would also delineate their respective future roles with regard to the infant formula issue and to each other. Clearly, the goals of the two sides were not similar. While both groups wanted to resolve the issue — which by then had become a foregone conclusion — the issue of "form" was equally critical because, to a significant extent, form had become an integral part of "substance" and could not be separated from it. It is, therefore, important for us to understand the strategic and tactical considerations that underlaid the actions of INBC and NESTLE during the formal phase of discussions-negotiations. Our analysis in this section is based on interviews with most of the actors, confidential documents including communications between NCCN operatives and Nestle — Switzerland and a careful assessment of the activities of various groups and individuals both during the meetings and in the period subsequent to the suspension and termination of the boycott.

Nestle's Strategic and Tactical Considerations

NCCN made three initial strategic decisions that were to influence its actions in the formal discussions-negotiations.

1.   Notwithstanding the need for face-to-face meetings, NCCN would not recognize INBC as a "negotiating" party. It did not want to concede to INBC — in a formal sense — the role of the authoritative spokesperson for those who had previously been opposed to Nestle. Nor did it want INBC and the activists seen as the spokespersons of the Third World on this issue in their dealings with Nestle. This would mean that there would have to be a third party present who would act as a facilitator in transmitting messages and interpreting intentions and commitments on the part of one group for the benefit of the other. Since it had become apparent that INBC would not accept either MTF or NIFAC in that capacity, NCCN decided to ask UNICEF to play that role. Previously, Nestle had attempted to enlist WHO's support in this endeavor which that organization had declined. UNICEF thus became the logical and perhaps the only choice that would be acceptable to the parties. UNICEF would lend further credence to the negotiations, and affirm to the world body, about the actions so far taken by Nestle in complying with the WHO Code. NCCN also decided that should it become necessary, it would accept UNICEF as the final arbiter of appropriate meanings of various code provisions. Such a move would preclude INBC from resorting to differing interpretation of the code in the future. It would also induce the company to accept those interpretations which it otherwise might have resisted.

To an outside observer, this would seem like an absurd position to take and, in terms of the real-world perception, quite irrelevant. Whether Nestle called these meetings discussions or negotiations, or talked to the other side directly or through intermediaries sitting in the same room across the able, seemed trivial and nit picking. However, NCCN had to keep up the fiction so that its actions would not run counter to the "stated and long observed" corporate policy. This would also help contain the resistance of those executives in Vevey who were adamantly opposed to dealing with the activists or giving them any quarter. In a sense, NCCN was anticipating internal dissention and was building external support for its actions.

2. Pagan decided that NCCN would not yield anything on its own to INBC. He felt that this hard ball tactic did not run any danger of derailing the discussions-negotiations. From his perspective: there were no significant differences of opinion between the two sides on INBC'S four points; and that having once entered the discussions-negotiations, INBC would be hard pressed to break them given that there had been a significant erosion in the strength of the boycott and public support of INBC. Any concessions, if they had to come, would result from UNICEF's interpretation, thereby relieving NCCN from the burden of making concessions and denying INBC of the credit for gaining them. This strategy was "vintage Pagan" in terms of risk, brinkmanship, and boldness.

3. In another move reminiscent of NCCN's *modus operandi* during the phase of its dealings with MTF, NCCN prepared a talking paper that spelled out Nestle's views on the four issues. This would be called the "Statement of Understanding." A great deal of thought had gone into drafting the statement. The objective was to control the tenor of discussions by forcing all parties to react and respond to the Nestle-provided statements and definitions and thereby making them assume the burden of justifying alternative definitions and interpretations.

INBC's Strategic and Tactical Considerations

INFACT-INBC realized that boycott as an emotional issue with high moral overtones was running out of steam and, except for the hard-core committed followers, could not be sustained at the mass level. Consequently, INFACT's leadership began working on a strategy that would help them claim victory at the national and international level and then mobilize resources to mount challenges against infant formula manufacturers at the local level. Since the passage of the code, INBC-INFACT had been devoting successively increasing amounts of time at the policy-making level dealing with political-government leaders and corporate executives. The work of guiding the boycott was delegated to less experienced, local, nonprofessional volunteers. According to Doug Johnson, INFACT soon realized that "once you take your leadership out of front line and assign secondary or tertiary leaders to work at that level, the basic issue then is to hold it, not to do any more with it. Therefore, it meant that in the area of the boycott we were on the defensive." He also acknowledged that "there was a decline in the membership because our leadership was not making strong efforts to enlist new members."

INFACT recognized that the boycott momentum had shifted from the streets to institutional level requiring different types of strategies and tactics. It broadened the scope of its negotiating position by designating INBC as the major entity for formal discussion-negotiations with Nestle. Such a move would provide for greater involvement on the part of the European contingent of the activists who had been expressing some dissatisfaction at being left out and relegated to the sidelines by their American brethren.

INFACT had all along operated on the assumption that corporations responded only under pressure because of institutional inertia and a bureaucratic aversion to change. Continued pressure was necessary to keep the corporate focus on the issue. However, once that objective was achieved, then other methods of pressure were needed to ensure that corporations would not retract from their commitments and that INFACT would continue to play a significant role as a monitoring agent. Constant pressure on Nestle through boycott activism had already yielded significant results by bringing about changes in the company's corporate culture, forcing the company to alter — often unilaterally — its marketing practices with regard to infant formula products, and a de facto recognition of INFACT-INBC as the spokespersons for the boycott movement. The focus for the next step would be on institutionalizing compliance with the code as an integral part of the company's operating procedures and to position INFACT-INBC as a permanent player with regard to the marketing of infant formula products throughout the world and as the conscience and watchdog of the Third World poor to ensure that infant formula companies would not regress from their efforts to promote breastfeeding and comply with the letter and spirit of the WHO Code.

Prelude to Discussions-Negotiations

NCCN still had to solve two problems before any formal discussions could take place: to get permission from Nestle-Switzerland to go ahead with the meetings, and to persuade UNICEF to participate as a moderator but not as an arbitrator. Pagan made a good start with Vevey by sending them the draft of his proposed Statement of Understanding. In his communications with Vevey he played to their concerns and sensitivities by projecting INBC to be much weaker and more willing to negotiate than was indicated by available information and prevailing circumstances. He also gave the impression of playing hardball with INBC. In order to assure Vevey further, he indicated that NCCN would welcome Fookes' participation at the meetings and would benefit from his expertise and knowledge about the infant formula issue from the perspective of Nestle's worldwide operations.

Wogaman advised NCCN against going the UNICEF route which he thought would be cumbersome and strewn with bureaucratic tangles. Pagan, however, decided otherwise. He mounted a determined and multisided effort to get UNICEF on board. He called James Grant, UNICEF's director general, and urged him to take the initiative in the interest of moving this "confrontation" off the center stage so that all parties could get on with the business of implementing the code. He complained that despite Nestle's best efforts, they have not received any help or guidance in interpreting the code and facilitating its compliance. While UNICEF people were quite forthcoming and supportive in private meetings, they were reluctant in making those observations in public. Grant promised to consult with his people to see whether and under what circumstances UNICEF might play the role of a peacemaker.

Pagan sought Wogaman's help in persuading Tim Smith of ICCR to accept NCCN's initiated role for UNICEF. He also had a personal meeting with Sister Regina Murphy, a major player within INFACT-INBC, and asked for her support in getting the activists to work with UNICEF. Initially, INFACT-INBC were not sold on the idea because an intermediary would dilute their demand for direct one-on-one negotiations. However, Pagan emphasized the fact that since Nestle — Switzerland would not allow him to negotiate with the activists, the only way this dialogue could take place would be through an intermediary such as the UNICEF. This put INFACT-INBC in a bind. Expectations had been raised all around that negotiations were in the offing. The activists needed a closure deal. Since they had already rejected MTF as an intermediary and were unwilling to accept NIFAC, their only remaining option was to go along with the UNICEF idea or risk a breakdown of the negotiation process before it had even started.

NCCN's Thad Jackson met with various UNICEF staff people in New York to persuade them to join in this effort. Among the people contacted were: Dr. Stephen Joseph, Mr. Bertil Matheson, Ms. Kathleen Cravero, and Mr. Yoon Goo Lee. Recall that Dr. Joseph was one of the USAID aides who had resigned his position to protest the U.S. vote at the 23rd World Health Assembly opposing the passage of the infant formula code. All others had spent long years working on issues of infant health and nutrition and, through direct involvement, had become very familiar with the infant formula controversy. Dr. Joseph turned out to be quite receptive to the idea and endorsed UNICEF's participation in the discussions. This set the stage and the forum in which UNICEF was going to help in clarifying the interpretation of the WHO Code.

The Meetings

The format of the meetings, their location, and identity of representatives for various parties were carefully negotiated and agreed upon through a series of discussions between INFACT's Doug Johnson and NCCN's Niels Christiansen. There were to be a total of six meetings, with three to be held at the UNICEF's offices and three in the offices of Jonathan Churchill, INBC's attorney. The two sites would be alternated. The meetings at UNICEF were chaired by Dr. Joseph. The three meetings at Churchill's office were each chaired by Dr. R. Campbell, head of the Baptist Church and NIFAC member, Mr. Michael Glenn, a partner in Senator Muskie's law firm, and Dr. Wogaman, chairperson of MTF and a NIFAC member. The entire process lasted from January 14–23, 1984. The organizations and people represented at the meetings were:

UNICEF: Stephen Joseph, Kathleen Cravero, Yoon Goo Lee, and Bertil Matheson.
NCCN: Rafael D. Pagan, Jr., Thad M. Jackson, Niels Christiansen, Geoffrey Fookes, Jack Mongoven, and Susie Ferrer (observer).
INBC: Doug Johnson, Jonathan Churchill, Sister Regina R. Murphy, David Hallman, Fred Zeimonds, Colleen Shannon Thornberry, Tim Smith (observer), and Leah Margulies (observer).
NIFAC: Robert Campbell, Philip Wogaman, and Michael K. Glenn.

The First Meeting: January 14, 1984

At the beginning of the first meeting, Stephen Joseph of UNICEF enunciated a number of rules — all previously agreed upon by INBC and NCCN — that would be adhered to in the conduct of all meetings. These were:

1. Nestle's Statement of Understanding would serve as the basic document/working paper during the meetings.
2. Discussion would be limited to the four areas of major concern specified in INBC's letter to Nestle — Switzerland.
3. Both sides would present their viewpoints on each issue. This would then be followed by a discussion, including clarifying questions, until a mutual agreement is reached on Nestle's Statement of Understanding.
4. In the event of a clear disagreement, the issue would be referred to UNICEF, which would then withdraw, caucus, and return to state which position was in compliance with the code.
5. The proceedings of the meetings were to be kept confidential by everyone including the observers. This was honored by all parties, indicating a real desire on everyone's part to see that these meetings produced the desired result.

At the end of the first day of the meeting, both parties had already reached an agreement on Nestle's understanding of the WHO Code on two major areas of health hazards warning on labels and personal gifts to health workers. They had also agreed to continue their discussions of the remaining two areas of educational materials and supplies on which both parties had substantial disagreements. UNICEF suggested that it would like to see both sides come to whatever points of agreement independent of UNICEF and if they still had some areas of negotiable differences, UNICEF would be glad to help them in arriving at an acceptable understanding.

Although the meetings were concluded in a short span of 10 days, the discussions were not always amicable, either between the groups or within each group. There were heated disagreements, innuendoes, and often loss of self-control as each party fought for "principles" and maneuvered for tactical negotiating advantages.

NCCN and Pagan had to maintain a fine balance between its external posture and internal intransigence reflected by Fookes. In more ways than one, Fookes represented the views of a powerful segment of Vevey's bureaucracy. In addition, he could authoritatively assert as to what would be acceptable to Nestle — Switzerland on various points of contention. There was also tension because Pagan was leading the Nestle delegation and Fookes had to restrain himself from publicly disagreeing with him. Fookes' personal confrontation style and disdain for the activists often ended up creating a negative charge among the participants. Thus NCCN's operatives would argue and plead with each other for long hours after each meeting to iron out their differences. The cable and telex traffic between NCCN and Vevey was invariably heavy, fast, and furious.

Reflecting on that phase of discussion, Thad Jackson observed:

> In a dynamic situation like the one we faced some tensions were inevitable. Fookes and Paternot were in a defensive-reactive mode more often than Pagan considered advisable given the rate of progress in negotiations. There were also differences in perspectives because of lag in time, distance, and the currency of the situation. Switzerlasnd, of course, not being here, not being caught up into it, had its reservations. And more importantly, people at Vevey didn't want us making commitments that we could not fulfill, or to write language that was impossible to live with later on, I think there was a genuine safeguard there. We would have caused more problems than we would have solved.

The next two meetings were held at Jonathan Churchill's office on January 15 and January 16, 1984, presided over by Dr. Robert C. Campbell and Mr. Michael Glenn of NIFAC, respectively. After each meeting, Nestle would update its statement of understanding, incorporating the suggestions of INBC and UNICEF. This revised draft then would become the basis for discussion for the following meeting. Of the remaining two issues, "educational materials" was resolved by the end of the fourth meeting on January 19, 1984. At the meeting on January 19, 1984, Doug Johnson of INBC wanted to present an INBC Statement of Understanding on the ground that it was an important part of communication and INBC's understanding of the issues discussed. However, Stephen Joseph overruled Doug Johnson on the ground of pre-agreed procedure of operation and reminded everybody that "The Nestle Statement of Understanding will be used as a reference point to proceed from, and INBC can use its paper as a source to comment from; not to belittle the INBC paper but rather to be consistent with our previous agreements."

The second and most controversial area of INBC's concern pertained to supplies. This kept both parties at loggerheads for the longest period of discussions in UNICEF meetings. This was one area in which the Nestle team had already decided not to compromise and had to consult with Vevey before coming to an understanding with INBC and UNICEF. After intensive discussions, three major areas of disagreement were isolated between Nestle and INBC: definition of "infants who have to be fed on breast-milk substitutes"; the propriety of discharge packs given to new mothers leaving the hospital which included, among other things, a supply of infant formula foods; and the nature and extent of Nestle's responsibility for limiting supplies. On the issue of discharge packs both INBC and Wogaman believed that Nestle had been less than candid with them. In earlier informal meetings, Doug Johnson felt that Niels Christiansen had led him to believe that Nestle's talking paper contained a statement to the effect that supplies were not to be used as discharge packs for breastfeeding mothers. Wogaman had also told Doug that Nestle had stopped giving discharge packs and free samples. Hence, discharge packs was not one of the issues to be discussed with Nestle. However, in the formal meetings, it appeared that discharge tins were still permitted to be distributed to mothers by hospitals and that Nestle considered discharge packs as part of supplies. Tim Smith immediately called Wogaman who was travelling in Central America. This was on January 13, 1984, a day before the UNICEF meetings, and expressed his great concern over Nestle's position on discharge packs. Wogaman told Tim Smith that based on Nestle's assurances, the MTF report to the Methodist General Conference had clearly stated that Nestle had refrained from giving discharge packs to mothers in Third World hospitals.

During the UNICEF meeting, Nestle had insisted that it would not change its policy on discharge packs. INBC's basic position was that discharge packs were samples. When Nestle had said that discharge tins were part of supplies, UNICEF ruled "No, they are not." Notwithstanding, Nestle kept on arguing against it even though all four people from UNICEF had interpreted Nestle's position as a violation of the WHO Code. On this issue, there was strong disagreement within the Nestle team, particularly between Pagan and Fookes. When Nestle realized that UNICEF considered its position in violation of the WHO Code, Nestle indicated that it would go back and check this issue with Vevey. Wogaman also talked to one of Nestle's staff people and conveyed his own concern that "if they were to stick to their guns on the hospital discharge tin question, it would put the MTF in an untenable position as it had already informed the General Conference about Nestle's intent not to allow hospital discharge packs. We would have to publicly indicate that we had been wrong."

Following the January 19 meeting, Nestle was under intense pressure from UNICEF, INBC, and Wogaman of MTF to resolve this issue. Pagan and Fookes had serious differences on the issue of hospital discharge packs. Fookes was quite adamant against accepting UNICEF's interpretation and asserted that Vevey would not make a change in its policy as it would have a devastating impact on the company's infant formula markets around the world. Pagan was inclined to accept the UNICEF position. He told Fookes that he had sent a telex to Carl Angst in Vevey expressing his own personal view that Nestle should accept the UNICEF definition of "have to be fed infant formula" which, in essence, would be the basis to provide supplies to hospitals and that supplies to hospitals were not to be used as discharge packs. Pagan also asked Vevey's confirmation that he had the authority, which Fookes had questioned, to commit Nestle on this issue in the UNICEF meetings. Angst endorsed the change recommended by Pagan. With this Nestle "bit the bullet and agreed to abide by WHO-UNICEF's interpretation." When Pagan told Fookes about his conversation with Angst, Fookes showed great displeasure and disappointment. At this point, Pagan told Fookes, "I am in charge here and this is the Nestle policy. If you don't like it, you can take the next plane to Vevey." Instead of Vevey, Pagan then sent Fookes to California to meet with some members of NIFAC and then on to Brazil. As a result, Fookes was absent from the remaining meetings. As it turned out, the resolution of the controversy was not clearcut. The language in the joint statement was deliberately crafted such that both parties could accept it at face value; yet, it left some leeway for the two parties to resort to differing interpretations. Thus the unresolved issue of gift packs and free supplies would eventually become a major point of contention between INBC and Nestle and lead to the launch of another boycott against Nestle in October 1988.

Nestle and INBC now had an agreement on all the four points raised by INBC. The final text of the *Nestle Statement of Understanding* was agreed to by the parties [Appendix A]. It was all over except a little bit of drama left. The last meeting, on January 23, 1984, was essentially devoted to administrative purposes.

Prelude to the Press Conference

The plans for the announcement of the boycott suspension were meticulously prepared and negotiated by the parties to satisfy their internal constituencies and with an eye toward maximum news media coverage. The two sides agreed to issue a single statement signed jointly by Nestle's Carl Angst and INFACT's William Thompson. It was agreed that the press release would include: (1) a statement recognizing the concerns of all those involved in the health and nutrition problems of infants in the Third World; (2) a reference to the fact that the ultimate solution of this problem lies in the adoption by national governments of national codes and their intensive efforts in improving water supply, educational system, and other infrastructure facilities; (3) a reference to the understanding reached on critical points of the WHO Code after discussions with UNICEF, WHO, NIFAC, church groups, and others; (4) an indication of the need for field testing on certain gray areas of the code; (5) an expression of thanks to UNICEF and WHO for developing the code and in helping its implementation by providing acceptable interpretation; and (6) an acknowledgment that the four concerns raised are valid. They deal with difficult areas of the code. Nestle has sought and will continue to seek advice from institutions with responsibility for resolving these issues. Nestle has also demonstrated its willingness to respond to constructive criticism.

Preparation of Joint Statement

NCCN continued to take the initiative and maintain control of the process in discussions with INBC. It prepared a draft statement for INBC's review and comment. Pagan also insisted that a "round table" discussion format was inappropriate for drafting a statement. Instead, the two parties should each delegate one person to hammer out a draft statement which could then be approved by the two organizations. Doug Johnson was becoming concerned that his "consensus building" posture was being increasingly strained and might contribute to internal discord and resentment within INBC's constituencies.

There were four sticking points: actual wording, the timing of the release, the persons who would sign the statement, and the structure of the press conference. NCCN refused to yield on the issue of timing and location.

It was initially suggested that once the meeting had resulted in an understanding, a joint statement would be issued. However, during a meeting with Niels Christiansen, Doug Johnson suggested that the joint statement should be withheld from release to the press until INBC had its meeting in Mexico and had the Statement of Understanding accepted by its constituents. NCCN rejected this idea. Pagan felt that they really had to push for closure. If INBC were to take the Statement to Mexico, it would open it up all over again. NCCN was determined to terminate these discussions when they did and to bind the two parties through a joint public announcement. In the case of INBC's Mexico City "big pow-wow, all the publicity would be centered on the activists and Nestle would be left out in the cold." NCCN insisted that if this were the case, there would be no joint signing of the Statement of Understanding until after the Mexico meeting. NCCN also stated that irrespective of the status of a joint statement, once the understanding between Nestle and INBC was reached, Nestle would announce that an understanding was reached and INBC has agreed to end the boycott.

After intensive negotiations lasting over seven hours, the language of the joint statement was finalized. It was agreed that the joint statement would be signed on Wednesday and the press release would be made on Thursday, January 25, 1982. The press conference took place as scheduled.* All the events of the conference were carefully choreographed and expertly stage managed. For once, all the players acted out their assigned roles and the "history was made" — as planned.

Epilogue

The discussion-negotiation process continued. On April 25, 1984, NCCN issued a communique[3] outlining the steps the company had taken toward the four points of the *Statement of Understanding*. The activists had been pressing Nestle to extend its code implementation to Europe. Although Angst was sympathetic to the activists' concern, he indicated that Nestle could not take such a step unilaterally and thereby risk serious loss of market share to its competitors. At the same time, he defended Nestle's position which advocated for strong national codes. He also indicated that Nestle would be willing to work closely with INBC in this effort once their adversarial relationship had been abandoned and the boycott termination made permanent.[4] On September 25, 1984, Nestle issued its Addendum to the Nestle Statement of Understanding. Among other things the addendum stated that the company was "against the provision of 'discharge tins' for breastfeeding mothers. We had notified hospitals of this policy. However, the company's goal is to seek an end to the provision of 'discharge tins' by all health systems and industry in developing countries for all mothers, whether breast-feeding or not."[5]

WHO had also become more active in the process. In a meeting in New York, Dr. D. Tejada de Rivero, WHO's director-general, agreed that some of the code's provisions needed clarification and that both industry and member government representatives needed to be brought into these consultations. However, WHO bureaucracy would not go along and instead suggested that it could be done only by the World Health Assembly,[6] which in the last analysis did not happen.

On October 4, 1984, INBC announced its end of boycott against Nestle. Following the already established pattern, the two sides issued a joint state-

---

*For details of the drama of the press conference, see Chapter 1, "The Infant Formula Controversy at Center Stage."

ment supplemented by individual statements from the representatives of Nestle and INBC.

Appendix A: Nestle Statement of Understanding

January 24, 1984

The following paper delineates Nestle's understanding of four areas of activity covered by the WHO Code and its policies regarding same.

Preamble

Nestle made a commitment to support the aim and principles of the World Health Organization Code on May 21, 1981, the day it was passed. Throughout the past three years Nestle has worked hard to keep that commitment and seeks to effectively implement the Code, but finds itself in the position of having to determine, without being able to obtain official endorsement for its policies, exactly what the commitment to the Code entails.

Initially Nestle hoped that the 118 nations which voted for the Code would quickly adopt national codes of their own that Nestle could then follow. When it was pointed out that few developing countries were treating the matter with sufficient priority, Nestle drew up comprehensive instructions to its markets in all developing countries as to exactly how to follow the WHO Code. Further, pursuant to Article 11.3 of the Code, it established an independent and objective body, the Nestle Infant Formula Audit Commission (NIFAC), to review the company's application of the Code and to make suggestions as to how the company could better follow the WHO Code.

NIFAC consulted with UNICEF, the WHO and several church bodies and made several recommendations to the company as to changes it thought would make the Nestle Instructions on the WHO Code more clearly in conformity with the Code. The company adopted those changes in October, 1982.

Since then the NIFAC has made other suggestions, and the company, after consultations with WHO and others, has taken additional steps to ensure compliance with the Code.

In the meantime Nestle has cooperated with NIFAC Chairman Senator Muskie and NIFAC in investigating more than 100 allegations that the company was in violation of the Code, and in remedying any deficiencies in the company's compliance procedures. In addition, the Commission has made several personal inspection trips to developing countries to observe the company's practices and to meet with local health authorities there and has released reports on their findings to the public.

The company has instituted an internal audit function to review and assess its marketing practices with the objective of ensuring that there is full compliance with the instructions relative to the Code in the field.

Now, several church leaders and some of the company's critics have asked Nestle to review four areas of its compliance with the Code. Nestle has agreed, and in doing so it is consulting with NIFAC, WHO and UNICEF.

Nestle is encouraged to see that The International Nestle Boycott Committee (INBC) and those churches and institutions represented therein have narrowed their concerns down to four points of the Code. Nestle, with the help of the Commission, has been trying to develop acceptable procedures dealing with these four points.

Educational Materials

Nestle will continue to seek professional advice from specialized consultants including those recommended by WHO and UNICEF, in the development and field testing of education materials.

The objective of the field testing is to ensure that these materials help the mother make the best informed choice about the method she decides to use in feeding her baby, after serious consideration of all the consequences of her choice as impled by Article 4. of the WHO Code. An additional objective of information dealing with infant formula is to teach and remind the mother about its proper use. As in the past, WHO and UNICEF have assured Nestle that it can approach them for their advice. Nestle is committed to this effort and to obtaining results as quickly as possible. Clear information will be included in all materials on all the points recommended by the WHO Code as listed below (treatment, such as detail and means of presentation of the information, will vary according to the purpose and type of material):

A. Materials dealing with the feeding of infants will include information on:
    1. The benefits and superiority of beastfeeding.
    2. Maternal nutrition and the preparation for maintenance of breastfeeding.
    3. The negative effect of introducing partial bottle feeding on breastfeeding.
    4. The difficulty of reversing the decision not to breastfeed.
B. Materials dealing with infant formula will also include information on:
    1. Possible health hazards of inappropriate foods or feeding methods; and in particular the health hazards of unnecessary or improper use of infant formula.

2. Social and financial consequences of the decision to use infant formula.

Hazard Warning on Labels

The second area of concern is the hazard warning that Nestle intended to print on its infant formula labels. This warning was developed in concert with NIFAC after consultations with WHO. Some concerned parties, nevertheless, pointed out differences of approach by different manufacturers and claimed that other companies had developed more effective warning statements. The matter was therefore rediscussed with WHO and UNICEF and efforts will be made to develop language that would be meaningful to Third World mothers most likely to need this information. No work has been done as yet to determine, in the field, which form of warning would be most appropriate. The decision was therefore made to test different statements in the Third World countries, with the help of specialized consultants recommended by WHO and UNICEF. The purpose of the testing is to ensure that effective warnings are given on the consequences to the health of infants of inappropriate or incorrect use arising from:

1. unclean water,
2. dirty utensils,
3. improper dilution, and
4. storage of prepared feeds without refrigeration.

While the intended audience of this warning includes all purchasers of the product, this educational message is particularly targeted at low-income, urban and peri-urban mothers.

Nestle is committed to obtaining results and implementing new warning statements expeditiously as part of an industry-wide solution.

Personal Gifts to Health Professionals

The third area of concern that we were asked to address was that of the provision of "personal gifts" to health professionals. The Code is not very clear on this point since it refers to "financial and material inducements."

Nestle has already made it clear that it will not provide financial or material inducements to promote the sale of infant formula.

Personal gifts of a non-professional nature, such as chocolates, key-rings, and pens, although not considered inducements, will now be considered inappropriate, and will not be given to health professionals by Nestle.

The provision of inexpensive materials of professional utility is in line with Article 6.8; it does not fall under Article 7.3 of the code. Nestle will not include proprietary information in such materials.*

The distribution of technical and scientific publications, such as the Nestle Nutrition Workshop Series, is considered to be in accordance with Article 6.8. This distribution is an important service to health professionals and is not to be confused with the question of gifts. No proprietary information (such as product brand advertising) will be included in such publications.

Supplies

The final subject raised was the provision of free or low-cost supplies of infant formula to health care institutions. Nestle recognizes that the church leaders who have raised this subject, as well as NIFAC members and the INBC, have a legitimate reason for concern where these supplies are used as the routine, normative manner of feeding infants in health care institutions.

In the development of the section dealing with supplies in the WHO Code, the World Health Assembly relied heavily on the results of the 1979 WHO/ UNICEF Joint Meetings on Infant Feeding where it stated:

Support through the health services.   "Health service staff must play a critical role in the initiation, establishment and maintenance of breast-feeding and should ensure that the mother has a source of sustained support for as long as breastfeeding continues, and thus health workers should be well informed and provide consistent information.

A baby who is not breastfed should receive special attention from the health care system. Adequate instructions for the use of infant foods as well as warnings about its problems should be the responsibility of the health care system. Supplies of infant formula would thus be required for distribution only where necessary and not as a routine."

It is for this reason that the WHO Code in intended to discourage routine bottle feeding in hospitals and that it is important industry policy be implemented in such a way that the provision on supplies does not bias the decision made by mothers and health professionals on how any infant is to be fed in the hospital.

Nestle therefore recognizes and supports the aim and spirit of the provi-

---

*Nestle will establish a list of accepted items falling under this definition. This will be sent to the markets. A market which wants to distribute an item not covered by the list will be required to obtain specific clearance from Vevey. This list will also be made available to NIFAC for use in their auditing procedures.

sions of the Code regarding limitations on the use of supplies to infants who have to be fed on breastmilk substitutes. It is recognized, however, that the definition of this term, "infants who have to be fed on breastmilk substitutes," requires further clarification in order to give practical guidelines to industry in its procedures for implementation, and to assist health professionals in reaching their decisions. The goal of Nestle policy is to restrict the distribution of supplies to three areas of need: medical, economic and social.

Nestle requests that these terms be further defined by WHO and UNICEF and that they then be communicated to health authorities and industry as the basis for government and company policies. Nestle recognizes that industry has a responsibility together with the health care system in limiting the provision of supplies to these defined needs, once defined, and will ensure that hospital administrators are aware of Nestle policy so that requests for free supplies will be formulated in the context of there needs only.

At the same time, Nestle offers cooperation to WHO and UNICEF in ensuring that the limitation of supplies to meet real needs as specified by the Code is uniformly applied.

Nestle will therefore write to the health authorities in all Third World countries where Nestle sells infant formula recommending that the WHO/UNICEF policy on supplies, once defined, be supported and implemented, and requesting precise government guidelines to health care institutions and industry.

This process could be facilitated by original or national seminars involving all concerned, sponsored by WHO and UNICEF. Nestle is ready to participate in such efforts.

The process should include, in addition to clarification and explanation of the term "infants who have to be fed on breastmilk substitutes":

• communication of the clarification and education of all concerned.
• implementation of the necessary procedures by health authorities and industry to limit supplies at the hospital and clinic level in accordance with that clarification.

Attachment 2 explains the procedure for adopting the Nestle supply policy.

Conclusion

Nestle has acted in good faith to fulfill its commitment to the WHO Code. This commitment is firm. The WHO recommendations provide an agreed framework for the marketing on infant formula. In spite of its imperfections, inevitable in an international consensus of the nature, the Code helps to define the role of the infant food industry in ensuring safe and adequate nutrition for infants. We take this issue very seriously, and we will remain firm in our commitment.

Attachment 1

Pack Shots

Nestle includes a product illustration (pack shot) on product instruction leaflets to be given to a mother by a health professional after a decision to use that product has been made. Nestle considers this product identification to be an important element of information which helps to ensure that the mother purchases the product to which the instructions refer. If the mother purchases another product, to which the instructions do not apply, this could result in serious misuse of that product and be harmful to the health of the baby. The WHO Code seeks to minimize risks of misuse.

In consulting with the UNICEF staff on this issue, Nestle was told that, in their opinion, such a product illustration is "promotional" in nature and therefore not in accord with Article 4.3 of the WHO Code. Nestle would like further clarification from WHO and UNICEF as to how they define the difference between "promotion" and "information." Nestle accepts that product instruction leaflets should only be given to mothers by health professionals after a decision to bottle feed has been made. Their purpose is therefore to ensure safe and correct use. They should not be used for promotional purposes.

These instruction leaflets will be developed in the future after consultation with WHO and UNICEF and as recommended and field tested by recognized Health Communications consultants to ensure that:

- they cannot be mistaken for promotional material.
- that the information on how that particular product is to be used will include effective warnings on the consequences to the health of infants in appropriate or incorrect use.
- they contain all the information required by the WHO Code, Article 4.2.

Nestle will make every effort to ensure that specific product instructions are not given to mothers who do not need them. Therefore, Nestle personnel will give theses materials only to health professionals and will strongly request that such product instructions not be displayed publicly in hospitals or other health care facilities.

Attachment 2

Summary of Procedure for Adopting the Nestle Supply Policy

As company policy, Nestle's goal is to have free low-cost formula supplied to hospitals used only for infants who "have to be fed" on breastmilk substitutes within the health facility, except as provided for in Article 6.7 of the Code. This goal must apply to the entire industry.

In order to implement this policy, Nestle believes that the following steps should be taken in the process of developing that policy by the entire industry and the health care system:

1. WHO/UNICEF define the term "have to be fed," to include consideration of the status of mothers who exercise their rights to free choice not to breastfeed. Nestle will support the WHO/UNICEF definition with health care system.
2. That definition will be transmitted to health authorities by WHO and UNICEF.
3. Nestle will cooperate with WHO/UNICEF in the implementation of educational programs for the health community that clarify the term "have to be fed."
4. Nestle will design its supply request forms reflecting only those uses intended by the Code, and will fill requests only for those uses.
5. Nestle will keep careful account of amounts of formula being provided to hospitals.
6. If amounts of formula requested appear to be incongruent with reasonable needs for free supplies as outlined above, this will be taken into account in filling future request for supplies.

It is obvious that this process of implementation, involving WHO, UNICEF, health ministers, health administrators and other concerned parties and industry requires adequate time to accomplish, and that each party must do its part if we are to succeed in our goal. Nestle reiterates its commitment to implementation of the WHO Code in all its facets and hopes that all concerned parties can move forward expeditiously and without unnecessary delay, so as to facilitate the promotion of breastfeeding in hospitals and assure standard practices by all manufacturers and hospital administrators.

Notes

1. Wogaman's letter to the author dated February 25, 1993.
2. INBC, Letter from Douglas Johnson to Dr. Carl Angst, Nestle — Switzerland, December 14, 1983.

3. Nestle Coordination Center For Nutrition, Inc., *Implementation Agenda - WHO Code of Marketing of Breastmilk Substitutes — Nestle Communique Number 1* (Washington, D.C., April 25, 1984).

4. Carl Angst, letter to Lisa Woodburn of INBC (Geneva: Nestle — S.A., September 17, 1984).

5. Nestle Coordination Center for Nutrition, Inc., *Addendum to the Nestle Statement of Understanding* (Washington D.C., September 25, 1984), p. 1.

6. K. Edstrom, "Note for Record on discussions WHO/UNICEF with INBC and Nestle (New York: United Nations, Liaison with Operational UN Agencies (LNO), August 1, 1984).

VI LESSONS LEARNED AND UNLEARNED

19 THE LESSONS OF ACCOUNTABILITY — THIRD WORLD GOVERNMENTS: EXPECTATIONS AND PERFORMANCE — WHO's NON-EXISTENT MONITORING

The passage of the infant formula code was a manifestation of strong opposition by a multitude of private and public groups to the unbridled promotion and sale of infant formula products, especially in Third World countries. The preamble to the WHO Code states that infant malnutrition is part of the wider problem of illiteracy, poverty, and social inequality within a society. The removal of these wider problems and the protection and encouragement of breastfeeding is the primary responsibility of local governments.

Prima facie, it would seem that any country that wants to impose conditions on the promotion and sale of infant formula, or for that matter on any other product, within its borders may easily do so through appropriate laws and regulations. Most countries do indeed regulate a variety of marketing activities without resorting to international mechanisms. Therefore, the need for the infant formula code would seem to be of questionable value. However, the activists and a great many Third World countries, scientific and health care professionals, and members of WHO and UNICEF had argued that, given the global magnitude of the problem and other related complexities, a worldwide collective solution was more desirable. In particular, it was suggested that:

1. Infant mortality was a global problem, with a greater incidence in the Third World. Governments in poorer countries lack the necessary expertise, administrative capabilities, and financial resources to handle the problem by themselves. They are also in a weaker bargaining position in dealing with

large and powerful foreign multinational corporations (MNCs). Therefore, they should seek solutions through collective effort at the international level.

2. An international code would provide member governments with a uniform set of standards and guidelines for developing a legal or administrative response, and suitable monitoring mechanisms, that are in harmony with their own social and cultural norms. Moreover, such a code would help these countries in developing appropriate monitoring procedures necessary for an effective enforcement of the code.

3. The code would help the health ministries and public health officials in Third World countries to pressure their own governments into assigning health issues a higher priority and increased budgetary resources.

In this chapter, we focus our attention on an analysis of the efforts by Third World governments in creating the necessary implementing and enforcing mechanisms with regard to the WHO Code in their respective countries. Second, we examine the actions of the World Health Assembly and the World Health Organization in mobilizing member governments and other interested parties in fulfilling the code's mandate.

An analysis of the available literature and activities of the various players since the enactment of the code in May 1981 indicates that the focus of the monitoring effort on the part of WHO as well as the activists has been primarily, if not exclusively, directed at the infant formula industry. While this effort is highly desirable, and quite legitimate in emphasis and intent, it offers at best a partial picture of the situation in view of the fact that both the Third World countries and WHO have an infinitely larger role to play in improving the environment relating to infant health and nutrition. It is, therefore, legitimate to ask what programs and actions have been undertaken by the WHO member governments, especially those in the Third World countries, and WHO itself, in carrying out the mandate of the infant formula code.

From any logical perspective, it would seem that the governments of the countries involved, especially those in the Third World, would have the greatest motivation to create mechanisms for implementing and monitoring the various provisions of the WHO Code. During the WHO deliberations, these countries forcefully argued for the enactment of the code on the premise that a collective worldwide effort was needed to enable them to resist the pressures from multinational corporations and to promote policies for increased breastfeeding and improved infant nutrition in their countries.

Provisions for Implementation and Monitoring of the Code

Monitoring of the code was the most contentious issue in its development. Under Article 7 of the first draft code, WHO/UNICEF were to assume the key responsibility for monitoring the code implementation and for adjudicating disputes over its interpretation. Supporting these monitoring activities, the draft code had provided the creation of a "Central Office" for WHO/UNICEF for collection, analysis, and interpretation of the necessary data. However, in the final and fourth draft this provision was dropped in favor of the following three-tier monitoring and enforcement system:

1.   The code devolves primary responsibility for monitoring its application on member countries, "acting individually, and collectively through the World Health Organization."[1] Member countries are required to take appropriate legal and administrative actions consistent with their social and legislative frameworks. These laws and regulations are required to be applicable equally to both domestic and foreign suppliers of infant formula products. *In developing local laws and regulations, member governments are encouraged to seek help from WHO, UNICEF, and other agencies of the U.N. system and to inform WHO each year on actions taken by them in implementing the code* [Emphasis added]. WHO, based on the information received each year from member states, is required to inform the World Health Assembly biennially in even years of the status of country compliance. This provision allows WHO to modify the code and change its scope if warranted by country compliance experience.[2] It should be noted here that in reporting to WHA, WHO relies solely on the information provided from member states. WHO does not undertake either to collect information on its own or to seek independent verification of data provided by member governments.

2.   Manufacturers and distributors of infant formula products, irrespective of any action taken by members states, are held responsible for monitoring their marketing practices in conformity with the principles and aims of the code and for taking steps to ensure that their conduct at every level conforms to them.[3]

3.   The code requires that "nongovernmental organizations [NGOs], professional groups, institutions, and individuals concerned should have the responsibility of drawing the attention of manufacturers or distributors to activities which are incompatible with the principles and aim of this Code, so that appropriate action can be taken. The appropriate governmental authority should also be informed."[4] The inclusion of NGOs — as the external watchdogs — in the monitoring process was a unique feature of the code. It was a tacit recognition of the key role played by the activist groups in the code's enactment process and their growing political power with the U.N. system.

Although member countries were assigned the primary responsibility for implementing the code, the code does not contain any mechanism for establishing national governments' accountability. While putting considerable pressure on industry compliance, both WHO and activists treat member governments with kid gloves when it comes to infant formula code compliance and monitoring thereof.

Code Compliance

Over 12 years have passed since the Code was adopted in May 1981. It is appropriate that we review the progress made by various parties in implementing the code, which was considered by the Assembly to be the "expression of the collective will of the membership of the World Health Organization" to eradicate the problem of infant morbidity and mortality in the Third World.[5]

By Industrially Advanced Countries

The industrially advanced (developed) countries, which claimed from the very beginning, and rightly so, that infant mortality was a Third World problem, have relied primarily on the voluntary code prepared by the infant formula industry itself. However, the European Economic Community has taken some serious steps to strengthen its commitment to the code. In 1986 the EC Commission revised its policy toward the code. It strengthened its commitment to marketing in general and the responsibilities of health care workers in line with the code. In the case of advertising, the Commission preferred to limit the promotion of infant formula products to media specializing in baby care.[6] In East European countries the infant formula production and distribution is controlled by their governments. Hence, it limits our evaluation of the code compliance to the Third World.

NGOs argue that the developed countries must implement the code so as to set an example for the Third World. It is ironic that NGOs are making this argument. It implies that Third World countries either lack an independent judgment or the willpower to improve their infant mortality and will follow simply what developed countries do. If this were indeed the case, it would be a strong indictment — and an unwarranted one — against the Third World governments and their people.

By Developing Countries

Our analysis of Third World code compliance covers 123 countries. They comprise the countries where the problem of infant mortality is acute. They also include all the nations that were most active in the World Health Assembly in the enactment of the code.

The Third World countries' compliance with the code suffers from serious limitations. WHO presents a biennial report on the code implementation status to the Assembly. These reports are based on the information supplied by member states following initial guidelines provided by WHO. In this sense, WHO is simply a recipient of information and lacks any formal authority over member governments to seek their compliance. WHO also does not make public the code compliance information, even where the information is furnished by the countries themselves. There is no indication of the format prescribed by WHO to collect country compliance information, its analysis of the information received, and specific guidance to countries in improving the quality of their compliance and reporting information. The data made public by WHO also do not provide any indication as to the consistency of the information provided and the problems that may have occurred in the process of data aggregation. Some indication of countries' code compliance efforts is available in the biennial proceedings of the Assembly where member governments provide this information through brief comments by their representatives on the code implementation. These statements are general and rarely give a definite indication on the specific progress made by a country on the code implementation. It is, therefore, impossible to undertake any independent analysis of the veracity or adequacy of the information furnished by individual country governments to WHO.

Another source of corroborating information is provided by the American Public Health Association (APHA), a Washington-based private organization funded by the U.S. Agency for International Development (AID), which collects information on country code implementation. Both these sources follow an identical pattern and a near-common basis in collecting and disseminating information of country compliance with the code. To wit, neither APHA nor WHO make any attempt at verifying the information provided by individual country governments, create uniformity in the system of reporting, or seek independent monitoring and evaluation of this information. Thus the best that can be said for the information generated by WHO and APHA is that it is simply a tally sheet or a report card indicating the extent of efforts reportedly being made by individual governments in implementing the WHO Code and not the actual outcome of these efforts.

Wherever possible, additional information has been gleaned from data made public by NGOs, mainly the International Baby Food Action Network (IBFAN) and the International Organization of Consumers Union. IOCU represents consumers throughout the world and has a membership of 164 consumer organizations in some 60 developing and industrialized countries. IBFAN also claims to have a worldwide network of more than 100 NGOs in 67 countries.

Given the severe limitations and deficiencies of available data, it is not possible to draw any definitive conclusions. However, the paucity of the data itself, and the unwillingness of WHO to collect and individual countries to report more specific information, suggests that a large gap exists between the rhetoric of intentions and the reality of implementation. The following analysis, based as it is on the somewhat superficial nature of country reported data, still strongly indicates that the Third World governments have been grossly negligent in fulfilling their part of the undertaking in implementing various provisions of the code. Furthermore, in many cases, where credit has been taken by the country governments for code compliance, more often than not, it refers to the actions that infant formula manufacturers were obligated to take under the provisions of the code.

The infant formula code compliance has two interrelated aspects: code implementation and code monitoring. The code implementation demonstrates the steps taken by various countries toward adopting the infant formula code either in toto or partially within their legal and administrative systems, and the progress made by them in this effort since May 21, 1981. These data would indicate the seriousness of purpose or the sense of urgency exhibited by a country in resolving its critical infant health problems. The effort at code monitoring would suggest the extent to which a country was enforcing the code provisions, after having been enacted in the first place. Furthermore, it would show what local administrative apparatus is in place in each country for monitoring such implementation. This would provide an indication of the extent of resource commitment made by individual countries. The score card of Third World countries is very disappointing on both these counts.

Code Implementation

Our analysis of the code implementation by Third World countries suggests the following key conclusions:

1. Only 10 countries, barely 8 percent of those reporting, had adopted the infant formula code in toto by the end of 1988, the latest year for which the data are available (Table 19-1). Consider the fact that Third World countries account for about 72 percent of the world population and contribute roughly 16 percent to the world gross national product (GNP). In contrast, the 10 countries mentioned in Table 19-1 represent less than 5 percent of the world population and less than 2 percent of the world's GNP. Of these, four countries enforce the code on a voluntary basis. There are 34 other countries that claim to have *adopted only some provisions* of the code either on a mandatory or a voluntary basis. Unfortunately, these countries also do not provide any details as to the specificity of the code provisions that they have adopted, the extent to which they have been implemented, and the resources that have been devoted to their enforcement.

Information from IBFAN/IOCU, APHA, and WHO biennial reports re-

Table 19–1.   The code compliance by Third World countries: 1981–1988

Regions	Compliance Status*					
	A	*B*	*C*	*D*	*E*	*F*
	Number of Countries					
Africa	1	12	3	3	22	11
Americas	5	7	0	1	17	3
Asia	4	8	4	4	15	7
Total	10	27	7	8	54	21

*Compliance status description:
A. The total code in effect as law in the country.
B. Some of the code provisions in effect as law.
C. Some of the code provisions in effect on a voluntary basis.
D. Government controls the supply and distribution of breast-milk substitutes.
E. The code being studied by a working group or by a government appointed committee or awaiting legislation.
F. No action at all.
Sources: IBFAN/IOCU, Documenting Center, Penang, Malaysia; APHA, Clearinghouse on Infant Feeding and Maternal Nutrition, Washington, D.C.

veals that, by and large, countries have zeroed in essentially on two key areas of the code: labeling, and promotion and education. Compliance with the labeling provision is simple because the industry has made these changes voluntarily. IBFAN/IOCU reported in their 1988 survey that the industry had made considerable progress in this area. According to this report, with the exception of five companies in Europe, Japan, and Korea, all other companies had complied, either partially or fully, with the code's labeling provisions. The survey disclosed that Nestle of Switzerland and three major U.S. companies (Ross Laboratories of Abbott Labs, Mead Johnson of Bristol-Myers, and Wyeth Laboratories of American Home Products) were in full compliance with Article 9 of the code.[7]

In the area of promotion and education (Articles 4,5, and 6), these countries have banned mass advertising of breast-milk substitutes to the general public. The potential impact of this activity, however, should not be overestimated. These countries suffer from a very high rate of illiteracy, low per capita income, and no nationwide television network. Under these conditions a ban on general advertising has little significance.

2.   Progress in compliance with the code was also uneven when analyzed region by region. In Africa, where the infant mortality problem is most severe, governments have shown a callous disregard for infant welfare. According to the World Bank, the infant mortality rate (deaths per 1,000 live births) averages about 65 in developing countries versus 9 in industrialized countries. The low-income Asian countries suffer an infant mortality rate of

95 while countries in sub-Saharan Africa have an infant mortality rate of 107, the highest in the world.[8]

In 1982, the Inter-Parliamentary Conference, attended by delegates from 23 African nations, had urged all regional governments to implement the code through local legislation. To date, only Kenya has implemented the code in toto. Thirty-three other countries, representing 43 percent of the region's population, either have taken no action at all or are still reviewing the code for legislative action.

3. Countries have been equally slow in developing their implementation response to the code and do not display any sense of urgency. Kenya, Mexico, and the Philippines, which have adopted the code in toto, took between five and six years to pass the necessary local legislation (Table 19-2). This slow and hesitant country response becomes even more apparent when country compliance is studied in terms of time progression.

During the eight years subsequent to the passage of the code, there were two distinct periods wherein many Third World countries showed significant activity in their code compliance reports, that is 1982 and 1986, the latter being the most active year in any country compliance report. In 1982, 17 countries reported for the first time that they were "studying" the feasibility of code implementation. Unfortunately, as of 1988, none of these countries had as yet crossed that stage. In 1986, 32 countries had disclosed the extent of progress made by them in the code implementation. Of these, 26 countries had disclosed for the first time, after waiting for five to six years, that either the infant formula code was under review by a committee or its draft was awaiting legislation.

This sorry state of affairs is confirmed by the report card issued by IBFAN/IOCU. Mrs. A. Allain of IBFAN/IOCU made the following comments at the WHA meeting in May 1988 on the global state of code implementation:

> Only six governments had adopted the entire code as law, 11 had relatively well-monitored voluntary codes, 24 had passed legislation on significant parts of the Code and 33 had drafts awaiting legislation, some of which had waited as long as four or five years. 34 countries had taken no action, 8 had an industry-written code in effect and 23 were still studying the situation seven years after their endorsement of the Code.[9]

Reluctant as it may be, even WHO obliquely acknowledges that developing countries have been negligent in the infant formula code implementation. In its 1984 biannual report to the 37th Assembly, WHO reported that countries "have been slower than originally hoped for" in implementing the code. Nevertheless, WHO was generous in giving credit to the member state governments by putting the issue of infant health and nutrition in a wider context.[10]

Table 19–2.   Time progression of the code compliance by Third World countries:
1981–1987

Provisions Complied	1981	1982	1983	1984	1985	1986	1987
A. The code as a law	—	2	3	1	—	1	3
B. Some provisions	4	4	6	4	2	5	2
C. Some provisions	1	3	—	1	—	—	3
D. The code under study	2	17	3	3	1	26	6
Total	7	26	12	9	3	32	1

Sources: IBFAN/IOCU, ALPHA, and WHO.

Five years after the 1979 WHO/UNICEF Meeting on Infant and Young Child Feeding it is possible to say with conviction that *real progress has been achieved, especially as regards heightened public awareness of (the Code) importance . . . . Obviously, awareness of a problem, while an indispensable condition for action, cannot serve as a substitute for it"* (Emphasis added).

In 1990, WHO presented to the Assembly a synthesis of its country compliance reports submitted between 1982–1990. The sole basis of this report was the information provided by member states. The tabular summary included in the report indicated the time when a member country informed WHO of its progress on the code implementation. The report did not distinguish between the countries that intended to take some action and those that had taken specific action toward implementing the code. The WHO tabular summary leaves one with the impression that "intent to act" is tantamount to action. The best interpretation one can put on the report is to call it an apology for the slow response on the part of Third World countries to the code. According to WHO, while many countries have taken partial action in implementing the code, most countries were still trying to find out the best way to implement the code "not in isolation but as part of their wider efforts to address the health, nutritional problems, and related social status of women and families."[11] As of 1990, nine years after the code adoption, 75 countries, representing 54 percent of the total Third World population, were still "considering" some suitable action for implementing the code.

Code Enforcement

Most developing countries have been silent on the issue of the code enforcement. Even IBFAN/IOCU, APHA, and WHO have not released any information in this aspect. There is only one inescapable conclusion. Despite all the agitation for the code's passage and their alleged concern for infant morbidity and mortality, most Third World countries have not taken even the minimal steps that they could have taken, even in the absence of any international code, to address these problems to the extent that they fall within their purview. The problem of lack of progress is compounded by a number of factors that are inherent in the structure and provisions of the code. For example:

1.   The code does not provide a specific mechanism for holding member states accountable for its implementation. There is no outside pressure to take action unless warranted by internal circumstances. Although the moral force of the U.N. system has been effective in seeking the code's passage, it has failed in ensuring effective and expeditious enforcement by member states.

2.   Most Third World countries, faced with the pressures of maintaining a balance between economic growth and social progress, and between concerns for national security and social welfare, seem to have opted in favor of weapons and economic growth and have given a short shrift to public health and welfare needs.

A number of examples of individual country efforts lend further evidence to this sad state of affairs. According to Health Alert 83, in the Philippines, which had adopted the code in toto in 1986:

> Almost 2 years after (its) enactment and despite the strong sanctions provisions of the Code, the Department of Health, which is responsible for monitoring and enforcement, seems unable to curtail blatant violations by infant formula companies. Also the "dominant method of infant feeding in Metro Manila continues to be bottle-feeding, and the infant formula companies continue to rake in profits.[12]

Malaysia, which since 1983 has banned all mass advertising and relies on voluntary code enforcement, monitors industry promotion and distribution activities through the Government Liaison Committee. According to the Consumers Union of Penang (Headquarter of IOCU) "formula companies' promotion in Malaysia continues as aggressively as ever" and the voluntary code is "weak with many loopholes."[13] Liberia has also banned advertising of breast-milk substitutes via mass media and health institutions. However, the Breast-feeding Advocacy Group (BAG), a private voluntary organization, reports that "substitutes and baby foods are widely available in shops and markets and continue to be imported as essential commodities."[14]

3.   Even given the necessary political will, most Third World countries lack financial resources to develop and maintain the required administrative and educational infrastructure for effective code implementation. One of the key responsibilities of local governments under the WHO Code is to ensure that health workers and, through them, pregnant women and young mothers receive "objective and consistent" information on the virtues of breastfeed-

ing and disadvantages of breast-milk substitutes. This is a serious responsibility, and its implementation requires major investments in updating and maintaining the existing administrative infrastructure, including building of additional health care facilities, revamping existing instructional materials, and retraining of existing health care workers. This is a tall order and is difficult and expensive to achieve in most developing countries. For example, between 1972 and 1987, the share of Third World countries' total budget expenditures on health declined from an average of 5.9 percent in 1972 to 4.6 percent in 1987 (Table 19-3).

Of the 34 countries that claim to have certain provisions of the infant formula code in effect either as a law or on a voluntary basis, all except Bangladesh and Ecuador, experienced a decline in government expenditures on health during this period. For example, the high-debt countries in Latin America and other regions reduced the share of their expenditures on health significantly, from 8.4 percent in 1972 to 5.9 percent in 1987 in order to meet their more urgent economic and debt service needs.

4. Developing countries face a dilemma regarding the infant formula code. They are anxious to promote and diversify their economies. They also want to protect domestic nascent industries against foreign competition. However, the code requires equal enforcement against both domestic and foreign suppliers of infant formula. Many countries fear that nondiscriminatory treatment would keep local manufacturers at a disadvantage against the well-entrenched foreign MNCs. For example, in 1985, the government of India had adopted a national code for the protection and promotion of breast-feeding. This national code barred foreign MNCs from advertising their infant formula to the general public and from direct contact between their marketing personnel and young and pregnant mothers. The national code, however, exempted the local infant formula companies from these provisions. Furthermore, in contravention to the WHO Code provisions, India's national code allows local companies to promote their products through health care workers and by handing out free samples.[15]

Table 19–3. Share of central government expenditures on health: 1972–1987

Countries	1972	1987
Developing countries	5.9%	4.6%
Low-income countries	5.4%	3.4%
High-debt countries	8.4%	5.9%
Upper-income countries	6.7%	n.a.
Developed countries	11.2%	12.6%

Source: World Bank, World Development Report, 1989, Table 11, Central Government Expenditures.

The Role of WHO

WHO defines its role as being merely a conduit between member states and the World Health Assembly. This may explain why WHO's biennial reports to the Assembly on the code implementation status are no more than collated and summarized versions of information provided by member nations. This is what the member nations want to make public, and WHO is only too happy to oblige. WHO argues that it does not have the authority, which it tried very hard not to have in the first place, either to interpret the code or to judge whether certain industry marketing practices are in violation of the code. It considers these matters to be the preserve of member states. Thus, along with most Third World member states, WHO is equally negligent in this respect and cannot escape responsibility.[16]

The World Health Assembly, in its 39th session held in Geneva in 1986, requested that WHO "propose a simplified and standardized form for use by member states to facilitate the monitoring and evaluation by them of their implementation of the Code and reporting thereon to WHO, as well as the preparation by WHO of a consolidated report covering each of the articles of the Code."[17] Even after a passage of four years, WHO's 1990 report failed to respond to the request of the Assembly. Thus one is led to an inescapable conclusion. To wit: it would appear that the WHO was unwilling to assume any responsibility for monitoring the code implementation and thereby risk the wrath of its political bosses.

Conclusion

Our analysis of the impact of the infant formula code is disheartening. The best that can be said is that the code succeeded in creating public awareness and political interest on the vital public policy issue of infant health in the Third World. There is also evidence to indicate that major multinational infant formula producers have made improvements in their marketing and promotion practices to comply with the code. However, the veracity of the industry's claims cannot be verified with any degree of objectivity. The industry's critics continue to charge infant formula manufacturers, notably Nestle and Wyeth, for continuing significant code violations. Notwithstanding, independent evidence is also lacking to assess the substance of their complaints in terms of overall patterns prevailing in various Third World regions and markets.

The code provided a framework within which Third World nations and multinational infant formula manufacturers could develop a mutually beneficial relationship. "The modern corporation has lived in relative harmony within the nation-state because the corporation has sought legitimacy for its operations and benefits for its owners within the framework of the broader welfare concerns of society."[18] The Third World nations, by not implementing the code, have failed to make use of this framework or to create more appropriate indigenous structures within which mutual cooperation and action would yield their social goal of reducing infant mortality.

The paramount question, however, remains unanswered and is unlikely to be resolved anytime soon. To wit, what if any difference has been made in reducing infants' sickness and deaths in Third World countries as a consequence of the infant formula code? According to WHO, in the Third World, the number of malnourished children between the ages of 0 to 5 increased from 126 million in 1963–1973 to 145.4 million in 1973–1983, and its proportion to the total population remains stubbornly high and constant.[19]

Notes

1. *International Code of Marketing of Breast-Milk Substitutes* (Geneva: World Health Organization, 1981), Article 11.2.

2. *Ibid.*, Article 11.7.

3. *Ibid.*, Article 11.5.

4. Ibid., Article 11.4.

5. *Ibid.*, supra note 1.

6. *Official Journal of the European Communities*, No. C285, (November 12, 1986), pp. 5–19.

7. IBFAN/IOCU, *State of the Code by Country 1988*, Code Documentation Center, Penang, Malaysia, May 1988.

8. The World Bank, *World Development Report 1991* (New York: Oxford University Press, 1991), Table 28: Health and Nutrition, pp. 258–259.

9. World Health Organization, Forty First World Health Assembly, Committee A, *Provisional Summary Report of the Second Meeting*, Geneva, May, 6, 1988, p. 6.

10. World Health Organization, Thirty Seventh World Health Assembly Provisional Agenda Item 21: *Infant And Young Child Nutrition (Progress and Evaluation Report; And Status of Implementation of the International Code of Marketing of Breast-Milk Substitutes)*, Geneva, April 6, 1986, p. 41.

11. WHO, *The International Code of Marketing of Breast-Milk Substitutes: Synthesis of Reports on Action Taken (1981–1990)* (WHO/MCH/NUT/90.1), p.44.

12. American Public Health Association, *Legislation and Policies to Support Maternal and Child Nutrition, Report No. 6*, Washington, D.C. (June 1989), p. 90.

13. *Ibid.*, p. 89.

14. *Ibid.*, p. 82.

15. American Public Health Association, *Ibid.*, p. 88.

16. World Health Organization Executive Board, Seventy First Session, Provisional Agenda Item 13: *Infant and Young Child Feeding*, Report by the Director General, November 11, 1982, p. 21.

17. WHO, Executive Board Eighty First Session, *Resolutions and Decisions Annexes*, Geneva, January 11–20, 1988, p. 153.

18. S. Prakash Sethi and Bharat B. Bhalla, "The Free Market and Economic Growth," *Business and The Contemporary World*, (Winter 1991), 100.

19. WHO, Thirty Ninth World Health Assembly Provisional Agenda Item 21, *Infant And Young Child Nutrition (Progress And Evaluation Report, And Status of the Implementation of the International Code of Marketing of Breast-milk Substitutes)*, Report by the Director General, April 7, 1986, p. 10.

20 CODE COMPLIANCE BY THE INFANT FORMULA INDUSTRY

The New Nestle — The More Things Change the More They Remain the Same

Article 7 of the WHO Code requires that the industry, that is, manufacturers and distributors, irrespective of any action taken by member states, is responsible "for monitoring their marketing practices conforming to the principles and aim of the Code and for taking steps to ensure that their conduct at every level conforms to them."[1] The code also proscribes, among other things, infant formula manufacturers and distributors from gaining market share by offering incentive bonuses or quotas set specifically for sale of breast-milk substitutes. However, the payment of bonus is permitted if it is "based on the overall sales by a company of other products marketed by it."[2] The industry representatives are disallowed to "perform educational functions in relation to pregnant women or mothers of young infants and young children." However, they can be "used for other functions by the health care system at the request and written approval of the appropriate authority of the government concerned."[3]

An evaluation of the code compliance by the infant formula industry is hampered by a variety of factors that makes all claims and counter-claims as to the industry compliance, or lack thereof, highly suspect. For example:

1. There are no objective, neutral, international monitoring mechanisms to evaluate the nature and extent of industry compliance with the code. The issue remains contentious until today. As was previously stated in an earlier part of the book, WHO has steadfastly declined to assume this responsibility arguing that it lacked specific legislative authority from the World Health

Assembly, and it did not have resources to undertake such a task. And yet, it has also strongly lobbied strongly against the WHA granting it such an authority (see Chapter 19).

2.   Another problem lies in the lack of a clearcut reporting system that is followed by all parties in monitoring the implementation of the code. Neither WHO nor any other country or group of countries has instituted uniform data collection and reporting systems, thereby making it impossible to verify any claims of compliance or code violations.

3.   In industrialized and developed countries, notably the United States and the European Community, infant formula marketing practices vary considerably based on country codes and local regulations. In the United States, companies follow the regulations prescribed by the Food & Drug Administration (FDA), their own voluntary codes and conventions established by the medical profession. In the 12-member European Community (EC), all companies have agreed on a voluntary code of conduct, the so-called IDACE Code (Industry Code of Practice for the Marketing of Breast Milk Substitutes in the EC), prepared by the Association of Dietetic Foods Industries of the EC. This industry code endorses the aims and principles of the WHO Code and is consistent with the social and legislative requirements of EC member nations and relevant to the needs of mothers and babies. It relates to the marketing practices — that is, direct advertising and labelling, mentioned in the WHO Code over which manufacturers have control. It excludes elements of the WHO Code that relate to the responsibilities of health workers and allow companies to sell infant formula directly to the consumers.[4] This IDACE-EC Code has been in effect since January 1, 1986, and is adhered to by all the companies operating in that region. The IDACE-EC Code will be replaced by the EC directive on infant formula and follow-up formulas which has been recently finalized by the EC Commission.[5]

4.   The situation with regard to the developing countries is even more troublesome. A number of major infant formula manufacturers — all of whom have agreed to abide by the principles and aims of the WHO Code — refuse to include countries like Hong Kong, Singapore, South Korea, and Taiwan in the list of developing countries and thus follow marketing practices more in line with applicable country codes and competitive marketing practices (Chapter 19).

5.   For the most part, developing countries, including almost all the largest ones, have been singularly reticent in enacting necessary legislation to implement the WHO Code and establish mechanisms for enforcing and monitoring compliance by companies (Chapter 19). In general, where domestic producers hold a substantial market share, the lack of compliance with the WHO Code is particularly glaring — for example, India. Thus any claims made by the industry members as to the level of compliance must be taken on faith or through spotty checks by the industry's critics. An important factor to remember in this regard, and the one that is generally ignored, is

that despite the fact that while a handful of large multinational corporations account for the major share of the worldwide infant formula sales, there are a large number of small and medium-size local manufacturers in various developed and developing countries that are not subjected to review, audit, and control by the industry's critics. Some well-known international companies such as Glaxo and Cow & Gate in the U.K., Varta in Germany, Meiji, Morinaga, and Snow in Japan, Dumex in Denmark, and CDC in Canada have generally remained outside the review process of the nongovernmental organizations (NGOs).

6.   Infant formula industry's own record of independent monitoring and reporting of code compliance is not exactly noteworthy. Furthermore, industry members and nonmember infant formula manufacturers have uniformly declined to disclose any data as to their sales of infant formula products (see Chapter 10). Consequently, it is difficult to assess what, if any, effect the code has had in promoting breastfeeding or reducing the sale of infant formula foods. To the best of our knowledge, no company has left any market because of declining sales or restrictive governmental regulation. On the contrary, there is evidence, at least in the United States, of infant formula manufacturers resorting to even more aggressive marketing and promotion practices in the sale of infant formula foods.

Prior to the passage of the Code, the International Council of Infant Food Industries (ICIFI), representing 14 major infant formula manufacturers, had formulated its own voluntary code of ethics governing the sale and distribution of breast-milk substitutes. This code, however, was seen by the industry's critics as grossly inadequate because it was voluntary in nature and lacked any enforcement powers. It was viewed as the industry's attempt to derail WHO's efforts in enacting a stronger code. The controversy surrounding some of ICIFI's actions during the battles around the WHO Code enactment and the widespread feeling among its critics that ICIFI was Nestle's handmaiden seriously eroded its credibility and effectiveness. As a consequence, ICIFI was disbanded and replaced by another, more broad-based industry organization (Chapter 10).

Code Compliance by the Infant Formula Industry

Nestle was one of the most vociferous opponents of the infant formula code during its formulation stages; it was the first one to embrace the code once it was passed. However, the company conditioned its acceptance only as far as it applied to Third World countries. Most other major international formula manufacturers soon followed with similar announcements. There is, however, no record of announcements of "intention to comply" by any of the major domestic producers of infant formula products in Third World countries. It should be noted here that some of these producers often hold significant shares of their domestic markets — India, for example (Chapter 19).

Although multinational companies contend to have made significant and sincere efforts to comply with the infant formula code provisions in most Third World countries, they have refused to implement its provisions in industrially advanced countries beyond what is required by local and regional laws and voluntary codes. At the same time, certain companies have initiated new marketing and promotional practices — for example, direct consumer advertising and promotion — in some of the developed countries that go beyond those currently used by the industry and frowned upon by the local medical community, health professionals, and activist groups. Furthermore, the companies introducing these new marketing and promotion tactics are often the ones that were previously chastised by industry's critics for being too aggressive in their marketing and promotion of infant formula foods in Third World and other markets. This has been especially true in the case of the United States where some companies, including Nestle, have flouted prevailing practice of promoting infant formula products only through the medical community and have opted instead to market their products through direct consumer advertising. It has been suggested that these companies have had to resort to more aggressive promotional practices in order to overcome the entry barriers erected by established marketers of infant formula producers in the United States.

From the very beginning, a major bone of contention between the multinational infant formula manufacturers, WHO and NGOs, in terms of the infant formula code compliance had to do with its "universal coverage." Infant formula companies argued that the "alleged" marketing and promotion problems, as well as unhygienic conditions, prevailed only in Third World countries. Moreover, since the consumer in industrially advanced countries had the means and capabilities to be informed about the product and the discretionary income to acquire the product, the consumer's right to choose could not be limited without overwhelming evidence of countervailing factors. To date, this issue remains unresolved.

In February 1984 the infant formula industry formed another group called the Industry Association of Infant Food Manufacturers (IFM), with 33 members varying in size from small to medium-size and large manufacturers. Although Nestle strongly denies it, the new group is also perceived to be heavily influenced by Nestle. Unlike ICIFI, IFM appears more moderate and has striven to provide a cohesive industrywide image and effort, and to undertake to answer some of the criticisms of the industry's efforts toward complying with the WHO Code.

Among IFM's objectives are: industry policy development relating to composition, utilization, labeling, packaging, and marketing of infant and young children foods; representation to governing industry bodies; and collection and dissemination of information pertaining to IFM members and their activities in the marketing of infant foods.* Participation by member companies in any and all of IFM activities, however, is voluntary. IFM has no provisions either to monitor an individual member's performance or to persuade member companies to improve their compliance efforts should such actions be called for. Among the major elements of compliance on the part of individual companies have been in the areas of: labeling, consumer advertising, instructional materials, and some of the other marketing activities. Disagreements, however, persist between the companies and the activists as to the degree of compliance of various code provisions by individual companies.

IFM has no mechanism or plans to collect industrywide data on the sale of infant formula foods in different parts of the world. It cites lack of resources and unwillingness on the part of member companies to undertake such a project.† The ineffectiveness of the IFM is made apparent by such a policy, and its own stated objectives are thereby undermined. To the extent that member participation and cooperation is voluntary and enforcement is nonexistent, the ability of the IFM to realize changes in marketing practices of members is highly suspect. The IFM's response was that it should be the national governments' responsibility to monitor local marketing practices. And yet, this explanation flies in the face of the very basis of the infant formula controversy and the WHO Code, namely, that international regulation of corporate practices and their monitoring was necessary because, for a variety of reasons that have been debated ad nauseum over the years, Third World country governments were found to be unable to initiate and enforce local standards regulating such marketing practices. To suggest, as IFM does, that it should be merely a passive organization waiting for the complaints to be filed before it could and would act, is to avoid the issue and abdicate responsibility both in terms of WHO Code provisions and also the spirit of their implementation. The leakage-prone character of IFM's complaint mechanism is further demonstrated by the fact that even where complaints have been filed with the association, and the affected member company has been asked to modify its behavior, there are no followup procedures to verify whether in fact the necessary changes have been put into effect.

---

*For more detailed information concerning IFM and its specific objectives, see Chapter 10: "Infant Formula Industry and Major Manufacturers Involved in the Controversy."
†Mr. John Zanzevoort, executive director, IFM. Interview with the author. Unless otherwise specifically stated, all direct quotes or paraphrased statements attributed to various individuals, are based on personal on-the-record interviews or written communications with the author.

In January 1991 IFM introduced a major innovation in the form of appointing an ombudsman who would endeavor to settle disputes between complainants and any of the IFM member companies (including Nestle) pertaining to WHO Code violations. Professor Frank Falkner, a pediatrician in the field of maternal and child health, accepted the post as IFM's first ombudsman.[6] The ombudsman, however, is a very weak and unsatisfactory response on the part of the industry. The ombudsman is intended to be a passive mechanism responding to complaints by outside parties against member companies or by the member companies against one another. It is essentially a one-person operation with no independent staff. IFM contends that member companies are the best watchdogs for other companies' performance as they affect their own sales and profits. The practical effect of this assumption is likely to be far more modest. Companies are likely to lodge complaints against other companies where the offending companies' practices differ significantly and are likely to cause serious competitive harm. However, companies would be less inclined to file complaints if they are all following similar practices and where they are vulnerable to complaints by other companies for alleged code violations. Thus, systematic industrywide violations are unlikely to be reported by IFM members. In an interview with the author, an IFM executive disagreed with this assertion and yet conceded that in 1990 there were five times as many complaints filed by the critics as those filed by all the member companies combined. The argument of complaint filing by NGOs is only partially true. It assumes that NGOs have the resources to constantly monitor and report industry performance in different parts of the world — a haphazard process under the best of circumstances. To date, IFM reports very few complaints, and industry officials lament the lack of complaints on the part of industry's critics.

The ombudsman also has no enforcement powers beyond persuasion. The most severe punishment that can be inflicted on a member company is expulsion from the group — a highly unlikely event. Moreover, since expulsion carries no penalties in the marketplace, it simply is more useful to keep even the worst offenders within the industry-association's fold so as to bring the combined pressure of other members to bear on the offending company to modify its practices. One wonders why the industry was unwilling to institute an organism like the NIFAC which had proved so successful in investigating complaints against Nestle and also undertaking independent studies of infant formula marketing practices in Third World countries. A broad-based support for a NIFAC-like organization, together with industrywide publication of sales data and marketing practices, would provide the best evidence as to the intentions and determination of the infant formula industry to comply fully with the code.

Infant formula industry has made some progress in one of the most contentious areas of disagreement between the companies and industry's critics. This relates to the distribution of free supplies to mothers in hospitals. In 1991, IFM members reached an agreement with WHO and UNICEF to cooperate in a new country-by-country initiative aimed at phasing out infant formula donations to maternity hospitals in developing countries by the end of 1992. Priority is given to those developing countries where infant formula donations are widely solicited. The goal of this initiative is to implement a withdrawal of free and low-cost supplies to maternity wards and hospitals in identified countries by working with their health ministries through the offices of WHO and UNICEF. Until this point, Nestle had supplied formula to Third World hospitals on a request basis, prompting objections from critics that this practice encouraged new, uneducated mothers in poor countries, with unsanitary conditions, to give up breastfeeding. Nestle's resolution to halt all such supplies requires that appropriate provisions be made for those babies who have to be fed breast-milk substitutes.

The Industry's U.S. Activities

Nestle was the only company to establish an independent monitoring system of its compliance with the WHO Code, and make public disclosure of its actions, through Nestle Infant Formula Audit Commission (NIFAC). None of the U.S.-based multinational corporations engaged in worldwide manufacture and sale of infant formula products undertook such measures. Instead they have either worked through IFM or promulgated their own codes in conformity with the WHO Code, but within the framework of FDA-instituted regulations. In a number of cases, they have also followed Nestle's lead in initiating changes in their infant formula marketing practices.

Finally, after years of recriminations and accusations of code violations, the activists again brought the issue to a new confrontational level. After a short truce and a boycott termination lasting less than four years, on October 4, 1988, the Action for Corporate Accountability (ACA) announced the resumption of its boycott of Nestle and a new boycott of AHP. ACA said the boycott against Nestle was reinstituted "to finish what we started," arguing that Nestle was routinely violating several provisions of the WHO Code. Of particular concern was the distribution of formula to mothers in the hospital. Critics believed that formula given with the imprimatur of a hospital encouraged women to choose bottle-feeding over breastfeeding — to the detriment of their children. "Children in developing countries live in very insulting life situations," said Doug Johnson, now board chairman of ACA. "Water is often unavailable or contaminated. It is virtually impossible to sterilize bottles. Formula tends to be over-diluted. Children are not getting the nutrition they need."

Nestle, however, regards infant formula as essential. "In developing countries, mothers do have to go out to work. They must supplement breast milk," said Dr. Thad Jackson, director of issues management at Nestle. The company stated that it was working with WHO and the U.N. Children's

Fund to support healthy infant feeding practices. "We should be working together to provide the best option for vulnerable mothers instead of fighting," said Dr. Jackson.[7]

ACA is a relatively new organization. However, it is being directed by the erstwhile leadership of INFACT and INBC. Based on their monitoring of industry's marketing practices in 42 developing countries, NGOs charged Nestle and American Home Products (AHP) with supplying free and low-cost infant formula to hospitals in violation of the code.[8] Although this boycott is still in effect, its practical impact today has been negligible in terms of press coverage or support by religious groups and other health and community organizations that had been a major force behind the original boycott against Nestle. During January-February 1991, both Nestle and AHP announced their decisions to stop providing free and low-cost samples to hospitals in Third World countries "except for the limited number of infants who need it." However, both companies planned to enforce this decision gradually. ACA was not satisfied with this gradual approach and has decided to continue its boycott of both the companies until it felt satisfied with their full compliance.[9]

The United States has become an intense battleground for competitive marketing in the infant formula industry as incumbent firms have sought to increase their market share while new entrants are striving to gain a foothold in this highly lucrative market. It is disturbing to note that in entering the U.S. market, Nestle undertook to use marketing strategies and tactics that (1) ran counter to both the existing practices of leading U.S. infant formula manufacturers and the prevailing medical opinion, and (2) for which Nestle, in particular, was attacked previously in Third World countries. It is not surprising that Nestle paid a high price in terms of adverse publicity, reawakening of public hostility, and an intensification of the renewed boycott launched against it by the activists.

Until quite recently, Nestle had not marketed its infant formula products in the United States. However, in June 1988 Carnation Company, a wholly owned subsidiary of Nestle, entered the U.S. infant formula foods market by introducing two infant nutrition products: Good Start H.A. and Good Nature. The two products were promoted as being more suitable for babies who were allergic to milk-based formulas. In order to create a special niche for its products and gain a marketing advantage, the company positioned its products as especially suited for very sick children. And yet, contrary to every established market practice in the United States, Carnation chose to advertise its products directly to consumers in print and television advertising and made them available for purchase in supermarkets instead of through pharmacies.[10]

Carnation's actions raised a storm of protest from activists and public health professionals, especially the American Academy of Pediatrics (AAP). Characterizing the move as a "shock to the physician community," Dr. Narkewicz, then president of the AAP, said that such advertising decreased breastfeeding, and asked Carnation to reconsider its marketing strategy.[11] Carnation maintained that it is simply giving women — the decision makers on infant feeding — information and choices. The ads commend breastfeeding as the best form of infant nutrition but also offer formula as the alternative when breastfeeding is difficult or not the mother's choice. In addition, the Food and Drug Administration (FDA) and various state health organizations initiated investigation of Carnation's claims that its product was hypo-allergenic, following numerous complaints of adverse reactions. The pursuant intense adverse publicity finally led to Carnation's cancellation of direct consumer advertising — for a short while — for its products and also withdrawal of all claims as to the uniqueness and suitability of its products for very sick children.[12]

Similarly, in October 1989 Gerber Corporation, a producer of baby foods, also initiated direct consumer advertising for a new line of artificial infant formula product, called "Gerber Baby Formula," under arrangement with Bristol-Myers Corporation, who manufactures the formula. Gerber's decision was based, in part, on an observed socioeconomic trend of mothers returning to work in increasing numbers within six months after giving birth, resulting in a rapid decline in breastfeeding. Moreover, research indicated to the company that parents were more and more inclined to making their own choices of infant formula, independent of physicians' recommendations.[13] Once again, AAP voiced its objections, citing primarily that such an advertising strategy undermined efforts to (1) promote breastfeeding as the optimal method of infant nutrition and (2) establish as primary the recommendations of health professionals as to the formula best suited to any individual child.

Gerber's plan to use direct advertising came soon after the barrage of criticism that had been leveled against Nestle's Carnation Company and that company's ensuing decision to discontinue its consumer-directed advertising. It would seem that Gerber was taking advantage of a market opportunity created by Nestle's withdrawal from direct consumer advertising. Perhaps the company felt that its small size would allow it to escape from activist criticism while improving its chances of gaining a foothold in the lucrative U.S. infant formula market. Gerber's response to the health community's disapproval was strikingly similar to Carnation's initial defense. Company officials pointed to their advertising slogan: "If it doesn't come from you, shouldn't it come from Gerber?" as evidence of reinforcement of the message that "breast feeding is best." Gerber also claimed, as did Carnation, that it was simply giving mothers a choice.

In January 1991 Nestle's Carnation Company reinstated its consumer-directed advertising after watching Gerber break into the market with its own aggressive direct-to-consumer campaign. The success of this strategy is apparent from the fact that the sales of the two Nestle brands made significant inroads in the infant formula market. Between 1991–1992, Good Start achieved a sales gain of 79 percent to $56.0 million, with Follow Up gaining 40 percent to $54.0 million. The two brands now hold a combined market share of 4.6 percent, which is remarkable for a company starting with a handicap of negative public image and in a hotly competitive market.[15]

Gerber's infant formula's direct consumer advertising campaign has not fared so well. It evoked a strong negative response from activist groups, pediatricians, and hospitals, who were even more concerned with the Gerber/Bristol-Myers product then they were with the Carnation/Nestle product, since the former is a formula for newborns where breastfeeding is even more critical, whereas the latter is a formula for babies over six months old. A number of hospitals even stopped using Bristol-Myers' lead brand Enfamil which lost 2.6 percent market share in 1992. Neither Gerber nor Carnation participated in the hospital sampling programs. Meanwhile, American Home products' Wyeth-Ayerst subsidiary has made significant progress in gaining market share by intensifying sales efforts through its traditional channels, that is, pushing more products through pediatricians.[15]

The loser in all these campaigns has been Abbott Labs, the market leader and the company that by some measures has pursued the most restrained promotional strategies in marketing infant formula in its domestic and international markets. In 1992, its two lead brands, Similac and Isomil, lost a combined market share of 1.9 percent although they still account for over 50 percent of all infant formula sales in the United States.[16]

FTC Charges Against the U.S. Manufacturers

A more disturbing picture of the marketing practices and profitability of the infant formula manufacturers was recently revealed when the U.S. Federal Trade Commission (FTC) charged the three major U.S. infant formula manufacturers with price fixing and other anti-trust activities, such as anti-competitive behavior, designed to enrich their profits at the expense of the U.S. consumer.[17] The FTC was slowly emerging from the laissez-faire attitude of the Reagan–Bush Administrations and was beginning to renew its interest in cases that affect the public's pocketbook. On June 11, 1992, FTC charged Abbott Labs (Ross Lab), AHP (Wyeth-Ayerst), and Bristol-Myers Squibb (Mead Johnson) with bid-rigging in the provision of infant formula in Puerto Rico.[18] The FTC indictment culminated a two-year investigation and charged the companies with conspiracy to set the bid prices to ensure that all three could sell their infant formula products in the U.S. territory. In making its charges, the FTC was relying on a relatively new antitrust theory which held that actions other than traditional written or spoken arguments might constitute price fixing or improper division of markets. The agency subpoenaed the records of all leading makers of infant formula after state welfare officials and consumer groups complained that the manufacturers had raised prices uniformly over the past decade.[19] The FTC investigations focused on what are called "facilitating devices" — signals between companies that lead to anti-competitive behavior.[20] The civil suit accused the companies of allegedly instituting a series of "lockstep" price increases since 1979, and restraining competition on bids for formula provided through WIC — Women, Infants and Children, an Agriculture Department feeding program that reached 5.4 million pregnant and nursing women, infants, and young children. As a result of the alleged bid-rigging, states administering the WIC program paid higher prices, lost million of dollars in potential rebates, and provided fewer poor people with food aid. Senator Patrick Leahy (D — Vt.) said noncompetitive practices by the companies cost taxpayers as much as $168.0 million each year through added expense to the federal food program for WIC which uses almost one-third of all infant formula sold in the U.S.[21]

In summary, the following are among the charges leveled by FTC against the three major U.S. infant formula companies:[22]

> *Abbott*: A civil antitrust suit accuses the maker of Similac and Isomil of bid-rigging in 1990 in connection with a two-year contract to provide formula to more than 40,000 infants through the government's food subsidy program for WIC in Puerto Rico. The government is seeking an unstated amount of restitution for money lost.

> *Mead Johnson*: The negotiated settlement concludes several civil antitrust charges against the company, which makes Enfamil and Prosobee. One accused it of engaging in unfair competition by sending letters to the WIC programs in four States — Nevada, Montana, Oklahoma, and Arizona — stating their bids, when the states had requested sealed bids.

> *AHP*: The settlement ends the FTC's civil antitrust accusation that the maker of SMA and Nursoy brands signalled its rivals during the Puerto Rico bidding.

Basically, the three had illegally limited competition in bidding on the WIC nutrition program subsidized by the federal government. The three companies together controlled 90 percent of the $1.5 billion industry in the United States, with Abbott representing about 50 percent, Mead-Johnson about 30 percent, and AHP about 8 percent. All the companies denied any wrongdoing. Both Mead and AHP claimed that the FTC charges were groundless but that they were settling the case as it was less expensive and easier than protracted litigation. According to Mead Johnson's nutritional group president, Donald Harris, Mead "absolutely and unequivocally" denied the charges filed by FTC; and John Skule, a vice-president of AHP, said that ". . . we disagreed with the charge completely."[23] In settling FTC charges, Bristol-Myers Squibb (Mead) paid $38.76 million in July 1992, and American Home Products (AHP) also negotiated a settlement. As part of the settlement, Mead and AHP donated 3.6 million pounds of powdered infant formula (worth about $ 25 million) to the Agriculture Department to be distributed to poor women and children.[24] Initially, Abbott refused to go along with other manufacturers and settle FTC charges despite the fact that allegations against the company were more serious than those against other companies that had agreed to settle. According to chairman and CEO Duane L. Burnham, Abbott, which sells formula through its Ross Laboratories unit, ". . . competed responsibly, aggressively and completely within the law and . . . will continue to vigorously defend this position." A trial date was set for June 1993.[25] However, shortly before the trial was set to begin, Abbott capitulated. "Facing federal antitrust allegations from 27 drugstore and food chains, along with charges from the Florida attorney general of bid-rigging, Abbott . . . settled for more than $140 million" in fines and other related payments.[26]

Nestle had not given up on its aggressiveness, however, and continued to push for greater penetration into the U.S. market. Around the same time, the U.S. infant formula manufacturers were settling their antitrust charges with the FTC, Nestle-U.S. weighed in by suing the U.S. manufacturers and the American Academy of Pediatrics alleging that the two conspired to block new competitors, i.e., Nestle, from the "lucrative U.S. market." In its suit, the company charged that its competitors entered into exclusive agreements with hospitals and set wholesale price increases in "lock step fashion" while concealing concerted action by alternating leadership in setting prices. The Academy of Pediatrics came under severe criticism from state and federal officials for receiving contributions from the infant formula manufacturers. It appears that between 1983 and 1991, these contributions amounted to more than $8.3 million, in addition to indirect funds from manufacturers' advertisements in its journals and donations toward the designing of hospital pediatric clinics.[27]

Following FTC's lead, whose investigations began in May 1990, state attorneys general in New York, Pennsylvania, Wisconsin, and Texas also looked into whether the producers rigged bids on contracts or overcharged consumers. The first state charges against infant formula manufacturers were filed by Florida in January 1991 in connection with price-fixing on the part of the three U.S. companies cited in the FTC federal cases. Florida Attorney General Bob Butterworth stated that since 1979, the companies have raised prices 155.4 percent, while the concurrent increase in the price of milk was 36.4 percent. In December 1992 Bristol-Meyers agreed to pay $4.0 million and AHP $1.0 million to settle in the State of Florida, though both continued to deny allegations.

Florida state attorney general Butterworth also claimed that the three companies, rather than selling their infant formula directly to consumers, encouraged physicians and hospitals to recommend the product to patients. In exchange for their endorsement, hospitals and doctors received free samples of formula and other baby products, as well as cash grants and research grants.[28] From the companies' perspective, this is an efficient way of marketing its product and also maintaining market control. Nutritionally, the major brands are virtually identical, since their content is regulated by the Infant Formula Act of 1980. The physicians' preference for breastfeeding creates a marketing problem for the industry: how to position a slightly-less-than-optimal product. The three U.S. leaders — Abbott, Bristol-Myers, and AHP — market directly to physicians or hospitals who usually give the formula free to mothers. The strategy works: research shows that 90 percent of women stick with the brand the hospitals gives them. "We don't do consumer promotion," said Cathy Babington, a spokeswoman for Abbott, in an oblique reference to the new and controversial practices of marketing directly to nursing women, which the industry giants oppose.[29] Industry leaders can apparently remain aloof from the vulgar area of consumer marketing which was the source of major criticisms against Carnation and Gerber, in part because of their market dominance.

The New Nestle

Notwithstanding the problems arising out of its infant formula sales and international boycott against its products, the 1980s were a period of aggressive expansion and growth for Nestle. Most of this growth came through mergers and acquisitions, including the United States, where at the beginning of the 1980s, Nestle had set a target of deriving at least 30 percent of its worldwide revenues from the U.S. market (see Chapter 10).[30] The absorption of this growth in the old Nestle culture, however, was not painless. In the past, Nestle was a largely decentralized company where many local subsidiaries were often perceived by the citizens of those countries as national companies. It was not uncommon for Nestle to downplay the company's Swiss identity. The proliferation of products, brands, and subsidiaries made decentralized structure even more difficult to manage, with the result that the headquarters was often found wanting in its knowledge of the company's far-flung operations and control of numerous subsidiaries' managers to ensure compliance with companies policies and procedures.[31] An added complexity, and one that is not often easily appreciated, was the clash of culture among different types of companies that were selling products and operating in markets that called for widely divergent entrepreneurial styles, risk taking, and response to market factors.

The company's U.S. operations provide a vivid example of the failure of the decentralized system, on the one hand, and the parent company's inability to manage diverse cultures among its various acquisitions in the United States, on the other hand. It should be remembered that it was the decentralized nature of the company's operations and wide latitude given to its U.S. managers that led Nestle — Switzerland to pursue policies and take actions dealing with the infant formula controversy, especially during the Kennedy Hearings and thereafter, that caused serious damage to the company's reputation and public credibility (Chapter 5). Recall that the company's growth had been derived through some major acquisitions, notably Stouffers Hotels and Carnation Corporation (Chapter 10). While the company has had tremendous success in its hotel business and processed food products, it also badly fumbled in other acquisitions. An analysis of some of these failures suggests that a major part of the blame lies with Nestle's lack of understanding of the diverse market conditions, corporate culture, and either too much or too little emphasis in integrating the culture of the acquired companies into that of Nestle — Switzerland. The case of Nestle's acquisition of Beech-Nut Nutrition Corporation and its further handling of its affairs aptly illustrates this point.

Nestle bought Beech-Nut from a group headed by Pennsylvania lawyer Frank Nicholas in 1979 for $35.0 million. Nicholas had bought the baby food manufacturer from Squibb Corp. in 1973 almost entirely with borrowed money and ran it on a shoe string budget. It is speculated that Beech-Nut's mounting losses and the millions it owed to suppliers led, in part, to its signing an agreement in 1977 with Interjuice Trading Corp., a supplier of apple juice concentrate, at a price 20 percent below the market. This proved to be a fatal error in judgment. Nestle inherited this judgment error along with Beech-Nut's lingering financial woes. The Swiss giant invested an additional $60.0 million in its new subsidiary, hiked marketing budgets, and succeeded in boosting sales. But cost pressures persisted in driving the company into the red. Nestle brought in Neils Hoyvald, a native of Denmark, in 1980, and he replaced Nicholas in April 1981 as president and CEO of Beech-Nut. Hoyvald was recommended by Ernest Saunders, then an executive of Nestle overseeing Beech-Nut.*

Hoyvald's career with Beech-Nut ended in a federal jury conviction in February 1988 for violation of the Federal Food, Drug and Cosmetic Act. A series of missteps paved the way to this finale, beginning with rumors of adulterated apple juice concentrate provided by Beech-Nut's low-cost supplier. Despite clear evidence from Beech-Nut's own research and development (R&D) scientists as early as 1981 that the concentrate was a blend of synthetics rather than the "100% pure juice" as claimed by the label, management (including Hoyvald) tended to ignore the issue. Hoyvald had promised Nestle that Beech-Nut would be profitable by 1982 and hence any suggestion was not tolerated that would result in increased operating costs to Beech-Nut. Attempts were made to silence Beech-Nut R&D director Mr. LiCari, who brought this issue up in what was later referred to as the "smoking gun" memo, by urging him to be a "team player." LiCari wrote the

---

*Saunders played a very active role in the Nestle's strategies in dealing with the activist groups pertaining to the international boycott of Nestle's products during the time of the Kennedy Hearings and the period immediately following it. He left Nestle soon thereafter to become the chief executive officer of Guinness, PLC, in the United Kingdom where he was involved in an insider trading scandal. For further details, see Chapters 5–7 of this book.

memo in August 1981 and resigned a few months later. What followed was an investigation of the manufacturing plant which revealed the truth of the rumor regarding the ersatz juice. In an entirely miscalculated strategy, Beech-Nut chose to stonewall officials and kept selling the product until March 1983, claiming a lack of unequivocal proof that the apple juice concentrate was bogus.

The controversy cost Beech-Nut an estimated $25 million in fines, legal costs, and slumping sales. Nestle financed a defense of Beech-Nut executives Neils Hoyvald and John Lavery, vice-president for manufacturing, trying to shift the blame on lower-level employees, another flawed tactic. Nestle also chose to hire the same lawyer that had defended Oliver North, whose disfavor in the eyes of the American public was glaring. Although Hoyward was able to get his conviction overturned by a federal appeals court due to a technicality, the reputation of Beech-Nut was severely tainted. By 1989 it was apparent that Nestle was preparing Beech-Nut for divesture, trying to distance itself from the incriminating evidence against operations in its subsidiary.[32]

Drive Toward Centralization

Nestle has undergone a number of significant changes in its organization, policies, and operating procedures, both in worldwide operations and also in the United States. However, in many ways the company has not changed at all, and manifestations of "old Nestle" invariably appear to remind both insiders and outsiders that the New Nestle is not deeply rooted in the corporate culture. Nestle took a series of bold and highly innovative strategic actions in an effort to combat the effect of a worldwide boycott against its products and the negative public image that the company had acquired during the entire history of the infant formula controversy covering the period 1974–1984 starting with the publication of *The Baby Killer*[33] and ending with the suspension of the boycott. The most notable of these were the establishment of NCCN and NIFAC, on the one hand, and a proactive strategic stance toward the company's critics and a willingness to effect changes in corporate practices, on the other hand.

After the termination of the boycott, Nestle's current chief executive officer, Helmut Maucher, launched an effort to reorganize and consolidate the company's highly fragmented operations into a more cohesive organization. The acquisition of Carnation Company provided a fillip in this direction by bringing into the company's fold a number of young and aggressive managers.

Up until 1986, Nestle — Switzerland was controlled by a special committee of three senior executives that managed an essentially matrix type of organization. Maucher, however, had an extreme dislike of the matrix type which he found to be unwieldy, unresponsive, and lacking in accountability.

He put into operation a new organizational structure, with him on top and seven managers reporting to him. Of these, five are line managers responsible for the operations of five zones representing Nestle's worldwide operations. These changes have resulted in a shift of power from headquarter staff specialists to line managers. In part, the new organizational structure reflects Maucher's orientation and work experience. He is steeped in the operations side of the business and takes pride in understanding details and minutiae of Nestle's far-flung operations undertaking extensive travel to remain in regular touch with a great many of the company's field operations and managers.

The U.S. operations have also gone through a process of consolidation. Prior to 1992, Nestle operated 32 subsidiaries and entities in the United States, each operating almost independently. A great many of them pursued their own growth and expansion plans that were not coordinated within the overall corporate goals. The situation often led to conflicting policies and actions in the marketplace, resulting in inefficiency and confusion. Nestle's U.S. operations have been consolidated into one holding company, Nestle — USA, headquartered in Glendale, California. Around 1990, Nestle's structure began to change and it was a question of whether Mr. Timm F. Crull, president of Nestle's Carnation Company, or James Bigger, then head of Stouffer's, would lead Nestle — USA. The decision was made to appoint Crull instead of Bigger, who retired at that point. The basis for the decision was twofold: Timm Crull was the younger of the two, and Carnation was a successful company. Nestle management believed that having somebody like Crull would help the reorganization and the subsequent consolidation of Nestle — USA.

The new company has six operating divisions, each headed by a president. They are: Nestle Beverage, Nestle Brands Food Service, Nestle Food, Nestle Frozen Food (Stouffer Foods and Nestle Ice Cream), Nestle Refrigerated Food Company, and Wine World Estates. Stouffer Hotels chain, one of Nestle's earliest acquisitions, was sold by the company in 1992. A part of the impetus for change came with the acquisition of Carnation and a shifting of the balance of power from the old guard dominated by the managers from Stouffers and aligned with the previous management at Nestle — Switzerland. The new management is dominated by the managers from the Carnation group.

Nevertheless, it is doubtful whether these changes have had a lasting effect on the company's psyche or operations except at a somewhat superficial level. Moreover, for reasons explained in earlier chapters, these innovative mechanisms were highly successful in getting Nestle to resolve its problems and manage a very serious crisis of public confidence and an attack on corporate legitimacy. However, the process of their operation and a lack of their integration into the company's structure in the post-crisis phase have created a perception that these institutional mechanisms were both Nestle-situation-specific and time-specific and that their generalizability to other situations involving other companies was somewhat limited. And that's a pity. I believe that a continuation of these institutions in some form, and their integration into the company's corporate structure and modus operandi would have gone a long way to demonstrate their pertinence for the business community in managing business and society conflicts in ways that are both highly effective and nonconfrontational.

Nestle's New Corporate Culture — Old Wine in New Bottle?

Maucher also claims to have made major changes in Nestle's corporate culture so as to make it more responsive to changing societal expectations. As an example of the changed corporate culture, he points to the company's novel approach in dealing with the infant formula controversy, establishment of NCCN, and dealing directly with the church leaders in the United States. However, as we pointed out in an earlier chapter of the book, the life tenure of NCCN did not last much longer beyond the termination of the boycott. The new Nestle seems to have poorly internalized the lessons of the boycott and the innovative strategies and tactics developed by NCCN. Rather than making sensitivity to external concerns, that is, non-market effects of its market related actions, an integral part of the responsibilities of its line managers, Nestle still sees it as a staff activity of essentially an advisory nature. In commenting about the infant formula affair, Nestle's new CEO, Helmut Maucher, commented that Nestle now did certain things differently and that Nestle's new department of corporate affairs had the job of sensitizing the Nestle's top management on measures whose economic nature could, nevertheless, "stir up hostile reaction among certain groups outside the company."[34]

Nestle's old guard has been intent on defending its strategies and tactics during the boycott campaign and suggesting that the setbacks suffered by the company were more of an aberration, brought about by its opponents who were motivated by anti-capitalist ideologies and who would resort to untruths and sensationalism; meanwhile the company was restrained because of its dedication to scientific truth, professionalism, and concern for the consumer in its overseas markets.[35] Subsequent events also showed that Nestle — Switzerland viewed these arrangements to be ad hoc and temporary, designed to take care of an unusual and one-of-a-kind situation. No sooner had the controversy been resolved when Nestle's culture reasserted itself. Viewing the events in the United States as temporary aberrations, the traditional culture did not choose to internalize that experience into institutional memory. Thus the company condemned itself to repeat the same mistakes eight years later when it decided to enter the U.S. infant formula market in 1988 and once again became the subject of public and professional criticism and a renewed boycott.

The entrenched bureaucracy at Nestle — Switzerland was, and still is, convinced that its strategy of domain defense, with its attendant tactics, was quite appropriate. It is not clear that any lessons have been permanently learned. If this is the case, then the whole tortuous process would have come to naught. It has been over 18 years since the Berne trial, and over 12 years after the passage of the WHO Code, and 9 years since the termination of the first boycott. And yet, Nestle's old guard is still trying to rewrite history and defend its activities. The latest attempt in this regard has been the publication of *Infant Feeding: Anatomy of a Controversy 1973–1984* (1988), edited by Dr. John Dobbing.[36] This book's description of the Berne trial and all subsequent events is so blatantly one-sided that it is hard to imagine what possible good it could do for the company. It does, however, offer a clear demonstration that the old guard, who had been relegated to the background during the later phases of the controversy, has regained its previous power. Given a supportive corporate culture, it has reasserted itself and is determined to rewrite history as it wishes to see it. The best defense of Nestle presented in the book is that of a naive and unworldly corporate management who was constantly outwitted and outmaneuvered by its unscrupulous, politically sophisticated, media-wise, and ideologically committed critics. In reading the book, it is hard to decide which is more deplorable, their actions and performance during the controversy or their account of its aftermath.

Notes

1. World Health Organization, *International Code of Marketing of Breast-Milk Substitutes* (Geneva, 1981), Article 11.3.

2. *Ibid.*, Article 8.1.

3. *Ibid.*, Article 8.2.

4. IDACE, *Industry Code of Practice for the Marketing of Breast Milk Substitutes in the EEC*, p. 2.

5. Dr. Rolf Reiss, Milupa F'Dorf, Letter addressed to Dr. S. Prakash Sethi, dated June 26, 1991.

6. Nestle Infant Formula Audit Commission, *Joint Statement by Nestle and the Nestle Infant Formula Audit Commission on the Dissolution of the Commission* (Washington, D.C.: June 1991), p. A-6.

7. Barbara Presley Noble, "Nestle — Battling The Boycotts," *The New York Times*, July 28, 1991, p. 5.

8. Alix M. Freedman, "Nestle Faces New Boycott Threat in Distribution of Infant Formula," *The Wall Street Journal*, June 29, 1988, p. 28; "Renewed Boycott of Nestle is Urged by Advocacy Groups," *The Wall Street Journal*, October 5, 1988, p. B10; "Boycott of Nestle to Resume," *The New York Times*, October 5, 1988, p. D2.

9. For details of the latest controversy see "Nestle to Restrict Low-Cost Supplies Of Baby Food To Developing Nations," *The Wall Street Journal*, January 30, 1991, p. B6; and "American Home Infant Formula Giveaway To End," *The Wall Street Journal*, February 4, 1991, pp. B1, B5.

10. For details see Amal Kumar Naj, "Nestle To Sell Infant Formula In U.S.; Step Likely To Hurt Competitors' Profits," *The Wall Street Journal*, June 6, 1988, p. 5; Alix M. Freedman, "Nestle's New Infant Formula Line Introduced In A Bid For U.S. Market," *The Wall Street Journal*, June 28, 1988, p. 38; Milt Freudenheim, "A Safer Infant Formula Prom-

ised," *The New York Times*, June 28, 1988, pp. D1, D22; Andrea Adelson, "Pediatricians On Carnation," *The New York Times*, June 29, 1988, p. D-5; "Carnation's Move In Infant Formula," *The New York Times*, June 30, 1988, p. D8; "Carnation Won't Use Name In Infant Formula Campaign," *The Wall Street Journal*, July 15, 1988 p. 20; Steven Greenhouse, "Nestle's Time To Swagger," *The New York Times*, January 1, 1989; "FDA Rejects Nestle Unit's 'Good Start' Label Claim," *The Wall Street Journal*, February 3, 1989, p. B7; Alix M. Freedman, "Nestle's Bid To Crash Baby Formula Market in The U.S. Stirs A Row," *The Wall Street Journal*, February 16, 1989, pp. A1, A9; "Nestle Ad Claims For Baby Formula Probed In 3 States," *The Wall Street Journal*, March 2, 1989, p. B6; "Nestle To Drop Claim On Label Of Its Formula," *The Wall Street Journal*, March 13, 1989, p. B5; "Nestle Rejects Militant P.R. Plan To Combat Renewal Of Boycott," *The Wall Street Journal*, April 25, 1989, pp. B6–7; M. Freitog, "Gerber Plan For Infant Formula," *The New York Times*, June 16, 1989, p. D5; Alix M. Freedman, "Gerber Unveils Its Baby Formula, Aims To Woo Parents Rather Than Doctors," *The Wall Street Journal*, June 16, 1989, p. B3; "Nestle's Carnation Co. Unit Settles Dispute Over Infant Formula Ads," *The Wall Street Journal*, July 7, 1989, p. B4; "Carnation Halts Formula Claims," *The New York Times*, July 7, 1989 p. D5; Michael Freitag, "The Infant Formula Debate Strikes Home," *The New York Times*, September 3, 1989, p. E5; Barry Meier, "Are Ads For Infant Formula Fit For The Eyes Of Parents?" *The New York Times*, December 29, 1990, p. 46; Julia Flynn Silver and David Woodruff, "The Furor Over Formula Is Coming To A Boil," *Business Week*, April 9, 1990, pp. 52–53; "A Flap Over Formula Is Coming To A Boil," *Business Week*, January 1, 1991, p. 47.

11. Andrea Adelson, "Carnation's Move in Infant Formula," *The New York Times*, June 30, 1988. p. D8.

12. Alix M. Freedman, "Nestle's Carnation Co. Unit Settles Dispute Over Infant Formula Ads," *The Wall Street Journal*, July 7, 1989, p. B4; and Michael Freitag, "The Infant Formula Debate Strikes Home," *The New York Times*, September 3, 1989, p. E5.

13. See Alix M. Freedman, "Gerber Unveils its Baby Formula, Aims to Woo Parents Rather than Doctors," *The Wall Street Journal*, June 19, 1989, p. B3; and, Michael Freitag, "Gerber Plan for Infant Formula," *The New York Times*, June 16, 1989, p. D-5.

14. Laura Bird, "TV Ads Boost Nestle's Infant Formulas," *The Wall Street Journal*, March 30, 1993, pp. B1, B14.

15. *Ibid.*

16. *Ibid.*

17. See "Makers of Baby Formula Charged," *The Boston Globe*, June 12, 1992, p. 66; Steven Morris, "Abbott Denies Formula Scheme," *Chicago Tribune*, June 12, 1992, p. 1; Kevin G. Salwen, "Infant-Formula Firms Rigged Bids, U.S. Says," *The Wall Street Journal*, June 12, 1992, p. A3; and, Robert Pear, "Top Infant-Formula Makers Charged by U.S. over Pricing," *The New York Times*, June 12, 1992, p. A1.

18. Barry Meier, "FTC is Re-Emerging as Watchdog on Prices," *The New York Times*, January 28, 1991, p. A16.

19. Paul M. Barrett, "FTC Steps Up Infant Formula Pricing Probe," *The Wall Street Journal*, January 2, 1991, p. A8.

20. Kathleen Day, "A New Activism on Antitrust Policy: The FTC Initiates Aggressive Inquiry into Alleged Price-Fixing by Infant Formula Giants," *The Washington Post*, January 13, 1991, p. H1.

21. Associated Press, "Baby Food Profits Hit in Congress," *The Chicago Tribune*, March 15, 1991, p. 8.

22. Robert Pear, *op. cit.*, supra note 17.

23. Steven Morris, *op. cit.*, supra note 17.

24. News Service, "FTC Files Antitrust Charges Against Infant Formula Makers," *The Atlanta Journal and Constitution*, June 12, 1992, p. 7.

25. Kevin Salwen, *op. cit.*, supra note 17; Laura Bird, *op cit.*, supra note 14.

26. Thomas M. Burton, "Methods of Marketing Infant Formula Land Abbott in Hot Water," *The Wall Street Journal*, (May 25, 1993), A1, A7.

27. "Nestle Unit Sues Baby Formula Firms, Alleging Conspiracy With Pediatricians," *The Wall Street Journal*, (June 1, 1993), A1; Barry Meier, "Battle for Baby Formula Market," *The New York Times*, (June 15, 1993), D1.

28. Glenn Ruffenach, "Florida Files Suit Against 3 Makers of Infant Formula," *The Wall Street Journal*, January 4, 1991, p. A4.

29. Robert Pear, *op. cit.*, supra note 17.

30. "Nestle: Centralizing to Win a Bigger Payoff from the U.S.," *Business Week*, February 21, 1981, pp. 58–60.

31. Robert Ball, "A 'Shopkeeper' Shakes Up Nestle," *Fortune* (December 12, 1982), pp. 1053–106; Marcia Berss, "Sleep Well or Eat Well," *Forbes* (February 13, 1984), pp. 62–63.

32. See The Corporation, "What Led Beech-Nut Down the Road to Disgrace," *Business Week*, February 22, 1988, pp. 124–128; Ann Hagedorn, "Two Ex-Officials of Beech-Nut Get Prison Sentences," *The Wall Street Journal*, June 17, 1988; Betty Wong, "Conviction of Nestle Unit's Ex-President is Overturned on Appeal in Juice Case," *The Wall Street Journal*, March 31, 1989; and, Alix M. Freedman, "Nestle Quietly Seeks to Sell Beechnut, Dogged by Scandal of Bogus Apple Juice," *The Wall Street Journal*, July 14, 1989.

33. Mike Muller, *The Baby Killer* (London: War on Want, 1974).

34. Graham Turner, "Inside Europe's Giant Companies: Nestle Finds a Better Formula," *Long Range Planning*, Vol. 19, No. 3 (1986), 12–19.

35. John Dobbing, ed., *Infant Feeding: Anatomy of a Controversy 1973–1984* (New York: Srpinger-Verlag, 1988).

36. *Ibid.*

21 EMERGING MODES OF BUSINESS–SOCIETY CONFLICT RESOLUTION — AN ASSESSMENT

The realms of competitive markets and collective public policy, the domains of rights and reciprocal obligations, the concepts of legitimacy of actions and distribution of just rewards, and the right of voluntarily contracting parties against those who are adversely affected by them while remaining outside the transaction — these have always proved to be among the major causes of social conflict in dynamic societies. They direct both the process and outcomes of evolving social order through their impact on relative bargaining power, rules of the game, and the legitimization of ensuing distribution of sociopolitical and economic gains and losses among groups and individuals. Adherents of free markets and individual choice recognize these strains as market imperfections and market failures, which should be corrected through minimal governmental intervention while ensuring that market imperfections are not aggravated further. Proponents of collective action for social good, however, start with the assumption that markets are never perfect. Even under the absurd condition of perfect markets, they may create income and wealth distributions that violate a society's sense of fairness and equity, are perceptibly disproportionate to one's *real* contribution to social well-being, and hurt those who are the most vulnerable and least able among a society's people.

It is also argued that economic system is but a tool to be used for the common good. Since markets are inherently imperfect, the dominant institutions of markets — large corporations and their leaders — are least accountable for their actions either to markets or to other instruments of social control.[1] Therefore, alternative, nontraditional mechanisms must be found

355

to control these economic behemoths so as to make them more socially responsible.

In the United States, there has been a profound change in the process of public policy formulation, shifting it away from the conventional institutional arena, such as legislative bodies, and more into a system of direct franchise. Private voluntary organizations (PVOs) of all ilks and persuasions have sought to influence existing social order through moral suasion, mass action, news media, and legislative-judicial means to bend the public weal to their vision of a just social order. What started out to be a fragmented movement against the Vietnam war, the degradation of the environment, the spread of poverty, and big brotherism of the big government and big business came to be institutionalized as the third force of social change, with its own vision of an ideal society, how it might be achieved, and who might be its leaders. In a sense, this is nothing new. We have been through similar cycles during our developmental history. The process of industrialization, economic growth, and a market economy created inequalities in opportunity for equal sharing, lack of obligation for equal caring, and a high proportion of society's rewards going to a few who were entrepreneurially daring. Their combined effect led to doubts in the minds of the populace about the legitimacy of large corporations and other established institutions that were identified with this socioeconomic order. There was a questioning of the concept of growth and well-being not only in the aggregate but in terms of those poor who were left outside the system. We were examining democratic capitalism not only for its grand design and institutional vestments but also in terms of the disenfranchised who did not count at all.

Lessons of the Eighties

Conflicts between business and other social institutions during the seventies and eighties covered a wide spectrum of issues, companies, industries, and nations. At a more fundamental level they raised the issues of "legitimacy" in terms of "right to exist" and the "scope of discretion" on the part of large corporations and PVOs. While the established institutions, such as the corporation, sought to define legitimacy in narrow legal and functional terms, the newly emerging groups defended their legitimacy in moral and ethical as well as constituency-representational terms, avowing to speak for the poor, the disenfranchised, and the unborn. Emanating from these diverse claims of superior legitimacy, the opposing groups have sought to rationalize their behavior and justify their actions against their opponents.

History tells us that social movements of major public import, like pathbreaking scientific discoveries, seldom occur in a vacuum. A multiplicity of related and seemingly unrelated actions by a multitude of people, extending over a long period of time, create the preconditions and ultimate acceptance of a major discontinuity in the existing sociopolitical arrangement. However, it is often a single event or person that gives focus to the turbulence in the environment and thereby marks and crystallizes a major social change. The history of the infant formula controversy, the dynamics of conflict between Nestle and the activist groups, and the process of conflict resolution involving religious institutions, national and international agencies, and well-meaning public citizens admirably fill this role. The controversy and the Nestle boycott have left an indelible mark on our collective psyche that would likely influence the perceptions and behavior of participants in similar conflicts in the future.

The Nineties — Large Corporations as the Prime Target

Once again, the large corporation, notably the multinational corporation (MNC), has in the nineties become the prime target of societal concern, especially on the part of PVOs. The sixties saw a spate of controversies against the overpowering influence of large multinational corporations in impacting the destinies of nations and peoples. There was the specter of the nation-less corporation moving its resources and technologies at will and holding hostage nations who must compete among themselves to attract these companies' investments. Even industrially advanced nations were not immune from this pressure and succumbed to the influence of MNCs by granting them tax benefits and other operational freedoms while overlooking their excesses — all in the name of protecting employments and their people's living standards.[2] The seventies and the eighties were a period of relative respite when earlier fears of the demonic powers of the MNC were found to be unreal, and the role of market economies to create ever-increasing living standards was forcefully demonstrated by the newly industrialized nations of the Pacific Rim. The point was made even more poignant when juxtaposed against the abject failures of many a command economies of the former socialist countries and their numerous emulators in the Third World.

We have come now full circle, but with a difference. There is clear recognition that private enterprise and competitive markets are essential to economic growth and political freedoms; they do not always ensure that MNCs would operate in a manner that necessarily fosters competition, minimizes negative externalities, and enhances general social welfare. MNCs are often seen as creating and exploiting market imperfections and causing general social harm to the environment, and public health and safety, while exploiting market opportunities for the benefit of the few. This view is further reinforced by social activists because they lay at the door of the MNCs most of what they perceive to be economic inequities in a society.

As we emerge in the nineties, the scope of activity arena involving MNCs and PVOs has vastly expanded. These groups have also developed a certain level of understanding about each other's goals, motives, and modus operandi. One can also predict the nature of strategic alliances between groups as they maneuver to gain competitive advantage during various phases of an issue's life cycle. This, however, is superficial learning. It would be sheer folly to assume that social activism as a phenomenon has matured and that its parameters have become fully defined. While many PVOs — for example, those related to religious institutions and conservation movement — have a long history of social action and have achieved a certain size and financial stability, scores of new groups are being constantly spawned as new issues arise and new victims are identified. They have become a recognized force under the rubric of nongovernmental organizations (NGOs) and are represented in the public policy debates at all levels of governments in the United States, a number of European nations, and the United Nations' agencies.

The seventies and the eighties were the time of learning for the public advocacy movement in terms of strategies and tactics, issues of legitimacy, and justification of ends. Business institutions were also in the learning phase, having had to confront an unconventional adversary that did not respond to conventional motives, modes of negotiation, or prevailing rules of the game. The complex character of the public advocacy movement is not yet well understood. It was seen during various phases of the infant formula controversy that Nestle, and to some extent other corporations, repeatedly failed to foresee the events as they were influenced and shaped by the PVOs; and the PVOs were equally unwilling to acknowledge attempts on the part of Nestle to rectify its mistakes. The intractability of the two sides, especially in the early stages of the controversy, caused damage both to the company and to the cohesiveness of the activist groups.[3]

The infant formula controversy provides us, the corporate community, social activists, international organizations, and national governments, with lessons in how to deal most effectively with similar issues as they emerge. It gives us an insight as to the impact of corporate culture on a company's responses to external pressures and the extreme difficulties in bringing about changes in that culture, value orientation, and self-image. In the pages that follow, we briefly discuss the new perceptions of MNCs and the activist groups, the nature of social arena where business-society conflicts emerge, are fought, and ultimately resolved in some fashion, only to reemerge again as each solution gives rise to new problems, new advocacy groups, and new conflict arenas. Also offered are specific guidelines as to how the process of conflict resolution can be made more constructive and efficient. Finally, procedures are suggested that business institutions might adopt so as to better anticipate and assess emerging sources of business-related social discontent and take proactive measures that would minimize the likelihood of these conflicts becoming major issues, and would constrain the potential for diminution in the corporation's autonomy to manage its own affairs. Of paramount importance for business institutions is the need to re-evaluate their sources of legitimacy in the changing societal context and to ensure that their claims to legitimacy — both as to type and extent — are in congruence with evolving social precepts.

The Multinational Corporation

It is desirable to focus on the large multinational corporation, not as that institution sees itself but as it is perceived by major segments of society, the PVOs, and a great many Third World countries. The globalization of economic activity has been progressing at a very fast pace, often spawning, but invariably led, by large multinational corporations. More recently, the collapse of the centralized economies of Russia and its satellite states has put renewed emphasis on the role of private economic institutions in economic growth in developing countries. Nevertheless, a number of factors that led many a developing nation to choose the state-controlled model of growth remain undiminished and may actually have worsened. The governments and people of developing countries — as well as the poor and disenfranchised in the industrially advanced countries — fear exploitation because of lack of comparative bargaining power, inaccessibility to technical expertise and information, and a desperate need for advanced technologies. The public advocacy movement has sought to fill this gap by acting as surrogates for many of these groups and nations to demand a "better deal" from the MNCs. In doing so, they have thrown a new light on the changing role of multinational corporations around the world. In the process, and in order to gain strategic and tactical advantage, PVOs have succeeded in creating a caricature of large multinational corporations as ruthlessly using their tremendous power against others while portraying developing nations as helpless victims of MNC exploitation.

At the aggregate level, the assumption that MNCs serve public interest in host countries through their activities in the private sector is largely supportable and easily defended. We have the example of such newly industrializing countries (NICs) as South Korea, Taiwan, and Singapore. There is also strong evidence to suggest that in the Third World the countries that seemed to have made the least progress in the economic and political spheres are also the countries that restricted the growth of private enterprise, relying primarily on state-owned enterprise and government-to-government assistance.[4] The munificence of the multinational corporation is not an unmixed blessing, however. Problems arise because the objectives of private-owned multinational corporations in investing abroad may not always agree with those of the host countries, especially the poor and less-developed ones. The host country may have unrealistic expectations of what it can expect, or extract, from the multinational corporation within its borders. There is a whole body of scholarly literature and polemical-political publications listing the MNCs' sins of omission and commission.[5] The movement for a new international economic order (NIEO) is one response by the Third World nations to seek a larger, and what they consider to be a more equitable, share of this world's resources from the industrialized world.[6]

Problems also arise at the level of a single company or industry in the Third World as a consequence of MNC operations. These may have to do with the inappropriate or ill-conceived transfer of technology and plant operations. The most recent, and by far the most tragic, example of this kind occurred in December 1984 in Bhopal, India. The specific causes of the accident and Union Carbide's culpability may never be fully known. The important thing, however, is to realize that the Bhopal accident was not a natural disaster that could not be foreseen and therefore prevented, given the operating experience of Union Carbide or for that matter of other MNCs in developed countries.[7] While a multinational corporation may not deliberately violate any laws, its normal business activities can and do have unintended, but nevertheless undesirable, social consequence. Each individual action, pursued in enlightened self-interest, does not always lead to collective good. Thus rational individual actions lead to irrational collective outcomes which, had we known before the fact, we would not have wanted to cause.[8] We become victims of the tragedy of the commons where collective responsibility becomes total irresponsibility.[9]

And yet, it is not difficult to see the fallacy of the MNC stereotypes as economic behemoths whose enormous wealth and economic power make them impervious to the needs of people in countries where they operate and whose governments are afraid and unable to control them. The power of the multinationals, by the very nature of the institution, must be exercised rationally, that is, in response to market opportunities. It is unreasonable to blame the multinationals for the economic and social ills of these countries or to expect them to exercise their economic power in a manner that would significantly harm their self-interest. The argument is based on inconsistent logic. Economic power can be abused only when it is exercised irrationally, illegally, or under the aegis of political dictatorships and command economies where people's freedom to assert their economic will is subjugated to the dictates of centralized authority. The extent to which a corporation can and must deviate from this narrow mandate depends on society's changing expectations of the functions and performance of economic institutions. Democratic societies impose tremendous constraints on the use of economic power on the part of its holders. Power also imposes its own discipline. It must be wielded in a restrained manner or the holder loses its legitimacy. The large corporation, therefore, must be flexible and proactive in responding to changing societal expectations.

PVOs

Earlier in this book, we presented a brief discussion of the contrasting core values and institutional cultural ethos of business institutions and public advocacy groups that invariably lead them into conflict situations against each other (Chapters 2 and 3). In this section, we discuss PVO strategies, their organizational traits, and operational patterns. Admittedly, it is a broad-brushed picture and in parts unflattering to the self-image of many a PVO. However, it is based on an in-depth analysis of the PVO activities during the approximately 15-year span of the infant formula controversy, supplemented by the author's research in scores of business-society conflicts encompassing over 22 years.[10]

The growth of the public advocacy movement has coincided with the general decline of public trust and confidence in major societal institutions, including business. An increase in their influence has been accompanied by an expansion of the public sector and a vastly enlarged regulation of business activities. Business accountability to market forces increasingly has been substituted or superimposed by performance reporting and evaluation to government agencies, and social activists representing special constituencies of ideas or people and projecting themselves as public interest groups. It seems hardly necessary to state that these new groups have been quite successful. One has only to look at the plethora of income transfer and entitlement programs and the vast body of governmental regulation of private enterprise, to grasp the magnitude of changes in the U.S. economic and sociopolitical system.

The organizational structures, leadership styles, and operational characteristics of large, well-established, and well-financed PVOs differ with those of small, emergent, single-issue groups. The former has more in common with those of large corporations while the latter bears resemblance to small, entrepreneurially driven business organizations. PVOs also employ patterns of interorganizational cooperation that are quite similar to those employed in the economic sector by both large and small business institutions (Chapter 3). Notwithstanding, given PVOs' radically different concept of legitimacy and sense of mission, their strategies and tactics are guided by a different set of motives and emotional drives endowing them with intensities of a different order. These characteristics provide them with strong internal bonds and unity of purpose, and create identifying traits that distinguish them from business institutions.

The Role of Charismatic Leader and Professional Reformer

PVOs, both well-established and emergent single-issue groups, are often the creation of professional reformers and charismatic leaders. The former are more prominent in larger PVOs while the latter provide the life-blood of emerging single-issue groups. The large well-established PVOs also differ from large corporations where institutional structures are quite resilient and self-sustaining, and the need for charismatic leaders is less apparent and may even be harmful to the well-being of the organization. For large PVOs, even where social activism is not the primary mission of the institution, their drive for social action is often fueled by individuals who are single-mindedly focused on the activistic agenda and consider the mission and resources of the parent organization as means to achieving their particular ends.

A central element to our understanding of the dynamics, vitality, and influence of activists is the role of the reformer activist whom Harvey Cox calls the "New Breed" of professional reformer.[11] PVOs, especially the single-issue-oriented emerging groups, seek legitimacy and operate through other more established groups, and above all are identified through a common adversary: for instance, the MNC. This is not necessarily the outcome of an ideological animosity against the capitalistic system or private enterprise. A more obvious reason is that the large multinational corporation, by the very nature of the size and scope of its operations, is susceptible to such pressure and has come to accept it as a fact of life. Consequently, an analysis of the role of PVOs is increasingly becoming an integral part of strategy development by the U.S. corporations because a failure to deal with PVOs can have a devastating effect on corporate survival, profitability, and growth. The working of the Interfaith Center for Corporate Responsibility (ICCR) in the case of the infant formula controversy clearly epitomizes the working of professional reformer at its very best.[12] However, for the professional reformer to operate successfully, he/she also needs the support and acquiescence of the leadership of the primary organization. Professional reformers achieve this in two ways:

1.   They encourage the ascendence of leaders sympathetic to its cause through control of information flows and the organization's decision-making structures. For example, the leadership of National Council of Churches (NCC) is elective and subject to regular turnover. The staff, on the other hand, is appointive, has a long tenure, has a stake in the organization, and tends to guide the organization in its own vision and with its own agenda which may not serve the best interests of the larger body politic. Through their control of budgets and internal resources, these bureaucrats can make a leader look good or bad during his/her tenure of office. Through his/her control of the organizational staff and resources, professional reformers are also able to advance the cause of second-tier leaders who are most likely to be the catalysts of change and supporters of action instigated by others. They criticize the traditional programs of churches and missions and societies, and advocate using the churches' resources for politically active mobilization of the poor and the disenfranchised.

2. They set up new organizational entities — for example, program agencies and task forces — where they can operate with relative freedom and call their own programming shots without clearing them with established governing structures. This facilitates action on their preferred projects without too much budgetary accountability and performance oversight on the part of the established hierarchy.

Notwithstanding the general mission of the parent organization, the program agenda of the professional reformer bears a remarkable resemblance to the agenda of other activist-oriented groups in other PVOs. This can be partially explained by the goals and objectives of the professional reformer and also the nature of his/her networking system.[13] For example, the ICCR-initiated strategies and tactics in the infant formula controversy have been used by that organization in a host of other business-society conflicts and have become standard operating procedures for a great many other aggressively activistic PVOs.

Linkages Between Organizational Structures Strategies and Tactics

Two critical elements in the survival and growth of PVOs are: (1) to create and sustain the support of a large grassroots organization of motivated volunteers, and (2) to maintain the saliency of an issue by keeping it alive in the news media and imbuing it with a sense of importance and social priority. A volunteer-based organization needs constant replenishment because of high turnover. It must be managed democratically with a large measure of local autonomy as to governance, means of action, sources of funding, and a high level of emotional intensity so as to keep the commitment of volunteers. It must also be strongly controlled and centrally directed to minimize the risk of losing momentum and focus. This twin dilemma of the need to have a strong, disciplined, but small cadre of leaders, along with an equally strong requirement for a consensual and participative system of decision making, is resolved through a variety of measures whose successful implementation is best exemplified by INFACT/INBC/ICCR in the case of the infant formula controversy. Similar measures are being increasingly used by many other emerging groups covering a wide range of issues and adversaries.

The *organization* of a typical PVO is tied together by a small group of highly dedicated professionals who control a decentralized network by strategically placing one of their own in local units or by co-opting, through training and indoctrination, like-minded local volunteers with leadership qualities and a strong commitment to the cause. The objective is to make each subgroup work as if it were a perfect clone of the parent. Thus, given a similar set of circumstances, each subgroup would react as if it were like any other group. In practice, this is not always possible. Local groups may have their own agendas and priorities. This situation was exemplified in the infant formula controversy when, during the remedy and relief stage of the issue life cycle, a number of local groups, coming from different church-based organizations, took a more conciliatory stance against their corporate opponents than was advocated by the boycott movement's leadership. When these situations occurred, the core leadership of the boycott movement was quite willing to suppress such a divergence of opinion by severely disciplining the individuals involved. Since the organization lacked any of the means of financial punishment, it used psychological pressures such as public ridicule, disloyalty to the cause, naivete and co-option by the companies, aspersions about one's integrity and ethics, and pressure from one's cohorts and peers.* At its core, the organization becomes like a small close-knit community that is exclusive, intolerant, and increasingly repressive. In the name of unity, it abhors giving equal time or even the platform to opposing views because "we have heard them all" and "we know what they are going to say anyway" or "what else can you expect from this." Unfortunately, once started, these repressive measures are hard to contain. In their effort to keep the troops in line, the group leadership stresses means and loses sight of ends with a consequent erosion of legitimacy.

It should be noted here that corporations are equally guilty of this mentality. As we shall see in a subsequent section, their treatment of internal dissent becomes even more pernicious because they can inflict additional inequities on the "deviant and unrepentant" through financial penalties and even deprivation of one's livelihood.

Rhetoric plays an important part as the glue that binds the organization and sustains the issue in the public's mind. PVOs, both broad-based, well-established, as well as single-issue emergent groups, must define their goals in broad sweep and often simplistic terms. The lifeblood of activists is rhetoric: the penetrating phrase, the daily portrayal of things as worse than they really are, the ongoing effort to exploit verbally the discontent of the populace. History shows that when massive social acquiescence is necessary, a one-parameter proposition will dominate the more refined proposal, especially when interests diverge and people who think there is a choice will exercise it. Facile rationalizations and even myths are easily believed as truths because they confirm previously held prejudices and a conviction of moral superiority. Simplified problems offer easy comprehensive solutions because they are not burdened with the necessity of evaluating unsatisfied

---

*Two incidents that illustrate these tactics involve Sister Marilyn Uline during the earlier phases of the controversy, and Father Theodore Purcell during the later phases. They are described in Chapter 7, "The Drive Toward Code Enactment: The Post-Kennedy Era."

competing needs. Position becomes an easy substitute for real concern. Quick solutions are preferred because they can be labeled as victories. There is a rush to jump to the newest wave of perception as long as it is widely shared and to ride it until it crashes into the beach as well.

In the early stages of the issue life cycle such a strategy offers certain advantages because the activist group's overriding concern is to keep the issue alive and to move it from the pre-problem stage and into the problem identification stage. However, this strategy often causes difficulties in the latter stages of the controversy. As critics they are not encumbered by the discipline of power. Skilled in the politics of opposition, they are also untutored in the defensive compromises of power. After a while they begin to believe in their own rhetoric whose shrillness and insistence increases with every setback in the group's ability to move the issue into the latter stages of the issue life cycle.

The infant formula controversy also provides us with an illustration of the dual set of strategies and tactics pursued by the activistic church-related organizations, on the one hand, and other secular social activists and corporate critics, on the other hand. It should be noted here that the degree of moderation or active confrontation in dealing with economic institutions is not necessarily a defining characteristic of one or the other group but can be found in groups of all religious and ideological persuasions. One can find church-groups resorting to direct pressure and confrontation tactics and often disregarding the niceties of means in achieving their desired goals. At the same time, other church groups and agencies could be seen to insist on a different posture — one that examines all relevant aspects of an issue and questions the strengths and deficiencies of various positions, including their own, and puts emphasis on rapprochement and alleviation of the problem.

Just as one cannot ignore the undesirable second-order effects of MNCs' activities, it would be equally unreal to assume that there are no problems associated with the programs and policies of PVOs, or to overlook some of the less palatable aspects of the strategies and tactics employed by different social activist groups. Two decades of social conflict have also brought to surface some of the more troubling aspects of the activities of public advocacy groups. At the extreme, social conflict and resulting social activism have led to the growth of single-issue causes and narrowly based political PVOs as a dominant feature, and not necessarily a salutary one, of the American sociopolitical arena. As pursued by the more radical and ideologically oriented elements of the activist movement, issues are invariably projected as good or evil, with social activists defending the good and the poor against the evil and the unscrupulous. This halo effect, especially when it acquires the imprimatur of the church, puts the opposition on the defensive regardless of the merit of the case. Issues are often selected not on the basis of their relative importance for the victims whose interests are being represented but the intensity of moral offense one feels against the offender and the relative ease with which an offender can be brought to one's preferred view of justice before the court of world opinion. While the opposition is accused for its disregard of facts, no such compunction is conceded on their own part, although at the least, selective articulation of the facts is a conscious strategy of many PVOs. According to one critic, the activist movement "selectively magnifies" its victories in its communications and uses newsletters as a vehicle for "spreading selective information about protest activities, about endorsement, about the alleged wrongdoing of industry and the way even more people are coming to understand this."[14] Those who are righteous don't have to worry about the rules and propriety. Moreover, this selfishness and self-centeredness are elevated to the status of a noble calling. We all become cloistered in our self-ordained virtues. Compromises are disdained because to see reason in an adversary is to sully one's own reputation. This behavior pattern is not typical of most PVOs and certainly not of those associated with organized religion. It is also true that corporate community has seldom criticized one of its own for socially undesirable behavior. However, to compare the two on equal terms would be begging the question. Ostensibly, the critics seek a higher moral ground and, therefore, must demonstrate a higher level of socially responsible behavior. While the business community is constantly exhorted toward self-analysis, soul searching, and development of codes of conduct, no such need is perceived on the part of PVOs.

To an extent some of the alleged excesses of activist groups are inherent in the nature of the movement itself and are common to most emerging groups who seek a greater share of power from the established sociopolitical order. While the power imposes its discipline, those who lack power are not so restrained. The activist mentality — a feeling of being under constant siege — creates an approach to problems that is born of reaction to the exercise of power rather than the wielding of it. Confrontation becomes their lifeblood, and they are energized by defeats and rebuffs. Issues are simplified because to allow for complexity is to concede that the issues might be multisided. Solutions become all-pervasive. They feel compelled to design comprehensive solutions to every problem, ignoring the ones that are difficult and messy. Imbued with the righteousness of their causes and correctness of their advocated solution, they ignore those aspects of the problem that don't fit their mold.

And herein lies one of the major dilemmas of our times. As activists become more and more influential in the process of social intervention, they become an important element in the process of social change. However, their value-set and self-perception may cause them to adopt attitudes and means in achieving their objectives that may have potential of causing great social harm through severe rupture in the established order with no better or effective alternative in sight.

Corporate Structure: Strategic and Tactical Approaches Involving PVOs

The success of a strategy presupposes the existence of a supportive organizational structure that facilitates its implementation. Strategies fail because they are hostile to the self-interest and culture of the organization that is called upon to implement them. Conversely, a radical change in the direction of the organization is not possible in the absence of a radical change in the organizational structure that existed for the support of strategies. Corporations, even the most forward looking ones, generally have not been very successful in generating effective responses to business–society conflicts. The reasons for such failures are not difficult to find, although they fail to explain a corporation's inability to learn from its own experiences and those of other companies and industry groups, or to affect changes in its organizational structures and strategic response patterns given the potential for their significant adverse effect on a corporation's autonomy of operations, revenues, and profits.

A corporation's organization structure and decision-making processes are invariably designed to manage an incredibly large number of routine repetitive decisions that constitute a large body of its operations and management functions.[15] Most corporations categorize their activities into two classifications. Activities dealing with production, manufacturing, and services are considered line functions and are placed under line executives who are responsible for managing profit centers. Activities dealing with public affairs, constituency relations, and government regulation are placed under staff executives, treated as cost centers, and are considered peripheral to the corporation's primary function, that of production and distribution of goods and services. This dichotomy, except for administrative convenience, is quite false and is likely to cause serious problems for the corporation in terms of planning deficiencies and implementation shortfalls. Since second-order effects are inextricably linked to a corporation's primary activities, it follows that the executives responsible for the primary activities must also take into account the second-order effects of these activities on society. They have the potential for becoming added costs for the corporation in terms of new laws, government regulation, adverse publicity, loss of goodwill, and even lawsuits. The potential costs and risks of these second-order effects must be integrated into a company's decision-making processes for its primary activities. Successful implementation of integrative strategies requires extensive skills on the part of top executives in managing diversity and uncertainty that go beyond narrow market and competitive factors. Mangers, who are highly steeped in narrow product or industry sectors, find such integration hard to achieve. One's experiential make-up, network of professional relationships, past commitments, and existing power structures defend status quo and are difficult to overcome.[16]

Innovative decision making is almost invariably concentrated at the top. It involves developing long-term strategy, risk assessment, and a substantial commitment of corporate resources. This is the province of senior management. Unfortunately, business–society conflicts do not fit this pattern. They are often one of a kind; there is little prior experience; they may involve factors that are largely outside management's control; and they may require dealing with groups and institutions whose value set and modus operandi are quite different from those of the corporation. A large organization also prizes stability and predictability. It calls for systems that can handle large quantities of decisions efficiently and economically. This approach makes their managers averse to taking challenges that are too unfamiliar, unconventional, and therefore risky. When confronted with public policy issues, they search for patterns of similarity between social problems and ordinary business problems. This filtering mechanism tends to discard information that is unusual — does not fit the familiar pattern — as extraneous and therefore irrelevant. And yet, this is precisely the information that the management should seek because it may hold the key to the problem resolution.

Ironically, the very bigness and required stability of large organizations make them too fragile to support an innovator or even a flexible manager at the top. The growing size of the corporation and its increasing complexity shifts the decision-making power within the organization to the techno-structure. Driven by the demands of economic efficiency, there is a corporate bias toward decentralization and functional specialization. Corporate managers are also solution-driven and tend to define problems in small, discrete chunks. Social issues and business–society conflicts do not neatly fit into the existing boxes of the organization chart.[17] When these problems don't respond within the projected time frame and solution criteria, there is a tendency to delegate implementation to lower ranks and move to other "more pressing" business problems. The distinction between "responsibility for policy" and "responsibility for implementation," however, is wholly fallacious and tends to aggravate the problems in the area of business–society conflicts. Those at the top of an organizational hierarchy cannot abdicate responsibility, they can only delegate authority.

Another consequence of this narrow specialization may be avoidance of issues that are not of immediate relevance to the business in hand. The business of business may be business, but this rationale would not survive the community test of legitimacy unless a meaningful and compelling explanation could be offered for the business function. Although top management in most companies is increasingly concerned with the battle for their share in the marketplace of ideas, this does not appear to be the case with the vast majority of young managers entering the corporate executive ranks. The narrow training of business school graduates has recently become the subject of considerable soul searching by the universities and corporate community.[19] The young managers, like the young lawyers, the young engineers, and the young scientists, are the product of professional schools and are steeped in the technical skills of their respective professions. They are at home with cash flow analysis, return on investment, sales forecasting, and management by objectives. Eager to demonstrate their technical skills, they carefully choose projects that lend themselves to deterministic and quantitative types of analyses. In this approach, they are amply assisted by a corporate environment which calls for systematic and sequential goal setting and program implementation. Starting with the problems that are straightforward and quantifiable, they end up assuming that those problems that cannot be quantified, are not immediate, need not be solved, and perhaps do not even exist. They become captives of concreteness, forcing qualitative values into quantitative variables, thereby producing solutions that are elegant, precise, but may be meaningless or even wrong. This lack of interest in abstract ideas and an unwillingness or inability to engage in substantive dialogue about them are tragic. It deprives the corporation of those leadership qualities in its future top managers on which the survival and growth of the company must ultimately depend.

Inadequacy of Prevailing Patterns to Conflict Resolution

When confronted by activist groups, a company's initial and almost reflexive response to criticism from any quarter has been to condemn it as if it were questioning the legitimacy of private property and the competitive free enterprise system. Business history is replete with examples of corporate and industry campaigns to educate the American people in defense of free enterprise which was not much in danger of being obliterated, and yet without explaining or correcting its own shortcomings that were the subject of public criticism in the first place.[19] As part of their initial response, companies deny the legitimacy and the right of the group to advocate the issue, indicating that the group is naive or uninformed; resort to legalistic defense of corporate actions which meets the letter and not necessarily the spirit of prevailing laws and regulations; and, when all else fails, meet and discuss the issue with their critics in the spirit of advancing mutual understanding and cooperation. These approaches can be grouped into three broad categories: public relations responses, legal responses, and industrial relations responses. Oddly enough, while these response patterns have certain inherent merit, their ritualized application without serious attention to the life-cycle stages of an issue and its saliency within the sociopolitical context and the critics' agenda can render them largely ineffective and even counterproductive.[20]

The public relations response emanates from the belief that corporate critics are either motivated by other than altruistic concerns or are ignorant and uninformed about the role of business in society in general and the social and economic contributions of the corporation in particular. The real or alleged gap between societal expectations and corporate performance is sought to be narrowed through public education and information. This approach is doomed to failure before it even starts because it is based on two faulty assumptions: (1) corporate critics lack information about the issues, and (2) the relevant "data or facts" are those that the corporation prefers to advocate. The fundamental flaw in this logic is that while the corporation is looking at the issue in narrow economic terms, its critics insist on viewing it in broad sociopolitical terms. A given set of events or facts is viewed entirely differently by different groups both as to veracity and sufficiency as a basis for developing new approaches to conflict resolution. This depends not only on the degree of scientific rigor demanded by different groups but also on how different groups perceive changes in existing approaches in impacting their vital interests. Finally, when corporations confine themselves to merely rejecting the reform proposals of their critics without suggesting alternatives, except the status quo, they surrender the initiative to their critics and thereby forego the opportunity of playing a proactive role in shaping the public policy agenda.

The legal response is used to defend the corporation's "legitimate" right to engage in activities that are under attack and at the same time question the legitimacy of its critics. When used exclusively or in combination with the public relations response, this approach may reduce the danger of litigation; it creates the image of a corporation under siege and hiding behind legalities, evasive tactics, and unwillingness to change. It may also end up enlarging the scope of public distrust and skepticism in the corporation and giving greater credibility to its critics.

The industrial relations-bargaining response is fashioned after the traditional employer-union negotiations and assumes that even in the area of social conflict, a modus vivendi can be achieved in a spirit of give-and-take where the opposing groups would reach acceptable solutions based on their competing needs, relative bargaining power, and support in the larger community. This approach, however, invariably fails because it is based on two faulty assumptions. First, the corporation's emphasis is on *managing* these new stakeholders just as it manages its traditional stakeholders, such as stockholders and employees. In the latter case the integrity of the corporate person and mission are not in question; the conflict is on the allocation of corporate resources and benefits. Second, the external stakeholders, however, could not be more different and do not respond to similar incentives and constraints. The new stakeholders represent people who are affected by corporate actions but who may or may not be directly involved in influencing those actions. Quite often, these groups represent not constituencies of people but constituencies of ideas, that is, pursuit of ethical and behavioral norms that may have been downgraded or ignored by the corporation, environmental preservation, and so on.

These new stakeholders also *do not want to be managed* within the corporate defined operational parameters, but instead may question the integrity of the corporate mission, its operational processes, and its allocation of corporate resources and outputs. In the case of large, well-established groups and under conditions where the issue has reached the remedy and relief stage and moving into the prevention stage, agreements can be reached and enforced provided the PVOs have been involved in *both* defining the scope of the problem and fashioning acceptable solutions.

The situation is even more difficult when corporate adversaries are emergent single-issue groups or are advocating causes not yet part of a society's mainstream agenda. These groups are perceived by the corporations, at least during the pre-problem and problem identification stages, to be of marginal relevance or, worse, a lunatic fringe. Companies are unlikely to yield them anything substantial except payment for "nuisance avoidance." These groups, however, make up in intensity and commitment what they lack in numbers and resources. Realizing that any positive corporate response is a measure of their "nuisance value," they use a strategy of ever-escalating demands and ever declining compliance.

When a company feels that after intense negotiations it has reached an agreement, it is confronted with a situation where the opposing group has not only failed to deliver on its part of the bargain but has also escalated the level of its anti-corporate rhetoric and scope of its demands from the corporation. This pattern was all too familiar during the better part of the infant formula controversy. It changed only after the entry of the Methodists into the fray and subsequent to significant changes in the strategic posture and tactics on Nestle's part. These included, among others, the establishment of the company's new organizational entity, the Nestle Coordination Center for Nutrition, Inc. (NCCN) in Washington, D.C., and the creation of the Nestle Infant Formula Audit Commission (NIFAC). As new groups continue to form and new issues emerge, this pattern will accelerate. This is already apparent to an increasing number of companies and industries as they confront new societal demands. And just as predictably, companies have been resorting to the aforementioned conventional approaches with equally disappointing results.

Development of New Corporate Response Patterns to Resolve Business–Society Conflicts[21]

Under conditions of democratic capitalism, corporations have no choice but to respond to changing needs of the community and play by the evolving rules of the game. They can play this role in a positive proactive manner by becoming agents of social change, or they will be forced to react to changes initiated by other social actors. A positive, proactive role would require that, first and foremost, corporations must consider social issues as an integral part of their strategic and operational decisions to be treated at par with the company's normal business operations. There are four areas that urgently need attention: environmental scanning and long-term planning; creation of new communication channels that are sensitive to receiving social issues-related information from the external environment; development of strategic assets to be used in the area of social issues management; and changes in the company's organizational structure and decision-making processes to make them respond more effectively to business–society conflicts.

1. **Environmental scanning**. Figure 21-1 briefly describes the process of diffusion by which social issues move from the idea incubation and creation stage to where they become part of public domain and "received wisdom." It shows that social activists become involved in the process at the earliest stage of the creation–diffusion process, increasing their identification with the social concern as it is embraced by various opinion leaders and groups. They are, therefore, able to inject themselves in the diffusion process, claim ownership rights, and also influence the choices of preferred solutions. The business community, on the other hand, is only tangentially involved in the early stages of the process. Their primary focus here is to monitor the prog-

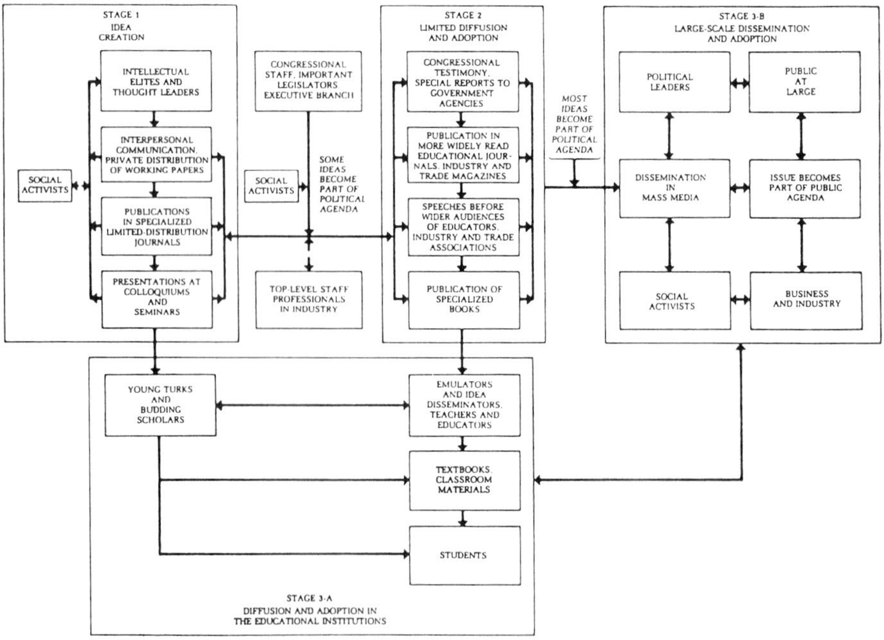

Figure 21–1.   Process of diffusion and adoption of ideas in the public domain

ress of the issue through various stages of the issue life-cycle. This is done at the lower levels of corporate staff and professionals in industry and trade associations. Senior executives are very rarely brought into the picture until the time when the issue has become part of the legislative agenda or has captured the attention of mass media and, through it, large segments of the population. This is already too late. The most business can do is to fight a rear-guard action. Each victory is achieved at a heavy cost of public good-will and credibility, and many more issues are lost than are gained.[23]

The objective of environmental scanning is to identify social issues that pertain to a corporation's business activities and are likely to become important in the foreseeable future (Figures 21-2 and 21-3). There are four areas of emphasis:

- issues relevant to the corporation must be identified at the earliest stage, and those issues selected that provide the best *fit* between issues and corporate resources and that *achieve* maximum social benefits;
- relevant strategies must be identified and a particular strategy developed that best meets the corporation's needs in responding to those issues;
- issues that *threaten* a corporation's survival and growth are never allowed to reach crisis stage, calling for desperate measures with inadequate time;
- corporate response mode is geared to constantly driving individual issues toward a lower level of intensity where more measured and deliberate response patterns can be developed.

2. **Communication Channels**. Corporate communications dealing with external social issues-related constituencies have a "window out" bias, that

Figure 21–2.   A grid pattern for determining the life cycle of an issue from "Emerging" to "Critical"

STAGES OF ISSUE EVOLUTION

———————————————— Intensity of the Issue ————————————————▶

Dimensions of Corporate Behavior	Preproblem Stage	Identification Stage	Remedy & Relief Stage	Prevention Stage
SOCIAL OBLIGATION				X CRITICAL ISSUE
SOCIAL RESPONSIBILITY				
SOCIAL RESPONSIVINESS	X EMERGING ISSUE			

Intensity of Corporate Responses

Figure 21–3. Strategic grid for social issues management

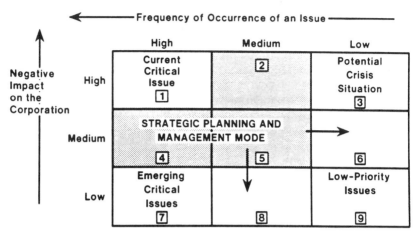

is, they are geared to disseminate information that the company wants its critics to hear. However, tracking new issues and emergent groups requires that corporate communication channels also have a large measure of "window in" element, that is, they tell the company what its critics are saying about it. A further element of efficient communication dictates that these channels filter out information not directly needed for the relevant corporate activity. This process is likely to be counter-productive when applied to emerging issues and new groups. The company does not have enough experience with issues-groups and cannot determine a priori the parameters of relevant information. Therefore, external communication channels should have a large element of "window in" and should be loose enough to allow for certain static in the system to signal management that something unusual is happening.

The development of effective communication channels requires that corporations must be willing to communicate with even those groups whose values may not agree with the traditional values or the position of the corporation. New institutions and value systems in their embryonic stages lack central direction and goal crystallization. They may even seem destructive — at least in the short run — as they are tied together only in their opposition to a common adversary, the corporation. For the business community, it serves no constructive purpose to engage in the essentially useless tactic of attacking its "opponents." By retaliating against these groups, when they are in their embryonic stage, companies will not eliminate the causes that gave rise to these groups, but instead will end up preparing the ground for breeding even more militant groups of the future. Corporations can best help achieve social harmony and contribute to social justice by focusing on the problems that have to be dealt with and not on the spokespersons who voice them. However, with few exceptions, the business community does not seem to have appreciated the need for such a change in focus.

In the pre-problem and problem identification stages, companies are confronted with a cacophony of voices, all claiming to represent valid interests, often making difficult, exaggerated, and contradictory demands. A gestation period is needed during which internal stresses may develop and be settled before strong and viable groups with effective leadership and a well-defined hierarchy of goals can emerge. During this period, there will be a large number of self-styled leaders struggling to enlarge their power-base among the competing PVOs for public acceptance, volunteer following, and financial resources. Coping with this problem, even for a well-intentioned and socially proactive corporation, is quite difficult. It requires an understanding of the process of social change and the maturing of new groups. The business community cannot help in the development of either effective leadership or crystallization of group objectives among these groups by direct assistance or interference in the process. However, it can help the process by remaining scrupulously out of the PVOs' internal struggles while at the same time creating an atmosphere that is more susceptible to the acquisition of power by more moderate and constructive elements of a particular issue-advocacy movement. Nestle used just such an approach through NCCN when it moved to rectify the causes of complaints on the part of its critics, and reached out to more moderate groups by yielding to them the right to independently investigate complaints against the company and verify its assertions of compliance. This had the effect of defusing the bases for the critics' complaints; ensuring that charges of WHO Code violations were specific and well documented; and when corrective actions by the company were verified, accepting them and having the charges removed.*

3. **Development of Strategic Assets.** Just as it is important for a company to have resources that could be strategically deployed to take advantage of market opportunities, it is equally important that companies create strategic assets for use in the public policy arena. The concept is that of *strategic slack*[23] — an organization's horde of resources that allows it to react to external conditions, either proactively or reactively, with greater degrees of

---

*For a detailed discussion of Nestle's strategies and tactics that led to the successful termination of the boycott against the company, please see: Chapter 15, "Nestle Coordination Center for Nutrition, Inc. (NCCN): Nestle's Change in Organizational Structure and Strategies to Deal with the Boycott"; Chapter 16, " "Winning" the Methodists: The Last Major Battle-Ground to Enlist the Religious Community's Support for the Boycott"; Chapter 17, "Nestle Infant Formula Audit Commission (NIFAC): A New Model for Gaining External Legitimacy for Corporate Actions;" and, Chapter 18, "Settlement of the Dispute and Termination of the Boycott: Discussions Between INBC/INFACT and Nestle - UNICEF in the Role of an Honest Broken".

freedom. When applied to social issues, strategic slack comprises of a *firm's accrued trust* on the part of sociopolitical leaders and the public-at-large such that its pronouncements and suggestions for change have public credibility and its management is trusted to follow up on promised actions without extensive external monitoring. A corporation possessing large strategic slack is able to intervene in the public policy process with greater credibility, counter the demands of PVOs in asserting its preferred course of action, and even resist demand for change from public unless it has been given an opportunity to present its viewpoint for public debate and scrutiny. A corporation's stock of public goodwill and trust, however, is quickly exhausted if by its actions, or those of the industry-at-large, issues reach the crisis stage, thereby forestalling any time for deliberate discourse.

4. **Organizational Structure and Decision-Making Processes..** An attitude of public concern needs to be fostered at all levels of corporate structure. Policy decisions are likely to founder at the operational level if the intent of top management is not clearly transmitted to operating level personnel. Corporate managers at all levels need to bring, consciously and intentionally, public interest factors to bear on their strategic and operating decisions. The reason for doing so should not be a moral obligation or a charitable attitude, but rather a real duty or obligation arising out of the causal interrelation between the corporation and the society-at-large.

Companies should consider employing a variant of Strategic Business Unit (SBU) in their internal handling of social issues management. This would involve development of "social responsibility centers"[26] similar in purpose and goals to a company's profit centers. These profit centers are organized on a rational basis since the SBU's performance has to be evaluated, isolated, and measured so as to reward responsible managers for superior performance. Thus, managers of social responsibility centers would be responsible for minimizing negative externalities and accountable for harm to a corporation's public trust and goodwill and the resultant loss of business and managerial autonomy where social issues are improperly handled. Ideally, both the product profit centers and social responsibility centers would have similar boundaries under the responsibility of common managers. However, this is not always possible. Social issues may affect different profit centers differently. Therefore, new forms of organization structures should be explored to handle these twin issues more effectively and efficiently.

Where an issue has reached the crisis stage, or where corporate reservoir or goodwill and public trust is largely depleted, the corporation needs to establish external sources of monitoring and verifiability of its actions in response to public concern of its previous, allegedly socially harmful, behavior. Just such a course of action was successfully employed by Nestle through the creation of the Nestle Infant Formula Audit Commission (NIFAC) under the chairmanship of former U.S. Senator and Vice Presidential candidate Mr. Edmund Muskie. Other companies, facing crisis of public confidence, have responded with a range of measures including: publication of Public Interest Report akin to a company's annual report outlining its activities in the social-public arena; appointment of in-house corporate critic, ombudsman, or toll-free telephone lines where employees, customers, and others can air their concerns to corporate management; and hiring of an outside counsel to investigate a corporate's alleged misdeeds and suggest corrective actions.

To date, these approaches have had minimal success, if any, in garnering greater public confidence. Most of these approaches are seen by the public as an attempt at whitewashing by management and at shielding itself from further public scrutiny. Inadequate resources and insufficient authority for action are devoted to these measures, portraying them as mere "window dressing" and indicating a lack of management's serious intent and commitment. Even when management is forced by circumstances to create truly independent measures of external accounting, it is only too anxious to get rid of them once the crisis has passed. This was indeed the case for NIFAC which was neither integrated into Nestle's organizational structure nor adapted by the infant formula industry once the successful termination of the boycott had been accomplished.

Selection of Appropriate Corporate Response Patterns

The next stage in our analysis has to do with the selection of an appropriate response pattern to a given social issue. This would depend, to a large extent, on the stage of the issue life cycle of the external environment, patterns of responses adopted by other corporations and industry groups similarly placed, the nature of constituency groups and the intensity of their advocacy, and prior public expectations based on a corporation's behavior in similar situations in the past.

One of the main objectives of developing appropriate corporate responses to societal problems and external constituency groups is to prevent erosion in management's discretion to manage corporate affairs in a manner that it considers best for the corporation, its dependencies, and society-at-large. In general:

- The opportunity for maintaining maximum discretionary decision-making authority is greatest in the pre-problem stage and lowest in the prevention stage.
- Public's perception of the use of management's discretionary power during the pre-problem and problem identification stages would determine the extent of available flexibility in the remedy and relief, and prevention stages.
- In case constituency groups succeed in the problem identification stage in

bringing an issue into the judicial and political arena and score gains, management's discretion is likely to be minimal in subsequent stages.
- During remedy and relief, and prevention stages, management's discretion is also impacted to a greater extent by what other corporations are doing than in the two earlier stages.
- A social obligation mode of corporate response is likely to yield maximum discretion in the early stage of issue life cycle. However, if this response pattern fails, the rate of decline in management's discretionary authority would likely be very steep in subsequent stages.
- A social responsibility mode of corporate response in the early stages of the issue life cycle is difficult to sell to the corporation. It may also give rise to more external constituencies who may otherwise not have become viable and could be counter-productive, at least in the short-run.
- Where a social responsibility mode is developed on the basis of accurate environmental scanning and constituency group analysis — especially in the issue identification stage — it could yield consistently higher degrees of discretionary authority for the management in subsequent stages.
- A social responsiveness mode is most conducive to maintaining management's discretion in the pre-problem stage where it becomes the essential core of strategic planning. In other stages of the issue life cycle, it must follow the social responsibility mode to establish credibility. It is unlikely to be acceptable to other groups in the remedy and relief stage, especially if the company followed a social obligation mode in the problem identification stage.

Some Concluding Thoughts

The endemic character of business–society conflicts in market economies and democratic societies has to do with the nature of public-collective goods and private goods. The former are viewed as society's endowments to be shared by all of its members without regard to one's ability to pay for them. The distributive criteria are those of need, social relevance, and collective enjoyment. Private goods are for the exclusive enjoyment of their owners and, within broad limits, to be bought, sold, and exchanged at their owners' discretion. Expansion of market activities, by its very nature, creates more private goods, often contracting the supply of public goods. While business institutions are applauded for their production of private goods and services, they also take the major blame for depleting the stock of public goods.

In one sense, society's moral and ethical values, concern for the less fortunate, and preservation of the natural environment are public or collective goods. All members of a society stand to benefit from an enhancement of these values regardless of their individual contributions to such enhancement. Here the nature of corporate mission and goals and those of private voluntary organizations stand in sharp contrast. It may partially explain the inherent discrepancy in public trust and goodwill enjoyed by public interest groups against that of the business community.[25]

The collective stock of a society's moral and ethical values will increase if more and more individuals and groups behaved with greater degree of altruism. In the case of PVOs, there is a presumption of altruism which is further strengthened by their espoused mission and goals. Even when individual PVOs act in a manner that could be construed anti-social in some quarters, they are still viewed as only hurting private greed for larger social good. The problem of free rider — that is, one who takes a greater share of public-collective goods without adequately contributing to the enhancement of their stock or being concerned about depriving other of similar enjoyment — is not considered serious. PVOs are expected to behave in the public interest. It is their raison d'etre. Ergo, there is no free rider.

Private firms face the exactly opposite problem. They must always try to maximize private gain by internalizing all possible profits and externalizing all possible costs. Given competitive markets, firms have a great deal to lose from contributing to general public trust and moral and ethical values and everything to gain from being a free rider. Since a firm cannot control the behavior of other firms, it must assume that other firms would behave equally aggressively as free riders. The exception to this rule would take place under conditions of imperfect markets, that is, where a firm is anxious to protect its strong market position and resultant nonmarket rent or above-normal profits by courting the goodwill of its customers, government regulators, or public-at-large.[26] The incentive to do so, however, is not altruism but a desire to preserve the firm's extra profits. Thus public goodwill is measured by its direct costs in terms of loss of potential profits. Both these conditions tend to undermine the value of business contributions to enhancing a society's ethical and moral values because companies are viewed to be primarily acting in self-interest, thereby discounting their claims of being good public citizens.

It is not now, and unlikely to be in the foreseeable future, that the traditional role of competitive markets, and corporations as their primary institutions, will be supplanted by other institutions in most democratic and industrially advanced societies. If anything, this role is gaining wider acceptance in other societies that had previously denigrated it or chosen to follow the path of a centrally managed, government-controlled system of economic growth. The areas of conflict rest almost entirely as to the means that business institutions allegedly use to circumvent the discipline of markets or to appropriate for their use gains from the marketplace arising out of their superior bargaining leverage, insufficient consumer information, and a host of other factors classified under the economic concept of "market failures" or "market imperfections." And yet corporations rarely if ever address issues of social conflict or their adversaries along those dimensions until such time that the issue has reached the remedy and relief, and prevention stages of the issue's life cycle, the adversaries have established firm positions in public's psyche, and the companies have been put on the defensive because of the positions taken during the earlier stages of the issue's life cycle.

Both the scale and scope of economic activities have expanded tremendously together with the proclivity of industrialized societies to seek ever more consumption of goods and services. It is no doubt influenced by our ethos of growth above everything else and encouraged by business institutions, the producers of economic goods and services. It has sharply constrained availability of social space between people of different resources and capabilities, between private goods and public needs, between those get ahead and those who are left behind, and between economic activities and negative externalities created by them. The corporation cannot consider the economic system as if it were operating in a vacuum, screened only by the economic test of corporate profit and viewing society primarily as markets to be exploited.[27] It is no wonder that corporate leaders react with hurt pride and injured innocence when their social contributions are discounted and they are taken to task for a variety of social sins of omission and commission.

The challenge for the society-at-large is to seek ways and means by which economic institutions and PVOs interact with each other in a harmonious and socially positive manner. At the micro level, it would require a new social compact where society would accommodate these evolving institutions of social control over the activities of economic institutions. It would also call for a better understanding of the objectives and resource constraints of the public advocacy movement so as to channel its emotive and people power into ways that serve society constructively. At the micro level, the challenge for the corporation is to understand the objectives and resource constraints of particular groups that it must deal with and then develop anticipatory and proactive response mechanisms given the nature of sociopolitical arena where such a conflict is taking place.

The last two decades have seen a distinct shift from the center in the United States, first to the left and then to the right. What we need is a perception of how a new center is to be found and how we might get there. The extremes are ultimately self-destructive of all rational human discourse. Democratic societies, and especially multiracial polyglots that United States is and most other societies are bound to become, cannot survive and cohabit without a large center where diversity of ideas and cultural norms must co-exist. This would be true not only for religious freedom and political thought but also for the nature of economic order and distributive justice.

The arenas of social conflict between business and society are not those of between right and wrong, between guilty and innocent, but between one type of inequity and another, between giving one group more while taking some from another group, between the virtue of frugality and sin of accumulation, and between morality of principle and morality of situations. In an unjust world, the distinctions between the guilty and innocent have become ambiguous. What we are confronted with is the realization that we live in an increasingly interdependent society where individual good is not possible outside the context of common good. It makes no sense to separate moral principles from institutional behavior, political power from material rewards. To do so is to divorce the social system from its basic element, the human being, who does not behave in a fragmented manner.

Notes

1. For a brief discussion of the economic concepts of market and regulatory failures, see Robert G. Harris and James M. Carman, "The Political Economy of Regulation: An Analysis of Market Failures," in S. Prakash Sethi, Paul Steidlmeier, and Cecilia M. Falbe (eds.), *Scaling the Corporate Wall: Readings in Social Issues of the Nineties* (Englewood Cliffs, N.J.: Prentice-Hall, Inc., 1991), pp. 24–35; Francis E. Bator, "Anatomy of Market Failure," *Quarterly Journal of Economics* (August 1958), 351–379; Oliver E. Williamson and Sidney G. Winter (eds.), *The Nature of the Firm: Origins, Evolution, and Development* (New York: Oxford University Press, 1991); Oliver E. Williamson, *The Economic Institutions of Capitalism* (New York: The Free Press, 1985); and Charles Wolfe, Jr., "A Theory of Nonmarket Failures: Framework for Implementation Analysis," *The Journal of Law and Economics* (October 1978), 107–139.

2. See, for example, Richard J. Barnett and Ronald E. Muller, *Global Reach: The Power of the Multinational Corporations* (New York: Simon & Schuster, 1974); C. Tugendhat, *The Multinational* (London: Penguin, 1973); Raymond Vernon, *Storm Over the Multinational: The Real Issues* (Cambridge, Mass.: Harvard University Press, 1977); Kari Levitt, *Silent Surrender: The Multinational Corporation in Canada* (Toronto: Macmillan of Canada, 1970); F.G. Lavipour and Karl Sauvant (eds.), *Controlling Multinational Enterprises: Problems, Strategies, Counterstrategies* (Boulder, Colo: Westview Press, 1976); Lee A. Tavis (ed.), *Multinational Managers and Poverty in the Third World* (Notre Dame University Press, 1982); and Theodore H. Moran, *Multinational Corporations: The Political Economy of Foreign Direct Investment* (Lexington, Mass.: D.C. Heath, 1985).

3. Oliver Williams, "Who Cast the First Stone?" *Harvard Business Review* (September-October 1984), 151–166.

4. P.T. Bauer, *Equality, the Third World, and Economic Delusion* (Cambridge, Mass.: Harvard University Press, 1981).

5. *Op. cit.,* supra note 2.

6. Willy Brandt, *North-South: A Program for Survival* (Cambridge, Mass.: The MIT Press, 1976); and Karl V. Sauvant and Hajo Hasenpflug, *The New International Economic Order* (Boulder, Colo: Westview Press, 1977).

7. S. Prakash Sethi, "The Inhuman Error — Lessons from the Union Carbide Plant Accident in Bhopal, India," *The New Management* (Summer 1985), 41–45.

8. Thomas C. Schelling, "On the Ecology of Micromotives," *The Public Interest*, 25 (Fall 1971), 59–98.

9. Garrett Hardin, "The Tragedy of the Commons," *Science*, 162 (December 13, 1968), 1103–1107.

10. S. Prakash Sethi, "Inhuman Errors and Industrial Crises," *Columbia Journal of World Business* (Spring 1987), 101–110; *The South African Quagmire: In Search for a Peaceful Path to Democratic Pluralism* (Cambridge, Mass.: Ballinger Publishing Co., 1987); "Interfaith Center on Corporate Responsibility (ICCR), A Sponsor-related Movement of the

National Council of Churches," in *Up Against the Corporate Wall: Modern Corporations and Social Issues of the Eighties,* 4th ed. (Englewood Cliffs, N.J.: Prentice-Hall, 1982), pp. 450–480; "The Marketing of Infant Formula in Less Developed Countries: Public Consequences of Private Action," *California Management Review* (Summer 1979), 35–48; *Japanese Business and Social Conflict: A Comparative Analysis of Response Patterns With American Business* (Cambridge, Mass.: Ballinger, 1975); *The Corporate Dilemma: Traditional Values and Contemporary Problems* (Englewood Cliffs, N.J.: Prentice-Hall, 1973), with Dow Votaw; and, S. Prakash Sethi, *Business Corporations and the Black Man* (New York: Harper & Row, 1970).

11. Harvey G. Cox, "'The New Breed' in American Churches: Sources of Social Activism in American Religion," *Daedalus* (Winter 1967), 135–149.

12. S. Prakash Sethi, "The Corporation and the Church: Institutional Conflict and Social Responsibility," *California Management Review* (January 1972), 63–74; S. Prakash Sethi, "Interfaith Center on Corporate Responsibility (ICCR), A Sponsor-related Movement of the National council of Churches," in S. Prakash Sethi, *Up Against the Corporate Wall,* 4th ed., *op.cit.,* pp. 450–480.

13. S. Prakash Sethi, "The Corporation and the Church," supra note 12, and references cited therein.

14. Luther P. Gerlach, "The Flea and the Elephant: Infant Formula Controversy," 17, 6 *Society* (1980), 55.

15. S. Prakash Sethi and Dow Votaw, "Do We Need a New Corporate Response to a Changing Social Environment? Part II," from *California Management Review* (Fall 1969), reprinted in Votaw and Sethi, *The Corporate Dilemma, op. cit.,* supra note 10, pp. 191–213.

16. In his research in international business strategies, Doz discovered that managers who are oriented toward responding to national demands find it difficult to alter their focus from purely national to a multinational and international orientation. See Yves Doz, *Management in Multinational Companies* (Oxford, England: Pergamon Press, 1986), pp. 16–17, 44–47, 96–100, 191–213.

17. S. Prakash Sethi and Dow Votaw, "Do We Need a New Corporate Response to a Changing Social Environment? Part II," from *California Management Review* (Fall 1969), reprinted in Votaw and Sethi, *The Corporate Dilemma, op. cit.,* supra note 10, pp. 191–213.

18. See, for example: "What Are They Teaching in the B-Schools," *Business Week,* November 10, 1980, pp. 61–69; Gene Maeroff, 'Harvard: A Real-Life Case Study-Derek Bob Asks Review of the Business School," *New York Times,* May 6, 1979, p. F11; Edward B. Fiske, "Education: Values Taught More Widely," *New York Times,* March 4, 1980, C1; John Henderson, "Change on Campus: More Colleges to Require a Variety of Courses to Broaden Students," *Wall Street Journal,* March 9, 1981, pp. 1, 15.

19. The ineffectiveness and inappropriateness of the so-called "defense of free enterprise" approach to muffle corporate criticism was first discussed in 1950 by William H. Whyte, Jr., a distinguished management scholar and commentator of societal mores and cultural values in "Is Anybody Listening." Since then, scores of other studies — both inside and outside academe — have made similar claims but to little effect. As late as 1992, International Advertising Association was promoting a public education campaign to defend private enterprise and the role of advertising in simplistic message that were at best silly and at worst insulting to the intelligence of even moderately informed viewers. See, for example, William H. Whyte, *Is Anybody Listening* (New York: Simon & Schuster, 1950); Daniel J. Boorstin, "Tradition of Self-Liquidating Ideals," *The Wall Street Journal* (February 18, 1970); Paul T. Heyne, *Private Keepers of the Public Interest* (New York: Wiley, 1986); Dow Votaw and S. Prakash Sethi, "Do We Need a New Corporate Response to a Changing Social Environment? Part I," from *California Management Review* (Fall 1969), reprinted in Votaw and Sethi, *The Corporate Dilemma, op. cit.,* supra note 10, pp. 170–191; S. Prakash Sethi, *Advocacy Advertising and Large Corporations* (Lexington, Mass.: D.C. Heath & Co.,

1977); and Irving Kristol, "On Economic Education," *The Wall Street Journal,* February 18, 1970, p. 20.

20. For a more detailed discussion of these response patterns, see: S. Prakash Sethi and Dow Votaw, "Do We Need a New Corporate Response to a Changing Social Environment? Part II," from *California Management Review* (Fall 1969), reprinted in *The Corporate Dilemma, op. cit.,* supra note 10, pp. 191–213; S. Prakash Sethi, "A Conceptual Framework for Environmental Analysis to Social Issues and Evaluation of Business Response Patterns," *Academy of Management Review* (January 1979), 3–14; and, S. Prakash Sethi, *Advocacy Advertising and Large Corporations, op.cit.,* supra note 19.

21. Some of the ideas presented in this section were originally elaborated in Votaw and Sethi, *The Corporate Dilemma, op. cit.,* supra note 10, pp. 167–213.

22. S. Prakash Sethi, "A Strategic Framework for Dealing With Schism Between Business and the Academe," Special Report, *Public Affairs Review* (1983), 44–59, reprinted in S. Prakash Sethi and Cecilia Falbe (eds.), *Business and Society: Dimensions of Conflict and Cooperation* (Lexington, Mass.: D.C. Heath & Co., 1987), pp. 331–352; see also Niels Christiansen and Sharon Meluso, "Environmental Scanning and Tracking of Critical Issues: The Case of the Life Insurance Industry," in Sethi and Falbe, ed., *Business and Society, op. cit.,* pp. 423–431.

23. Cecilia Falbe and S. Prakash Sethi, "Concept of Strategic Slack: Implications for Strategic Response Patterns by Corporations to Public Policy Options." Paper presented at the Ninth Annual Internal Conference of *Strategic Management Society,* San Francisco, California, October 11–14, 1989.

24. This suggestion was first made by the author in a Congressional Testimony. See S. Prakash Sethi, "Corporate Law Violations and Executive Liability," Testimony on H.R. 4973 before the Subcommittee on Crime of the House Judiciary Committee, December 13, 1979. Reprinted in S. Prakash Sethi, "The Expanding Scope of Executive Liability (Criminal and Civil) for Corporate Law Violations," in Sethi and Falbe (eds.), *Business and Society, op. cit.,* pp. 471–506.

25. In developing these ideas, I have greatly benefitted from the writing of Fred Hirsch, *Social Limits to Growth* (Cambridge, Mass.: Harvard University Press, 1976). See in particular, Section II, "The Commercialization Bias," pp. 72–114, and Section III, "The Depleting Moral Legacy," pp. 117–158.

26. William Baumol, *Perfect Markets and Easy Virtue* (Cambridge, Mass.: Blackwell, 1991); Thomas Schelling, "On the Ecology of Micromotives," *op.cit.,* supra note 8. See also Amartya Sen, "Behavior and the Concept of Preference," *Economica* (August 1973), cited in Hirsch, *op. cit.,* supra note 25, p. 139; and Robert H. Scott, "Avarice, Altruism, and Second party Preferences," *Quarterly Journal of Economics* (February 1972), cited in Hirsch, *op.cit.,* p. 78.

27. Votaw and Sethi, *The Corporate Dilemma, op. cit.,* pp. 173–175.

BIBLIOGRAPHY

Abbott Laboratories. *Annual Report, 1990.*

Adelman, C. "Infant Formula, Science and Politics," *Policy Review* (Winter 1988), 107–126.

Adelman, C. (ed.) *International Regulation.* San Francisco: Institute for Contemporary Studies, 1988.

Adelman, C. "Baby Feat; More Newborns Are Surviving Infancy Than Ever Before," *Policy Review* (Summer 1984), 80–83.

Adelson, A. "Carnation Won't Use Name In Infant Formula Campaign," *The New York Times,* July 15, 1988, p. 20.

Adelson, A. "Carnation's Move In Infant Formula," *The New York Times,* June 30, 1988, p. D8.

Adelson, A. "Pediatricians On Carnation," *The New York Times,* June 29, 1988, p. D5.

Alinsky, S.D. *Reveille for Radicals.* New York: Vintage Books, 1979.

Alinsky, S.D. *Rules for Radicals.* New York: Vintage Books, 1971.

American Academy of Pediatrics. "Report of the Task Force on the Assessment of the Scientific Evidence Relating to Infant-Feeding Practices and Infant Health," *Pediatrics,* Supplement, 74, 4 (October 1984).

American Home Products Corporation. *Annual Report, 1990.*

American Public Health Association. *Legislation and Policies to Support Maternal and Child Nutrition, Report No. 6,* Washington, D.C., June 1989, p. 90.

Anderson, J. "Washington Merry-Go Round: Big Business Pressure Swayed White House on Formula Vote," *The Washington Post,* June 2, 1981.

Associated Press. "Baby Food Profits Hit in Congress," *The Chicago Tribune,* March 15, 1991.

Ball, R. "A 'Shopkeeper' Shakes Up Nestle," *Fortune,* December 12, 1982, pp. 1053–1060.

Barnett, R.J. and Muller, R.E. *Global Reach: The Power of the Multinational Corporations.* New York: Simon & Schuster, 1974.

Barrett, P. M. "FTC Steps Up Infant Formula Pricing Probe," *The Wall Street Journal,* January 2, 1991, p. A8.

Barron's, "Nestle Crunch," Editorial Comment, *Barron's,* July 16, 1979.

Barros, F.C., Victoria, C.G., Vaughan, J.P. and Smith, P.G. "Birth Weight and Duration of Breast-Feeding: Are the Beneficial Effects of Human Milk Being Overestimated?" *Pediatrics,* 78 (1986), 656–661.

Bator, F.E. "Anatomy of Market Failure," *Quarterly Journal of Economics* (August 1958), 351–379.

Bauer, P.T. *Equality, The Third World and Economic Delusion.* Cambridge, Mass.: Harvard University Press, 1981.

Baumol, W. *Perfect Markets and Easy Virtue.* Cambridge, Mass.: Blackwell, 1991.

Baysinger, B.D. "Domain Maintenance as an Objective of Business Political Activity: An Extended Topology," *Academy of Management Review,* 9, 2 (1984), 248–254.

Bazerman, M.H. and Lewicki, R.J. (eds.) *Negotiating in Organizations.* Beverly Hills, Calif.: Sage Publications, 1983.

Berg, A. "Industry's Struggle with World Malnutrition," *Harvard Business Review,* 40 (1972), 50.

Berryman, P. *Liberation Theology.* New York: Orbis, 1987.

Berss, M. "Sleep Well or Eat Well," *Forbes,* February 13, 1984, pp. 62–63.

Bird, L. "TV Ads Boost Nestle's Infant Formulas," *The Wall Street Journal,* March 30, 1993, pp. B1, B14.

Boorstin, D.J. "Tradition of Self-Liquidating Ideals," *The Wall Street Journal,* February 18, 1970.

Borgoltz, B.A. "Economic and Business Aspects of Infant Formula Promotion: Implications for Health Professionals," in D. B. Jelliffe and E. F. P. Jelliffe (eds.), *International Maternal and Child Health,* Vol. 2. New York: Oxford University Press, 1982, ch. 12, pp. 158–202.

The Boston Globe. "Makers of Baby Formula Charged," *The Boston Globe,* June 12, 1992, p. 66.

Bourgeois, J.L. and Singh, J. "Organizational Slack and Political Behavior Within Top Management Teams," *Academy of Management Proceedings,* 1983, 43–47.

Brandt, B. *North-South: A Program for Survival.* Cambridge, Mass.: The MIT Press, 1976.

Bresser, R. and Harl, J.E. "Collective Strategy: Vice or Virtue?" *Academy of Management Review,* 11, 2 (April 1986), 408–427.

Bristol-Myers Squibb Company. *Annual Report, 1990.*

Burton, Thomas M. "Methods of Marketing Infant Formula Land Abbott in Hot Water," *The Wall Street Journal,* May 25, 1993, pp. A1, A7.

Business Week. "What Are They Teaching in the B-Schools?" *Business Week,* November 10, 1980, pp. 61–69.

Business Week. "Nestle: Centralizing to Win a Bigger Payoff from the U.S.," *Business Week,* February 21, 1981, pp. 58–60.

Caves, R.E. and Porter, M.E. "Market Structure, Oligopoly, and Stability of Market Shares," *The Journal of Industrial Economics*, 26 (1978), 289–313.

Chetley, A. *The Politics of Baby Foods: Successful Challenges to an International Marketing Strategy*. London: Francis Pinter Publishers, 1986.

Chetley, A. *The Baby Killer Scandal*. London: War on Want, 1979.

Child, J. "Managerial and Organizational Factors Associated with Company Performance — Part II: A Contingency Analysis," *Journal of Management Studies* (1975), 12–28.

Christiansen, N. and Meluso, S. "Environmental Scanning and Tracking of Critical Issues: The Case of the Life Insurance Industry," in Sethi and Falbe, (eds.), *Business and Society*, pp. 423–431.

Clegg, S.R. and Redding, S.G. (eds.). *Capitalism in Contrasting Cultures*. New York: Walter de Gruyter, 1990.

Cole, J. H. "Bolivia's 'Right' Not Likely to Endorse the Free Market," *The Wall Street Journal*, July 19, 1985, p. 21.

Cox, H.G. "The 'New Breed,' in American Churches: Sources of Social Activism in American Religion," *Daedalus* (Winter 1967), 135–149.

Cunningham, A. Congressional Hearing on "Infant Feeding Practices," before the Subcommittee on Domestic Marketing Consumer Relations and Nutrition. Washington, D.C.: U.S. Government Printing Office, June 22, 1988.

Cyert, R.M. and March, J.G. *A Behavioral Theory of the Firm*. Englewood Cliffs, N.J.: Prentice-Hall, 1963.

Dahl, R.A. *Democracy and its Critics*. New Haven, Conn.: Yale University Press, 1989.

Day, K. "A New Activism on Antitrust Policy: The FTC Initiates Aggressive Inquiry into Alleged Price-Fixing by Infant Formula Giants," *The Washington Post*, January 13, 1991, p. H1.

De Soto, H. *The Other Path: The Invisible Revolution in the Third World*. New York: Harper, 1989.

DeWire, N. Letter written to Tom Lee (General Manager, Stouffer's Dayton Plaza Hotel), May 11, 1981.

Dobbing, J. (ed.). *Infant Feeding: Anatomy of a Controversy 1973–1984*. New York: Springer-Verlag, 1988.

Dobbing, J. "Breast is Best — Isn't It?" Paper presented in a *Symposium on Health Hazards of Milk*, University of Manchester, September 13–14, 1983, pp. 1–2.

Dollinger, M.J. "The Evolution of Collective Strategies in Fragmented Industries," *Academy of Management Review*, 15, 2 (November 1990), 266–285.

Donaldson, T. *The Ethics of International Business*. New York: Oxford University Press, 1989.

Dowling, J. and Pfeffer, J. "Organizational Legitimacy: Social Values and Organizational Behavior," *Pacific Sociological Review*, 18, 1 (1975), 122–136.

Doz, Y. *Management in Multinational Companies*. Oxford, England: Pergamon Press, 1986.

Duncan, R.B. "Characteristics of Organizational Environments and Perceived Environmental Uncertainty," *Administrative Science Quarterly*, 17 (1972), 313–327.

Dunnette, M.D. (ed.) *Handbook of Industrial Organizational Psychology*. Chicago, Ill.: Rand McNally, 1976.

Ebrahim, G.J. *Breast Feeding — The Biological Option*. London: MacMillan, 1978.

The Economist. "The World This Week: Business and Finance," *The Economist*, February 20, 1993.

The Economist. "A Survey of the Third World: Poor Man's Burden," *The Economist*, September 23, 1989.

European Communities. *Official Journal of the European Communities, No. C285*, 12 (November 1986), 5–19.

Farmer, R.N. (ed.) *Advances in International Comparative Management*, Vol. 1. Greenwich, Conn.: Jai Press, 1984.

Ferry, B. *World Fertility Survey Comparative Studies, Cross National Summaries No. 13*. Voorburg, The Netherlands: International Statistical Institute, May 1981.

First Boston Corporation. *Report No. 813046*, June 3, 1989.

Fiske, E.B. "Education: Values Taught More Widely," *The New York Times*, March 4, 1980, p. C1.

Fortune. "The Fortune 500 — The Largest U.S. Industrial Corporations," *Fortune*, April 22, 1991.

Fortune. "The Global 500," *Fortune*, July 30, 1990.

Fortune. "The International 500: The Fortune's Directory of Largest Industrial Corporations Outside the U.S.," *Fortune*, August 19, 1985, pp. 182–201.

France, J. *Abbott Laboratories, Inc., Company Report No. 817163, July 21, 1988*. New York: Smith Barney Upham & Co., 1988.

Freedman, A.M. "Nestle Quietly Seeks to Sell Beechnut, Dogged by Scandal of Bogus Apple Juice," *The Wall Street Journal*, July 14, 1989.

Freedman, A.M. "Nestle's Carnation Co. Unit Settles Dispute Over Infant Formula Ads," *The Wall Street Journal*, July 7, 1989, p. B4.

Freedman, A.M. "Gerber Unveils Its Baby Formula. Aims To Woo Parents Rather Than Doctors," *The Wall Street Journal*, June 16, 1989, p. B3.

Freedman, A.M. "Nestle Rejects Militant P.R. Plan To Combat Renewal Of Boycott," *The Wall Street Journal*, April 25, 1989, pp. B6–7.

Freedman, A.M. "Nestle To Drop Claim On Label Of Its Formula," *The Wall Street Journal*, March 13, 1989, p. B5.

Freedman, A.M. "Nestle Ad Claims For Baby Formula Probed In 3 States." *The Wall Street Journal*, March 2, 1989, p. B6.

Freedman, A.M. "Nestle's Bid To Crash Baby Formula Market in The U.S. Stirs A Row." *The Wall Street Journal*, February 16, 1989, pp. A1, A9.

Freedman, A.M. "Renewed Boycott of Nestle is Urged by Advocacy Groups," *The Wall Street Journal*, October 5, 1988, p. B10.

Freedman, A.M. "Nestle Faces New Boycott Threat in Distribution of Infant Formula," *The Wall Street Journal*, June 29, 1988, p. 28.

Freedman, A.M. "Nestle's New Infant Formula Line Introduced In A Bid For U.S. Market," *The Wall Street* June 28, 1988, p. 38.

Freitag, M. "Gerber Plan For Infant Formula," *The New York Times*, June 16, 1989, p. D5.

Freitag, M. "The Infant Formula Debate Strikes Home," *The New York Times*, September 3, 1989, p. E5.

Freudenheim, M. "A Safer Infant Formula Promised," *The New York Times*, June 28, 1988, pp. D1, D22.

Geach, H. "The Baby Food Controversy," *The New Internationalist,* August 1973.

Gelardi, R.C. "The Infant Formula Issue: A Story in Simplification and Escalation," *Nutrition Today,* September/October, 1981, p. 29.

Gerlach, L.P. "The Flea and the Elephant: Infant Formula Controversy," *Society,* 17, 6 (September/October 1980), 51–57.

Gilpin, R. *U.S. Power and the Multinational Corporation.* New York: Basic Books, 1973.

Gluckman, N.G. and Woodward, D.P. *The New Competitors.* New York: Basic Books, 1989.

Greenhouse, S. "Nestle's Time To Swagger," *The New York Times,* January 1, 1989.

Greiner, T. "The Promotion of Bottle-feeding by Multinational Corporations: How Advertising and the Health Professions Have Contributed," *Cornell International Nutrition Monograph Series No. 2.* Ithaca, New York: Cornell University Publications Program in International Nutrition and Development, 1975.

Grinyar, P.H. "Strategy, Structure, Size and Bureaucracy," *Academy of Management Journal,* 24, 3 (1981), 471–486.

Hagedorn, A. "Two Ex-Officials of Beech-Nut Get Prison Sentences," *The Wall Street Journal,* June 17, 1988.

Hall, B. "Changing Composition of Human Milk and Early Development of an Appetite Control," *Lancet,* April 5, 1975, p. 779.

Hardin, G. "The Tragedy of the Commons," *Science,* 162 (December 13, 1968), 1103–1107.

Harris, R.G. and Carman, J.M. "The Political Economy of Regulation: An Analysis of Market Failures," in S. Prakash Sethi, Paul Steidlmeier, and Cecilia M. Falbe (eds.), *Scaling the Corporate Wall: Readings in Social Issues of the Nineties.* Englewood Cliffs, N.J.: Prentice-Hall, Inc., 1991, pp. 24–35.

Hedberg, B.L.T., Nystrom, P.C. and Starbuck, W.H. "Camping on Seesaws: Prescriptions for a Self-Designing Organization," *Administrative Science Quarterly,* 21 (1976), 41–56.

Henderson, J. "Change on Campus: More Colleges to Require a Variety of Courses to Broaden Students," *The Wall Street Journal,* March 9, 1981, pp. 1, 15.

Heyne, P.Y. *Private Keepers of the Public Interest.* New York: Wiley, 1986.

Hirsch, F. "The Commercialization Bias" and "The Depleting Moral Legacy," *Social Limits to Growth.* Cambridge, Mass.: Harvard University Press, 1976, pp. 42–114, 117–158.

Horwitt, S. D. *Let Them Call Me Rebel: Saul Alinsky — His Life and Legacy.* New York: Random House, 1991.

Hrebniak, L.G. and Snow, C.C. "Industry Differences in Environmental Uncertainty and Organizational Characteristics Related to Uncertainty," *Academy of Management Journal,* 23 (1980), 750–759.

Hymar, S.H. *The International Operation of National Firms: A Study of Direct Foreign Investment.* Cambridge, Mass.: MIT Press, 1977.

IBFAN/IOCU. *State of the Code by Country 1988,* Code Documentation Center, Penang, Malaysia, May 1988.

ICCR. *Nestlegate Memorandum — US Boycott — Conclusions Based on US Visit.* New York, August 2–4, 1980.

ICIFI. *Code of Ethics and Professional Standards for Advertising, Product Information and Advisory Services for Breast Milk Substitutes*, Zurich, 1975 (amended 1976).

IDACE. *Industry Code of Practice for the Marketing of Breast Milk Substitutes in the EEC*, p. 2.

INFACT. Letter to Dr. Paul Minus dated October 9, 1980.

Infant Formula Task Force. *Infant Formula Task Force Report*, April 1983.

Infant Formula Task Force. *Minutes of the Meeting*, April 2–3, 1982.

Infant Formula Task Force of the GCOM. "Second Report to GCOM," July 1982.

Infant Formula Task Force of the GCOM. "Report of the Infant Formula Task Force to the GCOM," October 30, 1981.

Infant Formula Task Force of the GCOM. *Minutes*, Dayton, Ohio, September 25–26, 1981.

International Association of Infant Food Manufacturers (IFM). *Summary Report on Complaints Relating to Marketing Practices of Infant Formula. Period from 1 November to October 1987, 1988, 1989 and 1990*, 75001 Paris.

International Association of Infant Food Manufacturers (IFM). *Statutes*, Article 2: Objectives. Paris, France, Undated.

International Council of Infant Food Industries. *Objectives, History and Activities*, Summer 1980.

International Management Development Institute. Case No. 9–81-A006. OIE-51, "Nestle and the Infant Food Controversy.

Jackson, J.H. and Morhan, C.P. (eds.) *Organization Theory: A Macro Perspective for Management*. Englewool Cliffs, N.J.: Prentice-Hall, Inc., 1978.

Dr. Thad Jackson, Testimony before the House Subcommittee on International Economic Policy & Trade Committees on Foreign Affairs, June 16, 1981.

Jelliffe, D.B. "Commerciogenic Malnutrition," *Nutrition Review*, September 30, 1972, 199–205.

Jelliffe, D.B. and Jelliffe, E.F.P. (eds.) *Advances in International Maternal and Child Health*, Vol. 2. New York: Oxford University Press, 1982.

Jelliffe, D.B. and Jelliffe, E.F.P. "The Volume and Composition of Human Milk in Poorly Nourished Communities: A Review," *The American Journal of Clinical Nutrition*, March 31, 1978, 492–515.

Jelliffe, D.B. and Jelliffe, E.F.P. *Human Milk in the Modern World*. London: Oxford University Press, 1977.

Jelliffe, D.B. and Jelliffe, E.F.P. "The Urban Avalanche and Child Nutrition," *Journal of American Dietary Association*, 57 (1970), 114–118.

Johnson, D.A. "Confronting Corporate Power: Strategies and Phases of the Nestle Boycott," in Janes E. Post (ed.), *Research in Corporate Social Performance and Policy*, Vol. 8. Greenwich, CT: Jai Press, 1986, pp. 323–344.

Johnson, D. and Margulies, L. and U.S. Congress. "Marketing and Promotion of Infant Formula in Developing Countries," Hearing Before the Sub-committee on International Economic Policy and Trade of the Committee on Foreign Affairs of the House of Representatives. Washington, D.C.: U.S. Government Printing Office, 1980.

Klitgaard, R. *Tropical Gangsters: One Man's Experience with Development and Decadence in Deepest Africa*. New York: Basic Books, 1990.

Kondel, J. "Breast-Feeding and Population Growth," *Science,* December 1977, pp. 1111–1114.

Kristol, I. "On Economic Education," *The Wall Street Journal,* February 18, 1970, p. 20.

Kristol, I. "When Virtue Loses All Her Loveliness: Some Reflections on Capitalism" and "The Free Society," *The Public Interest,* Fall 1970, pp. 3–16.

Kutner, R. *The End of Laissez-Faire: National Purpose and the Global Economy After the Cold War.* New York: Knopf, 1991.

The Lancet. "Infant Food Industry," *The Lancet,* editorial, June 10, 1978, p. 1240.

Latham, M.C. "Infant Feeding in National and International Perspective: An Examination of the Decline in Human Lactation and the Modern Crisis in Infant and Child Feeding Practices," *Annals of the New York Academy of Sciences,* 300 (November 30, 1977), 197–209.

Laventhal, J. M., Shapiro, E.D., Aten, C.D., Berg, A.T. and Egerter, S.A. "Does Breast-Feeding Protect Against Infections in Infants Less Than Three Months of Age?" *Pediatrics,* 1986, pp. 896–903.

Lavipour, F.G. and Sauvant, K. (eds.) *Controlling Multinational Enterprises: Problems, Strategies, Counterstrategies.* Boulder, Colo.: Westview Press, 1976.

Lazarus K.A. Letter dated January 27, 1981, to Ambassador Jean Kirkpatrick, U.S. Ambassador to the United Nations.

Ledogar, R.J. "Formula for Malnutrition," in *Hungry for Profits: U.S. Food and Drug Multinationals in Latin America.* New York: IDOC/North America, 1975, ch. 9, pp. 111–126.

Lee, L. and Mufson, S. "Angry New Leaders in Africa Are Trying To Right Past Wrongs," *The Wall Street Journal,* July 18, 1985, pp. 1,15.

Lefever, E.W. *Amsterdam to Nairobi: The World Council of Churches and the Third World.* Washington, D.C.: Ethics and Public Policy Center, 1979.

Leifer, R. and Huber, G.P. "Relations Among Perceived Environmental Uncertainty, Organizational Structure and Boundary Spanning Behavior," *Administrative Science Quarterly,* 22 (1977), 235–247.

Levitt, K. *Silent Surrender: The Multinational Corporation in Canada.* Toronto: Macmillan of Canada, 1970.

Lucinchi, V. "U.S. is a Dissenter as U.N. Agency Votes Baby Formula Code," *The New York Times,* May 21, 1981, p. A1.

Maeroff, G. "Harvard: A Real-Life Case Study-Derek Bob Asks Review of the Business School," *New York Times,* May 6, 1979, p. F11.

Maremont, M. and Templeman, J. "How Much Chocolate Can The Nestle Devour?" *Business Week,* May 9, 1988, p. 6.

Mason, J.M., Nieburg, P. and Marks, J.S. "Mortality and Infectious Disease Associated with Infant-Feeding Practices in Developing Countries," in AAP Task Force Report, *Pediatrics,* October, 1984, pp. 702–725.

McCall, M.W., Jr. "Making Sense with Nonsense: Helping Frames of Reference Clash," in Nystrom, P.C. and Starbuck, W.H. (eds.), *Prescriptive Models of Organizations.* Amsterdam: North-Holland, 1977, pp. 111–123.

McComas, M. "Origins of the Controversy," in J. Dobbing (ed.), *Infant Feeding: Anatomy of a Controversy 1973–1984.* New York: Springer-Verlag, 1988, pp. 36–38.

McComas, M., Fookes, G. and Taucher, G. *The Infant Formula Controversy — Nestle and the Dilemma of Third World Nutrition.* Vevey, Switzerland; Nestle, S.A., 1982, pp. 9, 26–29.

Meier, B. "Battle for Baby Formula Market," *The New York Times,* June 15, 1993, p. D1.

Meier, B. "FTC is Re-Emerging as Watchdog on Prices," *The New York Times,* January 28, 1991, p. A16.

Meier, B. "Are Ads For Infant Formula Fit For The Eyes Of Parents?" *The New York Times,* December 29, 1990, p. 46.

Melloan, G. "Nestle Courts the LDC Middle Class," *The Wall Street Journal,* June 4, 1990, p. A13.

Miles, R.E. and Snow, C.C. *Organizational Strategy, Structure and Process.* New York: McGraw Hill, 1978.

Miles, R.H. *Coffin Nails and Corporate Strategies.* Englewood Cliffs, N.J.: Prentice-Hall, Inc., 1982.

Miles, R.H. *Managing the Corporate Social Environment: A Grounded Theory.* Englewood Cliffs, N.J.: Prentice-Hall, 1987.

Minchin, M. *Breast-feeding Matters.* Sydney, Australia: George Allen and Unwin, 1985.

Minus, P.M. *A Background Paper on the Infant Formula Controversy: Prepared for the United Methodist Task Force on Infant Formula.* Dayton, Ohio: United Methodist Church, September 17, 1980.

Montanari, J.R. "Operationalizing Strategic Choice," in J.H. Jackson and C.P. Morgan (eds.), *Organization Theory: A Macro Perspective for Management.* Englewood Cliffs, N.J.: Prentice-Hall, Inc., 1978.

Moran, T.H. (ed.) *Multinational Corporations and the Third World.* Lexington, Mass.: D.C. Heath, 1985.

Moran, T.H. and Contributors. *Investing in Development: New Role for Private Capital.* Washington, D.C.: Overseas Development Council, 1986.

Morely, D. *Pediatric Priorities in the Developing World.* London: Butterworth, 1973.

Morris, S. "Abbott Denies Formula Scheme," *Chicago Tribune,* June 12, 1992, p. 1.

Muller, M. *The Baby Killer.* London: War on Want, 1974.

Muller, M. *The Baby Killer,* 2nd ed. London: War on Want, 1975.

Naj, A.K. "Nestle To Sell Infant Formula In U.S.; Step Likely To Hurt Competitors' Profits," *The Wall Street Journal,* June 6, 1988, p. 5.

Nestle, "What Led Beech-Nut Down the Road to Disgrace," *Business Week,* February 22, 1988, pp. 124–128.

Nestle Coordination Center for Nutrition, Inc. "Joint Statement of Nestle and the International Nestle Boycott Committee," *Press Conference,* Washington, D.C., October 4, 1984.

Nestle Coordination Center for Nutrition, Inc. *Minutes of Press Conference,* October 4, 1984.

Nestle Coordination Center For Nutrition, Inc. *Aide Memoir to The United Methodist Task Force,* Washington, D.C., September 25, 1981.

Nestle Infant Formula Audit Commission. *Joint Statement by Nestle and the Nestle Infant Formula Audit Commission on the Dissolution of the Commission.* Washington, D.C.: June, 1991, p. A-6.

Nestle Infant Formula Audit Commission. *Report No. 13*. Washington, D.C., June 30, 1989, p. 7.

Nestle S.A. *Annual Report, 1989*.

News Service. "FTC Files Antitrust Charges Against Infant Formula Makers," *The Atlanta Journal and Constitution*, June 12, 1992, p. 7.

The New York Times. "Carnation Halts Formula Claims," *The New York Times*, July 7, 1989, p. D5.

The New York Times. "Boycott of Nestle to Resume," *The New York Times*, October 5, 1988, p. D2.

Noble, B.P. "Nestle — Battling The Boycotts," *The New York Times*, July 28, 1991, p. 5.

Novak, M. *This Hemisphere of Liberty: A Philosophy of the Americas*. Washington, D.C.: The AEI Press, 1990.

Nystrom, P.C. and Starbuck, W.H. "Managing Beliefs in Organizations," *Journal of Behavioral Science*, 20 (1984), 277–287.

Nystrom. P.C. and Starbuck, W.H. "To Avoid Organizational Crisis, Unlearn," *Organizational Dynamics*, April 12, 1984.

Ohmae, K. *Borderless State*. New York: Harper, 1991.

Oliver, C. "Determinants of Interorganizational Relationships: Integration and Future Directions," *Academy of Management Review*, 15, 2 (April 1990), 241–265.

Pear, R. "Top Infant-Formula Makers Charged by U.S. over Pricing," *The New York Times*, June 12, 1992.

Perrow, C. *Complex Organizations: A Critical Essay*, 2nd ed. Glenview, Ill.: Scott, Foresman, 1979.

Pettigrew, A.M. *The Politics of Organizational Decision-Making*. London: Tavistock, 1973.

Pfeffer, J. and Leblebici, H. "The Effort of Competition on Some Dimensions of Organizational Structure," *Social Forces*, 52 (1973), 268–279.

Pfeffer, J. and Salancik, G.R. *The External Control of Organizations*. New York: Harper & Row, 1978.

Porter, M.E. *The Competitive Advantage of Nations*. New York: Free Press, 1990.

Porter, M.E. (ed.) *Competition in Global Industries*. Boston, Mass.: HBS Press, 1986.

Post, J.E. (ed.) *Research in Corporate Social Performance and Policy*, Vol. 8. Greenwich, Conn.: Jai Press, 1986, pp. 323–344.

Post, J.E. Stanford University, Case No. S-BPP-5A, Nestle Boycott (A to E), 1981, p. 4-A.

Post, J.E. "Testimony," U.S. Senate, "Marketing and Promotion of Infant Formula in the Developing Nations, 1978," Hearings before the Subcommittee on Health and Scientific Research of the Committee on Human Resources, 95th Congress, 2nd Session, May 23, 1978, p. 120.

Pruitt, D.G. "Achieving Integrative Solutions," in M.H. Bazerman and R.J. Lewicki (eds.), *Negotiating in Organizations*. Beverly Hills, Calif.: Sage Publications, 1983, p. 36.

Pruitt, D.G. *Negotiating Behavior*. New York: Academic Press, 1981.

Public Affairs Council. *Public Interest Profiles*, a bi-annual publication. Washington, D.C.: Congressional Quarterly.

Raphael, D. "The Role of Breast-Feeding in a Bottle Oriented World," *Food Nutrition*, 2 (1973), 121–126.

Reiss, R. and F'Dorf, M. Letter addressed to Dr. S. Prakash Sethi, dated June 26, 1991.

Roach, J. "Into The Mouths of Babies," *Transcript of CBS Reports*, 6th ed., Wednesday, July 5, 1978.

Ross Labs. Memorandum to IATF, dated July 9, 1980.

Ruffenach, G. "Florida Files Suit Against 3 Makers of Infant Formula," *The Wall Street Journal*, January 4, 1991, p. A4.

Salwen, K.G. "Infant-Formula Firms Rigged Bids, U.S. Says," *The Wall Street Journal*, June 12, 1992, p. A3.

Sauvant, K.V. and Hasenpflug, H. *The New International Economic Order*. Boulder, Colo.: Westview Press, 1977.

Schelling, T.C. "On the Ecology of Micromotives," *The Public Interest*, 25 (Fall 1971), 59–98.

Scott, R.H. "Avarice, Altruism, and Second Party Preferences," *Quarterly Journal of Economics*, February 1972, 1–18.

Scrimshaw, N.S. "Code Not Cure," *Nutrition Today*, July 1981, 11–15.

Scrimshaw, N.S. "Myths and Realities in International Health Planning," *American Journal of Public Health*, August 1974, 792–798.

Scrimshaw, N.S. and Underwood, B.S. "Timely and Appropriate Complementary Feeding of the Breast-Fed Infant — An Overview," *Food and Nutrition Bulletin*, 12, 2 (April 1980), 19–22.

Sen, A. "Behavior and the Concept of Preference," *Economica*, August 1973.

Sethi, S. Prakash. *The South African Quagmire: In Search for a Peaceful Path to Democratic Pluralism*. Cambridge, Mass.: Ballinger Publishing Co., 1987.

Sethi, S. Prakash. "Opportunities and Pitfalls for Multinational Corporations in a Changed Political Environment," *Long Range Planning*, 20, 6 (December 1987), 45–53.

Sethi, S. Prakash. "Inhuman Errors and Industrial Crises," *Columbia Journal of World Business*, Spring 1987, 101–110.

Sethi, S. Prakash, "The Inhuman Error — Lessons from the Union Carbide Plant Accident in Bhopal, India," *The New Management*, Summer 1985, 41–45.

Sethi, S. Prakash. "A Strategic Framework for Dealing With Schism Between Business and the Academe," Special Report, *Public Affairs Review*, 1983, 44–59.

Sethi, S. Prakash, *Up Against the Corporate Wall: Modern Corporations and Social Issues of the Eighties*, 4th ed. Englewood Cliffs, N.J.: Prentice-Hall, 1982.

Sethi, S. Prakash. "Interfaith Center on Corporate Responsibility (ICCR), A Sponsored-related Movement of the National Council of Churches," in *Up Against the Corporate Wall: Modern Corporations and Social Issues of the Eighties*, 4th ed. Englewood Cliffs, N.J.: Prentice-Hall, 1982, pp. 450–480.

Sethi, S. Prakash. "Corporate Law Violations and Executive Liability," Testimony on H.R. 4973 before the Subcommittee on Crime of the House Judiciary Committee, December 13, 1979.

Sethi, S. Prakash. "A Conceptual Framework for Environmental Analysis of Social Issues and Evaluation of Business Response Patterns," *The Academy of Management Review*, January 1979, 63–74.

Sethi, S. Prakash. "An Analytical Framework for Making Cross-Cultural Comparisons of Business Responses to Social Pressures," in L.E. Preston, (ed.), *Research in Corporate Social Performance and Policy,* Vol. 1. Greenwich, Conn.: Jai Press, 1978, pp. 233–267.

Sethi, S. Prakash.*Advocacy Advertising and Large Corporations: Social Conflict, Big Business Image, News Media and Public Policy.* Lexington, Mass.: D.C. Heath & Co., 1977.

Sethi, S. Prakash. *Japanese Business and Social Conflict: A Comparative Analysis of Response Patterns With American Business.* Cambridge, Mass.: Ballinger, 1975.

Sethi, S. Prakash. "The Corporation and the Church: Institutional Conflict and Social Responsibility," *California Management Review,* January 1972, 63–74.

Sethi, S. Prakash. *Business Corporations and the Black Man.* New York: Harper & Row, 1970.

Sethi, S. Prakash and Bhalla, Bharat B. "Free Market Orientation and Economic Growth: Some Lessons for the Developing Countries and Multinational Corporations," *Business in the Contemporary World,* III, 2 (Winter 1991), 86–101.

Sethi, S. Prakash, Etemad, H. and Luther, K.A.N. "New Socio-Political Forces: The Globalization of Conflict," *The Journal of Business Strategy,* Spring 1986, 24–31.

Sethi, S. Prakash and Falbe, Ceclica M. "The Concept of Strategic Slack: Implications for Strategic Response Patterns by Corporations to Public Policy Options," Paper presented at the 9th Annual International Conference of Strategic Management Society, San Francisco, California, October 11–14, 1989.

Sethi, S. Prakash and Falbe, Ceclica (eds.), *Business and Society: Dimensions of Conflict and Cooperation.* Lexington, Mass.: D.C. Heath & Co., 1987.

Sethi, S. Prakash and Falbe, Ceclica M. "Determinants of Corporate Social Performance," Paper presented at the Stanford Business Ethics Workshop, Graduate School of Business, Stanford University, Stanford, California, August 14–17, 1985.

Sethi, S. Prakash, Namiki, N. and Swanson, C.S. *The False Promise of the Japanese Miracle.* New York: Harper & Row, 1985.

Sethi, S. Prakash and Post, James E. "The Marketing of Infant Formula in Less Developed Countries: Public Consequences of Private Actions," *California Management Review,* Summer 1979, 35–48.

Sethi, S. Prakash and Steidlmeier, Paul. *Up Against the Corporate Wall: Modern Corporations and Social Issues of the Nineties,* 5th ed. Englewood Cliffs, N.J.: Prentice-Hall, 1991.

Sethi, S. Prakash and Steidlmeier, Paul. "A New Paradigm of the Business/Society Relationship in the Third World: The Challenge of Liberation Theology," in L.E. Preston (ed.), *Research in Corporate Social Performance and Policy,* Vol. 10. Greenwich, Conn.: Jai Press, 1988, pp. 29–43.

Sethi, S. Prakash, and Votaw, Dow. *The Corporate Dilemma: Traditional Values Versus Contemporary Problems.* Englewood Cliffs, N.J.: Prentice-Hall, Inc. 1973.

Sethi, S. Prakash and Votaw, Dow. "Do We Need a New Corporate Response to a Changing Social Environment? Part II," *California Management Review,* Fall 1969.

Sharfman, M.P., Wolf, G., Chase, R.B. and Tansik, D.A. "Antecedents of Organizational Slack," *Academy of Management Review,* April 13, 1988, 601–614.

Silver, J.F. and Woodruff, D. "A Flap Over Formula Is Coming To A Boil," *Business Week,* January 1, 1991, p. 47.

Silver, J.F. and Woodruff, D. "The Furor Over Formula Is Coming To A Boil," *Business Week,* April 9, 1990, pp. 52–53.

Starbuck, W.H. "Congealing Oil: Investing Ideologies to Justify Acting Ideologies Out," *Journal of Management Studies,* 1981, 3–27.

Starbuck, W.H. "Organizations and their Environments," in M.D. Dunnette (ed.), *Handbook of Industrial Organizational Psychology.* Chicago, Ill.: Rand McNally, 1976, pp. 1069–1123.

Starbuck, W.H. and Dutton, J.H. "Designing Adaptive Organizations," *Journal of Business Policy,* April 4, 1978, 21–28.

Starbuck, W.H., Greve, A. and Hedberg, B.L.T. "Responding to Crises," *Journal of Business Strategy,* February 9, 1978, 111–137.

Tarullo, D.K. "Logic, Myth and the International Economic Order," *Harvard International Law Journal,* 26, 2 (Spring 1985), 533–552.

Tavis, L.A. (ed.) *Multinational Managers and Poverty in the Third World.* Notre Dame, Ind.: Notre Dame University Press, 1982.

Tugendhat, Ç. *The Multinational.* London: Penguin, 1973.

Turner, G. "Inside Europe's Giant Companies: Nestle Finds a Better Formula," *Long Range Planning,* 19, 3 (1986), 12–19.

U.S. Congress. *Implementation of the World Health Organization (WHO) Code on Infant Formula Marketing Practices.* Hearings before the Subcommittee on International Economic Policy and Trade and on Human Rights and International Organizations of the Committee on Foreign Affairs, Ninety-Seventh Congress, First Session, June 16–17, 1981.

U.S. Congress. Statement by Dr. Stephen C. Joseph in Implementation of The World Health Organization (WHO) Code on Infant Formula Marketing Practices. Hearing before the Subcommittee on International Economic Policy and Trade and on Human Rights and International Organizations of the Committee on Foreign Affairs, 97th Congress, 1st Session, June 16–17, 1981, p. 154.

U.S. Senate. *Marketing and Promotion of Infant Formula in the Developing Countries, 1978.* Hearings before the Subcommittee on Health and Scientific Research of the Committee on Human Resources, U.S. Senate, 95th Congress, Second Session, on Examination of the Advertising, Marketing, Promotion, and Use of Infant Formula in Developing Nations, May 23, 1978, pp. 204–207.

United National Development Programme (UNDP). *Human Development Report 1990.* New York: Oxford University Press, 1990.

Vernon, R.A. "Sovereignty at Bay: Ten Years After," *International Organization,* Summer 1981.

Vernon, R.A. *Storm Over the Multinationals.* Cambridge, Mass.: Harvard University Press, 1977.

The Wall Street Journal. "Nestle Unit Sues Baby Formula Firms, Alleging Conspiracy with Pediatricians," *The Wall Street Journal,* June 1, 1993, p. A1.

The Wall Street Journal. "American Home Infant Formula Giveaway To End," *The Wall Street Journal,* February 4, 1991, pp. B1, B5.

The Wall Street Journal. "Nestle to Restrict low-Cost Supplies Of Baby Food To Developing Nations," *The Wall Street Journal,* January 30, 1991, p. B6.

The Wall Street Journal. "FDA Rejects Nestle Unit's 'Good Start' Label Claim," *The Wall Street Journal*, February 3, 1989, p. B7.

The Wall Street Journal. "Who Approves Limits on Sales of Infant Formula," *The Wall Street Journal*, May 21, 1981, p. 31.

Wells, L.T., Jr. *Third World Multinationals: The Rise of Foreign Investment from Developing Countries*. Cambridge, Mass.: MIT Press, 1983.

Whitehead, R.G. (ed.) *Maternal Diet, Breast-feeding Capacity and Lactational Infertility*, supplement 6, New York: U.N. University Food and Nutrition Bulletin, 1983.

The World Bank. *World Development Report 1991*. New York: Oxford University Press, 1991. Table 28: Health and Nutrition, pp. 258–259.

Whyte, W.H. *Is Anybody Listening?* New York: Simon & Schuster, 1950.

Williams, O. "Who Cast the First Stone?" *Harvard Business Review*, September-October 1984, 151–166.

Wogaman, P. Letter to MTF members and other church leaders, dated March 8, 1982.

Wolfe, C., Jr. "A Theory of Nonmarket Failures: Framework for Implementation Analysis," *The Journal of Law and Economics*, October 1978, pp. 107–139.

Wong, B. "Conviction of Nestle Unit's Ex-President is Overturned on Appeal in Juice Case," *The Wall Street Journal*, March 31, 1989.

The World Bank. *World Development Report, 1991*, New York: Oxford University Press, 1991.

World Council of Churches. *Structures of Injustice and Struggles for Liberation: A Report From Nairobi Assembly of the World Council of Churches, 1975*. Geneva: World Council of Churches, 1975.

World Health Assembly. *Provisional Verbatim Record of the Fifteenth Plenary Meeting*, Geneva, May 21, 1981.

World Health Organization. *The International Code of Marketing of Breast-Milk Substitutes: Synthesis of Reports on Action Taken (1981–1990)*, (WHO/MCH/NUT/90.1).

World Health Organization. Forty First World Health Assembly, Committee A, *Provisional Summary Report of the Second Meeting*, Geneva, May 6, 1988.

World Health Organization. Executive Board Eighty First Session, *Resolutions and Decisions Annexes*, Geneva, January 11–20, 1988.

World Health Organization. Thirty Ninth World Health Assembly Provisional Agenda Item 21, *Infant And Young Child Nutrition (Progress And Evaluation Report, And Status of the Implementation of the International Code of Marketing of Breast-milk Substitutes)*, Report by the Director General, April 7, 1986.

World Health Organization. Executive Board Seventy First Session, Provisional Agenda Item 13: *Infant and Young Child Feeding, Report by the Director General*, November 11, 1982.

World Health Organization. *67th Executive Board Summary Report* (EBSR).

World Health Organization. *International Code of Marketing of Breast-Milk Substitutes*. Geneva, 1981.

World Health Organization. *Contemporary Patterns of Breast-Feeding: Report on the WHO Collaborative Study on Breast-Feeding*. Geneva: WHO, 1981.

World Health Organization. *Thirty-Fourth World Health Assembly: Resolutions and Decision Annexes,* WHA 34/1981/REC/1, May 4–22, 1981, Geneva, May 1981.

World Health Organization. *WHO/UNICEF Consultation on Development of Drafts International Code Breast-milk Substitutes.* Geneva, August 1980.

WHO/UNICEF. *Joint WHO/UNICEF Meeting on Infant and Young Child Feeding: Background Paper and Themes for Discussion,* DOC FHE/ICF/79.3, Geneva, 1979.

WHO/UNICEF. "Meeting on Infant and Young Child Feeding," Part 2 — Themes for Discussion, (Geneva, October 1979).

WHO/UNICEF. *Infant and Young Child Feeding,* Geneva, October 1979.

Wray, J.D. "Feeding and Survival: Historical and Contemporary Studies of Infant Morbidity and Mortality," Unpublished paper, Center for Population and Family Health, Columbia University Medical School, New York, April 1979, pp. 1–45.

Yasai-Ardekani, M. "Structural Adaptations to Environments," *Academy of Management Review,* 11, 1 (1986), 9–21.

INDEX

Issues in Business Ethics

1. G. Enderle, B. Almond and A. Argandoña (eds.): *People in Corporations*. Ethical Responsibilities and Corporate Effectiveness. 1991   ISBN: 0-7923-0829-8
2. B. Harvey, H. van Luijk and G. Corbetta (eds.): *Market, Morality and Company Size*. 1991   ISBN: 0-7923-1342-9
3. J. Mahoney and E. Vallance (eds.): *Business Ethics in a New Europe*. 1992   ISBN: 0-7923-1931-1
4. P. Minus (ed.): *The Ethics of Business in a Global Economy*. 1993   ISBN: 0-7923-9334-1
5. T. Dunfee and Y. Nagayasu (eds.): Business Ethics: Japan the Global Economy. 1993   ISBN: 0-7923-2427-7
6. P. Sethi: *Multinational Corporations and the Impact of Public Advocacy on Corporate Strategy:* Nestle and the Infant Formula Controversy. 1994   ISBN: 0-7923-9378-3

KLUWER ACADEMIC PUBLISHERS • DORDRECHT/BOSTON/LONDON